Sexual Sites, Seminal Attitudes

Studies on Contemporary South Asia

A joint publication series
with South Asian Studies Association (SASA)
&
South Asia Research Unit (SARU)
Curtin University of Technology

General Editors: Peter Reeves, John McGuire and Jim Masselos

Series Editor: Howard Brasted

Other Titles in this Series

John McGuire, Peter Reeves and Howard Brasted (eds), *Politics of Violence: From Ayodhya to Behrampada* (1996, Sage Publications, New Delhi).

D.A. Low and Howard Brasted (eds), *Freedom, Trauma, Continuities: Northern India and Independence* (1998, Sage Publications, New Delhi).

Siri Gamage and I.B. Watson (eds), *Conflict and Community in Contemporary Sri Lanka: 'Pearl of the East' or the 'Island of Tears'?* (1999, Sage Publications, New Delhi).

Sexual Sites, Seminal Attitudes

Sexualities, Masculinities and Culture in South Asia

Editor
Sanjay Srivastava

Series Editor
Howard Brasted

Studies on Contemporary South Asia No. 4

SAGE Publications
New Delhi ◆ Thousand Oaks ◆ London

First published in 2004 by

SAGE Publications India Pvt Ltd
B1/I 1, Mohan Cooperative Industrial Area
Mathura Road, New Delhi 110 044
www.sagepub.in

SAGE Publications Inc
2455 Teller Road
Thousand Oaks, California 91320

SAGE Publications Ltd
1 Oliver's Yard, 55 City Road
London EC1Y 1SP

Published by Tejeshwar Singh for SAGE Publications India Pvt Ltd, typeset in 10/12 Galliard by Excellent Laser Typesetters, New Delhi, and printed at Chaman Enterprises, New Delhi.

Second Printing 2012

Library of Congress Cataloging-in-Publication Data

Sexual sites, seminal attitudes: sexualities, masculinities and culture in South Asia/ editor, Sanjay Srivastava.
    p. cm.
  Includes index.
1. Sex customs—South Asia. 2. Sex customs—India. 3. Masculinity—South Asia. 4. Masculinity—India. 5. Men—South Asia—Sexual behaviour. 6. Men—India—Sexual behaviour. I. Srivastava, Sanjay, 1960–

HQ18.S64S49   306.7'0954—dc22   2003   2003016651

ISBN: 0–7619–9777–6 (US–Hb)   81–7829–264–5 (India–Hb)

SAGE Production Team: Larissa Sayers, Radha Dev Raj and Santosh Rawat

In memory of
Vikash N. Pandey (1959–2003)
valued friend and colleague

Contents

8 ◆ Contents

List of Plates

List of Figures

1

Introduction

Semen, History, Desire and Theory[1]

◆ Sanjay Srivastava

Question: I am 36 years old.... When I was pregnant I lost the urge to have sex, which my husband thought was not true of other women. Please advise. **Response**: There are many women in your position who feel that sex during pregnancy may lead to ill effects on the foetus...during pregnancy, the sex urge may, in fact, increase and men adopt such positions as not to put pressure on the stomach.

Question: My wife is very shy and refuses to discuss sex-matters with me. I have often asked her if she too achieves orgasm. Can you please advise if this is the case for women as well. **Response**: Yes, you are correct.

---

[1] The essays included in this collection were presented at the conference on 'Sexualities, Masculinities and Culture in South Asia: Knowledges, Practices, Popular Culture, and the State', 6–8 July 1999, Melbourne, Australia. I would like to thank the Wenner–Gren Foundation for Anthropological Research for its generous sponsorship of the conference. Financial assistance was also provided by the South Asian Studies Association of Australia, the School of Literary and Communication Studies and the Faculty of Arts of Deakin University, Melbourne, Australia. My thanks to Stacy Pigg for extensive and valuable comments on an earlier draft of this essay; and also to Kajri Jain for raising certain issues. I have incorporated as many of their suggestions as possible.

Question: I have recently married and haven't yet had sex with my wife. However, I suspect that she has had previous sexual experiences. Can a medical inspection establish this?

Response: How incredible that you suspect her even before commencing sex-relations! The hymen may tear during any physical activity and it is impossible to determine if sexual intercourse is the cause. We suggest that you rid yourself of suspicious thoughts and aim to live a happy domestic life. Lack of trust destroys domestic life.

Question (a male reader): My nipples are very sensitive and I often get excited when they are touched, are men as liable to sexual excitement as women in this regard? **Response**: Yes, sometimes, so there is nothing to worry about.

Question (a female reader): My friend is having an affair with a man older than her father and is completely oblivious to the bad-name she is bringing to her family. **Response**: Often this is merely a sexual attraction and often dissipates, otherwise she may need to see a psychiatrist.

(From *Nar-Naari* [Man–Woman], Vol. 33 [1970], No. 2 'Your Questions, Our Answers:')

I wanted to begin with a fragment from the public culture of provincial India in order to position this introduction as part of a continuing conversation the sites of which are as far-flung as its concerns are diffuse. A variety of positions and knowledge regimes construct the world that gathers around *Nar-Naari*, pointing to the multiplicity of knowledges, and cultural and social strategies that make for an interstitial—though not 'fractured' in the sense of maladjusted—self. It is an archive, then, somewhat marginal to the exhortations of the 'official' family planning programme of the Government of India, but, one connected to the circuits of, let's call it, 'footpath capitalism'; contiguous to a space crowded with a variety of industrial and semi-industrial desiderata at the margins of neo-classical economics and subject to ineffably supple laws of supply and demand, these wares are really quite impossible not to notice unless one crosses the road at the hint of 'encroachment', or only drives. It is to these sorts of merchandise, moving between shelves marked 'official' and 'contraband', between spaces designated 'unauthorised' and those 'regularised unauthorised', that the contributors to this volume turn their attention. Either out of scholarly coyness, or through an inability to conceive of 'active' sexuality (as opposed to a sphere located in the context of prohibitions) as anything but a masculine concern, discussions of sexuality in the South Asian context have been remarkably focused on men's preoccupations. The few exceptions to this, such as Raheja and Gold's important book,[2] have served to demonstrate how narrow our scholarship has been. Further, in this context, there has in recent times been a conflation of what might be referred to as Gandhian perspectives on sexuality with the more general milieu of Indian life; given the salience of discourses of the body in Gandhi's political philosophy, and the relatively unquestioned assumption of the accessibility of his ideas to the 'masses', this is not an unsurprising consequence. It is hoped that the essays here, each in its own way, will serve to broaden the debate on sexuality, through providing accounts of a myriad sites and meanings of sexuality. Hence, for example, the essays in this volume suggest that though 'semen anxiety' is an important theme in Indian sexuality discourses, it should not be allowed to monopolise the analytical framework.[3]

For the Indian case at least, some clue to the choice of 'explanatory' variables in both popular and scholarly discussions lies in the excessive attention we still ascribe to the importance of religion (Hinduism, in particular) in everyday life. No doubt, religion continues to be an important variable in the life of people of South Asia, but it also just that: a variable, one that exists in a complex relationship to the various elements of modernity.[4] These may

---

[2] G. G. Raheja and A. G. Gold, *Listen to the Heron's Words: Reimagining Gender and Kinship in North India* (Berkeley, University of California Press, 1994).

[3] Cf. J. Alter, *The Wrestler's Body* (Chicago, University of Chicago Press, 1992); M. G. Carstairs, *The Twice Born* (London, Hogarth Press, 1958); and V. Lal, 'Nakedness, Non-Violence, and the Negation of Negation: Gandhi's Experiments in *Brahmacharya* and Celibate Sexuality', *South Asia* (n.s.) Vol. 22, No. 2 (1999), pp. 63–94.

[4] This is not to deny the value of accounts such as Kolenda's, who speaks of the religious basis of the sexual ideology of the 'untouchable Chuhras' of Western Uttar Pradesh; rather, it is a plea for the taking into account of those other factors that also constitute the swirl of modernity. P. Kolenda, 'Untouchable Chuhras through their Humor: Equalizing Marital Kin through Teasing, Pretence, and

include commodity cultures, media cultures, engagements with the imperatives of the state and its models of development, the actions of non-state organisations, gender activism and the unfolding politics of desire. So, when Kakar suggests that the 'Hindu version' of the 'mother–whore dichotomy ... is crucial for understanding the culture's public and official attitudes towards women and wives',[5] it would appear that the part is too readily pressed into service for the whole; it is not clear, in other words, that analytical recourse to *The Laws of Manu*—as attractive an option as it might seem—is adequate to an understanding of the sexual present. I hope that the tone of this essay as well as the diversity of materials covered by the essays in this collection will suggest the need for decentring the search for the 'core' values and concerns of South Asian sexualities.

This task is also crucial in as much as it is important to disrupt the tendency to read 'India' as metonymic for 'South Asia', a tendency that, as scholars of non-India South Asia have noted, tends to go largely unmarked; in any case, 'the "east" imagined by Foucault as possessing an *ars erotica* is not the subcontinent under British rule nor the present day state of India.'[6] In what follows I will frequently refer to 'Indian sexuality', however, I hope it will be obvious that it is an attempt to problematise it, rather than to establish a regional spatio-intellectual hegemony.

'Semen anxiety'—where 'loss' of semen is equated with a loss of masculine strength and 'life-force'—has an impressive career in India-related scholarship, and for *this* reason deserves the introductory space of this essay (rather than the privileging of a male concern); the scholarly preoccupation with it is almost as

---

Farce', in O. M. Lynch (ed.), *Divine Passions. The Social Construction of Emotion in India* (Berkeley, University of California Press, 1990).

However, Kolenda's view that 'the belief in mystical Hinduism that sexual interest distracts the holy man from his spiritual goal' (*ibid.*, p. 123.) seem to be at odds with Lynch's observation in the same volume that in Hindu thought 'asceticism, with its emphasis on thought and meditation, and emotionalism or eroticism, with its emphasis on feeling and emotion are not logical contradictions; rather, they are logical contraries, two aspects of the same thing.' O. M. Lynch, 'The Mastram. Emotion and Person among Mathura's Chaube's', in Lynch (ed.), *op. cit.*, p. 102.

[5] S. Kakar, *Intimate Relations. Exploring Indian Sexuality* (Chicago, University of Chicago Press, 1990), p. 17.

[6] Stacy Pigg, personal communication.

obsessive as what is sought to be described. This is not to deny the myriad concerns with semen (its production and its 'protection') in Indian life, but rather to suggest the significance of the slippage between the idealised texts of social life and the practices through which lives are led and such textual imperatives transgressed.

Quite clearly, we need to distinguish between normative rules of sexuality and those practices and beliefs that are contingent: a flux dictated by the overwhelming circumstances of social and cultural processes. In this context, we also need to keep in view the sociological significance of the pronouncements of the legal system on matters sexual, or on matters that in some way impinge upon the notion of sexuality. For quite often, a normative bias is built into the law through the gendered reality of the legal system, where judges 'bring to their interpretation of the law very masculinist sex-role stereotypes while manifestly upholding the cause of women.'[7]

Combined with the Gandhian gloss on the necessity of overcoming desire,[8] and a more general ethic of *brahmacharya* and 'self-control' such as that articulated by the *pahalwan* (wrestler) community of Banaras,[9] 'semen-anxiety' has taken on the appearance of an irrevocable truth of the Indian (male) milieu. Indeed, the stoic father, whose sexual activity remains confined to the imperatives of reproduction, and whose daily routine is one of unremitting frugality and discipline, is almost a stock figure of many twentieth century biographies (as, for example, in the memoirs of the poet Bachchan, and the writer Kashinath Singh).[10] However, this sexual landscape—or rather, a landscape where sexuality is an unspoken spectre—is only one of many social topographies, and a fuller picture must include other, 'little', traditions that are too frequently regarded as aberrations and not

---

[7] P. Uberoi, 'When is a Marriage not a Marriage? Sex, Sacrament and Contract in Hindu Marriage', *Contributions to Indian Sociology*, (n.s.) Vol. 29, Nos. 1 & 2, p. 321.
[8] See, for example, Kakar *op. cit.*, and B. Parekh, *Colonialism, Tradition and Reform. An Analysis of Gandhi's Political Discourse* (New Delhi, Sage Publications, 1989).
[9] Alter, *op. cit.*, especially Chapters Five and Six.
[10] H. R. Bachchan, *Kya Bhooloon, Kya Yaad Karoon* (Delhi, Rajpal and Sons, 1969/1993); K. Singh, 'Apne Bare Me' (About Myself), *Dus Pratinidhi Kahaniyan* (New Delhi, Kitab Ghar, 1994).

representative of an underlying 'truth'. In fact, for much of the twentieth century the theme of 'sexual energy turned in upon itself in a motif of contained, recycled essence'[11] has been, as if, shadowed by parallel narratives of non-reproductive sexual activity concerned with questions of modern subjectivity and its 'fulfilment'.

The focus on the colonial era, while it has opened up new areas of research and constitutes an indispensable resource for understanding the postcolonised present has also had a curiously occlusionary effect on research that might provide a complex entry into that present. It may not be an exaggeration to say that in recent times, a certain kind of scholarly work on India has become so 'over-determined' by history research that there is a tendency to render the present as almost a direct and unmediated consequence of the past. To speak of this propensity is not an incitement to ahistoricism, rather, an invitation to think about the present with as much finesse as that which marks so much of recent historiographic research on South Asia. So, for example, the relationships that contemporary populations have with that past[12] and the contingencies of the present as they articulate with imagined futures, appear not to interest many analysts; the present is, almost, not interesting enough. This, coupled with the lack of endeavours that seek to brush historical insights against the fabric of contemporary social life—the disdain for 'ethnography' in its various forms—has led to a situation where we do not have as theoretically sophisticated a sense of the post-colonial present as we do of the colonial past.[13] Certain versions of 'postcolonial theory'—those that often collapse different experiences of postcoloniality into a monolithic category—have, ironically, only compounded this situation. Their substantial reliance on English

---

[11] Alter, op. cit., p. 156.

[12] One that is nicely explored in Nita Kumar, 'Children and the Partition: History for Citizenship', (Calcutta, Centre for Studies in Social Sciences, 1998), Occasional paper No. 167.

[13] The issue, succinctly stated by Nita Kumar in another context, is of the following sort: 'How do you talk about weavers without ever encountering one face to face? How do you effectively describe rituals without witnessing the power of one?' Nita Kumar, Friends, Brothers, and Informants. Fieldwork Memoirs of Banaras (Berkeley, University of California Press, 1992), p. 10.

language texts produced by local and global elites—where, say a Rushdie novel comes to take on *Weltanschauung* status—and the resort to too-easy dismissals of 'ethnography', has led to simplistic representations of the postcolonised condition. It is hoped that this collection, which contains a variety of perspectives—historical, ethnographic, as well as those that seek to combine the two—will go some way towards exploring the complexities of the present in a similar manner to that which marks the efforts of historians of South Asia in their dealings with the past.[14]

'A focus on the conspiracy of silence regarding sexuality in India, whether within political and social movements or in scholarship', Mary John and Janaki Nair point out (following a broadly Foucaultian framework), 'blinds us to the multiple sites where "sexuality" has long been embedded.'[15] The outline of the history of the research on sexuality in South Asia provided by John and Nair in their introductory remarks to their edited collection *A Question of Silence? The Sexual Economies of Modern India* seeks to clear the way for critical cultural and social analyses of the sites, processes and discourses of sexuality. However, it also raises, I think, some interesting questions about modes of analyses. So, notwithstanding the valuable historical outline in their introduction, the dominance of history as *the* language of critical social analysis in South Asian studies is worth thinking about. There is need, in other words, to think about the relationship between history (or, rather, the history of specific processes such as sexuality) and contemporary non-scholarly subjectivity. So, while subjectivity in any area is the accretion of the events and processes of the past, how is this past interpreted in 'lay' engagements with it? We sometimes assume too readily that because we understand the historical construction of identity, this is the same thing as formulating a politics of the present.

As John and Nair also suggest that 'questions of male sexuality have rarely been a focus of scholarly analysis, except for celebrated

[14] My thanks to Kajri Jain for alerting me to an article by Vivek Dhareshwar that shares some aspects of the perspective outlined in this paragraph. V. Dhareshwar, 'Valourising the Present', *Seminar*, 446 (October 1996).

[15] M. E. John and J. Nair, 'A Question of Silence. An Introduction', in M. E. John and J. Nair (eds), *A Question of Silence? The Sexual Economies of Modern India* (Delhi, Kali for Women, 1998), p. 1.

instances of celibacy',[16] and that 'Celibacy has long been valorised as a cultural ideal for men, especially among Hindus.'[17] However, my own contribution to the collection attempts to argue that we may have placed far too much emphasis on celibacy as a central organising principle of (Hindu) male lives in South Asia; that, in fact, there exist unexplored sites of discourse on sexuality where the dialogue on celibacy is, in fact, far more ambiguous. Similarly, Kajri Jain's discussion about continuities and ruptures in the discourse on Indian popular culture also points to alternative lines of inquiry into the masculine realm.

However, in some respects John and Nair's discussion of the history of anthropological work in its engagements with sexuality appears to be unduly harsh, and they find very little of value in its vast corpus. It is in this vein that they pose the following question: 'could it be', they ask, 'that the caste/community/gender nexus framed by anthropology, so critical for any approach conceptualising sexuality in rural and urban India, has largely turned into a lost opportunity?' That anthropology is (and has been) a discipline in transition, and that there may be different models of anthropological inquiry does not seem a major concession to make; nor should it be difficult to devise anthropological frameworks that incorporate historical insights towards a sense of the present that attempts to make sense of the place of the past within it. Anthropology need not become history, but neither should we leave matters at history's door, assuming a straightforward mapping of the past onto the present; we may be subjects of history, but we make sense of it in a myriad ways. Nevertheless, John and Nair are quite correct to point out that:

> taken together, the discourses and practices of the law, of anthropology and demography leave us with a mixed legacy of hesitations, of questions opened up in one domain only to be shut out elsewhere, but also with an explicit concern over the details of sex that in any other context would be pornographic.[18]

The 'ancient' history of a 'liberal' sexual culture in India has, of course, been the subject of much popular and scholarly literature,

---

[16] *Ibid.*, p. 15.
[17] *Loc. cit.*.
[18] John and Nair, *op. cit.*, p. 26.

having been given a particular fillip through Sir Richard Burton's 1883 translation of the Vatsayayana's *Kamasutra*.[19] From Michel Foucault to the manufacturers of condoms in India, many have found satisfying uses for this text. Other, less well known, texts such as Kalyanamalla's *Ananga Ranga*[20] have also added to the lustre of the East as a place of once free sexual souls. However, texts have their own history of production and reception and these histories are as fascinating as the texts themselves. The *Kamasutra* and its cohort manuscripts also have their pasts, most importantly the past that is inextricably bound to the processes of colonial rule, and the reactions to it.[21] If I choose not to devote any length of space to a discussion of the centrality of this text to the development of Indian sexual cultures, it is not because it possesses no interest for contemporary scholarship; rather, it is because of the belief, considerably emboldened by Roy's discussion, that the importance of the 'classical indian love text' lies not so much in seeking connections between its recommendations and Indian sexual culture, as in its career as an object historical inquiry. In any event, even its role in the formation of an actually existing sexual culture is highly tenuous. Its importance may lie more in Western concerns with the difference between a technologised West and a 'free-flowing' East (as reflected in Michel Foucault's work, for example),[22] and in Indian middle class nationalistic pride in its 'great' civilisational past. This much we may speculate on the basis of recent arguments put forward by historians of modern South Asia. These are important topics that require separate research agendas, and I am constrained to leave matters at that.

During the early part of the twentieth century, sex and sexuality were part of another, more curious register, a context that brought together sexuality, *swarajya* and eugenics. This was the field explored, for example, by N. S. Phadke, Professor of Mental and

---

[19] Trans. by Sir Richard and F. F. Arbuthnot, introduction by Dom Moraes, John Muirhead–Gould (ed.), Vatsayayana, *The Kamasutra of Vatsayayana* (London, Kimber, 1963).

[20] Trans. by Sir Richard Burton and F. F. Arbuthnot, Kalyanamalla, *The Ananga Ranga of Kalyana Malla* (London, Kimber, 1963).

[21] For a discussion see K. Roy, 'Unravelling the *Kamasutra*', in John and Nair (eds), *op. cit.*, (1998).

[22] M. Foucault, *The History of Sexuality: An Introduction, Volume 1* (London, Penguin Books, 1990).

Moral Philosophy at Rajaram College in Kolhapur, Maharashtra. The foreword to Phadke's book, which was published in 1927,[23] was written by Margaret Sanger, 'the pioneer birth controller',[24] a fact that illustrates the localisation of a Western movement in an altogether different context within the colonial sphere. Phadke pointed out that his discussion was concerned with the issue of how to maintain the vigour of a 'declining race', for 'who could deny that physical strength and military power will be for us an indispensable instrument to keep *Swarajya* after it is won?'[25]

In many ways, Phadke articulated two important and recurrent themes of twentieth century nationalist discourse, viz., that of 'ancient Indian wisdom', and the importance of 'scientific thinking' for the development of a post-colonial society; President Radhakrishnan's *The Hindu View of Life*,[26] presents a good example of this, as did that of the proponents of modernising institutions such as the Doon School,[27] and of 'reformist' movements such as the Brahmo Samaj and the Arya Samaj. So, Phadke was to suggest that:

> any attempt to work out a Eugenic programme in India will have to take careful account of the principle of Heredity; and the Indian Eugenist will have, for instance, to subject the present Indian marriage institution to impartial and thoroughgoing criticism, and make constructive suggestions for its reform, induce the people to overhaul the whole mass of conventions and ideas about the act of procreation, and inspire then to leave the orthodox superstitious attitude towards sex questions for a scientific and healthy one.[28]

Further, he was to add,

> it need never be supposed that that the ancient Aryans were ignorant of the first principles of Eugenics and that India will have

---

[23] N. S. Phadke, *Sex Problem in India: Being a Plea for a Eugenic Movement in India and a Study of all Theoretical and Practical Questions Pertaining to Eugenics* (Bombay, D. B. Taraporevala Sons & Co., 1927).

[24] C. Haste, *Rules of Desire: Sex in Britain, World War I to the Present* (London, Pimlico, 1992), p. 24.

[25] Phadke, *op. cit.*, p. 8.

[26] S. Radhakrishnan, *The Hindu View of Life* (New York, Macmillan, 1975).

[27] S. Srivastava, *Constructing Post-Colonial India: National Character and the Doon School* (London, Routledge, 1998).

[28] Phadke, *op. cit.*, pp. 14–15.

to learn them anew at the feet of the Western scholars. [For] even in the Vedic and Puranic times our ancestors had realised the value of Eugenic principles with remarkable fulness of vision and depth of anxious insight, and how they had applied them to social laws and customs with conspicuous skill and foresight. ...a goodly harvest of Eugenic literature can be collected from Manu, Yadnyavalkya and other Smritis, some Brahmanas, the Ashvalayan Griha Sutras, medical treatises like the Vagbhatas and Sushruta, and the great epic of Mahabharata.[29]

There were also other instances during the early parts of the twentieth century of the 'ease with which the upper class agenda of Malthus and the Brahmanical Hindu agenda of upper caste India men could come together and reduce women to reproductive bodies requiring male control.'[30] Writing of colonial Madras, Anandhi also points out that 'the opposition between "desexualised" reproductive bodies as the ideal norm of "respectable" female sexuality and "sexual bodies" as its other, representing "immoral" and "disreputable" sexuality, was articulated by [several] political groups'.[31] We could generalise from this and say that a great deal of the discussion concerning sexuality has, implicitly and explicitly, been about the desexualisation of the female body, in which context the object of sexual acts becomes, exclusively, procreation.[32] This, of course, was an important aspect of the nationalist constructions of the 'ideal' Indian woman. However, other voices such as those of the Self-respect Movement and its founder Periyar E. V. Ramasamy argued the case for 'recasting desexualised reproductive bodies trapped within the endogamous/monogamous Hindu family, as sexual bodies capable of

---

[29] *Ibid.*, pp. 18 19.

[30] S. Anandhi, 'Reproductive Bodies and Regulated Sexuality. Birth Control Debates in Early Twentieth Century Tamil Nadu', in John and Nair (eds.), *op. cit.*, (1998), p. 145.

[31] *Loc. cit.*.

[32] The sexuality of the woman was often not an issue in another context, that of the inviolability of marriage as a sacral union. Hence, as in the case of the 'high caste "virgin" or "child" widows', Uberoi points out, 'the marriage was to be considered complete and binding even without consummation', Uberoi, *op. cit.*, p. 325. And, on the other hand, an implicit aspect of the Hindu Marriages Act of 1955 is that 'consent to marriage is also taken to be consent to sexual intercourse throughout the course of marriage', *ibid.*, p. 333.

breaking free from such regulations. For [Periyar], desire was natural and socially confining it amounted to a form of slavery.'[33] There was in Madras an overlap 'between the positions of the neo-Malthusians, nationalsists and the AIWC on birth control which...privileged women's reproductive role and delegitimised other forms of female sexuality.'[34]

However, in contexts others than the above—by which I mean other than those of the 'major' public discourses and movements—and during the second half of the twentieth century at least, female sexuality and female desire have had a reasonably well established, albeit silent, career in the annals of the 'minor' literatures of pornography, advice booklets and vernacular (in the cases I am familiar with, Hindi) journals of 'sex-education'.[35] In this, these are quite at odds with normative pronouncements regarding the boundaries of debate on sexuality. Discussions on female desire abound in contemporary mainstream women-directed magazines such as *Grihashobha* (The Splendour of the House/Home Beautiful) and *Meri Saheli* (My Girl-Friend), and articles with titles such as 'Sex: not only for entertainment but also an integral aspect of our lives', and 'Menopause should not

---

[33] Anandhi, *op. cit.*, p. 155.

[34] *Ibid.*, p. 157.

[35] As my primary objective is to survey terrain not usually covered by South Asia related social science literature, I do not intend to go over the substantial body of literature and debate devoted to the supposed 'cultural' split in Hindu life between 'women's sexual potency and their procreative and nurturing capacities', Raheja and Gold, *op. cit.*, p. 30. Raheja and Gold provide a summary of this position and of the various critiques, including their own, directed at it. Their account also highlights the fact that, contrary to conventional scholarly wisdom, 'sex-talk' is a common and important feature of women's lives. There is also, of course, a different context of female desire in India, viz., the debate over prostitution in the modern period. Whether as a threat to British military manliness (and hence the object of the Indian Contagious Diseases Act of 1868, see K. Ballhatchet, *Race, Sex and Class Under the Raj: Imperial Attitudes and Policies and their Critics* [New Delhi, Vikas, 1980]), or as a beguiling presence seducing Indian men, as in Premchand's, *Sewasadan* (New Delhi, Rajkamal, 1921/1994), the Indian prostitute has always had a negatively inflected agency in colonial and postcolonial debates. However, there was also a British opinion that suggested that prostitution in India was not always marked by 'the abhorrent feelings that obtain in Protestant England and other western countries' (Lt. Col. E. Tyrwhitt, DIG Police, NW Provinces to Secy. to the Govt. of NW Provinces, 'Kidnapping for Immoral Purposes', 22 Feb. 1870.)

mean a lack of sexual desire' (both in *Meri Saheli*, [March 1999])
are common fare. These themes were also common in an earlier
genre of 'advice' and 'discussion' magazines such as *Nar Naari*
and *Hum Dono*. The former was published from Patna from 1959
onwards. The latter magazine covered similar terrain and was
published from Ranchi in Bihar. I have been unable, however, to
ascertain the dates on which it started and ceased publication.

Such concerns as topics of public discussion—usually within
the framework of heteronormativity and domesticity—have, for
long been part of a semi-illicit circuit of debate and discussion,
the dialogue drawing its participants from small towns and
cities not part of the 'official' discourses on sexuality and 'sex-
education'. Its chief modes of articulation have been the quickly
produced 'pornographic' and 'advice' booklets, sold openly—
bound with trademark yellow cellophane paper—and circulated
surreptitiously among friends and relatives. Prior to its 'domestication' by 'women's magazines' as a topic proper to the familial
sphere, female sexuality and desire found in these publications
furtive audiences, solicitous advice-givers and, sometimes, anxious inquiries—from both men and women—about the nature of
and the necessity for female 'satisfaction'.[36]

Till quite recently, female desire—hetero or homoerotic—has
not been part of the feminist agenda in the Indian context, feminist
concerns (and those of non-feminist 'women's groups') having
been largely focused on issues of social, cultural and legal oppression of women. As a trope of subversion—to the domestic, for
example—it does, however, have a presence in literary and ethnographic works; *Mitro Marjani*, Krishna Sobti's great novel of
the 'recalcitrant' woman,[37] and the women's songs of North India
recorded by Raheja and Gold[38] provide excellent starting points
for more detailed research in this area. This challenge is slowly
being taken up by scholars of varied persuasions and recent
collections edited by Ruth Vanita and Saleem Kidwai mark a

---

[36] This is not a claim regarding the actual identities of the letterwriters. Rather,
that even if they are fictional creatures invented by the publishers, the continuing
popularity of their publications must say something about their role as 'true'
proxies for their readers' queries and anxieties.
[37] K. Sobti, *Mitro Marjani* (Delhi, Rajkamal Paperbacks, 1967/1994).
[38] Raheja and Gold, *op. cit.*.

promising beginning.[39] However, the incorporation of female sexual desire as an 'everyday' topic of discussion in the milieus of the 'woman's' magazine, one not otherwise sympathetic to feminist perspectives, presents an interesting situation; for it may mark not so much the circulation of feminist perspectives within wider circuits of readership, as the breakneck consolidation of a commodity culture, within which 'proper family life', sexuality and modernity become conjoined with the imperatives of choice.

And finally in this context, we should remember that an important impetus for the contemporary focus on sexuality in South Asia (and indeed in many other contexts) derives from something that is far more easily defined and more devastating in its consequences than scholarly reflection: the rapid, and seemingly unstoppable, spread of AIDS. Research on masculinity and sexuality in the Indian context has assumed a new urgency in the context of the reported trends on the pandemic in the subcontinent. In a recent report the World Bank has warned that as the AIDS axis 'pivots to Asia', the Indian subcontinent will come to 'dominate the picture in terms of the total numbers infected'. More specifically, it has been noted that in the Indian case 'the epidemic may be more likely to follow an exponential curve'[40] and that even the most reliable figures may only be underestimates. Further, the World Health Organisation (WHO) reported that during 1991 the Indian government revised its own estimate of HIV infection in India to include an almost hundredfold increase: from 4,515 cases at the beginning of the year to between 300,000 and 400,000 as at the end of the year.[41] As of 1 January 1995, India was estimated to have 1.5 million cases of HIV infection,[42] for the same period there were 20,000 cases of HIV infection in Australia.[43] From denials of the possibility of the occurrence of this 'Western'

---

[39] R. Vanita (ed.), *Queering India: Same-Sex Love and Eroticism in Indian Culture and Society* (London, Routledge, 2002); R. Vanita and S. Kidwai (eds), *Same-Sex Love in India: Readings from Literature and History* (New York, St. Martin's Press, 2000).

[40] J. M. Mann et al., *AIDS in the World/The Global AIDS Policy Coalition* (Cambridge, Mass., Harvard University Press, 1992), p. 26.

[41] *The Advocate*, 9 Nov. 1991.

[42] *HIV/AIDS in South-East Asia: An Update*, World Health Organisation Regional Office for South-East Asia.

[43] *Australia HIV Surveillance Report* (1996).

disease, we are now at a point where, for example, the government of Delhi is in the process of establishing a separate department for 'AIDS control awareness'.[44]

However, as Pigg and Pike point out in this volume, the emergence of AIDS as a major threat to public health is also linked to the consolidation of discourses of 'civil' and 'uncivil' life in the postcolonised situation. It is a context that entwines sexual economies with those of class privilege, nationalism, the urge to modernity and the imperatives of 'rational' behaviour. Of course, it is the clamour of these other voices that, in one way or another, concern all the contributors to this volume.

Cross-Cultural Modernities

It is important to situate current research into the sexual cultures of South Asia within a cross-cultural perspective. The importance of cross-cultural work on sexuality lies in the subsequent ability to contest the idea that sexuality is a thing in itself, rather than a process, an identity, or an event, that is a site of many other social and cultural processes. This should not, however, be taken to mean that the 'non-West' (for that is what we have come to understand when the term 'cross-cultural' is invoked) is a space of absolute difference, one with no historical linkages with what we understand as the 'West'. Rather, what is required is to foreground the *specificity* of locales—the accretions of 'culture' and history—that may invite unique readings on 'common' themes; I am speaking then of complicating analysis, rather than positioning it within the fiction of autochthonous development. This is of particular importance with respect to societies undergoing rapid cultural and social change. For in such situations, the construction of sexuality, and the discourses that gather around it (whether homo, hetero or others) have a fundamental connection with the entire gamut of processes—cultural, economic, political, 'global'—with which people must engage. Sexuality then becomes one of the many sites around which social and cultural ideas may be expressed. This does not deny the idea that the greater voice gained by certain marginalised sexual identities in

---

[44] *The Times of India*, 23 Feb. 1999.

India is not an important political process in itself, rather that it is also a part of the cultural politics of our time. To put it in another way, we might say that sexual identity 'is not destiny but choice',[45] and to formulate the issues in the terms of this paragraph is to seek to investigate the cultural, historical and political contexts of such choices.

The benefits of positioning questions of sex and sexuality within cross-cultural frameworks are well illustrated in a volume of articles edited by Patricia Caplan. Writing on 'notions of sexuality' among the Kikuyu of Kenya, Nicki Nelson suggests that

> just as men are thought to have a strong sexual drive, so are women, and both men and women recognise this fact. This is the reason migrant men give for forbidding their wives in the rural area to use any form of contraception. They fear that while they are gone their wives will have affairs and will not be found out.[46]

In the same volume, Caplan points to historical research that:

> shows how the dominant Anglo–American definition of women as especially sexual creatures was reversed and transformed between the seventeenth and nineteenth centuries into the view that women were less lustful than men. Cott's [1978] work on the ideology of what she terms female 'passionlessness' links it to the rise of evangelical Christianity between the 1790s and the 1830s. Ministers portrayed women as more sensitive to the call of religion than men, but the tacit condition for their elevation was the suppression of female sexuality, or, as another historian of the same period puts it, 'The mutation of the Eve myth into the Mary myth' (Basch 1974: 9).[47]

Clearly, what we require is a framework where a historically informed anthropology both establishes the haphazard trajectory of the past and is able to account for the contemporary complexities of the present.

Frameworks such as those in the Caplan edited volume may allow us to extend our discussion in various directions. So, in an

---

[45] J. Weeks, 'Questions of Identity', in P. Caplan (ed.), *The Cultural Construction of Sexuality.* (London, Tavistock Publications, 1987), p. 47.

[46] N. Nelson, 'Selling Her Kiosk: Kikuyu Notions of Sexuality and Sex for Sale in Mathare Valley, Kenya', in Caplan (ed.), *op. cit.,* p. 220.

[47] P. Caplan, 'Introduction', in Caplan (ed.), *op. cit.,* p. 3.

interesting contrast to an important strand in Indian thought, among the Kikuyu:

> it is thought that celibacy, as a voluntary state of abstention from sex, is a physical and psychological impossibility. Indeed there is no Kikuyu word for celibacy. ... There is no concept of a man or woman who is uninterested in sex.... Neither is there any word for frigidity in women, since granting a husband sexual services is an essential part of a wife's duty'.[48]

Hence, the juxtaposing of non-Western material has as much potential for problematising any notion of a homogeneous non-West, as does the usual comparison of West and 'non-Western' for the purposes of dismantling the universalism of categories.

Nelson goes on to point out that there is (and has been) a relative lack of distinction among the Kikuyu between 'married women' and 'free women' (that is, those who are part of the commercial sex economy). She observes that the relationship between husbands and wives in Africa lacks the 'mystical, romantic "soul mates till death do them part" elements which European monogamous marriage has developed over the last few hundred years'.[49] The Kikuyu stigmatise 'free women', Nelson says, not because of their perceived 'strong sex drive': rather, 'They are immoral because they have separated sex from procreation for the patrilineage. Uncontrolled sexuality is not a sin because of its venality or its essentially nasty character, but because it denies the lineage its future generation'.[50] This conclusion may well have resonance with aspects of the Indian situation.

'Cross-cultural research' does not, however, imply the retrieval of a once lost perspective, submerged by the wash of Western modernity. For, notwithstanding the current 'postcolonial' preoccupations with giving voice to 'other' knowledges and cultural positions, it would be ingenuous, not to say analytically simple-minded, to simply imagine away the West as a site of validation and performance. This is not to suggest, however, that non-Western engagements with the West have not been active and have not yielded fruitful frameworks of analysis and thinking.

---

[48] Nelson, *op. cit.*, p. 221.

[49] *Ibid.*, p. 234.

[50] *Ibid.*, p. 236.

Either way, it is no longer even possible to conceive a pristine theoretical and cultural world of 'non-Westernness', unmarked by a history of asymmetrical interactions. Given this context—where both the continuing potency of master narratives and a history of active participation within them structure our debates—fieldwork (conceived in the broadest possible sense and which can form the basis for cross-cultural analysis) in other places offers us one of the potent avenues of intervention in the naturalisation of universalist arguments. This is not really a strategy for 'improving' the West, but primarily one of re-centring the non-West. So, speaking of the Sambia of Papua New Guinea, the anthropologist Gilbert Herdt points out that to explore sexual cultures in 'other' places:

> is to re-examine the basic principles of late modern sexuality in the West. [Hence] To understand Sambia sexual subjectivity, for instance, we have to deconstruct the meaning of 'homosexuality' as a Western category.[51]

And further, that:

> while it is true that the Sambia practice homoerotic insemination, they lack the category 'homosexual' and have no 'homosexuals' to fill the category even if they did![52]

Cross-cultural work such as the above may, then, allow us to rethink the idea of identity in general and that of 'sexual identity' in particular. However, a caveat is in order. I am not suggesting that such a perspective should be accepted without problematisation, for, it is not difficult to see that it leaves Herdt open to charge of 'mining' his Sambia ethnography in order to 'improve' the West.[53]

---

[51] G. Herdt, *Sambia Sexual Culture. Notes from the Field* (Chicago, University of Chicago Press, 1999), p. 16.

[52] Herdt, *op. cit.*, p. 17.

[53] I am grateful to Kajri Jain and Stacy Pigg for raising this issue. There are, I think, some other works more ripe for criticism for their 'improving the West' perspective. See, for example, G. Marcus and M. Fischer, *Anthropology as Cultural Critique: An Experimental Moment in the Human Sciences* (Chicago, University of Chicago Press, 1986), and R. Rosaldo, 'Whose Cultural Studies?', *American Anthropologist*, Vol. 96 (1994). The urge to view anthropology's future as fundamentally linked to a doctrine of self-improvement is also, somewhat disappointingly, present in Nancy Scheper–Hughes' sentiments that 'Anthropological work, if it is to be in

There may, however, be another way of viewing this: as the possibility of 'decentring' knowledge. In any case, in the contemporary global cultural economy we ought not to make inflated claims for anthropology and this may be all that we can say.

Problematising 'Heritage'

To return to the Indian case, the discourse of 'Indian heritage' has, for the past one hundred years or so, had a prominent career in public discussions on individual behaviour, and like 'patriotism', it has been, till quite recently, one of the most naturalised of all social categories. A long history of social science research on the 'core' aspects of Indian life has also contributed towards the consolidation of a national imaginary of normal and abnormal Indianness; practice and custom as constituents of 'heritage' have, as recent scholarship has pointed out, had a rather marginal place in this imaginary that itself derives so much of its modern impetus from the *practices* of the nationalist movement that transformed the political landscape and allowed Indians to view themselves as other than deserving of perpetual colonial subjection.

Heteronormative perspective within the mainstream media, political parties, and those women's groups organised around preserving and promoting the 'sanctity' of domestic life has tended to structure debate on male and female homosexuality as a defence of Indian traditions. It is, by now, common place enough to point out that an important adjunct to these debates—Section 377 of the Indian Penal Code of 1861 that provides strict penalties for 'unnatural sex'—is itself a legacy of colonial rule. However, while it is important to point to the perversity of a situation where 'Indianness' may have come to be defined through the agency of British colonial rule, the extent to which the whimsy of history exhausts public opinion is not clear. Again, this is not an argument for ahistorical political practice or social theory, rather, one that seeks to problematise the uses of history. For the purposes of

---

the nature of an ethical and a radical project, is one that is transformative of the self but not (and here is the rub) transformative of the other.' N. Scheper–Hughes, *Death Without Weeping. The Violence of Everyday Life in Brazil* (Berkeley, University of California Press, 1992), p. 24.

contemporary critical practice, a strategy of analysing the present that theorises the relationship between the past and the present as less than deterministic would seem to be an important step towards identifying those processes of legitimisation that may sometimes be overlooked.

An important part of the landscape of sexuality—and that of 'heritage'—in the subcontinent has been the characterisation of non-Hindu and 'tribal' populations as particularly prone to sexual 'excess' and specially lascivious in their dealings with women of their community and with those of the (caste) Hindu groups. And, though twentieth century popular culture—films in the case of 'tribals' and written materials for that of Muslims—has played an important role in this process, it is certainly not a recent phenomenon. However, it could certainly be said that, the various processes of the twentieth century—nationalist and electoral politics, the Hindutva phenomenon, the ongoing tensions between India and Pakistan, among others—have served to embellish it.

There was no dearth of the sexual stereotyping of the Muslim and tribal populations during the colonial period. Further, there was a continuity of opinion that conjoined the Muslim and the tribal—both of whose sexual peculiarities had to be drawn out and carefully constructed—with those who were seen to be more obviously deviant. A kind of criminality came to be attached to all these groups. So, in the discussions that preceded the enactment of the Criminal Tribes and Castes Bill of 1872, not only were 'criminal tribes' sought to be controlled by legislative means, but a member of the Council of the Governor General of India 'moved for leave to introduce A Bill for the registration of criminal tribes *and eunuchs.*'[54] Further, it was suggested that 'it is proper to compel eunuchs to register, to render them liable to punishment for possession of a minor, and to declare them unable to adopt a son or to act as guardian to a minor.'[55] And from there, to the place of the Muslim in this 'unnatural' scheme of things:

---

[54] 'Extract from the Abstract of the Proceedings of the Council of the Governor General of India, assembled for the purpose of making Laws and Regulations under the provisions of the Act of Parliament 24 & 25 Vic., cap. 67, dated 3rd October 1870'. Home Department Files, National Archives of India, New Delhi (hereafter NAI). No. 1744, 27 Sept. 1870, (Emphasis added). See also Nigam 1995.
[55] Elliot to the Offg. Secy. to GOI, Legislative Dept., NAI, No. 640, 21 April 1871.

The provisions of the Bill, if strictly carried out, would reduce a considerable number of people to destitution. It is probable that in the three towns of Farrackabád ... there are not less than 1,500 persons of the *hijra* and *zánána* [i.e., non-castrated transvestite] classes. Their condition arises from immemorial usage, and degrading as it is, their practices are...sanctioned by public opinion of all Mussulmans....[56]

These sentiments were, of course, important echoes of colonial British opinions that had also been expressed in other contexts and at other times. So:

> when General Sir Lionel Smith stressed the importance of a lock hospital [for 'diseased women'] at Ahmadnagar, in 1830, he argued that one reason for the prevalence of VD was the presence of a large number of Muslims, 'the most debauched of any caste in this part of India'.[57]

The official records of the deliberations that preceded the Bill of 1872 present themselves almost in the nature of rites of self-affirmation, with those investigated for 'unnatural acts' tending mainly to be Muslims. So, in 1871 the Magistrate of Mathura noted that a eunuch by the name of Fyeman was reported to have been living with a twelve year old boy called Moolah (also referred to later as Moollah), and that the latter had been adopted during a famine. According to police reports, Moolah/Moollah identified one Eliah Jan as an associate of Feyman's, and as the musician to whose tunes he had danced wearing 'women's clothes and anklets'.[58] Particularly close attention was paid to Moolah/Moollah in a subsequent medical examination carried out by doctors Pain and Playfair, an examination which may perhaps be read as being an evaluation of native Muslim character:

> **Question:** Two doctors have examined your anus, and state that you bear clear marks of unnatural crime, who has had connection with you?
>
> **Answer:** About 18 months ago ... four eunuchs came from Futtehpore.... They came in a 2-bullock gharry. A Mahomedan

---

[56] *Loc. cit..*
[57] Ballhatchet, *op. cit.*, p. 20.
[58] Hardinge to the Commissioner, Agra Division, NAI, No. 18, 26 Jan. 1871.

drove them. A young man, beard just coming, dark complexion, was left with me alone. About noon he shut the door
and fastened it... and had unnatural intercourse with me.[59]

But of course, it was not only the 'criminal tribes' who shared
affinities with sexual errants such as eunuchs and Muslims; in
general, the spectre of peculiar (or uncontrollable) sexuality haunted
all tribal peoples. Speaking of Orissa during the nineteenth century, Felix Padel points out that 'the focus of the British campaign
to suppress human sacrifice was on saving [those] *meriahs*'[60] who
were to be sacrificed by the Konds. The usual practice consisted
of going into villages where the *meriah* were kept and taking them
away. Captain John Campbell, the first officer in charge of these
operations:

> was particularly proud of drafting 25 *meriah* into his *sebundy* corps,
> which he probably drilled in person.... [61] But the *meriah* children
> kept at his base in Russelkonds caused him endless problems.
> ...Campbell sent the girls to Sorada in order to put many miles
> between them and the boys, at Nowgam, for fear of sexual adven-
> tures—a segregation completely foreign to children from tribal
> background![62]

In 1848, the Captain reported that

> the large number of *meriah* girls are very unmanageable.... [And
> that] these girls are made to pound rice and prepare their food
> which keeps them employed, though not sufficiently either to
> prevent the necessity of the most constant vigilance and supervi-
> sion, or to remove the grounds of much anxiety regarding them.[63]

At present, the legacy of colonial and 'respectable' Indian opinion notwithstanding, a diversity of voices and practices characterise
the sexual cultures of South Asia.[64] The emergence of the homoerotic

---

[59] *Loc. cit.*; see Ann L. Stoler, *Race and the Education of Desire* (Durham, Duke
University Press, 1995) for a comprehensive discussion of the colonial discourse
on race and sexuality in the Dutch East Indies.

[60] F. Padel, *The Sacrifice of Human Beings: British Rule and the Konds of Orissa* (Delhi
and New York, Oxford University Press, 1995), p. 144.

[61] *Ibid.*, p. 145.

[62] *Ibid.*, pp. 145–46.

[63] Quoted in *ibid.*, p. 146.

[64] Here I am reverting to the traditional definition of sexuality as related to very
specific, goal oriented practice.

sphere into public life is a good example of this.[65] However, as in many other aspects of Indian life, this public presence is often dependant upon the whimsy of its 'translatability'—both as creative artefacts and lived experience—into the English language and as western concepts. So, while the writer and essayist Rajendra Yadav's remarkable 1956 proto-lesbian short story *Prateeksha* (The Wait)[66] is hardly referenced in gender and sexuality studies, Ismat Chugtai's much praised story *Lihaaf* (The Quilt) also owes its current visibility to its appearance in the English language. In India, as in other parts of the non-Western world,[67] male homoeroticism as both theory and practice has not been a particularly secret or unknown activity. This is true of both 'serious' and minor literature in non-English languages,[68] and social science research that cares to record it.[69] What has been relatively rare, however, is the ascription of a sexual identity to accompany it. This, of course, is part of an ongoing debate as to whether 'gay' and 'lesbian' identities are universal or part of, in societies such as India, the identity projects of middle class 'English educated' Indians [see, for example, the interview with prominent Indian gay rights activist Ashok Row Kavi in POZ (1998)].[70] The 'outreach' work carried out among men-who-have-sex-with-men (MSM) by non-governmental organisations such as the Delhi based Naz Foundation, indicates that same-sex relationships among men belonging to non-middle class contexts does not easily equate to

---

[65] I have deliberately employed varying nomenclature in the article as, for the Indian context at least, the debate over 'sexual identity' is by no means a resolved one.
[66] In R. Yadav, *Prateenidhi Kahaniyan* (New Delhi, Rajkamal Paperbacks, 1991).
[67] Herdt, *op. cit.*.
[68] Such as the ones analysed in L. Cohen, 'Holi in Banaras and the Mahaland of Modernity', *GLQ: A Journal of Lesbian and Gay Studies*, Vol. 2 (1995), and in the 'pornographic' literature referred to in my contribution to this collection.
[69] Though not specifically about male homoeroticism, Shrilal Shukla's, *Raag Darbari* (Delhi, Rajkamal, 1968/1991) presents an eminently analysable discussion of a provincial 'semen-economy' connected with masculinity. Curiously, despite its translation into English, *Rag Darbari: A Novel* (New Delhi and New York, Penguin Books, 1992), and incarnation as a television serial, its possibilities have remained largely unmined.
[70] W.M. Hoffman, 'Ashok to the System', an interview with Ashok Row Kavi by Willaim M. Hoffman, in *The Body: An AIDS and HIV Information Resource* (*http://www.poz.com/archive/july1998/inside/ashok.html*).

the adoption of a 'purely' homosexual identity:[71] indeed, sexual relationships between young men, and men and boys, are a common staple of the letters pages of magazines such as *Nar-Naari* and *Hum Dono*, without necessarily amounting to the affirmation of gay identities.[72] 'Fieldwork' data from Bangladesh seems to indicate a similar situation there.[73] Gay identity is, however, an important part of the contemporary Indian social landscape and magazines such as *Bombay Dost* and the recently established Delhi based *Darpan*[74] are part of it as both contributors to the process as well as consequences of a consciousness in the making.

Female homoeroticism as a consolidated site of public articulation has a more recent history. Part of this has to do with its position as an 'invisible' sexuality, an invisibility born both of a general incredulity at even the possibility of such acts, and a relative lack of legal proscriptions as to its occurrence. This lack of public presence, Indian lesbian activists have increasingly come

---

[71] Stacy Pigg has reminded me that the category 'MSM' has a history that deserves attention. It was, and remains, a gesture at opening up the question of the complexities of identities. And while I am not able to further explore this issue here, it is important to say that its circulation in the South Asian milieus speaks of the overlapping of a number of 'global-local' discourses, class contexts and the processes of engaging with local categories. I would like to thank the staff at The Naz Foundation (India) Trust for discussions on this issue and for making available their annual reports.

[72] I am aware of the perspective that 'gayness' can also be a political position. So, a recent review of a collection of *'Gay Writing from India'* points out that despite the editor's disavowal of a 'political' position, 'the act of editing an anthology of 'gay writing' is a political act.' S. Kugle's review of Hoshang Merchant (ed.), *Yaraana: Gay Writings from India* (New Delhi, Penguin Books, 1999), in *Darpan*, (Jan.–Mar. 2000), pp. 10–11. The recognition of an ambivalence over sexual identity (well captured through the expression men-who-have-sex-with-men) need not mean a denial of the political importance of gay identities. Further, the MSM category need not suggest a more progressive attitude towards women, since most men involved in MSM activity may not recognise a similar right (or possibility) of women to engage in same-sex activities or in relationships outside the marriage. This much we can deduce from a general understanding of scholarly literature on gender issues in India. See also, J. Seabrook, *Love in a Different Climate: The Meaning of Men who have Sex with Men in India* (New York, Verso, 1999).

[73] S. Ahmed, 'Risky Sex Among MSM in Public Sex Environment in Dhaka', paper presented at the conference on 'Sexualities, Masculinities and Culture in South Asia: Knowledges, Practices, Popular Culture, and the State, 6–8 July 1999, Melbourne, Australia.

[74] *Darpan*, however, covers issues of both gay and lesbian interest.

to realise, may be akin to the safety of a prison (see, for example, various discussions in the 1999 publication by the Campaign for Lesbian Rights [CALERI]).[75] One of the most salient consequences of the lack of a publicly articulated position on female homoeroticism has been its absence as a political platform within the strategies of the feminist movements. This has been in keeping with a general lack of engagement with the wider issue of female desire. However, some recent episodes have served, sometimes in tragic ways, to bring this context into public prominence; the suicide in 1998 by the two young women, Mamta and Monalisa, who had 'signed a notarized partnership deed in which they agreed not to marry, to stay together for the rest of their lives, to start a business venture and work together for the upliftment of women',[76] is one of these instances.

The Public Sphere: Debates, Forums and 'Experts'

It has been suggested that during the late nineteenth century, a prominent theme that underlined the 'sex question' in Britain concerned 'the aim to reconcile the sexual impulse to a new ethical order'.[77] So, a diverse cast of characters—Havelock Ellis, the novelist Olive Schreiner, the mathematician Karl Pearson, Beatrice Webb and the socialist Edward Carpenter among them—fired by a range of ethical ambitions and politico–philosophical predilections sought to reimagine the Victorian sexual landscape as a realm through which a reform of the 'private' would forever alter the contours of the 'public'. There exists a parallel, though largely uncharted, history of the 'sex question' as a public aspect of Indian modernity. It is a history whose archives are sprawled across a concatenation of minor printing presses in provincial cities, and over a loose networks of earnest men and women devoted to the task of grasping the 'truth' of sexuality in the cause of human 'satisfaction' and the explication of desire; it is an archive of the

---

[75] Campaign for Lesbian rights. A Citizen's Report, *Khamosh! Emergency Jari Hai. Lesbian Emergence.* (New Delhi, CALERI, 1999).
[76] Darpan. *The LesBiGay Mirror to the World* (New Delhi, The Naz Foundation, January–March 2000), p. 15.
[77] Haste, *op. cit.*, p. 8.

life of the province in a time of the consolidation of a metropolitan postcolonised modernity. The annals of the 'sex question' and issues of masculinity in India gather, then, around sincere missives to magazines such as *Nar-Naari* and *Hum Dono*, upon the shoddily-produced pages of 'advice' booklets such as *Kaam Samasyaen* (Sex Problems), and in the interstitial moments of the narratives of Indian cinema . These chronicles of postcolonised modernity may be found, as well, in the establishment of forums such as the *Nar-Naari Milan Manch* (Friendship Group), many of whose members expressed an interest in 'sex-related' literature and 'sex-knowledge', and sought to meet like minded men and women through the auspices of the above magazine.

Publications such as *Nar-Naari*, it need hardly be pointed out, constitute the encyclopaedia of the variety of the projects of the self in the postcolonised period. There is a certain assiduousness here in the recording of desires, fantasies, anxieties and intimacies that gains from not keeping to scholarly rectitude. In the pages of *Nar-Naari*, we find discussions of urolagnia, partly drawing upon psychoanalytic theories but also pointing to 'ancient belief according to which there is almost no difference between urine and semen.' Hence, it is pointed out, the saying, 'This boy was born from so and so's urine'. The discussion shares space with quotations from the Vedas, an article on the 'Sex-customs of Ancient Egypt' which concludes that, 'The [Egyptian] customs of devdasis, the worship of genitalia ... prove that ancient Egypt and ancient India must, in some way, have been linked', and discussions on the 'New Shape of the Family'. A 'Look at Sex in a Scientific Manner' is juxtaposed with a piece on 'Bajikaran: Restoring Potency through Traditional Medicines', and a discussion on 'Sex According to the Seasons' which enumerates, 'the pleasures of sweating and that of sweat drying upon the skin.... The cold weather is considered the best for sexual intercourse ... during winter, mutual oil massage is recommended.'

Corporeality as an aspect of the construction of the erotic is, of course, an important location of desire and fantasy. However, this does not in itself imply an exclusive identification between either desire and corporeality or desire and sex-eroticism, such that desire is exhausted in these denotative contexts. 'Desire' is the shard that splits from the body in order to reconstitute the self in the image of the most valorised social processes, as well as through objects that are not 'sexual' per se but become imbricated in an array of life-projects. 'Sexuality', in this sense, is an empty category, forever filling up (and evacuating) with the urge to be the 'satisfying' husband, the modern man, the wife as companion, the modern woman, the consumer of industrial commodities, the 'good' national subject and so on.[78] In the Indian case, the desires and fantasies that gather around sex and sexuality have also to do with the political economy of the province (versus that of metropolitan spaces and cultures), the unequal distribution of educational and other resources, and the competition for legitimacy by 'traditional' healing systems (against each other and against allopathy) in the dispensation of the postcolonised nation-state.

For the European context, 'with the rise of industrial society', Featherstone points out, 'passionate love became extended throughout the population. The literature on love of the eighteenth and nineteenth centuries (confessions, novels, pornography) became socially important by helping to provide "codes" between men and women, especially in the increasingly urbanised world of strangers.'[79] And yet, there is something more in the Indian public sphere of sexuality: a telescoping of a variety of processes of modernity—changes in family structures, the decline of established cultural zones and the rise of new immigrant spaces in the metropolis, the cultural and economic factors we have come to call 'globalisation'—that may not have been present to the same degree in the European case.

Simon points out that in the West 'sexology was born in [the] modernist tradition', where:

the modernisation of sex critically involved the naturalisation of sex; the sexual was to be subjected to the perspectives of natural science, which, in turn, required the quest for taxonomies, structures, and mechanisms of change that paralleled the vocabulary of the natural sciences as they were applied to all other life forms.[80]

---

[78] I do not mean to suggest a kind of instrumentality that sutures 'desire' to 'social process'; it may also, of course, be simultaneously subversive of the social. However, it is worth thinking about the degree of mutual exclusiveness between desire and the social. What social landscapes does subversion create?

[79] M. Featherstone, 'Love and Eroticism. An Introduction', in M. Featherstone (ed.), *Love and Eroticism*. (London, Sage, 1999), p. 5.

[80] W. Simon, *Postmodern Sexualities* (London, Routledge, 1996), p. 20.

In the Indian context, however, it seems more appropriate to say that a branch of sexology was formed as a by-product of (non-Western) modernity, but that many other, non-formal, systems of sexology pre-date the processes of modernity. Further, several non-formal systems of sexology (those that have neither the approval of the state nor that of the expert bodies of modernity: the professional associations) constitute not merely sites of engagement with modernity, but also attempts to contest modernity. One of the ways in which the latter is manifested is through claims to authority by the non-formal sexology sector in the name of alternative medical systems such as *Ayurveda*; in this way, these contests are not just articulations of the 'modernity of traditions', but also of the relevance of 'traditions' as sites of the discourses of intimacy at a time of increasing bureaucratisation and corporotisation of intimacy. Of course, I do not mean to suggest that contemporary 'traditional' sexological practices are not also part of an rapidly consolidating market economy, only that they may often contain parallel worlds of imagining the social self: both as supplicant and antagonist to the commerce in intimacies.

Assaying Sexual and Masculine Cultures

Covering the late eighteenth century period in India, Sudipta Sen's essay 'explores early versions of racial difference, especially as they intersected with other barriers that kept colonial societies such as British-India in place: blood and sex.' At this point in the career of colonialism, Sen points out, many of the features of the colonialism of later periods—'explicit racism', and the 'emasculation of the native in the service of British hyper-masculinity'— may not serve as useful framing devices. 'The family' he argues, 'was ... a strong organizing metaphor for the [English] state in the eighteenth century', and the imperial context of the civilizing mission owed much to this 'experience of the paternalistic, authoritarian state at home' where the male head of the household had already been theorised as being in a hierarchised relationship to the women and servants of the family. In the context of a situation of a substantial degree of social and sexual relationships between English men and native women, there developed a specific colonial discourse. This, it was argued was a situation prone to 'degeneracy', for 'an orderly middle class household was the site of respectability, happiness and discipline, but the despotic customs of the Orient in India thwarted this possibility.' The 'half-caste' emerged as a site of colonial fear, viewed as it was as creating a link between the rulers and the ruled and hence eroding the 'exclusive position of the rulers.' Here, sexual acts also became translated into political imaginaries organised around the defence of empire. Finally, sex was given a political and judicial biography: in April 1791, the Court of Directors of the East India Company (EIC) passed a resolution that barred Eurasians from gaining appointment with the company. Slightly later, 'purity' of parentage was further institutionalised as a principle for recruitment into the EIC's army, for gaining succour from charitable funds, and for widows wishing to establishing claims upon their husband's assets.

It was also assumed that those of mixed parentage would identify with a European heritage, inasmuch as it was inconceivable that a white woman would marry a non-white, and that the father's blood would 'dictate' the child's ancestry. There subsequently emerged an elaborate classificatory system that bound sex, race and power with the twine of legitimacy and its obverse. Hence, British and Indian subjects were produced according to whether the union between white men and brown women was 'legitimate' or not. In Sen's study, blood and sex become intermingled, contributing to a bio-politics of difference among the colonisers: the presence of 'Indian blood'—indicating proscribed intimacy between European men and Indian women—came to represent a degeneracy of character, and an unsuitability towards securing the appellation 'English'. In an important sense, Sen suggests, underlying the various discourses on purity and the taint of the tropics, was the visage of the English conjugal household. Finally, sex and economic prospects also became conjoined in as much as sexual relations between the Europeans and Indians also came to be seen as the path to 'deracination' and emasculation and hence virulent threats to 'the political ambitions of a commercial and trading nation like Britain.'

If the heterosexual family served as a model for colonial authority, then what of non-heterosexuality as a subversive force? Taking up a slightly later period, Zahid Chaudhary's discussion tracks the contours of colonial authority as inflected through the cultural politics of race and homoerotic desire. Focusing his attention to J. R. Ackerley's *Hindoo Holiday* (1932), Chaudhary points out that while the 'Near East' has been the focus of considerable scholarship on sexuality and travel writing, the Indian subcontinent has not received much attention. In particular in this context, despite the prominence of writers such as E. M. Forster and J. R. Ackerely and knowledge of their sexual preferences, the homoerotic sphere has tended to remain underexplored. *Hindoo Holiday*, Chaudhary suggests, is a text 'rife with the pressures of power dialectics, colonialist (sexual) anxieties and orientalist authority, all three of which are interdependent.' Ackerely arrived in India to take up the position of 'English tutor' in the household of the Maharaja of Chhatarpur, a position situated at the juncture of the colonial political, cultural and sexual imaginary. And, irrespective of his attempts to present himself as distant from the structural matrix of colonialism due to his 'marginal' sexuality, Ackerely's location, Chaudhary points out, never escaped the 'structure of [colonial] dominance; in his writings, he is always "on top", and interactions with the natives, sexual or otherwise, always take place on his terms. 'In this sense, Chaudhary suggests, sexual marginality does not 'cancel' imperial authority but only circulates within it (or rather, within the colonised space) as a differently inflected adjunct to it.

The career of alternative identities in the *Indian* context is the object of Kathryn Hansen's paper. Her essay explores 'the buried trove of theatrical transvestism that existed in western urban India in the Parsi, Gujarati and Marathi theatres between approximately 1850 and 1940' and attempts to position it within the context of the changing public culture of the metropolitan space. The urban theatre developed as a 'respectable substitute' for the vulgarities and immoralities of the 'folk' form. We also have here the slow but sure process of the consolidation of the 'moral' public space, its area delineated by the discourses of nationalism, upper caste politics, and the politics of 'proper' gender and sexuality. However, this move towards 'respectability' also introduced the socially well-positioned female impersonator, hence opening up new questions about homosociality. Hansen makes an important point about the *positive* nature of the demand for female impersonators through arguing that they found employment not simply because not enough women could be found to act on stage, rather, there may also have existed a *preference* for female impersonators who competed with female actors for roles. This, of course, moves us into an entirely different terrain of exploring homoeroticism and homosociality that existed within the interstices of heteronormative milieus. Hansen's discussion attempts to position these as not just alternative sexualities but as parts of the 'norm'.

Carla Petievich's contribution takes up the issue of the gender politics of the mainstream *ghazal* through a focus on the marginalised Urdu poetic genre known as *rekhti*. Developed by the literary figure Sa'adat Yar Khan 'Rangin' (1756–1834), rekhti differentiated itself from the mainstream ghazal through the device of utilising a feminine narrator, even though its public audience and all the major composers have been men. Twentieth century evaluations of rekhti, Petievich suggest, have been marked by 'moralistic judgements and a great deal of evasion' over its proclivity towards salacious narrative. However, she also points out, what may trouble the critics most is the supposed 'female-to-female' content of some of the rekhti poetry. This, she goes on to say, may only be a 'ruse' to efface a more subversive aspect of rekhti: that by unambiguously specifying the gender of the narrator and of the narrator's beloved, rekhti questions the naturalisation of male homoeroticism at the expense of female homoeroticism.

However, the terrain of gender and sexual politics is complicated by the fact that rekhti may not have been as much genuinely insurrectionary politics as male parody of female desire; it is the simulacrum of a desire inflected out of the political conditions of women. The subversive possibilities of rekhti, Petievich suggests, are undermined by the reductionism inherent in narrating female desire as unambiguously carnal, shorn of any of the complexities inherent in the male homoeroticism of the *rekhta* (mainstream) ghazal. Petievich warns us, then, against the tendency to read 'resistance' into the appearance of forms. During the postcolonial period, the politics of reading resistance, and what John and Nair refer to as 'the narrative of "decline" of "our" traditions has become a dominant tendency in spheres as divergent as social reform movements and contemporary radical sexual politics.'[81] If we follow Petievich's discussion, then we are forced to confront the possibility that just as the past cannot be used to

---

[81] John and Nair, *op. cit.*, p. 12.

account for all the 'evils' of the present, neither does it offer us much scope for its deployment as an uncritical resource for the present.

'Marginality', we have increasingly become aware, may not be sufficient grounds for insurrectionary forays upon the realms of dominant systems. For, the marginal space is also internally differentiated, its fault lines and fissures variously articulated with the discourses of dominance. Ethnographic work is often fruitful in overturning our most cherished fantasies through which we theorise the realm of the possible; the fantasies in which the 'marginal' performs a variety of transformative tasks assigned it. It is a fissured space of same-sex sexuality that concerns Gayatri Reddy's discussion. Her ethnographic site is Hyderabad and she combines a focus on contemporary transnationalism with an analysis of 'the relationship between different models of same-sex sexuality' current in India in order to denaturalise homosexuality-in-practice. Reddy juxtaposes two quite different kinds of male sexuality, one 'traditional' and the other 'modern'. The traditional *hijra* sense of the self is organised around notions of kinship, the desirability of 'controlled' sexual activity (frequently articulated through the vocabulary of Hindu life cycle discourses) and the dicta of authenticity, connected to surgical removal of the male genitalia.

In many respects, then, the codes of self-definition among the hijras are contiguous with those followed in 'mainstream' Hindu society; that is to say, that, the hijras articulate a difference that both interrogates and validates 'mainstream' social positions. Self-identified 'gay' identities in Hyderabad appear to be constructed through a more oppositional matrix, with being gay positioned as radically different from being heterosexual, with the public and private sense of 'gayness' fostered through a series of domestic and global developments in the cultural, economic and political sphere. There also appear to be no spaces of contiguity between 'gay' subjectivity and the wider cultural cache of religious and social ideas. Perhaps the most striking aspect of 'gayness' in Hyderabad is its subscription to the ideology of equality, the hierarchisation implicit in hijra categories of the self is done away with in favour of a position within which 'acknowledging desire for other men makes all such individuals *equally* gay' (italics in the original). Reddy concludes by pointing out that not only do these two senses of same-sex sexuality co-exist in India, but also that there are many points of borrowing rather than a strict demarcation of 'traditional' and 'modern' sexualities.

South India is also the focus of Chandra Balachandran's report on a preliminary project 'on emerging gay geographies' in Bangalore'. Adopting an approach influenced by geography, Balachandran attempts to develop a spatial mode of analysis for non-heterosexual identities. His framework derives from a number of variables: the internet as a tool of information exchange, the divide between English speaking and non-English speaking groups, the significance of class, and the various contexts of 'tradition' in a situation of rapid change among them. Through the outline of his vision for future research in the area Balachandran enunciates a position that combines both activist and scholarly ambitions.

Public debate over sexual identities is the topic broached by Vikash Pandey in his essay on Deepa Mehta's controversial film, *Fire*. The film, Pandey states, 'articulates the split between eroticism and emotional attachment in the heterosexual relationship: when wives threaten to become unavailable, the men of the house are erotically charged, and when the women are caring, they are percieved as sexually unstimulating by the husbands.' However, Pandey contends, the transgressive possibilities within the film are only partially realised, and perhaps even undermined by the filmmaker's reliance on essentialist resolutions to the politics of gender and sexuality. For, the narrative, rather than subvert masculinist ideologies merely pays them homage by seeking to imbue femininity with essences of its own, through a discourse of 'the authentic female self'. Such a position, Pandey concludes, effectively effaces the political and social complexities of the experience of womanhood, in effect, constituting an 'erasure of women' from the social *mise en scène.*

Leena Abraham's study focuses on the discourses and practices of sexuality among low-income, college going urban youth in Mumbai, and in this provides us with access to an arena that is not as well covered as research in higher socio-economic categories. Her study of youth sexuality is located, Abraham points out, at the juncture of a persistent belief system that valorises notions such as *pativrata*, and another space containing the often contrary messages that are a part of the burgeoning popular and commodity cultures of urban India. The specific socio-cultural circumstance of the group surveyed by Abraham—their language of everyday communication, their parents' occupations, their modest access to the commodities of their desires, for example—makes their location in a time of rapid change, a particularly interesting phenomenon. For, in the postcolonised situation, it is this group which, in many ways, must adapt most rapidly to briskly transforming social and cultural relations. Abraham points out that any automatic connection between the 'liberal' milieu of the metropolis and the transformative effects of globalisation on the one hand and their 'emancipatory' effects on women needs to be regarded with caution. For, as her study shows, many young women in Mumbai continue to be part of the regime of pativrata which places an unequal burden of 'goodness' and 'purity' upon men and women. 'The practices of silence' which constitute an important aspect of the socialisation of girls about their bodies and their sexuality are one of the several constituents of the cacophony of the city.

Young Nepali women working in Indian brothels have received considerable global attention as objects of pity and 'welfare'. Sushma Joshi's thought-provoking paper on the 'trafficking' of women between Nepal and India attempts to problematise the very concept through an exploration of the discourse that gathers around it; these include the contexts of social policy, activist non-governmental organisations (NGOs) and those of 'gender, citizenship and the nation'. Joshi points out that her task is to clear the way for an understanding of the 'trafficked' woman as a subject in the face of a well ensconced anti-trafficking discourse dominated by middle class upper caste women that has succeeded in 'reifying the notion of women-as-kin while obfuscating the need to define women as citizens of the nation.' In this, the latter position borrows from state level perspectives within which women are, in the first place, daughters (cheli-beti), sisters and wives, subject to male authority. The women-as-kin viewpoint finds further elaboration in the work of certain prominent anti-trafficking NGOs and in national policy through the discursive institutionalisation of the idea of the 'maiti': the natal home. The maiti discourse—which assigns a 'loving' but subservient position to the married-out daughter/sister—finds play in anti-trafficking activism through similarly prescriptive manoeuvres; 'trafficked' women come, then, to be defined as younger kin, in need of state (read, male) protection and 'rehabilitation', a position that simultaneous effaces the issue of the rights of women (to education, landownership, etc.) that may lead to transformation of their place in society.

As for 'rehabilitation', Joshi points out that rehabilitation homes in Nepal are eerily similar to the brothels from which the girls have been rescued and that each is, in turn, contiguous with a 'fear' discourse of the home: that women and girls need to be protected and must be careful not to stray too far from its confines. These spatialised narratives of fear have combined, Joshi suggests, to create 'women who are vulnerable and need protection.' Trafficking also serves as a national myth; serving to as a narrative of self-representation where a small and 'virginal' Nepal is 'violated by its far bigger neighbour; as a myth of national solidarity (against India), it pre-empts the necessity of a domestic dialogue over the need for internal reform of Nepalese institutions and norms.' Themes of Nepalese 'purity' and its 'desecration' are also reinforced through a process that sutures the *kumari* (virgin goddess) figure of Nepalese mythology to the cheli-beti whose purity must be protected; in both cases, male 'honour' comes to depend crucially on female purity. Joshi concludes by pointing to a collusive project between Nepalese and non-Nepalese participants that reinforces and promotes 'black and white' images of 'trafficking'. Hence, she suggests that the Western media and fund-raising bodies have been implicit in presenting 'Orientalist' images of the 'trafficked' women that accord with preconceived ideas.

Nepal is also the focus of discussion of the paper by Stacy Leigh Pigg and Linnet Pike. The collaboration is the result of two distinct projects carried out by the authors. Pigg's research has focused on 'the production of public knowledge about AIDS' with particular emphasis on the NGO sector, while Pike worked among sex workers in mid and western Nepal. The discussion is, therefore, situated at the juncture of caste, class, knowledge and 'respectability'. Between them the authors account for both the (middle class) formulators of anti-AIDS strategies as well as their (non-middle class) target groups; and, as is the hallmark of postcolonised situations in particular, this is a context ripe for the production of discourses on the 'primitive' and the 'civilised', the 'disreputable' and the 'respectable', constituents of Nepalese modernity.

Pigg and Pike suggest that AIDS education programmes in Nepal have been characterised by representations of homosexuality as alien to Nepalese society, minute cataloguing of sexual acts that mimics a nineteenth century European obsession with categorisation, as well as the effacement of the fluidities of local life and custom. The recent 'public attention to sexuality' has been accompanied by a public health dialogue that speaks to the problem from within upper caste and masculinist perspectives where both the non-upper castes and women tend to be cast as ignorant or naïve, or both; the latter characterisation is often reserved for upper caste women who are seen to have been seduced by the wiles of (Western) modernity. Most importantly, they suggest, the subtext to this dialogue is derived from development discourses that utilise universalising 'scientific' terminology, and which, implicitly, strive to make 'civil-society' synonymous with a homogenous upper caste culture. The authors conclude through a discussion of the case of the *Badi* people of mid and far west Nepal, an entire community that has come to be seen as inclined to 'commercial sex-work'. Pigg and Pike argue that the case of the Badi points to the complicities between the (global) development discourse and the dialogue of Nepalese modernity.

The prerogatives of maleness which have been an important theme in the various discussions thus far finds a more explicit focus in the two essays that follow. Kajri Jain explores the terrain of popular culture and masculinity and her paper seeks to 'open up some questions about the links between masculinity, muscularity, power and the work of mass-cultural image in post-independence India.' Her discussion focuses on muscularity in iconographic images in order to gain a perspective on the intersection of modernity and 'tradition' at which such images are positioned. She argues against a teleological understanding which reads the current muscularity of Ram images as in a direct relationship to earlier non-muscular iconography. The main issue, she suggests, is to understand how, after such a long history of the 'humanising' of Ram (and other divinities), the muscular god has achieved such popularity in contemporary times.

In calendar art, Jain suggests:

figuring [the] strapping male bodies [reified through the slogan *Jai Jawan, Jai Kisan*] is legitimised by their servile, devotional relationship to the state in much the same fashion as the muscular *shakti* of Hanuman's body becomes permissible, and indeed available for mimetic incorporation, within the framework of his *bhakti*. The *Jai Jawan* soldier and the *Jai Kisan* farmer... thus occupy an homologous position to that of Hanuman within a structure of devotional abjection.

Jain makes the important point that the adoption of realist techniques by the calendar industry does not signify the emergence of a 'post-sacred' subject, rather that its terms of reference are unequivocally lodged within—and derive their legitimacy from—the realm of the sacred'. The context for the elaboration of the iconography of calendar art, she argues, is the cultural economy of the 'bazaar', a term used to signify the domestication of capitalism through scraping against the social fabric of local concerns and preoccupations.

The masculinised version of Ram, Jain goes on to suggest, may not have been possible without the emergence of the very 'non-abject' worker figure portrayed by Amitabh Bachchan. For, 'the Bachchan persona [made] visible and available a bodily modality—and therby a ground for subjectivity—where the male body becomes a libidinised site for the production of value through its engagement with other bodies and objects.'

Even as Bachchan's 'modality of bodily agency did not *replace* existing forms, its very availability in the field of images posed a threat to the canonical symbolic order, to which Hindutva's response was a *defensive reappropriation* of the muscular body in the form of the aggressive Ram.'

My own contribution is based on 'fieldwork' in the 'sex clinics' of Delhi and is a preliminary exploration of the forum of discussion and debate that gathers around these and Hindi language 'footpath pornography'. The paper outlines a series of contexts that appear to be important for the study of non-middle class sexual cultures in India.

An important aspect of this forum is that most of its audience has little or no voice in the metropolitan postcolonial culture of the nation-state: it is not the 'reading-formation' of the civil-society constituted through *India Today* or *The Times of India*, nor does it take part in the formation of the idea of 'postcoloniality' that has gathered around writers such as Salman Rushdie and Vikram Seth. It does find some voice, however, in the writings of certain others such as Manjul Bhagat (*Anaro*), Nagarajun (*Ugratara*), and Krishna Sobti (*Mitro Marjani*).The context of this arena of debate and discussion is the milieu of the urban poor, rural-urban migration, and a variety of other aspects that impact upon the consciousness of the contemporary self. It is in this context that many new questions are being asked about the 'modern' self. The factors that go towards the formation of this context include: a new commodity culture, masculine anxiety, the marginalised position of 'traditional' medicine, and a new urban sensibility that is formed by but not reducible to the processes of globalisation.

Of course, other varieties of discourses on sexuality and masculinities—such as the Gandhian and the 'traditional Hindu' one's, for example—also make an appearance on this stage, but their presence does not appear to be either overarching or determining. They do not, in other words, form master-narratives of discourse and opinion. The Delhi 'sex clinics' are an important site for the investigation of this process, functioning, as they quite often do, as sites of therapy for marginalised populations. My discussion moves between the 'sex clinics' and footpath pornography, for the two are linked, both in the sense that many sex clinics publish the latter, and the clientele for the two is often the same. The important thing is that they are both part of a site for the discussion of many aspects of modern subjectivity in India.

2

Colonial Aversions and Domestic Desires

Blood, Race, Sex and the Decline of Intimacy in Early British India

◆ Sudipta Sen

T homas Babington Macaulay, liberal reformer and polemicist, found eastern India populated by a class of subjects enervated by a soft climate who were weaker in character than other Asiatics, just as the Asiatics were weaker than the bold and energetic children of Europe. Comparing Bengalis to other Hindus, and Hindus to Europeans, he famously quipped:

> ...the physical organization of the Bengali is feeble even to effeminacy He lives in a constant vapour-bath. His pursuits are sedentary, his limbs delicate, his movements languid. During many ages he has been trampled upon by men of bolder and more hardy breeds. Courage, independence, veracity, are qualities to which his constitution and his situation are equally unfavourable. His mind bears a singular analogy to his body. It is weak even to helplessness for purposes of manly resistance.[1]

---

[1] T. B. Macaulay, *Critical, Historical and Miscellaneous Essays and Poems*, Vol. 2 (Boston, Estes and Lauriat, 1880), pp. 566–67.

Decades later in 1899, G. W. Stevens, one-time special correspondent of the *Daily Mail*, made a similar observation:

> By his legs you shall know the Bengali. The leg of a free man is straight or a little bandy, so that he can stand on it solidly: his calf is taper and his thigh flat. The Bengali's leg is either skin and bone, and the same size all the way down, with knocking knobs for knees, or else it is very fat and globular, also turning at the knees, with round thighs like a woman's. The Bengali's leg is the leg of a slave.[2]

Although a Bengali clearly represented the worst kind of unmanly Indian, the general effeminism of subject races articulated first in British India by Robert Orme in the eighteenth century persisted through much of the nineteenth, alongside biological race, Social Darwinism and even early eugenics. These observations were not just capricious; they represented over the course of a century the cumulative and residual mythologies of race under colonial rule. The appearance of emasculated and enslaved subjects of the British empire, I would like to argue in this essay, was not simply a product of explicit racism, or of the need for an assertive, self-serving masculine identity for Englishmen in the tropics. During the period of imperial expansion, caricatures of a new subject population emerged in the process of the 'naturalisation' of colonial subjects. Even in 1836, a Select Committee appointed by the House of Commons to consider what measures ought to be adopted for native inhabitants of countries of British settlement, explained its task thus:

> The situation of Great Britain brings her beyond any other power into communication with the uncivilized nations of the earth. We are in contact with them in so many parts of the globe, that it has become of deep importance to ascertain the results of our relations with them, and to fix the rules of our conduct towards them. We are apt to class them under the sweeping term of savages, and perhaps, in doing so, to consider ourselves exempted from the obligations due to them as our fellow-men.[3]

---

[2] G. W. Stephens, quoted in Nirad C. Chaudhuri, *Thy Hand, Great Anarch! India: 1921–1952* (Reading, Addison–Wesley, 1987), p. 673.

[3] *Imperial Parliament, House of Commons* (publication details missing), p. 1, Salem Phillips Library, Peabody Essex Museum.

These obligations and beliefs anticipated, and even existed along with, the results of systematic and scientific examination of non-European races at a later period.

This essay explores early versions of racial difference, especially as they intersected with other barriers that kept colonial societies such as British India in place: blood and sex. In tracking such dissemination of racial ideology, especially toward the end of the eighteenth century, one needs to look away from some common associations that are Victorian in terms of history, Darwinian in terms of bio-ideology and politically contemporaneous with the high meridian of empire. It charts the racial divide in India during a formative period of British rule, when the colonial political economy was still burdened with the ideological work of sorting out the relationship between authoritarian rule, subjecthood and the division of labour. Distinctions between nation, race and subject had yet to harden into civilisational and biological certitudes.

Forms of inequality within the state and society in England had always impressed ideas of colonial rule as much as the encounter with people newly under British rule. In the denial of civilisation, sovereignty, property and liberty to the mass of inhabitants within the newly expanded reaches of empire in the later eighteenth century, various inferior subjects were authored: timid and rebellious savages, noble and ignoble barbarians, sturdy and effete workers, indentured bodies and slaving bodies, docile and treacherous subjects, Indians and Irishmen, the Negro, the Kaffir and the Fingoe, the Moor and the Gentoo. It is difficult to overlook the overtly gendered and sexually charged aspects of such nomenclature.

Recent work on the relationship between the sites of bourgeois sexuality in Europe and ideas of race has emphasised the many-stranded legacy of colonialism. Some historians have offered a straightforward explanation of the formation of male sexual identity, as in the case of young men in search of sexual exploitation and adventure in the colonies;[4] others have suggested an underlying sublimation of sexual danger and the threat of racial

---

[4] Ronald Hyam, *Empire and Sexuality: The British Experience* (Manchester & New York, Manchester University Press, 1990), p. 211.

difference *within* the walls of a European domestic scene.[5] According to Robert Young, perceptions of race were tied to the hidden articulations of sexual desire.[6] The misadventure and anxiety of the English household in early British India framed the discourse on race, and also contributed to sanguinary lines intended to keep the different subjects in place.

Historians of India and the British Empire have long regarded the last decade of the eighteenth century as a significant divide. This was a time when the Company government began to categorically discourage, liaisons and marriages between Englishmen and Indian women, remove the sons of 'mixed-blood' from service in the civil and military departments, and encourage the presence of English-born white women.[7] I reappraise here the significance of this dispossession in order to sift through colonial social formations and extract the particular histories of the relationship between blood, inheritance, race and sexuality. Why India never did become a major settler colony or, indeed, produce a significant population of mixed Indo-Anglican descent toward a more widespread mestizo society, can be traced back to both the eroticisation and radicalisation of cultural difference.

The Colonial State and the New Domestic Order

With the emergence of newly constituted subjects, some significant tensions and contradictions surfaced in the formulation of the East India Company's colonial polity. Consider, for instance, the rising ideology of the domestic household in British India as a crucible for the larger conceptions of state and political economy. The political discourse of the Enlightenment had produced an

---

[5] Ann Laura Stoler, *Race and the Education of Desire: Foucault's History of Sexuality and the Colonial Order of Things* (Durham and London, Duke University Press, 1995).

[6] Robert Young, *Colonial Desire: Hybridity in Theory, Culture, and Race* (London, New York, Routledge, 1995), pp. 25–26.

[7] See for instance Percival Spear, *The Nabobs: A Study of the Social Life of the English in Eighteenth Century India* (London, Curzon Press, 1980); Kenneth Ballhatchet, *Race, Sex and Class under the Raj: Imperial Attitudes and Policies and their Critics, 1793–1905* (New York, St. Martin's Press, 1980), and more recently Hyam, *ibid.*, pp. 115–16.

overt reference to paternalist authority in the conception of state-hood. In the despotic state, following Kant, subjects are likened to immature children who do not have the means to judge their own good or evil and look up to the head of the state for guidance, whereas in the patriotic state everyone 'regards the common-wealth as the maternal womb.'[8] In this, and various other rendi-tions, the eighteenth century, it might be argued, interrogated and received the Aristotelian relationships between *oikia*, *oikos* and the *polis*. An important instance in this debate in the English context was Locke's rebuttal of Robert Filmer's *Patriarcha*, where he re-pudiated the Biblical injunction of filial submission to the figure of the king, and suggested a much wider arena of relationships in society in the conception of a meaningful polity: man and wife, parents and children, master and servant. I do not have the opportunity here to elaborate upon the interrelated series of enclosures through which the negative markers of civilisation were produced—non-male, non-adult, non-white, non-gentrified, and so on. The crucial point here is that the regulative framework of the bourgeois household was being reified in the course of the formation of the English state, particularly through the Georgian period. In this contention I follow Corrigan and Sayer's sugges-tion that we relate the so-called private realm of the household to the 'public sphere' of rule, for throughout the eighteenth and nineteenth centuries, 'the centrepiece of the social fabric was the family, its patriarchal order and society reflecting that of society as a whole.'[9] The family was certainly a strong organising meta-phor for the state in the eighteenth century.

The orderly family, as Lawrence Stone has shown, was part and parcel of the orderly nation state, and both represented a search for stability in a world of rapid material upheaval and uncertainty of station and rank for men who had long been apprenticed in hierarchy.[10] A significant aspect of this process related to the ambitions and constraints of the gentrified family, with the decline

---

[8] Immanuel Kant, 'Von den vershiedenen Racen der Menschen' [1775] in Earl W. Count (ed.), *This is Race* (New York, Henry Schuman, 1950), p. 74.
[9] Philip Corrigan and Derek Sayer, *The Great Arch* (Oxford, Blackwell, 1985), p. 12.
[10] Lawrence Stone, *The Family, Sex and Marriage in England, 1500–1800* (New York, Harper & Row, 1979), p. 146.

of clientage constituted by retainers, servants and tenants, and the sanguinary limits of inheritable property. Without doubt, the family and household provided the formative and legitimising domain for the exercise of and apprenticeship in power for younger men in society. Extant literature on the formation of the English middle class confirms that the growth of large extra-familial institutions, and widening and diverse fields of occupation in commerce, finance and industry, accelerated the divide between the family and the world, the home and the workplace, and the private and public spheres.[11] Indeed, the mutually reinforcing ideas of liberty and property, natural endowments of many trueborn middle class Englishmen, may be related to the gradual sequestration of the immediate family and home from external domains defined by manly pursuits. 'The man, bold and vigorous', wrote Lord Kames in the 1770s, 'is qualified for being a protector: the woman, delicate and timid, requires protection.'[12] The man, as a protector, was endowed 'by nature' to govern; the woman due to her infirmity, was 'disposed to obedience.' Kames, true to the discourse of Scottish moral enlightenment, was of the opinion that feminine intellectual powers correspond to the 'destination of nature'; men had what women did not, 'penetration and solid judgment to fit them for governing'. While the master of the family was directly a part of the body politic, his wife, his children and his servants could be connected to the country only through him. A much larger conception of the state as an extended and gendered domestic arena was thus being articulated in contemporary political thinking. Extrapolated from the concrete materiality of the family at home, such an arena could provide a valuable political space where men could *place* themselves in the nation state. In the imperial context, the notion of a free but conquering people bringing the fruits of civilisation and government to the rude inhabitants of the tropical and Oriental realms was shaped to a large degree by the experience of a paternalist, authoritarian state at home.

---

[11] Leonore Davidoff and Catherine Hall, *Family Fortunes: Men and Women of the English Middle Class, 1780–1850* (Chicago, University of Chicago Press, 1987), pp. 229–31.
[12] Lord Henry Home Kames, *Sketches of the History of Man* (Edinburgh, Bell, Bradforte and W. Creech, 1774/1800), Vol. 1, pp. 168–69.

Anarchy, Despotism and Moral Governance

In the first decades of the rule of the East India Company, however, the government in India was considered to be in great disarray. The English in India had inherited the despoiled, tyrannical and fragmented government of the Moorish conquerors. As Warren Hastings pleaded during his trial, the political confusion in India could only be redeemed if all of the British acquisitions could be brought together under a 'uniform compact body by one grand and systematic arrangement', an arrangement that would 'do away with all the mischiefs, doubts and inconveniences, both to the governors and the governed.'[13] Only with the full assumption of power could such an unsettled state of society be brought to order and rescued from the 'unavoidable anarchy and confusion of different laws, religions and prejudices, moral, civil and political, all jumbled together in one unnatural and discordant mass.' In fact the distinction between state and civil society as in England simply did not obtain in India. As Burke saw it, the English nation in India was no more than a 'seminary for the succession of officers' and a republic without a people.[14] The inevitable consequence of this situation was that the power of office was arbitrary in India, and the ruling class of Englishmen, held together by an *esprit de corps* that was not related either to England or India, could not be controlled or opposed by people who understood their language or their laws. Both these responses are characteristic of an era of vigorous parliamentary debate over the future of British rule in India and the limits to the sovereignty of the East India Company's state in eastern India. In this period the British formally acknowledged territorial government in India, and public trials of illustrious Company servants such as Warren Hastings brought home to the British public the romance, exoticism and strangeness of British India.

What is remarkable in this spectacle of imperial profligacy is a rather unprecedented national condemnation of the British moral conduct in India *after* the fact of military conquest (1757–64) and the establishment of a revenue extracting state (1765). The

---

[13] A. B. Keith (ed.), *Speeches & Documents on Indian Policy*, Vol. 1 (New Delhi, Anmol Publications, 1985), p. 146.

[14] Speech at the Hastings trial, 15 Feb. 1788, from Keith, *ibid.*, p. 128.

inquisition into the affairs of the East India Company followed by a series of parliamentary acts has been characterised by Francis Hutchins as the rise of a 'just idea of rule.'[15] A new moral accountability of government in this era also subtends a new configuration of the society and self-awareness of the English in India which relates as much to the anxiety of race as to the anxiety of culture. Along with the satirical description of the newly enriched Anglo-Indian *nabob* there was emerging a deep-seated misapprehension of the society of the colonial, which unlike that in the New World could not be established *ex nihilo*. Clive, who for some opponents of the Company at home epitomised all that was despicable about the reprobate life of the English adventurer in India, reviled Anglo-Indian Calcutta as 'one of the most wicked places in the universe' where 'corruption, licentiousness and a want of principle seem to have possessed the minds of all the civil servants' who had become 'callous, rapacious and luxurious beyond conception...'.[16] The arrival of the nabobs in England and their attempt to purchase titles and respectability with their newly found wealth was derided by the public and the press in London. They were pilloried in the Haymarket production of *The Nabob or Asiatic Plunderer* in 1772, and according to a line engraving from 1797 given the epithet 'Count Roupee'.[17] In a later era Macaulay condemned General Richard Smith of the eighteenth century Calcutta circle who had already been lampooned in Forbes's play (*The Nabob*) as 'an Anglo-Indian chief, dissolute, ungenerous and tyrannical...hating the aristocracy yet childishly eager to be numbered among them, squandering his wealth on pandars [*sic*] and flatterers...'.[18] During the impeachment of Hastings, Burke had to debate forcefully against the position of 'geographical morality' which amounted to the principle that the private and public duties of men were governed by the degrees of latitude and longitude. That geography and climate rivalled divine providence and the laws of human

---

[15] Francis Hutchins, *The Illusion of Permanence: British Imperialism in India* (Princeton, Princeton University Press, 1967), p. 19.
[16] Cited in Dennis Kincaid, *British Social Life in India, 1608–1937* (London, George Routledge, 1938), p. 79.
[17] Mildred Archer, *India and British Portraiture, 1770–1825* (London, New York, Karachi, New Delhi, Oxford University Press, 1979), p. 39.
[18] Kincaid, *ibid.*, p. 80.

society, and that after Englishmen had crossed the line of the equinox their virtues simply expired.[19] In a peculiar inversion, then, the founders of British rule in India by the end of the century had been accused of despotism supposedly endemic to the Orient. This had, after all, been the defence of Clive and Hastings: that they had tried to govern an Oriental people with 'arbitrary and despotic ... Oriental principles.'

Domestic Dislocations

The fear of tyranny was tied from the very beginning to the life-style of the Company factors, servants and soldiers who had been absorbing facets of indigenous culture over a period of more than a hundred years in the cities and ports of India. What was most visibly at stake was the state of their domestic affairs, their extravagance, ostentation and their sexual relationships with native women. What little work has been done on the subject, notably by Percival Spear and Kenneth Ballhatchet, indicates a relatively uncharted history of English settlements in India during which both marital and extramarital relationships between European men and local women were tolerated and even encouraged. Modes of dress, cuisine, the smoking of the hookah, modes of entertainment, all suggest that British subjects could, given time, be assimilated into Indian society and culture. Even in the later eighteenth century, Company servants lived with their 'unofficial' Indian wives and mistresses or *bibis*. Captain Thomas Williamson writing in the early years of the nineteenth century defended such behaviour from the charges of libidinousness and licentiousness by asserting that they were simply the product of the 'disparity in numbers between British men and British women in India.'[20] Spear notes in passing the temporary marital unions between soldiers and Christian or Eurasian women whose children lived with their 'pariah or prostitute mothers' and after reaching their adolescence 'disappeared into the interior' or 'drifted into the bazaars'.[21] In the

---

[19] Keith, *op. cit.*, pp. 143–45.
[20] Captain Thomas Williamson, *East India Vademecum* [1810] quoted in Archer, *op. cit.*, p. 51.
[21] Spear, *op. cit.*, p. 62.

seventeenth century it was not uncommon for factors to induce soldiers to marry native women because it was too expensive for the Company 'to import women for their white subjects.'[22] An order from the Court of Directors of 1688 plainly suggested to the factors that they 'induce by all means you can invent our soldiers to marry with the Native women, because it will be impossible to get ordinary young women as we before directed to pay their own passages.'[23] In contrast to this were the unions of wealthy Anglo-Indian officers whose Indian wives were permanent members of the household and presided over an extended *zanana*.[24] The offspring of such families referred to by the curious term 'natural children' were given the opportunity of education, and if their skin colour permitted, attempted to blend in with the greater society of metropolitan London. Lieutenant Colonel Skinner, Major Hyder Hearsay and James Forbes were well known for their marriages into Indian aristocratic families. Others like William Hickey of Calcutta were noted for their attachment to native mistresses. Hickey writes fondly in his memoirs about his 'cheerful and sweet-tempered Jemdanee' whom he lost in childbirth, a 'gentle and affectionately attached ... girl' with a 'strong natural understanding, with more acuteness and wit than is usually found among the native women of Hindostan.'[25] She left him with 'a fine, strong, healthy-looking male child' who was then entrusted to the care of Mrs. Turner, the wife of Hickey's business partner, who adopted him into her large family and procured a nurse for his care.

During the period of ascendancy of Company rule in question, such extended Indian households were beginning to be looked upon with disdain. Soon after British victories in India, administrators in the newly established presidencies, while admitting irregular unions of Englishmen and natives, began to impose restrictions on marriages. By the first decades of the nineteenth century the company of native women, especially of entertainers and prostitutes was seen by observers from England to have the

---

[22] Kincaid, *op. cit.*, p. 51.

[23] Harry Hobbs, 'Old-Time European Women' in H. S. Bhatia (ed.), *European Women in India: Their Life and Adventures* (New Delhi, Deep and Deep, 1979), p. 15.

[24] Spear, *op. cit.*, p. 63.

[25] W. Hickey, *Memoirs of William Hickey*, Vol. 4 (London, Hurst & Blackett, 1913/1925), pp. 140–41.

most baneful effect on the English character. Mary Sherwood in her travels commented on the association of young Englishmen in India with the infamous 'nautch girls' and lamented on how these 'once blooming boys, who were … slowly sacrificing themselves to drinking, smoking, want of rest, and the witcheries of the unhappy daughters of heathens and infidels.'[26]

A related and equally pernicious aspect of the Indian influence was the presence of an immoderate number of servants, bearers, middlemen and sycophants within the elaborate household constructed around a successful Company official. Burke spoke at length on the figure of the go-between, or 'black *banya*', as a testament to the moral anarchy of the European household in India:

> He is a domestic servant. He is generally chosen out of that class of native who, by being habituated to misery and subjection can submit to any orders, and are fit for any of the basest services. Having been themselves subject to oppression, they are fitted perfectly—for that is the true education—to oppress others. They serve an apprenticeship of servitude to qualify them for the trade of tyranny. They are persons without whom a European can do nothing.[27]

An orderly middle class household was the site of respectability, happiness and discipline, but the despotic customs of the Orient in India thwarted this possibility. Forbes in his Oriental memoirs observed:

> This system of oppression, so completely pervades all classes of society under every form of oriental government, that it is almost impossible, out of the British dominions, to find an Asiatic of any caste or tribe, who, like the English *country gentleman*, in the middle walk of life, enjoys his patrimonial inheritance, surrounded by domestic happiness and rural pleasures.[28]

It has been argued that the possibility of the development of a mixed society, of Anglo-Indians and Eurasians, located in the

---

[26] Ketaki Kushari Dyson, *A Various Universe: A Study of the Journals and Memoirs of British Men and Women in the Indian Subcontinent, 1765–1856* (New Delhi, Oxford University Press, 1978), p. 81.

[27] Keith, *op. cit.*, p. 138.

[28] James Forbes, *Oriental Memoirs: A Narrative of Seventeen Years Residence in India*, Vol. 2 (London, Richard Bentley, 1834), p. 52.

kin-networks and households of India, was checked by the introduction of an increasing number of English and European women
in the settlements. After the era of political reform introduced by
Lord Cornwallis, the newly established Board of Control mandated that Europeans should not be allowed to settle freely in the
Company territories, for the presence of a large body, including
settlers of the middle and lower classes, would be detrimental to
the native respect and reverence for British authority.[29] Spear has
suggested that this was the crucial turning point during which
there was a 'widening racial gulf' that separated Englishmen from
Indians. In the pages to follow, I will try to qualify this *prima facie*
equation between the fear of the *déraciné* and the restoration of
conjugal relationships between white men and women in India.
The incrustation of race in the pre-Victorian era entailed unstable
associations between notions of national exclusiveness and sexual
identity whose historical and specific outlines still have to be
mapped out beyond the usual analytics of ethnicity, gender and
class.[30]

One notable aspect of this process was surely the beginnings
of a powerful domestic ideology exercised in the small compass
of the Anglo-Indian household, the paternalist implications of
which spread through the emergent colonial political economy. In
early-Victorian India the vignette of the orderly colonial household could be rendered almost complete, and the native subjects
most familiar to the English men and women could become servants and maids. Thus Colesworthy Grant could put together
letters to his mother in the form of *An Anglo-Indian Domestic Sketch*
(1849) where the various servants of the house included the
khidmutgar, the *bawurchee*, the *mushalchee*, the house bearer, the
durwan, the *mehtur*, the *ayah*, the *dhobee*, the *durzee* and the *hookka
burdar*.[31] He noted that a 'great gulf ... exists between Europeans
and their dependents' and that Anglo-Indian children 'seldom see

---

[29] See especially Kenneth Ballhatchet, *op. cit.*, pp. 96–97 and Spear, *op. cit.*, pp. 140–
41.
[30] Catherine Hall, *White, Male and Middle Class: Explorations in Feminism and History*
(New York, Routledge, 1992), pp. 205–07.
[31] Bishop Heber describes a similar number of servants in his travel narrative. See
Reginald Heber, *Narrative of a Journey through the Upper Provinces of India, from
Calcutta to Bombay, 1824–1825* (London, J. Murray, 1828), p. 25.

anything in the manners of their parents towards the servants to impress their minds with any strong feelings of respect for them.'[32] The natives were after all 'with very rare exceptions, the *only servants* whom they see in the country.'[33]

Colonial Society and the Sanguinary Divide

Regulation of the territorial possessions of the Company-state was to a degree complicit with the ordering of race, sex, marriage and reproduction in the last two decades of the eighteenth century. In order to explore this growing distance between the British and the natives in India, I turn to Winthrop Jordan's signal analysis of the development of racial consciousness in early North American colonial society. English settler society, in this context, differentiated by statute the offspring of unions between whites and Native Americans, and whites and Africans.[34] Not only was interracial union seen as contrary to the laws of nature, but also as the introduction of inferior blood in the body politic in various proportions. In the absence of the genetic theory of human reproduction, Jordan inferred, blood was indeed seen as the virile essence that passed on the essential attributes of a society and race. In the context of slavery, of course, the admixture of African blood was seen as instantly contaminating, and thus for social and economic purposes the mulatto was considered a Negro.[35] In the case of the Native Americans, as Kathleen Brown points out in a recent essay reconsidering Jordan's conclusions, the possibility of assimilation through sexual union was seen as much stronger than in that of the Africans.[36] As she shows elsewhere, while sexual relations with Indian women could be seen as an extension of commerce

---

[32] Colesworthy Grant, *An Anglo-Indian Domestic Sketch: A Letter from an Artist in India to His Mother in England* (Calcutta, Thacker and Company, 1849), p. 87.

[33] *Ibid.*, emphasis in the original.

[34] Winthrop D. Jordan, *White over Black: American Attitudes Toward the Negro, 1550–1812* (Chapel Hill, University of North Carolina Press, 1968), p. 163.

[35] *Ibid.*, p. 168.

[36] Kathleen Brown, 'Native Americans and Early Modern Concepts of Race', in Martin Daunton and Rick Halpern (eds), *Empire and Others: British Encounters with Indigenous Peoples, 1600–1850* (Philadelphia, University of Pennsylvania Press, 1999).

and exchange, and thus compatible with the rise of English dominance in northern America, those between Englishmen and Negroes threatened the stable distinctions between slave and free, especially as far as the law was concerned.[37] In the seventeenth century, exemplary punishment was handed out to white women attempting to marry a black, a Native American or a mulatto. The newly emerging legal definitions of race were thus tied to the details in which the sexuality of women, especially white women, was regulated.[38]

Since India was never considered a colony of settlement, the presence of people of mixed parentage did not directly threaten the rights of white British-born subjects in India, as they did in the British West Indies or the Cape.[39] This situation began to change in the era of the expansion of the East India Company's territorial ambitions. It is possible that in the wake of the rebellions in the creolised Spanish Americas, their growing numbers were seen to be particularly menacing. Scholars of Anglo-Indian background in the modern era such as H. A. Stark have emphasised this threat voiced in contemporary newspapers and travel accounts, such as that of Viscount Valentia who was in India between 1802–06, and whose *Voyages and Travels* reported on the state of the East India Company's eastern possessions. Valentia saw a grave danger in the rising numbers of 'half-caste' children, the 'most rapidly increasing evil of Bengal', who by creating a 'link of union' between the English and the natives were eroding the exclusive position of the rulers.[40] Other, recent histories have pointed out that at the root of discrimination against the East Indians or Eurasians, as they were called at the time, lay the security concerns of the Company-state keen to hold on to its territorial acquisitions in India in the face of European

[37] Kathleen Brown, *Good Wives, Nasty Wenches, and Anxious Patriarchs: Gender, Race, and Power in Colonial Virginia* (Chapel Hill, University of North Carolina Press, 1996), pp. 66–67, 131–34.

[38] *Ibid.*, pp. 181–86.

[39] Peter Marshall, 'The Whites of British India, 1780–1830: A Failed Colonial Society?', in *Trade and Conquest: Studies on the Rise of British Dominance in India* (Hampshire, Varorium, 1993), pp. 26–44.

[40] Valentia quoted in H. A. Stark, *John Ricketts and His Times, Being a Narrative Account of Anglo-Indian Affairs During the Eventful Years from 1791 to 1835* (Calcutta, Wilsone, 1934), pp. 19–20.

rivals.[41] In addition, the rapidly rising career prospects in the government of India alerted the Court of Directors and shareholders of the Company to the valuable source of patronage available to the Indian-born 'sons of the Company', many of them begotten through legitimate or illegitimate union with Indian women. Up until the 1780s it was customary among those who could afford it to send their children to be educated in England; to be absorbed thereafter into the covenanted and the commissioned services.[42]

None of these concerns fully explain why between 1786, which marks the arrival of Cornwallis as the Governor General of India, and 1791, there were a series of measures passed that would banish the sons of mixed parentage as significant members of the East India Company's civil and military establishments. In the March of 1786, the Court of Directors suddenly refused to entertain the Bengal Military Orphan Society's proposal (1784) that the wards of the Upper Orphanage School of Calcutta, both British and British-Indian born, be sent to Britain for further education. An order had been issued that only legitimate children born to European parents on both sides would be allowed to return to Britain. A firmer decision followed in 1791 when John Turing, whose father was the Commissioner of the Coromandel (Resident at Ganjam) and mother, a southern Indian woman, was barred from joining the Company's army as a commissioned officer.[43] In April that year the Court of Directors passed a resolution that no person of Indo-British or Eurasian extraction could be appointed to the civil, military or marine services of the Company.[44] In 1794 Governor General Cornwallis drafted a plan for the amalgamation of the King's troops and the Company's army in India in which he laid down a fundamental principle that 'the European and Native branches of the service...should be entirely separated'[45] and that no persons 'who are not descended on both sides from European parents, can be admitted into the European branch of

---

[41] C. J. Hawes, *Poor Relations: The Making of a Eurasian Community in British India* (Surrey, Curzon Press, 1996), pp. 71–72.

[42] H. A. Stark, *Hostages to India, or; The Life Story of the Anglo-Indian Race* (Calcutta, Fine Art Cottage, 1926), pp. 56–57.

[43] *Ibid.*, p. 60.

[44] Hawes, *op. cit.*, p. 55.

[45] Charles Ross (ed.), *Correspondence of Charles, First Marquis Cornwallis*, Vol. 2 (London, John Murray, 1859), p. 570.

the service, except as drummers, fifers, or other musicians: nor can such persons be hereafter admitted on the establishment of European officers in Native troops.'[46]

A similar prejudice surfaced with regard to the claims of the widows and children of civil and military servants on long-established charitable funds. The Bengal Civil Fund was all of a sudden closed to Indian women and their Eurasian children in 1804; similar measures followed in the military. In 1805 a major controversy emerged with regard to the management of the Military Fund (or Lord Clive's Fund), a charitable institution founded by Robert Clive, from which financial support had once been extended to the native wives of European officers 'in common with persons of European descent.'[47] However, despite petitions to the Board disputing claims denied to widows 'born in India', a widow seeking charity had to make an affidavit that she was not of native blood, and her certificate of birth attested by a surgeon was a crucial part of the application.[48] First at Madras and subsequently at Bombay, funds were being disbursed only to children of unmixed European blood.[49] Article 14 of the proposed legislation for the Bombay Military Fund in 1810 guaranteed full benefits to the wives and legitimate children of all officers in service at that time, but categorically stated that for all marriages contracted thereafter, it would be:

> ...an indispensable qualification that both the parents of any and every claimant shall have been European, or of unmixed European blood, though born in other quarters of the world, four removes from an Asiatic or African being considered as European blood.[50]

---

[46] *Ibid.*, p. 576.

[47] Extract, Military Letter from Fort St. George, 8 Sept. 1805, Board's Collection (hereafter BC), India Office Library and Records, London (hereafter IOR), F/4/211, No. 4716.

[48] For example, Mary Christie, the widow of one Sergeant James Dick was identified as a 'native of India' from her marriage certificate, and her claim on her late husband's pension was denied. Similarly, the widow of Sergeant Samuel Vinon, although legally married, was not allowed a share in her husband's assets as she appeared to be a 'Malabar woman' and a 'native of India'. (Extract Military letter to Fort Saint George, 7 Sept. 1808, BC, IOR, F/4/360, No. 8774.)

[49] Stark, *John Ricketts*, p. 27; Hawes, *op. cit.*, pp. 66–67.

[50] Extract, Military Letter to Bombay, 17 Jan. 1810. The proposals were adopted in 1816; see Extract, Military Letter to Bombay, 4 May 1816, BC, IOR, F/4/538, No. 12948.

It is clear that colonial habituation demanded legal sanction for the separation of blood, although the incidence of sexual contact between Britons and Indian women continued through the early nineteenth century, especially in the army. The purity of blood, actualised through law, stood as a measure of racial autonomy that safeguarded the idea of an undiluted British presence in India.

Conflicted Hierarchies: Blood, Race, Gender

In the light of what has been said above, it may be argued that while the colonial state tried to enforce the separation of blood, administrative rhetoric simply acknowledged the divide as absolute. Colonial and colonised subjects could in this way be naturalised through the category of race as a primordial, unchangeable entity, much like the essence of a nation or civilisation. Contemporary terms[51] such as 'legitimate', 'illegitimate', 'European', 'Eurasian', 'native' and 'half-caste' describing the status of children in India, all thus denoted a degree of divergence from a pristine natural state.

There was a great deal of disagreement about the consequences of the dilution of English with native blood. It is clear that British attitudes toward such admixture varied predominantly according to the gender of the offspring. Eurasian women appealed to Englishmen in India; they were even considered eminently nubile. Many Indo-British and half-caste women were raised by the orphanages of Madras and Calcutta so that they would be able to 'earn a respectable livelihood', and even provided with a modest dowry if they could marry their way out.[52] Eurasian families of Madras even in the 1830s tried their utmost to socialise with young English gentlemen and offer their daughters in marriage. Such

---

[51] See Extract, Military Letter from Madras, 11 Aug. 1817, BC, IOR, F/4/557, No. 13666.

[52] Female orphans in the Bengal Military Orphan Society were instructed in the arts of milliners and stay makers. Their relatives, guardians or trustees received an annual sum of £40 for their upkeep till they could find their own husbands and homes. See, Memorial of the General Management of the Bengal Military Orphan Society, 1824, BC, IOR, F/4/712, No. 19454.

liaisons were common according Albert Hervey, an ensign in Madras during 1833–43:

> ...officers belonging to regiments stationed in Madras are fre-
> quently thrown amongst these dark-eyed bewitching syrens, and
> are very liable to become smitten with their charms. I must say the
> young women are very pretty, notwithstanding their color. The
> consequences of associating with them are almost inevitable. Young,
> unthinking ensigns and lieutenants easily fall into the trap set for
> them.[53]

The presence of native blood in these 'pretty, handsome young women, full of Oriental ardour'[54] was seen as a mark of explicit sexuality. In a quatrain dedicated to a 'beautiful East Indian' in the *Asiatic Journal* of 1816, Thomas Moore exhorted:

> Oh for a sun-beam rich and warm
> From thy own Ganges' fervid haunts
> To light thee up, thou lovely form
> All my soul adores and wants![55]

This tribute was consonant with the natural sexual attractiveness of Indian women for contemporary Englishmen. 'Nature seems to have showered beauty on the fairer sex throughout Indostan' wrote Orme in his *Fragments*, 'with a more lavish hand than in most other countries.'[56] The author of *Sketches of India* offered that the 'Hindoostanee women...are in general exquisitely formed, after the truest models of symmetry and beauty' and that it was no surprise that otherwise prudent Englishmen fell victim to their charms.[57] Marriages took place between well-positioned English-men and Eurasian women even through the 1820s. The *Bengal Hurkaru* of March 1825 reported that many 'elegant and accom-plished half-Indian girls' had been respectably married, 'whose blood may soon mingle with that of the proud nobility of England;

---

[53] Captain Albert Hervey, in Charles Allen (ed.), *A Soldier of the Company: Life of an Indian Ensign, 1833–43* (London, Michael Joseph, 1988), p. 77.
[54] Hervey, *ibid.*, p. 79.
[55] 'On a Beautiful East Indian', *The Asiatic Journal and Monthly Register for British India and its Dependencies*, Vol. 2, [June–Dec. (1816)], p. 581.
[56] Orme, *Fragments*, p. 301.
[57] 'Sketches in India', quoted in Stark, *Hostages to India*, pp. 167–68.

and *en passant*, will not degrade it either.'[58] At the more profane end of the scale, contemporaries reported the widespread practice of concubinage in India by Europeans, tacitly sanctioned by British-Indian society. The author of the *Sketches* calculated that at least one-third of unmarried Englishmen in India kept native women as sexual companions, and among them about half had fathered children through such illegal liaisons.[59] It was partly the very climate in India which resulted in a 'great propensity to sexual intercourse' and a certain 'fever of the blood' hitherto unknown to these 'frigid sons of Europe'.[60] The young servants of the Company were thus quickly infatuated and wont to form easy attachments with native women, leading to children, debt and ruin.

And yet, the possibility of a widespread colonisation of India through a dispersion of European blood seemed remote to contemporaries. Implicit in this denial was the conviction that men of mixed blood were not in the last instance fit for gentlemanly office and rank because of their racial provenance, and also the deep seated assumption that Europeans and Indians were the farthest apart in racial terms. Sir Robert Grant, son of the philanthropist, abolitionist and statesman, Charles Grant, who had spent the first eleven years of his life in Bengal (and later became Governor of Bombay), wrote during the period of the passage of the Regulating Act in 1813 that Europeans should be 'for a very long course of time...divided by the strongest marks of distinction from the original inhabitants.'[61] He assumed that an unbridgeable difference "arising from diversity of colour, genius, manners, opinions, and institutions' existed between the two communities, which was further confirmed by the 'essential incompatibility between political authority and political subjection', as well as 'hereditary feelings and recollections' which could neither be renounced or reconciled.[62] For centuries, then, the 'purely Indian' and the 'purely European population' would continue. And even if there were to

---

[58] *Bengal Hurkaru*, (26 Mar. 1825) quoted in Stark, *John Ricketts*, p. 23.
[59] 'Sketches in India', quoted in Stark, *Hostages to India*, pp. 164–65.
[60] *Ibid.*, p. 166.
[61] Robert Grant, *The Expediency Maintained of Continuing the System by which the Trade and Government of India are now Regulated* (London, Black, Parry and Co., 1813), p. 226.
[62] Robert Grant, *ibid.*, p. 227.

be a large number of people of 'mixed order' with various grada-
tions of 'race and privilege' as in the Americas, they would clearly
identify with the European lineage.[63] This order would prevail,
according to Grant, not so much because people would prefer to
claim a 'nobler descent', but that the mixing of blood could only
happen where the father was European and the mother Indian, and
it was 'consonant with both nature and with experience' that the
character of the offspring would be dictated by the father's blood.
Grant could not imagine white women ever marrying Indian men.
European women in India were relatively scarce, and the prospects
of an 'Oriental haram' added to the 'obvious degradation' resulting from such a union could inspire in them nothing but horror and
disgust. The colony, he concluded, could not then descend by
degrees into the native population, but must be laid out as a society
of 'distinct and separate' entities.

While maintaining that a clear racial separation of the Indians
and the English was inevitable, Grant commented at length on the
acclimatisation of more than thirty thousand British subjects residing in India from their early youth, some from their very
childhood. They gradually become habituated, and even attached,
to the 'climate, manners, and the mode of living, which belong to
the country' he wrote, observing in passing that some 'enter into
less reputable connections with the native races.'[64] This contradic-
tion between the fact of miscegenation and the assertion that a
full-blooded ruling race would continue untainted in India implies a degree of apprehension regarding the hierarchy of various
subject races in the Indian context. Along with the categorical
denial of intimacy between Englishmen and Indians, one can
detect the beginnings of a particular aversion towards people of
mixed blood, which helps to explain the severity with which the
Eurasians of colonial India were marginalised.

The 'Intermediate Tribe'

The very presence of a body of subjects of mixed blood presented
a potential threat to the legitimacy and exclusiveness of the ruling

---

[63] *Ibid.*, pp. 227–28.
[64] Grant, *op. cit.*, p. 182.

community. On the point of law, the Supreme Court at Calcutta held that the legitimate offspring of a British-born subject and a native Indian woman was a British subject, while illegitimate children of such parents were Indians.[65] Thus an English officer of the East India Company who consorted with native women could father both Indian and British subjects, and the widow of an English officer returning to England with her children had to leave behind in India an offspring of her husband from a previous marriage to a native woman.[66]

The *Asiatic Journal* of 1825, in addressing the legal disabilities under which the Eurasians of India suffered, declared that the 'whole fabric' of Britain's 'Eastern Rule' was anomalous and unprecedented. Not only were the Eurasians denied a post in military and civil society, but also the 'very circumstances' of their birth made them 'outcastes in the eyes of their superstitious fellow nations.'[67] This was not only prejudicial, but 'cruel and unjust'.[68] These were also the grounds on which the East Indians of Bombay petitioned the Court of Directors of the East India Company, opposing the resolution passed by the Directors of the Bombay Military Fund in 1833, that widows of 'mixed-extraction' and children of 'mixed-blood' not be allowed to partake of its benefits.[69] The East Indian community of Bombay thought that such a resolution '… cast a stigma not only on those who suffer in their immediate persons … but also on every individual of the class which by implication it proscribes as a *degraded* body.'[70] Since many East Indians had held commissions and had risen to the highest ranks in the army, it was often the case that their own sisters had married brother officers of European descent. The new regulation in such cases worked 'to the prejudice of the weaker sex, so characteristically barbarous' that it appeared 'singularly

---

[65] Stark, *John Ricketts*, pp. 37–38.
[66] Memorial of the General Management of the Bengal Military Orphan Society (1783), BC, IOR, F/4/712, No. 19454.
[67] *The Asiatic Journal* (1825), quoted in Stark, *John Ricketts*, pp. 38–39.
[68] *Ibid.*, p. 76.
[69] See Military Letter to Bombay, 8 Feb. 1832, BC, IOR; Military Letter from Bombay, 4 Dec. 1833, BC, IOR; Directors of the Military Fund to Chief Secretary Norris, 15 Aug. 1833, BC, IOR; and 'Petition of the East Indians to the Court of Directors', 13 Nov. 1833, BC, IOR, F/4/1454, No. 57236.
[70] 'Petition of the East Indians.' Emphasis in the original.

out of place' in an institution, the patrons and members of which belonged to a 'highly civilized nation'.[71] What the East Indians found particularly onerous was the charge against widows of mixed origin, 'calculated to discourage illicit and immoral connections'. The rule, they argued, was not aimed so much at the 'moral nature' of such sexual relations, permitted or illicit, nor was it meant to protect the conventional assumptions of social rank based on the respectability of a woman's maternal family. It was based rather on an 'animal standard' which implied that without a certain proportion of European along with Asiatic and African blood flowing in their veins, these women were physically degraded.

Eurasians in India thus laboured under the accusation that there must be some 'inherent defect of body or mind' in the offspring of mixed descent. An order passed as early as 1786, that proscribed the wards of the Upper Military Orphanage in Calcutta from being educated in and settling in England, explained that it was 'a political inconvenience because the imperfections of the children, whether bodily or mental, would in the process of time be communicated by intermarriage to the generality of the people in Great Britain, and by this means debase the succeeding generations of Englishmen.'[72] Five years later a crucial proviso in the regulations adopted by the Court of Directors on the 9th of November, 1791, barred their participation in the higher and covenanted offices of the civil and military services: persons receiving any such appointment could not be 'the son of a native of India'.[73]

In 1830, the Eurasian Christians of Calcutta petitioned the British Parliament regarding their disqualification as subjects of the British Empire; they had neither the privileges of full-blooded Europeans, nor of the native Indians, and were excluded from all civil, military and naval posts, as well as the King's commission. Debating the East Indians' petition at the House of Lords in the same year, Ellenborough expressed some sympathy for 'the

---

[71] 'Petition of the East Indians'.

[72] Stark, *Hostages to India*, p. 65.

[73] 'Petition of the East Indians to the Honorable Commons of the United Kingdom of Great Britain and Ireland in Parliament Assembled'. See Stark, *John Ricketts*, Appendix A, p. 5.

unfortunate situation of the class to which the petitioners belonged.[74] Their condition, he felt, should be addressed as long as it did not violate the principles that were fundamental to the maintenance of the British government in India. When the Earl of Carlisle asked about the difference between first and second generation 'half-castes', Ellenborough confirmed that the children of 'illegitimate offspring' could be considered as closer to the natives, and thus eligible for services where natives had traditionally been admitted. However, they should not be asking for privileges in excess of their basic civil rights or for considerations that illegitimate children did not enjoy anywhere else in the world. The same petition on the floor of the House of Commons elicited a more pronounced sympathy for the plight of the East Indian community in India. Sir James Mackintosh warned against the consequences of debarring good, faithful Christians from holding respectable administrative offices. Branded as an inferior class, the East Indians would be 'visited by evils of a deeper dye'.[75] C. Pote, a member of the East Indian's Petition Committee which met in the Town Hall of Calcutta (1831) to receive their agent to the British Parliament, John Ricketts, admonished that the legislation disqualifying Indo-Britons from service would 'degrade that class below what the vilest barbarism and ignorance could effect...degrade them below their self-esteem...left for the support even of the rudest savages'.[76] John Ricketts himself at these meetings voiced the fear that 'political degradation' inevitably implied a 'moral degradation'.[77] Judging by the high standard of living enjoyed by Englishmen in India at the time, the abject financial plight of many of these East Indians made them particularly vulnerable to these charges.[78]

---

[74] 'Petition of the Christian Natives of India,' in *Hansard's Parliamentary Debates* (London, Baldwin and Cradock; Booker, Longman, Rees, Orme etc., 1830), Vol. 23 (n.s.), pp. 962–63.

[75] 'Parliamentary debate on the occasion of the presentation of the East Indian's Petition to the House of Commons by the Right Honorable Mr William Wynn, MP, on the 4th May, 1830'. Stark, *John Ricketts*, Appendix D, p. 34.

[76] 'Proceedings of the Public Meeting held on the 28th March, 1831 in the Town Hall, Calcutta, to receive the Report of Mr J. W. Ricketts, the Agent of the East Indians, just returned from his Deputation with their Petition to the British Parliament'. Stark, *John Ricketts*, Appendix F, p. 49.

[77] *Ibid.*, p. 88.

[78] Heber, *op. cit.*, p. 57.

Quite apart from the curious history of the dispossession and plight of what was to become the future Anglo-Indian community in India, I find such discussions highly illuminating in that they reveal contemporary attitudes toward racial degradation or degeneration beyond even the accepted doctrines of natural history. It is clear that victims of sanguinary and racial discrimination often submitted to such standards, especially as the question of extraction further implicated status, rank and class in colonial society. A contemporary observer remarked that 'the British blood and the native blood in their veins are alike hateful' to Eurasians.[79] Pote, who so vociferously defended the innocence of his fellow East Indians in the Town Hall of Calcutta, based his genuine outrage on the fact that his people were being denied the true birthright of British subjects, subjected to 'contumely and scorn' even though they 'stood in many ways in the relation of consanguinity to Britons' and, therefore, in effect under the protection of the 'noblest, freest and the most enlightened government of the modern and ancient world.'[80]

Race and the Splitting of Colonial Subjects

The very premise that native Indian blood was defiling and thwarted the rights and liberties of trueborn British subjects elucidates the early racial configuration of colonial India. I have already noted how the question of degeneracy was entangled with the question of gender. The taint of native blood devolved around the racial character of native women themselves. The author of the *Sketches* (1816) feared the 'vast and increasing number of *demibengalees*' in Calcutta, who were 'characterized by all the vice and gross prejudices of the natives, but devoid of their pusillanimity.'[81] They inherited all the 'faults and failings of the European character, without its candour, sincerity or probity.'[82]

While ascription of blood and character conferred on the English the genuine attributes of civilisation, they also produced

---

[79] 'Sketches in India', quoted in Stark, *Hostages to India*, p. 119.
[80] 'Proceedings of the Public Meeting', Stark, *John Ricketts*, p. 49.
[81] 'Sketches in India', quoted in Stark, *Hostages to India*, p. 165.
[82] *Ibid.*.

the negative racial profiles of native subjects. In the remaining section of this essay I shall explore the way in which the colonial discourse on race derived and diverged from the prevalent natural history of the races of mankind. Given the limits of conjugal English domesticity in colonial India and also the fear of wanton dissipation of blood, both manliness and racial exclusivity were jealously defended. It is hardly surprising in this context that the dependent Indian subjects would appear childlike or effeminate in the eyes of imperial rulers.

The assertion of a free, benevolent, paternalist, authoritarian colonising agency produced a split image of the generic Indian subject: the slavish Gentoo (Hindu) and the despotic Moor (Muslim). The Moor had been forcibly removed from his seat, not just because he had been vanquished, but crucially because he had forfeited the right to rule because of his own degenerate actions. And beneath the Moor was the Gentoo, consigned to timeless and irredeemable slavery in his own nation and abode. Despite the respect given them by Orientalist scholars for their sacred texts, the bodies, habits and character of living Hindus were looked upon with a mixture of odium and curiosity. William Carey, a Scottish missionary known for his benevolence and friendship with the natives of Bengal could still remark that the Hindus lacked the 'ferocity of American Indians' but were 'abundantly supplied with a dreadful stock of low cunning and deceit.'[83]

The twin figures of the despot and the slave emerged in late eighteenth century India with the categorical repression of sexual and social intimacy between the rulers and the ruled. Despotism and slavery had characterised the Indian polity centuries prior to the arrival of the British, and they were regarded as the consequence of climate and character. Excessive references to despotism in colonial accounts indicate a deep anxiety over the loss of true English character in India: a fear of miscegenation and degeneration was writ large. There was not much that was new in this, for both in the case of Ireland and North America, especially since the seventeenth century, excessive familiarity with inferior ways of life presented the danger of Englishmen turning into savages.[84]

[83] William Carey (1794) quoted in Spear, *op. cit.*, p. 197.
[84] James Muldoon, 'The Indian as Irishman', *Essex Institute Historical Collections*, Vol. 3, No. 4 (1975), pp. 284–85.

India under Company rule presented a further, Oriental version of this possibility: luxury and enticement. An anti-monopoly pamphlet warned against such temptations: 'Luxury not only mollifies, but depresses and debases the mind, and renders those who are immersed in it, incapable of any elevated sentiment, of any useful, active or patriotic exertion.'[85] Along with debauchery, despotism also threatened the moral fibre of the British in India and their national character. Despotism was endemic to India. Under the spell of the despot, all produce of the earth, and whatever was nourished by it, was engrossed, and hence, no form of property was safe.[86] This was a complex repudiation of a feudal European past. Having destroyed the possibility of a legitimate dominion, archaic or medieval, the charge of despotism kept alive a generic master–slave narrative of rightful colonial conquest. The division of subject races in India was also seen as the extension of this failed polity.

Colonial ideas of race derived in part from contemporary predilections of natural history. Ideas relating to the natural order and classification of mankind during the late eighteenth and early nineteenth centuries occupied not only naturalists, but jurists, statesmen, moralists and political philosophers. Aristotle's ideas of genus and species had been re-appropriated in the writing of Descartes, Hobbes and Locke, who laid the foundations for a systematic study of the place of man in the natural order of things. The four-stage theory of human progress posited by thinkers of the Scottish moral enlightenment such as Millar and Ferguson also had a significant impact on this field. As ideas of national and racial difference began to appear in the biological description of humans, the time-honoured principle of the great Chain of Being began to accommodate temporal change. By the second half of the eighteenth century, following the naturalist explorations of John Ray, Montesquieu and Buffon, ideas of racial distinction became more commonly accepted.[87] Kant had divided mankind into four races: White, Negro, Hunnic and Hindu.[88] Linnaeus, more directly

---

[85] *A Demonstration of the Necessity and Advantages of a Free Trade to the East Indies* (London, C. Chapple, 1807), pp. 138–39.
[86] Alexander Dalrymple, *Measures to be Pursued in India for Ensuring the Permanency, and Augmenting the Commerce of the Company* (London, J. Nourse, 1772), p. 3.
[87] A. J. Barker, *The African Link* (London, Frank Cass, 1978), pp. 59, 66.
[88] Kant, 'Von den vershiedenen Racen der Menschen', pp. 17–18.

attuned to colonial stereotypes had classified men as: Wild, American, European, Asiatic and African. Europeans were fair, sanguine and brawny, their manner gentle, acute and inventive, governed by laws. Asiatics were sooty, melancholy and rigid, severely haughty and covetous in manner, and governed by opinions.[89] There were two competing explanations of such diversity. One derived from the pre-Adamite theory of Isaac la Peyrère which posited that a vast majority of people in this world were outside the purview of the Bible and the history of the Jewish nation. The other was the idea that all humankind had a common ancestry, argued forcefully by Buffon (1749) in his *Histoire Naturelle;* different branches had undergone changes on account of climate, diet mode of living, diseases and the mixing of blood, as they spread throughout the habitable world. Blumenbach (1776) carried this contention further, arguing that there were five principle varieties: Caucasian, Mongolian, Ethiopian, American and Malay, but one species. Yet, the notions of continuity and gradation of different subspecies of *Homo sapiens* persisted through this period. Climatic explanations of diversity dating back to Montesquieu enjoyed renew currency in the colonial tropics in the context of early mortality, exotic diseases and racial degeneration.

It is worth nothing that monogenetic explanations of racial diversity in a way accentuated the hierarchy of races, with Caucasians emerging expectedly at the top. They also bolstered the more commonplace ideas of racial degeneration, borrowing from the theories Kames, Goldsmith and Blumenbach, which suggested that Orientals and Africans were degraded versions of the idea human form which was in essence European. Alongside proponents of the common origin of the human species, a body of ideas Richard Popkin calls 'liberal racism',[90] there were competing polygenetic theories of race gaining ground in the nineteenth century, especially in North America. Popular and less scholarly versions of these often conflicting theories of race based on skin

---

[89] See Richard H. Popkin, 'The Philosophical Basis of Eighteenth Century Racism', in Harold E. Pagliaro (ed.), *Racism in the Eighteenth Century* (Cleveland and London, Case Western Reserve University Press, 1973), pp. 245–62.

[90] Richard H. Popkin, 'The Philosophical Bases of Modern Racism', in Craig Walton and John P. Anton (eds), *Philosophy and the Civilizing Arts: Essays Presented to Herbert W. Schneider* (Athens, Ohio University Press, 1974), p. 132.

colour, geographical distribution and technological backward-
ness, abounded in the period under consideration here.

Such taxonomies were carried back and forth between European scholars and amateur scholar–administrators in India. William Watts, a participant in the Battle of Plassey and Senior Member
of the Calcutta Council, gave an exemplary account of the races
in the East Indies:

> The two great nations, inhabiting this part of the Indies, differ
> widely from each other in their complexions, languages, manners,
> disposition and religion. The Moguls who are commonly called
> Moors or Moormen, are a robust, stately, and, in respect to the
> original natives, a fair people ... they are naturally vain, affect shew
> and pomp in everything, are much addicted to luxury, fierce,
> oppressive, and, for the most part, very rapacious ... The Gentoows,
> or native Indians, are of a swarthy aspect ... a mild, subtle, frugal
> race of men, exceedingly superstitious, submissive in appearance,
> but naturally jealous, suspicious, and perfidious; which is princi-
> pally owing to that abject slavery they are kept in by the Moors.[91]

The Moor in this unruly capacity was disruptive of the stability
in the economy, while the Gentoo was the natural slave, submissive and the ideal domestic subject, with whom a direct paternal
relationship could be forged. The Mughal Empire had destroyed
every possibility of settled authority and regular collection of
revenue, and had rendered the Indian polity bereft of all equity
and reason. Disinvesting the Indian political landscape of the
Moorish regime would thus free the reproductive capacity of
Indian society for the sustenance of the British Empire.

Robert Orme, officially appointed as the historian of the East
India Company, emphasised the reproductive plenitude of this
society, relating it to the effects of climate. Due to the extreme
mildness of climate, sustenance was easily afforded; 'productions
peculiar to the soil of India', wrote Orme, 'exceedingly contribute
to the ease of various labours'.[92] Women in India were inordinately
fertile, and the propensity of men to propagate their species equal
to it. Gentoos thus took as many wives as they wanted, and this

---

[91] William Watts, *Memoirs of the Revolution in Bengal* (Calcutta, K. P. Bagchi, 1760/
1983), pp. 2–3.
[92] Robert Orme, in J. P. Guha (ed.), *Historical Fragments of the Mogul Empire* (New
Delhi, Associated Publishing House, 1782/1974), p. 262.

plurality of sexual union did not enervate their reproductive spirit and decrease their numbers, as noticed in the more severe climates of Europe. Orme's climatic explanations followed Comte de Buffon's theory of the degenerative effects of non-temperate latitudes, and echoed Lord Kames, Blumenbach and Oliver Goldsmith. Orme's *Government and People of Indostan*, one of the earliest studies of India, became a widely known natural history of Indians as newly acquired imperial subjects.

In the figure of the submissive Hindu the colonial body politic located the weakest section, signified both by the inferiority of the slave and the passivity of women. The body of the Gentoo was weak, his livelihood easy. As Orme observed, 'people born under a sun too sultry to admit the exercise and fatigues necessary to form a robust nation', were naturally weak in their constitution. As a result of this general lack of strength, the most popular source of livelihood was the manufacture of cloth, spinning and weaving. The weavers of India were deprived of the tools and machine skills available in England or other parts of Europe, yet their cloth was of exceptional quality. Such remarkable skills were accounted for in the fact that the Indians, in the form of their labouring bodies, possessed qualities unique to women and children.

Book Five of the *Fragments* proposed two registers of effeminacy. The first was physical appearance and strength. Hair colour, the shape of the lips, the eyes, the eyelid and the nostrils were compared with the features exhibited by the 'Coffrees' of Africa, the nations of Malay, the people of Tartary, the Spaniards and the Portuguese, and then they were compared to those of the inhabitants of northern Europe. Descriptions of the physical attributes of Indians in Orme bears a striking similarity to the treatises of Montesquieu and Buffon, seen as directly affected by the severity of the monsoons affecting the 'texture of the human frame.' Thus races residing in the northern and western extremes of the subcontinent were comparable in stature, muscularity and robustness to Europeans, while the combined effect of the monsoon and extreme heat in the great plains and river valleys, throughout the rest of India had resulted in 'a race of men, whose make, physiognomy and muscular strength, convey ideas of an effeminacy which surprises when pursued through such numbers of the species, and when compared to the form of the European who is making the observation.'[93] The Hindus were thus confirmed in their domestic servitude as passive subjects bearing the brunt of labour and reproduction. In so far as they were capable of reform and improvement and aspiring to the benefits of freedom and property, their tutelage in the higher aspects of civilisation had to be restricted or carefully graduated. As Dalrymple contended, the establishment of freehold tenure in the land revenue settlements in India was not desirable, as the natives would then be able to claim a legal status that would weaken the very colonial authority over them; and further, free tenures would not impart 'real freedom' to them for it would have the effect of increasing their licentiousness and indolence.

Conclusion: Furthering the Racial Divide

The idea that a majority of Indians were inherently unfree created a lasting impression. Robert Grant wrote in 1816 that the Hindus could not be 'like the negroes, personally slaves', and that a distinction ought to be made between 'personal and political servitude'.[94] At the same time,

> the feebleness and timidity of the Hindoo confer on the Englishman a moral superiority, which does not differ in kind, though it greatly differs in degree, from the dominion of a personal master, and which, unless subjected to powerful restraints, is not perhaps less susceptible of abuse.[95]

John Crawfurd, one time British Resident at the court of Java wrote in his *Free Trade Pamphlet:*

> The Indians know not what freedom is; they are for the most part a timid, often an effeminate, and as a nation a feeble race of semi-barbarians.[96]

---

[93] Orme, *op. cit.*, pp. 298–99.
[94] Grant, *op. cit.*, p. 236.
[95] *Ibid.*.
[96] J. Crawfurd, 'Free Trade Pamphlet' as quoted in *The Political Commercial & Financial Condition of the Anglo-Eastern Empire in 1832* (London, Parbury, Allen and Co., 1832), p. 37.

A report on the East India Company's Charter published in 1832 declared:

> The Hindoos, it is true, have not had iron fetters, on their wrists and ankles like the slaves of the West-Indies, but they have for centuries fetters of the mind, far more efficacious for the debasement of the immortal spirit of man...it must be a matter of astonishment that they possess so many amiable qualities in spite of the mental and bodily slavery to which for ages they have been subjected.[97]

Colonial India was thus seen as a deeply fissured civil society. According to Robert Grant, the 'associated community of British and natives' presented one of the 'most curious and interesting spectacles ever witnessed'.[98] Here were 'two races of men' distinct in origin, language, complexion, dress, manners, customs and religion, and completely 'disproportionate in energy both of body and mind.' On the one side there was 'extreme feebleness of frame joined with extreme effeminacy, dependence and timidity of spirit', while on the other there was 'vigour, hardiness, courage, enterprise and ambition.' Such inequality was not only natural, argued Grant, but both groups were aware of the fact that the 'feeble race is politically subject to the stronger'. Hindus in common usage had become the archetypal subject race.

Colonial perceptions of race did not always obey the laws of natural history that would place subjects in the appropriate hierarchy of creation, but borrowed freely from various ideas of climate, degeneracy, blood and civilisation, factors that both complemented and contradicted one another. The racial divide in India continued to encourage polygenetic accounts of difference among subjects of empire even while theories of the common origin of mankind began to dominate the scientific community in Europe. Climatic ideas of race which were in circulation in the 1830s continued well into the latter half of the nineteenth century. One in particular was the medical contention that 'unmixed European stock' could not survive more than two generations in the Indian plains and deltas, which was why surgeons advised that children should be sent back to England after the age of five or

---

[97] *Ibid.*, p. 50.
[98] Grant, *op. cit.*, p. 174.

six.[99] Colonial deracination in the end always entailed a fear of degeneration and emasculation, which, as Lord Kames had warned, distinctly threatened the political ambitions of a commercial and trading nation like Britain.[100]

During the period under consideration, however, the commonplace view was that all Indians were inferior. As Emma Roberts observed in her advice to outbound cadets, European residents in India not only 'despised native opinions' but also treated natives with 'rude indifference' and arrogance. Contempt often led to outright hatred:

> ... a considerable portion of Anglo-Indians entertain the strongest aversion to the people whom they have alienated by their haughty and imperious manners. A black fellow, the invidious epithet with which they designate every native, however high in the scale of intellectuality, is, according to their opinion, scarcely superior to the brute creation....[101]

She suggested that new arrivals try to 'think well of the natives', acquaint themselves with the local language as much as possible so that they could avoid their commands being misunderstood or disobeyed, and refrain from outbursts of rage and indiscriminate beating of domestic servants.[102] Similar incidents of racial antipathy occurred in the army, especially after 1797 with the rigid separation of the native and European officers of the infantry enforced by Cornwallis.[103] East Indians too were liable to be branded with the taint of race, depicted as proud, lazy, indolent, extravagant, ignorant and miserable. Bishop Heber had described the financial burdens of supporting a large number of 'European poor and half-castes' in Calcutta who led a life of considerable distress.[104] Agents of charitable societies only furthered the circulation of such epithets. A sympathetic reader wrote to the editor

---

[99] J. R. Martin, *Notes on the Medical Topography of Calcutta* (1837), pp. 173, 175.
[100] Kames, *op. cit.*, Vol. 2, pp. 5–7.
[101] Emma Roberts, 'The East India Voyager', *Oriental Herald*, Vol. 1, No. 3, British Library 1509/1014, p. 397.
[102] *Ibid.*, pp. 397–98.
[103] 'The East India Company's Army', *Calcutta Gazette*, 26 Oct. 1797, W. S. Seton-Karr, *Selections from the Calcutta Gazettes*, Vol. 3 (Calcutta, Microform Publication, 1987), pp. 115–19.
[104] Heber, *op. cit.*, p. 57.

of the *Government Gazette* in 1830, contending that their indolence was a 'moral result from their physical condition.'[105] Captain Hervey observed that the European community in Calcutta distinguished themselves from the Eurasians by calling them by the Hindusthani epithet of 'Chee-Chee' (shameful) while referring to themselves as 'Koi-Hai' (notable), and declared that the man who married a half-caste was 'a fool to be pitied' and that he 'would rather marry an Ourang-outang'.[106]

In the course of the nineteenth century the experience of empire mediated the turn away from these shifting categories of racial distinction posed by natural history towards the predestined superiority of a conquering, civilising, technologically superior nation rather than one conquering race among many—Briton rather Anglo-Saxon, Celtic or Teutonic.[107] How the historical progress of nationhood became analogous to the progressive natural development of man in the later Victorian era is a question beyond the breadth of this essay. This development of nation *as* race was articulated, perhaps not altogether accidentally, during the greatest extent of Britain's Asiatic empire by anthropologists like Kelburne King in tracts such as *An Inquiry into the Causes that have led to the Rise and Fall of Nations (1876)* where he dismissed geography, climate, forms of government and religion as factors that brought about the predominance of nations, and argued in favour of the merging of superior races to produce a dominant stock. The discovery of a common proto-historical Aryan ancestry complicated the picture, but the fallen state of the Hindu civilisation could be explained by the fact that centuries of Moorish tyranny had corrupted the character of these Aryans producing parasitic and un-martial Rajas. India was thus caught not in a barbaric but a savage state, or as Sir Henry Maine had it, in a state of arrested development.

The relative wildness or timidity of subject peoples was a reflection of the ambiguity of the colonial ideology of race as

[105] Letter of Monday, 5 April 1830 to the Editor of the *Government Gazette*, in Anil Chandra Das Gupta (ed.), *The Days of John Company: Selections from the Calcutta Gazette, 1824–1832* (Calcutta, Government Printing, West Bengal, 1959), pp. 492–93.
[106] Hervey, *op. cit.*, p. 79.
[107] For ideas of the technological superiority and global hegemony of European nations see M. Adas, *Machines as the Measure of Men* (Ithaca, Cornell University Press, 1989).

blood, and the unstable association of national, imperial and racial identities. I have tried to suggest in this essay that an important way in which racial differences were being articulated in the late eighteenth century and early nineteenth century was through new definitions of the colonial domestic order. The regulation of both casual sex and marital union between Indians and Britons was a response to the fear of a mestizo society on the American or West Indian model that could not be tolerated in a colonial dependency. In such a situation, the figure of the Indo-Briton could stand only as a figure of dispossession and marginality. In this, the history of colonial India can be likened to the history of colonial North America where, despite the long existence of a 'sexual frontier'[108] between colonists and Native Americans, the idea of racial segregation emerged triumphant despite all the evidence pointing to the crossing of racial boundaries. In order to locate this divide we need attentive studies of the early years of the colonial encounter in India when crucial links were established between the search for paternalist authority, domestic order, sexual moderation and national exclusivity, anticipating stable and enduring templates of colonial selfhood.

---

[108] I borrow the term from Richard Godbeer's 'Eroticizing the Middle Ground: Anglo-Indian Sexual Relations', in Martha Hodes (ed.), *Sex, Love, Race: Crossing Boundaries in North American History* (New York, New York University Press, 1999), p. 92.

3

Controlling the Ganymedes

The Colonial Gaze in J. R. Ackerley's
Hindoo Holiday

♦ Zahid Chaudhary

T he tradition of the colonial travel journal, by the early twentieth century, was well-institutionalised as a genre; travel journals produced, for the European, the world 'out there'. British writers such as Richard Burton in the nineteenth century, and T. E. Lawrence, E. M. Forster and J. R. Ackerley in the twentieth century, engaged in the production of the Orient, speaking on its behalf, purporting to represent its people and culture. However, as Edward Said explains, such production relies upon a:

> flexible *positional* superiority, which puts the Westerner in a whole series of possible relationships with the Orient without ever losing him the relative upper hand.[1]

Hence representation in travel journals inevitably becomes laden with the politics of both power and knowledge as the writer assumes authority from a superior position.

---

[1] Edward Said, *Orientalism* (New York, Vintage, 1979), p. 7.

Queering the Travelogue

One of the many configurations of this dominance emerges through imperialism's investment in patriarchy; specifically, as Edward Said elaborates in his discussion on Gustave Flaubert, the masculinised Occident strives to penetrate a feminised, fecund Orient.[2] Using erotic imagery, travel writers circulated colonialist phantasms of sexual promiscuity and deviance.[3] Certainly colonialist travel writers were intrigued and perhaps, in some cases, even motivated by sexuality—whether voyeuristically recording sexual practices, or actively pursuing sexual encounters in foreign lands:

> the Orient was a place where one could look for sexual experience unobtainable in Europe.... What [writers] looked for often...was a different type of sexuality, perhaps more libertine and less guilt-ridden.[4]

Pondering on the ambiguity surrounding Said's phrase, 'different type of sexuality', and his discussion of Flaubert's relationship with an Egyptian courtesan, Joseph Boone criticised Said's analysis of 'colonialist erotica' for remaining 'ensconced in conspicuously heterosexual interpretive frameworks.'[5] Boone argues that while the East has been gendered as feminine in Orientalist discourse, 'a close analysis of several specific Western experiences and representations of the Near East reveals that that which appears alluringly feminine is not always, or necessarily, female.'[6] The writings of Richard Burton, T. E. Lawrence and Gustave Flaubert attest to the prevalent homoerotic concerns running through much travel writing on the Near East. Since both Boone and Said take the Middle East and the Maghreb as their examples

---

[2] Ibid., p. 187.

[3] Trans. by Myrna Godzich and Wlad Godzich, Malek Alloula, *The Colonial Harem* (Minneapolis, University of Minnesota Press, 1986). This work elaborates on the eroticising and exoticising of the Orient through an analysis of early twentieth century colonial postcards, mailed home by the French in Algeria.

[4] Said, *op. cit.*, p. 190.

[5] Joseph Boone, 'Vacation Cruises: Or, The Homoerotics of Orientalism', *Publications of the Modern Language Association of America*, Vol. 110, No. 1 (1995), pp. 89–107.

[6] Ibid., p. 92.

of the Orient, the Indian subcontinent is left outside the purview of their analyses. Two of the most prominent colonialist travel writers of India, E. M. Forster (*Hill of Devi*) and J. R. Ackerley (*Hindoo Holiday*), practiced sexual relations with other men, and their experience of the Indian Orient was filtered through their own sexual identifications. The homoerotics of Ackerley's *Hindoo Holiday* are less coded than Forster's *Hill of Devi*, which suppresses homoerotic tensions. Ackerley's 'open secret', therefore, serves to highlight all the more issues of power relations, difference and representation in a colonial frame.

Literary criticism has paid very little attention to J. R. Ackerley, a close friend of E. M. Forster. Ackerley was born at the close of the nineteenth century (1896) and wrote most of his non-fiction, including *Hindoo Holiday* (1932), in the thirties. His only play, *The Prisoners of War* (1925), details the relationships of two homosexual couples after World War I, and was surprisingly successful in London's West End theatre district. He wrote two novels in the 1950s, based on his beloved Alsatian dog, Queenie, and his autobiography, *My Father and Myself* (1968), was published one year after his death, in which he describes in detail his innumerable liaisons with working class men against a backdrop of an ambivalent relationship with his father.[7] The dearth of criticism on Ackerley, especially on his travel-memoir, *Hindoo Holiday*, is surprising, since it is only one of two such memoirs, and provides an illustrative text for the intersection of postcolonialism and queer theory. Even when Eve Kosofsky Sedgwick mentions Ackerley in her seminal work, *Between Men*, she cursorily lists him alongside T. H. White, Charles Kingsley, Havelock Ellis, T. E. Lawrence and others as examples of 'English gentlemen' without a 'predetermined sexual trajectory'.[8] Her second, and final, mention of Ackerley again sets him against a list of others who objectify 'proletarian men'.[9] However, Sedgwick's work does provide a useful guide for elaborating on the function of the

---

[7] The most extensive analysis of J. R. Ackerley's autobiography was provided by Joseph Bristow, *Effeminate England* (New York, Columbia University Press, 1995), pp. 146–53.
[8] Eve Kosofsky Sedgwick, *Between Men: English Literature and Male Homosocial Desire* (New York, Columbia University Press, 1985), p. 173.
[9] *Ibid.*, p. 174.

male homosocial continuum, even if it does not examine such dynamics within Ackerley's writing. Christopher Lane, in *The Ruling Passion*—the only book to deal exclusively with colonialist homoerotics—produces a very brief, reductive reading of Ackerley's autobiography, aligning the ego in Ackerley's writing with a 'white man', and the unconscious with a 'black man'. Ronald Hyam refers to Ackerley in a footnote, as an example of a European who found his 'pederastic experiences' at the court of an Indian prince.[10] On the other hand, David Bergman lumps *Hindoo Holiday* with all of Ackerley's other writings, imposing upon them a singular interpretation: 'all of Ackerley's work deals with the same obsessive theme: losing the Ideal Friend.'[11] Bergman takes the figure of the 'Ideal Friend' from Ackerley's autobiography and illustrates this ideal, then point-by-point shows the search for the ideal, implying that the search would logically end at an incestuous resolution: Ackerley's own father as his ideal friend. Unfortunately, Bergman's own search for the-search-for-the-Ideal-Friend leaves him blind to the ambivalent workings of homoeroticism itself in Ackerley's work, especially in *Hindoo Holiday*. Perhaps more importantly, he fails to take into account the varying cultural resonances between Ackerley's travel writing and his autobiographical work.

All in all, the critics who do mention Ackerley refer more often to his autobiography than to his travel memoirs. I propose that a closer look at Ackerley's *Hindoo Holiday* would prove instructive not only for its contribution to the small body of English travel writing in India, but also because of its production of a homo-eroticised Indian Orient, viewed through the optic of middle class English colonialist and racialist ideology in the early twentieth century. As such, *Hindoo Holiday* yields a text rife with the pressures of power dialectics, colonialist (sexual) anxieties and orientalist authority, all three of which are interdependent. Ackerley remains, throughout the text, in a superior position, as the 'Sahib', which invests him with the authority to speak on behalf of the 'natives', while he implicitly wields power over them, whom he

[10] Ronald Hyam, *Empire and Sexuality, Studies in Imperialism* (New York, Manchester University Press, 1990), p. 136, n. 37.
[11] David Bergman, 'J. R. Ackerley and the Ideal Friend', in Peter Murphy (ed.), *Fictions of Masculinity* (New York, New York University Press, 1994), pp. 266–67.

finds both sinister and sexually attractive. While previous criticism, such as Lane's, has focused on the psychodynamics of race and homoeroticism, or in Bergman's case, biographical criticism, I wish to examine the structural relations that inform the observations, delineation of relationships and projections in Ackerley's travel journal, keeping in sight the dynamics of homoeroticism in this colonial encounter.

Perhaps what sets *Hindoo Holiday* apart from other travel journals is that it is a record of the observations of colonial life by an 'English tutor', whose authority is implicit in his role. Ackerley's visit to India was prompted by E. M. Forster who suggested that Ackerley visit India for a change of scenery since Forster's friend, the Maharajah of Chhatarpur, was offering a position for 'a companion secretary' or a tutor.[12] Ackerley writes in the opening 'Explanation:'

> He wanted someone to love him—His Highness, I mean; that was his real need, I think. He alleged other reasons, of course—an English private secretary, a tutor for his son.[13]

Whatever the Maharajah's motives, Ackerley's excursion into India is validated through the guise of tutorship, or at least through the position of a private secretary. In either case, the implications for Ackerley's place in India remain the same: a tutor and an English private secretary would both be positioned so as to simultaneously allow access to the 'inner spaces' of the native world, and also to be outside of that world altogether. Furthermore, since tutors and secretaries were—in colonialist tradition—generally men working with and for men, Ackerley's journal is, at its inception, partaking of a structure that allows knowledge to be circulated only between men, serving to cement bonds between men.

However, Ackerley is never fully assimilated into the Indian homosocial order because he is both an outsider and an insider; although he is in the service of the Maharajah, it is clear that he retains the more powerful position of a colonial Sahib. Ackerley

---

[12] Neville Braybrooke (ed.), *The Ackerley Letters* (New York, Harcourt Brace Jovanovich, 1975), p. 25.

[13] J.R. Ackerley, *Hindoo Holiday: An Indian Journal* (New York, Poseidon, 2nd edn 1990), p. 1.

assumes the role of the tutor in his attempts to answer Maharajah's questions regarding relationships, metaphysics and religion ('Cupidity. What does it mean?'; 'Is there an Absolute? Is there a God? Is there a future life?')—in fact, the Maharajah admits that he looks upon Ackerley as a 'kind of *weezard* [sic]'[14] and that he likes Europeans 'because he [a European] is so wisdom [sic].'[15] While Ackerley acts as a tutor to the Maharajah (he never does meet the Maharajah's son), his journal is meant to teach the western reader about India. Periodically—rather, randomly— Ackerley adopts an informative, pseudo-anthropological stance, detailing Hindu customs and religious beliefs; in short, to bring the Indian Orient 'home' to the English reader. Although Ackerley adds in the explanation that his knowledge of India 'is not exhaustive', the 'anthropological' passages nevertheless retain an authoritative veneer through their very referencing of anthropological discourse. That is, the intrusion of anthropology into the loose travel narrative bolsters the truth-content of both that narrative and, reflexively, of the pseudo-scientific passages themselves. Moreover, Ackerley's assumption of authority—as evident in his facile assimilation into the role of one who is 'so wisdom', and the authoritative tone of his 'anthropological' passages—is a function of his colonialist, middle class, English background. I am alluding here to Said's elaboration of the fundamental arrangement of Occidental knowledge-production that takes the Orient as its subject:

> For if it is true that no production of knowledge in the human sciences can ever ignore or disclaim its author's involvement as a human subject in his own circumstances, then it must also be true that for a European or American studying the Orient there can be no disclaiming the main circumstances of *his* actuality: that he comes up against the Orient as a European or American first, as an individual second.[16]

Since, in the case of the empire, political boundaries (English/ Indian, coloniser/colonised, powerful/powerless, civilised/ uncivilised) are so highly charged and patrolled at a very material

---

14 Ackerley, *op. cit.*, p. 25.
15 *Ibid.*, p. 42.
16 Said, *op. cit.*, p. 42.

level,[17] and since the existence of the empire itself rests upon a recognition of these important distinctions, Ackerley's role in Chhatarpur is foremost a political one, and his *positional* superiority' consciously and unconsciously pervades his observations, thoughts and writing.

Hindoo Holiday: Desiring Gazes, Positional Authorities

The journal opens with Ackerley's arrival in Chhatarpur, and his introduction to the Maharajah. The subsequent entries describe Ackerley's frequently bemused exchanges with the Maharajah on their daily rides through the surrounding countryside. The Maharajah is an odd mixture of childish whims, authoritative opinions and homespun philosophy. In the course of the journal, we are introduced to the other principal characters: Babaji Rao, the devout Hindu secretary to the Maharajah who faces existential angst for feeding his son chicken stock while the latter's health was in a critical condition; the stubborn Dewan, or 'Prime Minister', appointed by the Empire to oversee the Maharajah's state; Abdul Haq, Ackerley's Hindi tutor who persistently attempts to improve his rank through Ackerley's influence as a 'Sahib'; and Narayan, Sharma, Hashim and Habib, the servants who variously become the objects of Ackerley's desire.

This objectification takes place within a specular dimension where Ackerley's gaze binds 'native' identity to binary opposite: sinister/safe, invisible/visible, dirty/clean, ugly/beautiful, educated/uneducated and simple/experienced. The binaries sinister/safe and visible/invisible are codependent, and point to Ackerley's anxieties as a coloniser. He describes the guest house waiter, Hashim, as 'a queer, inscrutable man' who 'seems vaguely

---

[17] I am bracketing here the question of the ambivalence of colonial discourse, as propounded by Homi Bhabha (see Bhabha, *The Location of Culture* [New York, Routledge, 1994]), mostly because this discussion in postcolonial studies has remained at the level of the symbolic, with a corollary disregard for the material effects of colonialism. I am influenced here by Pheng Cheah's critique of Bhabha in *Cosmopolitics* (Minneapolis, University of Minnesota Press, 1998), pp. 290–328. Furthermore, the Bhabhian colonial subject, though split and hybrid, is not only universal but also problematically homogenous. See Ania Loomba, *Colonialism/ Postcolonialism* (Routledge, 1998), pp. 173–83.

hostile': 'He is a little alarming ... and since he walks with bare feet I can't hear him move about and am frequently startled to find him beside me or close behind my chair.'[18] Hashim is sinister because he is invisible; he alarms the white man who cannot locate him, and who unexpectedly finds him close beside him. The unseen, unheard, 'vaguely hostile' native is a continual source of anxiety for the coloniser. In Ackerley's case, however, the invisible is further linked with the erotic: after all, Hashim is 'rather handsome in his blue-and-white turban and his long close-fitting blue uniform coat'.[19] The closet that Hashim inhabits is the same mysterious space in which a Maharajah can have a wife as well as boy-lovers, a 'native' space from which, in Ackerley's mind, inexplicable contradictions arise without being solved.

Ackerley's insistence on knowing is an attempt to penetrate through the doors of a 'closet' that rests on epistemes foreign to him. The need to know the location of the sinister servant is linked to the need to know the complexities of caste/religious structures, as the journal breaks unexpectedly into strictly informative prose in which Ackerley begins to elaborate on Hindu mythology or the position of marriage in Hindu society. Superimposing the episte-mological need for the location of the invisible native onto the need to know the caste and marriage complexities, we find Ackerley's text complicit in the imperialist dialectic of surveillance and control, a preoccupation that underpins every observation and litany of 'Indian' cultural practice. Thus, it is clear that Ackerley must, and will remain on the outside, and the sort of understanding he desires will always elude him; India and its people will remain 'a strange, wild country, ... and strange, wild companions.'[20] In fact, Ackerley's contact with Hindu taboo and ritual constantly leaves him in an 'inferior' position: when entering the Maharajah's room before the spectacle of the 'Gods', Ackerley is told not to touch the Maharajah because he is 'holy'; Babaji Rao, the Maharajah's secretary, leaves Ackerley's presence before drinking water, so as to keep the water 'pure'; Narayan, a servant, refuses to take a cigarette that has been in Ackerley's mouth.

---

[18] Ackerley, *op. cit.*, p. 28.
[19] *Ibid.*, p. 27. There is a connection to be made here between colonial anxiety and colonial sexual fantasy.
[20] *Ibid.*, p. 185.

As a homosexual, furthermore, Ackerley himself is well-versed in the intricacies of the visible/invisible. Hashim, while representing a mutinous threat, also remains for Ackerley the alluring, yet hidden source of homoerotic tension. Ultimately, however, the binaries employed by Ackerley cannot hold—homoerotic acts are both visible and invisible. From his experiences in London,[21] Ackerley is aware of the importance of the closet and the safe invisibility it ensures; while in India he is presented with a world in which male bonds are more fluid. Upon a temple wall, Ackerley observes 'a long file of soldiers marching gaily along, and another, smaller, more elaborate, design which was frequently repeated. They were both sodomitic.'[22] The temple, as a public space, dismantles the visible/invisible dichotomy which regulates western notions of heterosexual, and especially homosexual, erotica. In Chhokrapur, or 'boy-town' (the city name chosen by Ackerley for the purposes of his travel memoir),[23] there is a distinct continuity between the homosexual and the homosocial. Eve Kosofsky Sedgwick in *Between Men* describes 'homosocial' as 'social bonds between persons of the same sex'; while 'homosocial' is derived from 'homosexual', it also marks a difference from the homosexual. 'To draw the "homosocial" back into the orbit of "desire", of the potentially erotic, then, is to hypothesise the potential unbrokenness of a continuum between homosocial and homosexual—a continuum whose visibility, for men, in our society, is radically disrupted.'[24] Bonds between men in western societies, according to Sedgwick, are simultaneously the most crucial and the most policed of all bonds. However, in Ackerley's Chhokrapur, there is no disruption between homosocial and homosexual bonds.[25]

---

[21] See Ackerley's autobiography, *My Father and Myself* (London, Pimlico, 1968).

[22] Ackerley, *Hindoo Holiday*, p. 18.

[23] All names, including the name of the city, Chhatarpur, were changed by Ackerley when *Hindoo Holiday* went to press, in order to protect the privacy of the Maharajah.

[24] Sedgwick, *op. cit.*, p. 2.

[25] It is vital to keep in mind, at the outset, that my analysis takes as its assumption that *Hindoo Holiday* is an emphatically 'western' text, constructed by a European whose observations of India are filtered, structured and selectively defined through his 'western' positioning. Therefore, the application of Sedgwick's 'western' formulations of the homosocial continuum in Ackerley's Chhokrapur is apt and useful.

Most men that engage in homoerotic activity, including the Maharajah and Narayan, are also married. While marriage secures male homosocial bonds through the exchange of women, homoerotic relationships secure erotic investments. In a section of *Hindoo Holiday* deleted from all editions,[26] the continuity between the homosocial and the homosexual is strikingly apparent. In the course of a dialogue with Narayan, a boy-servant, Ackerley discovers that Sharma, the Maharajah's 'valet', is not only the Maharajah's lover, but that the Maharajah forces Sharma to have sexual intercourse with the Maharani while he watches, and, indeed, her son is Sharma's son, not the Maharajah's. While the woman serves as an object of pleasure for both males—Sharma, through genital contact, and the Maharajah, because he likes to watch—she remains a child-bearing vessel under the imperative to produce males. In the meantime the two males in her life have regular sexual intercourse with each other—the homosexual flows into the homosocial, and vice versa, without disruption.

The performance of the 'Gods' is yet another illustration of this continuity. The Maharajah invites Ackerley to see the 'Gods', pubescent boys, dramatise through dance and song stories from Hindu mythology. Ackerley and the Maharajah sit in a small chamber, 'His Highness's private closet',[27] unobserved by the rest of the audience, and watch the show through a window. The Maharajah openly questions Ackerley, asking him to rate each boy's beauty. The homoerotics of the performance are abundantly obvious in the Maharajah's quest to find the most beautiful boys, and a later hint to Ackerley that some performances are naked. Later, at another performance, Ackerley remarks, 'It was not, of

---

[26] Apparently Chatto & Windus, the original publishers of *Hindoo Holiday*, asked Ackerley to omit certain passages which may have been considered libelous to himself or to others. Before the second edition was printed in 1951, Ackerley asked to restore the omissions, and the publishers agreed, since Ackerley had changed all names and the state of Chhatarpur was by then: 'dissolved'. However, the review copies of *Hindoo Holiday* were simultaneously released with review copies of Arthur Cunningham Lothian's *Kingdoms of Yesterday*, in which Lothian referred to Ackerley and identified both the Maharajah and his state. Since the Maharajah's son was still alive, the publishers asked Ackerley to omit one particular page which questioned the son's parentage, while Lothian was told to omit all references to Ackerley. Ackerley's 'missing page' was reprinted much later in an appendix to a selection of his letters (See Braybrooke, *op. cit.*, pp. 10, 95, 133, 334).

[27] Ackerley, *Hindoo Holiday.*, p. 32.

course, a private Palace entertainment like the other I had seen, for the women would never have been invited.'[28] The private Palace entertainment which parades homoerotics on a stage is reserved only for men, to strengthen the bonds between them. While watching the performance, the figure of the invisible, handsome servant reappears from the darkness of the Maharajah's chamber:

> From the shadows behind the *charpai*, where, unnoticed by me, he had been squatting, a white-turbaned servant rose and left the chamber by the other door.... He was young and tall, with bony hands and feet, but his face was strikingly handsome—fairer than usual and lighted by large glowing dark eyes, which every now and then rested curiously upon me.[29]

The emergence of the handsome male (Sharma) from the shadows gestures toward Ackerley's western imaginary, in which invisibility must regulate homoerotic desire. From this reassertion, at least in Ackerley's mind, of the visible/invisible dichotomy, to the openly homoerotic interaction between the performance and the gaze of the male audience, two continuities can be drawn: one from the homosexual to the homosocial (the homoerotics serving to strengthen male–male bonds while necessitating the effacement of female presence), and another from Ackerley's gaze (which constructs through binaries) to the Maharajah's gaze (which moves fluidly from one side of the binary to the other, not asserting either side of it), for which the emergence of the male servant from the dark is of no surprise or consequence. The tensions between the two different gazes and Ackerley's position in the colonial hierarchy come to the surface when the Maharajah asks the boy servant to step into the light again so that Ackerley may inspect him:

> He ... stood there facing me, motionless, expressionless, awaiting my inspection. But I couldn't manage that—sitting there studying him as though he were a slave; so I hurriedly murmured my satisfaction, and another motion of the royal hand restored him to his shadows.[30]

---

[28] *Ibid.*, p. 70.
[29] *Ibid.*, pp. 37–38.
[30] *Ibid.*, p. 38.

The presentation of a handsome boy to Ackerley's desiring gaze makes him acutely conscious of his own superior position as a Sahib. The anxiety caused by this crisis, precipitated by a recognition of himself as a master of sorts, momentarily dispels desire and the boy is immediately asked to recede.

In order to allay the anxiety of such colonial self-recognition, Ackerley tries to mark a difference between himself and other English people in India: he pokes fun at the English living in the guest house, and tries the sweetmeats and betel juice shunned by most colonials. However, the inequality between himself and the Indians, marked by his own racial makeup, follows him everywhere. Intentionally going against the advice of Mrs. Montgomery, an English caricature residing at the guest house, Ackerley walks through Chhokrapur alone. Soon he becomes the object of the colonised's gaze as the townspeople stop their chores to stare at him.

> Now I found *myself* an object of curiosity…I felt intrusive and self-conscious in my English clothes, and omitted to return salutes in case the saluters should be encouraged to speak to me and I should not understand what they said.[31]

The anxiety of his complicity mingles with the ever-present anxiety of being attacked by the 'natives': 'I hurried along in a panic…. The street became narrower and narrower as I turned and turned, until I felt I was back in the trenches, the houses upon either side being so much of the same colour and substance as the rough ground between.'[32] He seems to be running from an inescapable crowd of Indians, and as the roads become narrower and he feels more trapped, the association with warfare signals a willingness, on his part, to fight back. His relationships with Indians are infused with anxiety and both conscious and unconscious antagonism, despite attempts to set himself apart from other English colonials. The prospect of himself becoming the object of scrutiny (that is, an object of knowledge for the Indian) triggers Ackerley's colonial defences.

Nevertheless, Ackerley tries to insert himself into the Indian spectrum of sexuality via the Maharajah, whose polymorphous

---

[31] *Ibid.*, p. 16. Italics in original.
[32] *Loc. cit.*.

sexuality includes a fascination with the Greeks and Romans, precursors to the formation of Ackerley's own 'English' culture. Through this link Ackerley attempts to step into the realm of a diffuse sexuality. During a discussion of male beauty, or what the Greeks considered (male) beauty, Ackerley remarks, 'if I come back here to remain with you we will join in cultivating beauty in Chhokrapur; we'll wed beauty to beauty and beget beauty. In fact, we will turn your realm between us into a classic Greek state.'[33] This fantasy, informed by Platonic ideals, would underscore the continuities between the homosocial and the homoerotic; although the remark is undoubtedly facetious, it attempts to assert Ackerley's presence in the erotic registers of Chhokrapur. Later in the journal, Ackerley writes, 'I spoke to His Highness yesterday about a tutor for myself … and taking advantage of some remark of his on Zeus and Ganymede, asked whether I might not have his valet to teach me.'[34] Ackerley knows that the valet, Sharma, is the Maharajah's boy-lover, and by associating Sharma with Ganymede, Ackerley lumps himself with the Maharajah as Zeus, thereby directly placing himself in the midst of what he considers to be Chhokrapur's sexual imaginary. However, Ackerley's perceived inclusion into Indian sexuality is problematic because it is figured as the Maharajah's fantasy, who is himself entrenched in a colonialist dynamic of power and rule, and Zeus and Ganymede are figures of Western mythology. The Maharajah's status, although held in check by the more powerful Political Agent, is itself a colonial construction, as he depends on the empire's largesse himself. Thus both Ackerley and the Maharajah are implicated in taking part in the dominant sides of the ruler/ruled and coloniser/colonised binaries, and Ackerley's insertion into the spectrum of 'native' sexual identity is drastically limited, if not altogether spurious.

Ultimately, his attempts to align himself with the figure of a benevolent coloniser, whose sexual difference would 'neutralise' his dominant positioning and whose supposed inclusion in the erotic indexes of Chhokrapur would 'equate' him with the locals, fail. Ackerley's identity in India is defined by his dominant positionality, and the overarching structure of dominance pervades his thinking in unconscious ways. In describing Habib,

---

[33] *Ibid.*, p. 32.
[34] *Ibid.*, p. 46.

another servant, Ackerley uses the language of animal psychology:

> Whenever I ran out of cigarettes and drew attention to this, which otherwise would not have been noticed, by placing the Gold Flake tin in the centre of the verandah, it was always Habib who, apparently suspecting some connection between the emptiness and the exposure of the object, brought it back to me to elicit, by gesture, the reason for its having been placed where he found it.[35]

Habib, is like an animal which must be conditioned by Ackerley's superior knowledge and position, through a system of stimuli and response so that he can perform his duties and serve his role competently. The condescending language which reduces Indians to the status of animals is pervasive throughout the text: 'Hashim is easy to dismiss; one can do it with a nod, for he is accustomed to Europeans,'[36] or 'Munshi is always the most moved, and indeed seems endowed with a special faculty for sensing the approach of his royal master.'[37]

Ackerley enjoys his position as the served superior—when servants do not live up to his expectations, he shouts and bullies them. His gifts of cigarettes to certain attractive servants transcend no barriers, but serve as baits. Ackerley's text, therefore, presents us with a study in ideological confinement. Joseph Boone writes:

> In narratives where the occidental traveller by virtue of his homosexuality is already the other, the presumed *equivalence* of Eastern homosexuality and occidental personal liberation may disguise the spectre of colonial privilege and exploitation encoded in the hierarchy white man/brown boy.[38]

Although Boone focuses on western travellers to the Maghreb, the implications of travel writing by western homosexuals travelling in the East are equally relevant to J. R. Ackerley. Asymmetrical relations between Ackerley and Indians are perhaps most evident when Ackerley initiates erotic physical contact with the boy-servants. Such contact is always pre-codified in a colonial framework. In a 'dark roadway, overshadowed by trees', Ackerley

---

[35] Ackerley, *ibid.*, p. 144.
[36] *Ibid.*, p. 54.
[37] *Ibid.*, p. 36.
[38] Boone, *op. cit.*, p. 104.

kisses Narayan on the mouth, 'and this time he [Narayan] did not draw away.'[39] Their kiss takes place in the darkness, against the will of Narayan who had refused to share a cigarette with Ackerley because he ate meat, and who has therefore asked Ackerley not to kiss him on the mouth. Erotic contact occurs on Ackerley's terms because he, ultimately, holds the power, of which he is far too aware. Writing to E. M. Forster, Ackerley reflects:

> It is the power of authority.... They are blindly obedient to it. They prostrate their minds before it (as before all other manifestations of power) whether it proceeds from their parents, their chief, or the conquering European.[40]

Aside from the condescending tone of voice, Ackerley confesses to a full awareness of his own power over Indians.[41]

Reinforcing Structures: Appropriated Homoerotics

The pre-codified positioning of J. R. Ackerley in the colonial machinery ultimately serves to keep the imperial system in place. His potentially counter-frictional homoerotic relations with the boy-servants do not subvert the larger colonial structure or transcend any boundaries. The status quo remains unchallenged; colonial binaries (powerful/powerless, ruler/ruled) remain in place. This result is ensured by the creation of a space in which homoeroticism functions without subversion, and instead is subsumed in the overarching imperial framework—a space which acts as a 'buffer zone' of sorts, in which the potentially subversive bends to the laws and forces of the greater colonialist machinery.

This space is a product of the respective mechanics of Ackerley's 'positional superiority' and Chhokrapur's undisrupted homosocial continuum. According to Eve Kosofsky Sedgwick, in Western patriarchal configurations of sexuality, the continuum between the homosocial and homosexual 'is radically disrupted'.[42] Moreover,

---

[39] Ackerley, *Hindoo Holiday.*, p. 218.

[40] Braybrooke, *op. cit.*, p. 13.

[41] This is also apparent in *Hindoo Holiday*, when Ackerley visits a jail and feels obliged to give each prisoner 'equal attention', in case his 'visit was as important to them as are the visits of the Prince of Wales on tours of inspection in England'. (Ackerley, *Hindoo Holiday*, p. 43).

[42] Sedgwick, *op. cit.*, p. 2.

in western society, if 'homophobia directed by men against men is misogynistic, and perhaps transhistorically so',[43] then it necessarily implies that male homosexuality is structurally counter-patriarchal. Thus, in Ackerley's England, with its disrupted homosocial continuum, homoeroticism proves subversive, and hence homosexual activity is criminalised. Since the Western imperial project is ensconced in heterosexist, patriarchal frames, homoerotics would further serve to challenge the underpinnings of colonialism. Yet this is not the case in *Hindoo Holiday*, in which interracial homoerotics take place against the backdrop of (white) colonial rule upon an undisrupted homosocial continuum. While Chhokrapur is patriarchal, its homoerotics merely become yet another configuration of a polymorphous sexuality—given the fluidity between male homosocial and homoerotic bonds—rather than a threat to patriarchy. Amongst the most effectual men of Chhokrapur, such as the Maharajah, a classic Greek state is the ideal, a structure in which 'institutionalised social relations are … carried out via women'—that is, 'marriage, name, family, loyalty to progenitors and to posterity' all depend on the use of women by men in a manner that does not oppose the men's bonds to each other.[44] In Chhokrapur, then, the Maharajah's homoerotic relation with Sharma does not upset societal order, but perhaps enforces it through an assertion of power and class relations, if it has any effect at all.

While it would appear that homoeroticism between a white man and a 'native', given Western configurations of sexuality, would potentially overthrow colonial boundaries, the encounter between Ackerley and the eroticised figures of Chhokrapur suppresses structural upheaval on both sides. While homoeroticism becomes a non-disruptive subset of Chhokrapur's sexual imaginary, Ackerley's dominant racial and political position leave him with no vantage point from which to dismantle his colonialist, racialist assumptions. Hence every contact—sexual or otherwise—with the 'natives' is informed through his superior positionality. While interracial homoeroticism does not subvert the structures of Chhokrapur, it also does not undermine colonial hierarchies.

---

[43] *Ibid.*, p. 20.
[44] *Ibid.*, p. 35.

4

Theatrical Transvestism in the Parsi, Gujarati and Marathi Theatres (1850–1940)

◆ Kathryn Hansen

Female impersonation, the practice of men playing women's roles, has a long history in South Asian theatre. In Patanjali's grammatical text, the *Mahabhasya* (c. 150 B.C.), a male actor who plays female roles is described as a *bhrukumsa*, one who 'flutters his brows.'[1] The well known dramaturgical compendium of ancient India, the *Natyasastra* (c. 2–4 A.D.), mentions both men assuming the female role, an impersonation termed *rupanusarini* (imitative) and women taking on the male role.[2] Female impersonation continues today in regional theatrical arts such as the Kathakali of Kerala, the Ram Lila of Uttar Pradesh and numerous local and folk forms.[3] However, theatrical transvestism as a customary mode of enacting female characters has vanished from the urban cultural

---

[1] V. Raghavan, 'Sanskrit Drama in Performance,' in Rachel Van M. Baumer and James R. Brandon (eds), *Sanskrit Drama in Performance* (Honolulu, University Press of Hawaii, 1981), p. 13.

[2] Cf. *Natyasastra* xxxv: 31–32, cited in Syed Jamil Ahmed, 'Female Performers in the Indigenous Theatre of Bengal,' in Firdous Azim and Niaz Zaman (eds), *Infinite Variety: Women in Society and Literature* (Dhaka, Dhaka University Press Limited, 1994), p. 265.

[3] Jiwan Pani, 'The Female Impersonator in Traditional Indian Theatre,' in *Sangeet Natak*, Vol. 45 (July–Sept. 1977), pp. 37–42.

zone. It surfaces in current film and drama either in the mimetic representation of the *hijra*, the transgendered social actor (for example, the protagonist of Amol Palekar's film *Dayra* [The Square Circle, 1996], or the minor character who appears during the riots in Mani Ratnam's film *Bombay*, 1995) or as a self-conscious interrogation of the earlier female impersonator (in, for example, Anuradha Kapur's theatre piece, *Sundari: An Actor Prepares*, 1998).

With this disappearance, a cultural space that valorised crossgender role play and its associated spectatorial pleasures has vanished. Theatrical transvestism not only enabled actors to transform their own gender identities, it sustained and eventually reworked viewing practices predicated on an interest in transgender identification and the homoerotic gaze. This article excavates the buried trove of theatrical transvestism that existed in western urban India, in the Parsi, Gujarati and Marathi theatres, between approximately 1850 and 1940. Within the public culture of that time, female impersonators like Naslu Sarkari, Jayshankar Sundari and Bal Gandharva achieved the renown of a Madhuri Dixit or Lata Mangeshkar of today. The present essay will address this phenomenon, in the context of late colonial cultural formations, as the historical resurgence of a longstanding practice. It will explore the ramifications of theatrical cross-dressing for the constitution of gendered subjectivities, posing questions about homoerotic pleasure and homosexual culture that may be extrapolated to a wider range of spaces and times.

The analysis presented here challenges the time-honoured but fundamentally homophobic premise that female impersonators were mere surrogates for missing women. Women in the nineteenth century were, of course, disenfranchised both as social actors and as theatrical performers. My argument is that female impersonators were desired, in their own right, as men who embodied the feminine. Contrary to popular notions, they often coexisted with stage actresses and were chosen by their fans in preference to them. Moreover, these cross-dressed actors with their huge followings were vital agents in the redesign of gender relations and roles. They set new standards for feminine conduct and fashion, transforming the visual construct of womanhood into an image of bourgeois respectability. Simultaneously, female impersonators crafted a new sense of the interior person. They formulated attitudes of modesty and vulnerability that became the hallmark of the new femininity, paving the way for the emergence of the dutiful, demure *bharatiya nari* (Indian Woman) of the nationalist era.

Contours of the Bombay Stage

Soon after 1850, Bombay developed a metropolitan theatrical culture structured by the overlapping practices of the Parsi, Gujarati and Marathi theatres. Although separated to a certain extent by language, these theatres shared much beyond their orientation toward female impersonation. They participated in a commercial entertainment economy based on corporate ownership of theatrical companies, which arose in tandem with the city's rapid population growth and prosperity. Music, dance and dramatic entertainments, once restricted in circulation by aristocratic patronage, were transformed into commodities of mass consumption with the rise of a bourgeoisie and the institutionalisation of public space and leisure time. The appropriation of European stage technologies and new styles of drama deepened the divide between the older representational arena of court and countryside and the new public of the metropolis. Impersonations of gender, although continuous with earlier practices, entered the modern era and assumed meanings specific to the reconstituted audience.

That this audience was not bounded by the geographical perimeters of Bombay adds to the importance of the phenomenon for the construction of gendered subjectivities. Beginning in the 1870s, Parsi theatrical companies routinely traveled as far as Madras (Chennai) and Ceylon, Calcutta (Kolkata) and Rangoon, Peshawar and Sind. In each locale, companies sprang up styled after the Parsi companies, often adding the glamourous phrase 'of Bombay' to their names. Their popularity within these regions extended the Parsi theatre's impact far beyond its point of origin. Even within Bombay the Parsi theatre was a broad-based institution, the historical identity of which was never coterminous with the Parsi community.[4] Writers, actors, company managers, musicians and

---

[4] As immigrants to India from Iran after its conquest by Islamic rulers, the Parsis preserved their distinct Zoroastrian faith while adopting the Gujarati language and the customs of the surrounding society. In the eighteenth century many

stage hands belonged to a mix of class, caste and religious backgrounds. Audiences, comprising initially of British officials, the military and wealthy Parsi merchants, were soon joined by a growing class of educated professionals. Textile workers, artisans, and small traders formed a large share by the end of the nineteenth century, accommodated by low ticket prices that ensured a heterogeneous public.

Although much has been made of the derivative, colonial character of the Parsi theatre, largely on account of its fascination for Shakespeare and Victorian stagecraft, the overwhelming majority of the productions were in Gujarati, Urdu and Hindi. Indic poetry and song genres embedded in Sanskritic and Persian narratives formed the dominant literary substratum. The stage medium was fluid and polyglot; modern forms of the languages had not yet stabilised, and the association of community and region with linguistic identity was yet to become fixed. Bombay's theatre houses, although owned mostly by Parsis, were available for use to theatre companies regardless of language or community affiliation. Most of these were built on Grant Road, in what was rapidly developing into a red light district, but the prestigious Gaiety and Novelty theatres near the Victoria railway terminus also attracted large audiences. A great deal of imitation and rivalry existed within the entire urban theatre economy, allowing popular trends like female impersonation to circulate fluidly.

The rise of these urban theatres can be directly linked to the desire of the urban professional and mercantile classes for 'rational amusement' in respectable public spaces. Prince Albert's dictum, 'Rational entertainment, in which popular amusement was combined with moral instruction and intellectual culture,' was printed in English and Gujarati translation on the title pages of the earliest published Gujarati dramas.[5] Authorial prefaces to the plays stressed the efficacy of the drama as an instrument of moral

---

migrated from Gujarat to Bombay. Collaboration with European traders and the British East India Company enabled the Parsi mercantile elite to achieve extraordinary financial success. Middle class Parsis eagerly sought English education in the second half of the nineteenth century, filling a disproportionate number of seats at the recently established Elphinstone College. It was here, in mid-century, that amateur theatricals became fashionable among Parsi students.

[5] K. N. Kabra, *Jamshed* (Mumbai, Ashkara Press, 1870); K. N. Kabra, *Faredun* (Mumbai, Ashkara Press, 1874).

improvement. This principle was reinforced by the coverage of theatre shows in print journalism. Newspapers in English and Gujarati carried playbills, synopses, reviews and letters to the editor on the subject of theatre, with the explicit intention of building an audience and nurturing the theatre 'in its infancy'. Theatrical discourse thereby allied itself with the adjacent discourses of bourgeois respectability, civic order and moral reform, and patronage of the theatre became a demonstration of public virtue.

Theatre pioneers, including playwrights, managers and company owners, were careful to demarcate their efforts at constructing a new culture of educative leisure in contradistinction to older forms of entertainment. In a Gujarati preface that begins by contrasting *natak*, the Sanskrit term for drama, with *chetak*, 'sorcery, or witchcraft', playwright 'Delta' takes pains to discriminate between acceptable and unacceptable styles of performance:

> In short, rather than the black stamp of immorality that is slapped on the mind of the viewer by the dance of prostitutes, the shows of Mahlaris, and the Bhavai of the folk-players, the blameless amusement of theatre enlarges the mind, gladdens the heart, cools the eyes, and speeds morality.[6]

For Delta, immorality resides in the prevalent styles of popular entertainment, the nautch ('dance of prostitutes'), the folk drama: Bhavai, and the shows of itinerant performers such as the Mahlaris. It is known that the Bhavaiyas and Mahlaris were designated as low caste primarily because of their occupation as hereditary performers, whereas dancing girls were marginalised on account of their violation of normative gender codes. Patronising such performers, although widespread among the British and Indian elite as well as ordinary people in the eighteenth and early nineteenth centuries, had become at least somewhat stigmatised by 1850. Part of the success of the emergent public theatre lay in its ability to offer itself as an alternate site of respectable, 'blameless' entertainment, in contrast with these increasingly denigrated artistic traditions.

---

[6] Trans. by Samira Sheikh, Delta, *Romyo ane Julyat* (Mumbai, Fort Printing Press, 1876), preface.

Each of these older practices, nonetheless, contributed to the spectatorial economy of the urban theatres and is particularly salient to an understanding of the changes in theatrical transvestism that emerge in this period. In the case of Bhavai, a form of rural folk theatre from Rajasthan and Gujarat, the actors came from a hereditary caste called the Targalas (also called Bhojaks or Nayaks). The Targalas traced their descent to Asaita Thakur, the originator of Bhavai, a brahmin who is said to have lost his purity by dining with a Muslim and an untouchable. This narrative of origin asserts the non-hierarchical, non-sectarian character of the tradition. Bhavaiyas often targeted moneylenders, priests and other figures of authority, bringing a strong flavour of social critique to their skits. Female roles in Bhavai were played either by boys or by mature males who specialised in female impersonation. Termed *kanchalias*, in reference to the woman's blouse (*kanchali*) which they donned for their performances, these transvestite performers satirised women and male–female relations, while delighting audiences with dances such as the *ras* and *garba*.[7]

As the theatre-going public consolidated itself in Bombay, the urban elites withdrew their support from Bhavai, as indicated in statements like that of Delta. Although Bhavai performances were allegedly eschewed for their lewdness, separation from Bhavai must have been largely motivated by the desire to mark one's distinction in terms of caste and class. Moreover, the informality of Bhavai contrasted unfavourably with the Parsi theatre's elaborate proscenium stage. Buttressed by stage technologies that privileged spectacle and realism, dramatic narratives were moving toward tight plots divided into fixed acts and scenes. Grandiose melodramas of ancient glory and virtue, replete with luxurious costumes and large painted sets, replaced the rustic satiric thrusts of Bhavai. Nonetheless, continuities with older forms remained, particularly in the performative vocabularies of music, mime and movement. Late in the nineteenth century, the Targala community contributed significantly to the professional urban stage, when talented actors such as Jayshankar Sundari, Amritlal Nayak and others entered the ranks of female

---

[7] Sudha R. Desai, *Bhavai: A Medieval Form of Ancient Indian Dramatic Art* (Ahmedabad, Gujarat University, 1972); Balwant Gargi, *Folk Theater of India* (Seattle, University of Washington Press, 1966), pp. 51–72.

impersonators in the Parsi and Gujarati theatres and achieved extraordinary success.

Tamasha, another regional dramatic tradition, had developed in Maharashtra by the late eighteenth century into a multi-act folk drama.[8] A Persian word signifying 'entertainment' or 'show,' Tamasha incorporated several earlier styles such as Gondhal, Povada and Turra–Kalagi, while increasingly becoming infused with *lavani*-singing and erotic dancing. During the late Peshwa period, female concubines and slaves were kept at court to perform sexually explicit *lavanis* in the *natakshalas* (royal playhouses).[9] *Nachya poryas* (dancing boys) were also common in Peshwa times, and courtesans are said to have learned their melodies and dance movements from them.[10] The British takeover in 1818 forced Tamasha performers to seek new sources of patronage. The folk theatre retreated to rural Maharashtra where it was patronised by rural landlords. Whereas earlier it had attracted brahmin performers like Ram Joshi, it now became the province of two low caste groups: the Mahars and the Mangs. Entering the urban theatrical arena in the nineteenth century, Tamasha still employed 'effeminate males' in opposition to the ideal of manhood projected in the 'national theatre' of Vishnudas Bhave.[11] During the first decades of the twentieth century, if not before, Tamasha performances had become a regular offering in Bombay's gentrified theatres. According to Gargi, the Tamasha troupe of Patthe Bapu Rao and Pawala performed five times a week in three of the major Parsi theatre houses.[12]

Dance recitals by female performers, who came to be known as nautch girls, formed a customary part of celebrations like birthdays and weddings in Indian aristocratic families. The practice of holding a nautch (from the Hindi *nach* or dance), was adopted by the British in the early nineteenth century both for

[8] Kathryn Hansen, *Grounds for Play: The Nautanki Theatre of North India* (Berkeley, University of California Press, 1992), p. 66.

[9] Sharmila Rege, 'The Hegemonic Appropriation of Sexuality: The Case of the *Lavani* Performers of Maharashtra,' in Patricia Uberoi (ed.), *Social Reform, Sexuality and the State* (New Delhi, Sage, 1996), pp. 23–38.

[10] Gargi, *op.cit.*, p. 75.

[11] Neera Adarkar, 'In Search of Women in the History of Marathi Theatre, 1843 to 1933,' *Economic and Political Weekly*, Vol. 26, No. 43 (26 Oct. 1991), WS–87.

[12] Gargi, *op. cit.*, p. 75.

private enjoyment and to honour a guest. D. E. Wacha writes of Bombay in the 1860s, 'Dancing girls, both Hindu and Mahomedan, were invited to enliven every important domestic entertainment of a joyous character.' It was a 'social duty' for Parsis as well as Hindus and Muslims to host such occasions.[13] Missionary-led aversion to the nautch took root in mid-century and prompted Indian and British elites to look for alternative entertainments. In the columns of newspapers and letters to the editor, the urban theatre was often proposed as a respectable substitute. Nonetheless, the taint associated with the female performer, on account of her presumed sexuality and low social origins, carried over into attitudes towards actresses in the urban theatre. The stigma accompanying the presence of actresses, who were viewed as prostitutes, was often cited as the rationale for certain theatrical companies hiring only men to play female roles. Yet, fondness among spectators for erotic genres of song and dance such as the *thumri* and the *ghazal* dictated that these items be retained within the performative structure of the urban drama. In consequence, female impersonators took on the double burden of enacting noble womanly characters even as they inherited the arts of the women of the *kotha*.

The theatrical transvestism of urban Bombay, then, in one sense was formed at a point of convergence among older living traditions of erotic performance and gender impersonation. The *kanchalia* of Bhavai and the *nachya porya* of Tamasha, both roles that involved male-to-female impersonation, contributed to the reconfiguration of the actor-as-woman in the new urban theatre. Equally, the female *lavani* performer and the nautch girl served as templates for the reworking of the performer in female guise. While (s)he was required, to a great extent, to deliver the same kinds of pleasure as these earlier models, the particular moment at which the female impersonator entered the Parsi theatre required further adjustments to the formulation of the gendered performer. Before considering these additional attributes, however, I examine the explanatory apparatus that is so often given for the phenomenon of female impersonation.

[13] Dinshaw E. Wacha, *Shells from the Sands of Bombay: Being My Recollections and Reminiscences—1860–1875* (Bombay, The Bombay Chronicle Press, 1920), pp. 697–98.

Prohibition or Preference?

The most common reason offered for the prevalence of female impersonation in South Asia, as in China and Japan, is that it was a theatrical compulsion imposed by the social taboo against women appearing on stage. By the eighteenth century, the gendered segregation of public and private spheres forced the seclusion of women within the households of socially prominent families. Singing, dancing and other performance arts were relegated to stigmatised classes of women (for example, the *devadasis* of south India, the *maharis* of Orissa, the *naikins* of Goa and the western coast, and the *tawaifs* of the north). 'Respectable' women were thus at an extreme social disadvantage with respect to the stage, and were not only unwilling to become actresses but were ill-equipped for its rigours and lacking in skills. As to the question why professional performing women were not available to the nineteenth century public theatre, it is claimed that they kept themselves away from the stage because of the excessive degree of publicity, relative to the more private encounter between patron and performer in the setting of the *kotha* or salon. It is also mentioned that while professional women were trained in music and dance, they had little by way of dramatic experience and required extensive coaching.

This simplistic notion of substituting men for absent women must be questioned. Even in the ancient period, actresses (*natabharya* in Patanjali, *nati* in Bharata's *Natyasastra*) existed alongside with female impersonators in theatrical troupes. Ahmed documents the presence of both male and female performers from the earliest times in Bengal, noting that the gender of the performer was never made to conform to the gender of the character; 'both male and female performers have portrayed both male and female characters.'[14] In the Tamasha, female performers and men performing women's roles filled complementary functions. As for the Parsi theatre, the unavailability of performing women is a certain fallacy. Actresses were recruited to the Parsi stage as early as 1874, when actor–manager Dadi Patel brought back four *begams* from the *zanana* (harem) in Hyderabad to play the parts of the *paris* (fairies) in the *Indar Sabha*. Khurshed Baliwala, the popular actor-manager

---

[14] Ahmed, *op. cit.*, p. 280.

who led the Victoria Theatrical Company on a number of foreign tours, introduced a series of women—Miss Gohar, Miss Malka, Miss Khatun, Miss Fatima—whose courtesan origins were thinly veiled under the anglophilic classifier 'miss'.[15]

The preferences exercised by publics and patrons for female performers, male-to-female impersonators, or both, need to be understood as shifting over time in conjunction with strictures relating to caste, class, gender and codes of morality. Historical and regional variations in the popularity of female impersonation are not always easy to explain. In Calcutta, actresses from the class of rejected and outcast women ('prostitutes'), like Binodini Dasi, proved their merit to bourgeois audiences and directors early on. With the acceptance of actresses in the public theatre, female impersonation in that city ended in the 1870s. To explain this, Bhattacharya asserts that 'change in forms of representation required same-sex impersonation,' citing the influential playwright Michael Madhusudan Dutt, who stated that 'clean-shaven gentlemen just would not do any more' for his heroines.[16] Yet in western India, where forms of representation were also changing under conditions in many ways comparable to those in Calcutta, female impersonation entered a cosmopolitan phase and developed into a beloved art that continued through the 1930s. Even in Bombay, the reception was mixed. With the arrival of the Anglo-Indian actress Mary Fenton, in the 1880s, the female performer began to compete successfully in the Parsi theatre. Nonetheless, companies like the Natak Uttejak Mandali and the New Alfred solely employed female impersonators. The latter banned women from the stage until the death of director Sohrabji Ogra in the 1930s. For these companies and their audiences, performing women were undesirable rather than unavailable.[17]

---

[15] Somnath Gupta, *Parsi Thiyetar: Udbhav aur Vikas*. [Parsi Theatre: Origin and Development] (Allahabad, Lokbharati Prakashan, 1981), pp. 109, 210–12.

[16] Rimli Bhattacharya (trans. and ed.), *Binodini Dasi: My Story and My Life as an Actress* (New Delhi: Kali for Women, 1998), p. 11.

[17] The difference between Bombay and Calcutta parallels the variation in response to female impersonation found in Renaissance Europe. England barred actresses and preferred boys; Spain chose theatrical women over the spectacle of transvestite boys. See Stephen Orgel, 'Nobody's Perfect: Or Why Did the English Stage Take Boys for Women?' *South Atlantic Quarterly*, Vol. 88, No. 1 (winter 1989), pp. 7–29.

The ruse of unavailability may have been constructed to deflect attention from the extraordinary popularity of female impersonation. Although correct in acknowledging the widespread exclusion of women from public life, this explanation confuses the agency of company managers and publics with that of performing women. The historical record indicates that rather than filling in for absent women, female impersonators competed against them, and actresses competed against female impersonators for female roles within the theatrical troupe. These roles may have been divided by character type, replacing competition with cooperation in certain cases. In any event, it is clear that companies and publics made choices about whom they wished to see representing women on stage, and many times they chose men over women.

Present-day attempts to naturalise theatrical transvestism as a sociological imperative suggest an underlying anxiety, a tension of more recent origin regarding cross-dressing and the implications of effeminacy. Even as a relatively compartmentalised theatrical practice, female impersonation appears to threaten the construction of masculinity. Bringing it into the limelight seems to reinvigorate stereotypes of weakness and inferiority among the male population, a bitter legacy of colonial domination. As Sinha, Nandy, Chakravarti and others have shown, late nineteenth century Indian reformists responded to British disdain for Indian civilisation and morality, and the concomitant characterisation of Indian men as effeminate, both by recasting womanhood in the image of Vedic purity and by reinventing a belligerent style of masculinity.[18] Luhrmann similarly documents the process of hypermasculinisation among Bombay's Parsi community, who were closely allied with the British in entrepreneurial ventures.[19] Not only was a particular kind of masculinity cultivated as a defensive strategy during colonial domination, it has been revived and

[18] Mrinalini Sinha, Colonial Masculinity: The 'Manly Englishman' and the 'Effeminate Bengali' in the Late Nineteenth Century (Manchester, Manchester University Press, 1995); Ashis Nandy, The Intimate Enemy: Loss and Recovery of Self under Colonialism (New Delhi, Oxford University Press, 1988); Uma Chakravarti, 'Whatever Happened to the Vedic Dasi? Orientalism, Nationalism, and a Script for the Past,' in Kumkum Sangari and Sudesh Vaid (eds), Recasting Women: Essays in Colonial History (New Delhi, Kali for Women, 1989), pp. 27–87.
[19] T. M. Luhrmann, The Good Parsi: The Fate of a Colonial Elite in a Postcolonial Society (Cambridge, Massachusetts, Harvard University Press, 1996).

restyled by advocates of Hindu nationalism in the postcolonial period. Thus the god Ram, the divine hero whose temple in Ayodhya has become a mobilising symbol for the right wing Bharatiya Janata Party, has been widely represented in calendar art and visual imagery as a deity with bulging muscles, a depiction formerly associated only with his monkey attendant, Hanuman.[20]

Femininity Re-formed

In another work, I have demonstrated how the theatrical representation of *stri bhumika* or *stri pat* (women's roles) by men's bodies was crucial to the visual construction of the feminine in this period.[21] In that analysis, the effects of theatrical transvestism are understood to reach beyond the reification of existing gender boundaries, or the transgression of those boundaries for the purpose of generating laughter.[22] In the South Asian context, where women of status had long been secluded within private domestic spaces, masquerades of gender were productive of new ways of imagining and viewing the female form. Through the transvestite performer, the external look of the 'woman' was regulated by minute attention to the details of fashion and feminine accoutrement. This reworking of the surface was conjoined to a new focus on the interiority of character. Whereas the sexuality of the new woman became subsumed within norms of modesty, the feminine ideal was henceforward associated with inner sensibility and the capacity to suffer.

My emphasis here is on how the operation of female impersonation, within the reforming, educative programme of the late

---

[20] Anuradha Kapur, 'Deity to Crusader: The Changing Iconography of Ram', in Gyanendra Pandey (ed.), *Hindus and Others* (New Delhi, Viking, 1993). Similar ideas relating to virility, masculinity and Hindu chauvinism are explored in Anand Patwardhan's powerful documentary film, *Father, Son, and Holy War*.

[21] Kathryn Hansen, '*Stri Bhumika:* Female Impersonators and Actresses on the Parsi Stage,' *Economic and Political Weekly*, Vol. 33, No. 35 (29 Aug. 1998), pp. 2291–2300; Kathryn Hansen, 'Making Women Visible: Gender and Race Cross-Dressing in the Parsi Theatre,' *Theatre Journal*, Vol. 51 (1999), pp. 127–47.

[22] These are the outcomes most discussed in the literature on theatrical cross-dressing in the West. See Lesley Ferris (ed.), *Crossing the Stage: Controversies on Cross-Dressing* (London, Routledge, 1993); and Laurence Senelick (ed.), *Gender in Performance: The Presentation of Difference in the Performing Arts* (Hanover, New Hampshire, University Press of New England, 1992).

nineteenth century Parsi theatre, also complicated the viewing of the male body and the construction of masculine subjectivity. For men as well as women, performances of cross-dressing opened up an arena in which gender could be articulated in complicated ways. I propose that transgender masquerades, in addition to renewing a preexisting culture of homosociality within the context of a reconstituted urban public, introduced new possibilities for homoerotic pleasure and expression. As in the construction of heteronormative roles, these possibilities were predicated on exchanging devalued, 'traditional' ways of encoding gender difference, or more accurately gender ambiguity, for esteemed, updated, 'modern' ones. These urban theatres moved away from a burlesque, transgressive mode of female embodiment, often associated with folk practice, to a high mimetic style emphasising naturalism. The display of overt sexuality was replaced by an elaborate code of modesty, propriety and respectability that identified the 'new woman', in heteronormative terms. But equally they positioned the homoerotic gaze toward a refined, transgendered performer who aroused a different kind of desire.

These distinctions emerged within the first two decades of the Parsi theatre. The young Parsi men who pioneered the cosmopolitan practice of female impersonation were of high social standing, unlike their forebears in the rural or 'folk' theatres, who were traditionally of low rank. When the students of Elphinstone College in Bombay formed a club to rehearse Shakespeare and try out new Gujarati plays, it was probably obvious that some of them would play women's roles, although it is not known by what criteria they were chosen. The first on record to play female roles was D. N. Parekh, later a medical doctor and lieutenant colonel in the Indian Medical Service. While at Elphinstone College, he played Portia in *The Merchant of Venice* and Mrs Smart in G. O. Trevelyan's *The Dawk Bungalow*. These performances were held under the patronage of Sir Jamsetji Jeejeebhoy, a leading Parsi businessman and philanthropist, and Jagannath Shankarsheth, a wealthy Hindu banker, both of whom had been active in the public campaign to open the Grant Road Theatre.[23]

---

[23] Somnath Gupta, *op. cit.*, pp. 133–37; Vidyavati Lakshmanrao Namra, *Hindi Rangmanch aur Pandit Narayanprasad 'Betab'* [The Hindi Stage and Pandit Narayanprasad 'Betab'] (Varanasi, Vishvavidyalaya Prakashan, 1972), pp. 93–95;

Even at a time when theatrical activity was principally conceived as an amateur pastime, anecdotes suggest that a considerable premium was placed on successful female impersonators. Framji Joshi completed his matriculation in 1868, and in the same year played the female lead in a Gujarati version of Bulwer-Lytton's *The Lady of Lyons* presented by the Gentlemen Amateurs Club. His performance was so impressive that the club's director feared his star performer would be lured away by another company. Indeed, Joshi left the Gentlemen Amateurs and went on to new female roles with the Alfred Company, before he retired from the stage to become superintendent of the Government Central Press.[24]

The social prominence of the actors, the prestige of their wealthy patrons, and the location of amateur dramatics as a supplement to college life all established the early Parsi theatre as a 'rational' form of amusement, in contrast to the older nautch performances sponsored by 'feudal' aristocrats. By the end of the 1860s, the fondness for 'theatricals' was such that Parsi businessmen were drawn to theatre as an investment opportunity. With the establishment of the Victoria Theatrical Company in 1868, the Parsi theatre entered a period of capitalist reorganisation and professionalism. Productions became more lavish, and audience size expanded. A premium was now placed on young men of pleasing figure and superlative voice, who would ensure company profits through their virtuosity in women's roles. The split in the Victoria Theatrical Company in 1873 supplies an example. The former manager, Dadi Patel (1844–76), took his leading female impersonator with him when he separated to form the Original Victoria Theatrical Company. C. S. Nazir, the new manager of the Victoria, was at a complete loss and immediately organised a group of recruiters to look for new boys. This was particularly urgent as Nazir wanted to make a strong showing before the princes at Lord Lytton's imperial assemblage, the Delhi Darbar of 1877. He could not outdo his rivals and win a sizeable audience without top-notch female impersonators.[25]

Kumud A. Mehta, 'Bombay's Theatre World—1860–1880,' *Journal of the Asiatic Society of Bombay* (n.s.) Vol. 43–44 (1968), pp. 262–64.

[24] Gupta, *op. cit.*, pp. 122, 147–48, 174–75.

[25] *Ibid.*, pp. 109–10.

The Parsi theatre invested in the recruitment and training of boys because it needed their labour to ensure its economic viability. An acting career normally began in a period of apprenticeship with schooling in female roles such as the *saheli* or *sakhi*, companions of the heroine. This practice continued well into the twentieth century. The actor Fida Husain, who began his apprenticeship in the New Alfred Company around 1918, became famous first for his female roles.[26] Certain actors became known as 'all-rounders,' performing the hero, heroine or comedian, as needed. With age and a changing physique, others shifted from female to male roles. Khurshed Baliwala (1852–1913), who later managed the Victoria Theatrical Company and became one of the most renowned Parsi theatre personalities, played a female role when he was 18 in *Rustam and Sohrab*.[27] A year later he appeared as the hero of *Sone ke Mul ki Khurshed*, and from then on he acted primarily in male roles.[28]

Other actors specialised as female impersonators. Success in a role led to the public affixing the name of the character to the actor's name or nickname. It is only through this assignment of feminine stage names that the identity of many female impersonators can be determined from the record. Two brothers of the influential Madan clan acquired this popular status. Nasharvanji Framji became famous as Naslu 'Tahmina' for his performance as Sohrab's mother in *Rustam and Sohrab*. Naslu's younger brother, Pestanji Framji, was called Pesu 'Avan,' after the heroine in a Gujarati version of Shakespeare's *Pericles*.[29]

Female impersonators performed various types of stage roles. One was the romantic heroine, beloved of the hero and the embodiment of feminine perfection and modesty. A mellifluous voice became a valuable adjunct to such a role as songs gained ascendancy in the format of the musical drama. When Jehangir Khambata founded the Empress Victoria Theatrical Company in 1877, he took full advantage of the talents of a popular female

---

[26] Namra, *op. cit.*, p. 83; Pratibha Agraval, *Mastar Fida Husain: Parsi Thiyetar men Pachas Varsh* [Master Fida Husain: Fifty Years in the Parsi Theatre] (Calcutta, Natya Shodh Sansthan, 1986).

[27] Namra, *op. cit.*, p. 52; Gupta, *op. cit.*, p. 108.

[28] Namra, *op. cit.*, p. 55.

[29] Gupta, *op. cit.*, p. 201.

impersonator known as Naslu Sarkari. Famed for his sweet 'cuckoo' voice (*kokil kanth*), Naslu played the Emerald Fairy to Kavas Khatau's Prince Gulfam in the *Indar Sabha*.[30]

Then there were the female magician roles, like the *jogin* (female ascetic) in *Harishchandra*.[31] During the Victoria Company's tour of Delhi in 1874, Kavasji Manakji Contractor, a female impersonator affectionately called 'Bahuji' (daughter-in-law or bride), created a sensation in this role by delivering countless lashes to the tormented dancing figure of Baliwala playing Lotan. This particular gesture was later to become a trademark of the actress Nadia, known as 'Hunterwali' (Lady with the Whip), who appeared in stunt films in the 1930s and 40s. Nadia took on the androgynous aspect of womanhood, an extension of the construct associated with the *virangana* or warrior queen in Indian myth and popular culture.[32] Such virtuous embodiments of female power were also common on the Parsi stage, as seen in the warlike demeanour of Master Nainuram.

Female impersonation continued on the Parsi stage well into the twentieth century, retaining its popularity with audiences and with company managers. The long list of men who played women's roles in the history of Parsi theatre is remarkable; they seem to form the majority rather than the minority of the class of actors. Unfortunately, these actors have been virtually forgotten. Written documentation of their lives, their habits, even their careers is extremely limited. No biography or autobiography has emerged to illuminate this important institution. Records are somewhat more complete in the case of two non-Parsi actors, Jayshankar Sundari (1888–1967) from the Gujarati stage and Bal Gandharva (1889–1975) from the Marathi musical theatre. Both excelled in the embodiment of feminine sensibility and decorum, creating prototypes for the ideal Indian woman. Their tremendous success was recognised during their active careers and also later in life, by the award of the Padma Bhushan, the Government of India's prize for

---

[30] S/he was Laila with Khatau as Majnu; Bakavali with Khatau as Tajulmulk; and performed a number of other classical themes opposite Khatau, the actor known as 'India's Irving', *ibid.*, pp. 118–19.

[31] Gopichand, *ibid.*, pp. 111, 166.

[32] Kathryn Hansen, 'The *Virangana* in North Indian History: Myth and Popular Culture,' *Economic and Political Weekly of India*, Vol. 23, No. 18 (30 April 1988), WS–25–33.

achievement on the national cultural stage. Sundari's Gujarati autobiography, an English biography by B. B. Panchotia, and two English biographies of Bal Gandharva by Dnyaneshwar Nadkarni and Mohan Nadkarni supply a number of incidents that enlarge the picture of female impersonation as it flourished earlier in this century.

Legendary Heroines

Sundari launched his career on the Gujarati stage at the age of twelve, starring in *Saubhagya Sundari*, the role of the auspicious young wife that gave him his stage name. Before that, he had served an apprenticeship for three years in Calcutta with the Parsi theatre company of Dadabhai Thunthi. On a salary of six rupees a month, he performed in the chorus of 'girls' every night at the Thanthania Theatre. His first important role was the Emerald Fairy in Amanat's *Indar Sabha*, and he starred in a number of other Urdu-language plays. During his Calcutta training, Sundari perfected the distinctive feminine gait and stage entry that secured his fame as a modest yet alluring heroine.[33]

Returning to Bombay, he played Rambha, the milkmaid, in the Gujarati drama *Vikram Charitra*. The play was performed every Saturday night between 1902 and 1905; a total of 160 times. At the time Sundari was between thirteen and sixteen years of age. In his most memorable scene, he entered the stage with a pot on his head and offered milk to the hero, singing *Koi dudh lyo dilrangi*. The Vaishnava trope of the youthful lord Krishna with his adoring *gopis* (female cowherds) associated sexual/mystical enjoyment with the pleasures of oral consumption. As the bestower of 'milk' from her 'pot', the transvestite heroine maintained a demure, inward-turned posture that legitimised her seductive gesture. Her carefully arranged hair, jewellery, bodice and sari border worked to produce a sublimation of sexuality, an interiorisation of virtue as 'moral character'. This song became so popular that Bombay textile companies printed it on the milled lengths of cloth that were sold for men's dhotis and women's saris.[34]

---

[33] B. B. Panchotia, *Jayashankar Sundari and Abhinayakala* (Bombay, Bharatiya Vidya Bhavan, 1987), pp. 2–23.

[34] *Ibid.*, p. 42.

Moral purity and its counterpart, forbearance in distress, were invoked by impersonators like Sundari in scenes of pathos and tragedy, as found in the epics based on Hindu mythology and contemporary domestic melodramas. In *Kamalata* (1904), an adaptation of the Shakuntala story, he played his part with such finesse that it moved the entire audience to tears. Similarly, Bal Gandharva was acclaimed for his 1911 performance in Khadilkar's drama *Manapman*, which he refused to cancel even though his eldest child had died on the very day of the drama's debut. The ability to summon up pathos distinguished these impersonators from transvestite entertainers who aimed to titillate or ridicule. The histrionic power of these actors and their capacity to transform themselves into vulnerable, unfortunate females served to expand the emotional field of the male viewer/subject. A desire to explore and experience the interior realms associated with feminine feeling, thereby expanding one's humanity through the test of suffering, seems to have been a large part of the fascination with transgender roles at this time.

Sundari as a female impersonator crafted a self which, in its entry into feminine subjectivity, found deep sources of satisfaction. In his autobiography, he describes the first time he dressed himself in a woman's bodice:

> I saw a beautiful young girl emerging from myself. Whose shapely, intoxicating limbs oozed youthful exuberance. In whose form is the fragrance of woman's beauty. From whose eyes feminine feelings keep brimming. In whose gait is expressed the mannerisms of a Gujarati girl. Who is not a man, but solely a woman—a woman. I saw such a portrait in the mirror.... Reflecting the difference the mirror was saying, 'This is not Jayshankar. It is a shy and proud young Gujaratin. That graceful movement, that expressivity, that enchantment.' A sweet shiver ran through my body's limbs. For a moment, I thought that I was not a man—not a man at all.[35]

This rare self-reflective glimpse of the process of transformation from man to woman illuminates the possibilities for transgender identification and behaviour opened up by the practice of theatrical transvestism.

---

[35] Trans. from the Gujarati by Sunil Sharma and Kathryn Hansen, Jayshankar Sundari, *Thodan Ansu Thodan Ful* [Some Teardrops, Some Blossoms] (Ahmedabad, Gandhi Sombarsa, 1976), p. 73.

In his autobiography, Sundari described the methods he used to give versimilitude to his impersonations. He carefully studied the manners of female acquaintances, whom he observed in social situations where his own presence was unobtrusive. One of the most captivating for him was Gulab, a young girl who was soon to be married. Her shyness coupled with budding excitement and self-consciousness about her body and dress fascinated him. He even asked for the address of her tailor so that he could have the blouses that he wore for his performances tailored in the same style that she favoured.[36] To perfect his understanding of what it meant to be a 'complete human being' (*sampurn manav*), he also read a number of manuals of womanly conduct, books considered 'useful for women' (*stri-upyogi*), from which he learned about cooking, embroidery and how to manage a household.[37]

He reflected on feminine characters like Kumud Sundari and Kusum, whom he encountered in Govardhan Ram's *Sarasvatichandra*, the monumental Gujarati novel in four volumes:

> Having found here the woman of Gujarat that I had been research-
> ing, I began to sport with the depicted creation.... I found a new
> way to practice [the part]...I would take the novel and read it
> aloud in front of the mirror and practice the parts while looking
> into the mirror. In this way, I tried to match my feelings with the
> feelings in the hearts of the characters.[38]

Although narrated as testimonials to his artistic dedication, these accounts point to an engagement with transgender identification that goes beyond technique. Whereas it is commonplace to read that both Bal Gandharva's and Sundari's stage movements, attire and speech became models for women offstage, one suspects that they also were compelling examples of transgender exploration for men. The very earnestness of Sundari's portrayals would recommend such theatrics not only as stimulants of desire but as templates for incorporation into the affective and somatic domains of the spectator's being.

Bal Gandharva, born Narayan Shripad Rajhans, was Sundari's contemporary. He was born into a middle class Maharashtrian

---

[36] Sundari, *op. cit.*, pp. 80–81.
[37] *Ibid.*, p. 114.
[38] *Ibid.*, p. 70.

family, where he came under the tutelage of male relatives with strong interests in music and drama. In 1905 at the age of sixteen, he joined the Kirloskar Drama Company replacing Bhaurau Kolhatkar, the first successful female impersonator of the Marathi musical theatre, who had just died. He debuted in the title role in *Shakuntala* on a newly built stage before the prince of Miraj. The object of adoration and esteem from the start, Bal Gandharva became the pet of the students at the Deccan College, where he was frequently invited to sing, and he struck up a special friendship with one of them, Balasaheb Pandit.[39]

In the accounts of Bal Gandharva, the erotic allure of his impersonations is striking. When he entered the stage as Shakuntala surrounded by her 'companions,' the college boys would greet him with 'lusty applause,' according to one biography. Similarly, actor Londhe recalls 'all the sensuousness of female beauty' that Bal Gandharva emitted when he played opposite him, such that a 'unique thrill' passed through his veins as he stood close by.[40] One way that Bal Gandharva exploited his seductiveness was by displaying his long hair, which flowed down to his waist. In *Manapman* he entered the stage with his hair hanging loose, indicating that the heroine had not yet had her bath, while in another scene he turned his back to the audience to reveal a long braid.[41] Photographs show him flirtatiously casting sidelong glances at the hero while partially concealing himself behind a fan, or beckoning the hero with a certain bend backward from the waist. These gestures, rather than being read as crude, were understood as modest and charming representations of the educated young women of the day. As a contemporary noted, 'The manner in which Bal Gandharva made himself up and the way he moved on the stage fully evoked the *persona* of the contemporary young woman of the middle or upper middle classes.'[42]

The pleasures of homoerotic spectatorship and transgender performance were linked in the urban theatre with the satisfactions of social and economic privilege. Both Jayshankar Sundari

---

[39] Dnyaneshwar Nadkarni, *Bal Gandharva and the Marathi Theatre* (Bombay, Roopak Books, 1988), p. 41.
[40] Dnyaneshwar Nadkarni, *op. cit.*, p. 106; Mohan Nadkarni, *Bal Gandharva: The Nonpareil Thespian* (New Delhi, National Book Trust, 1988), p. 17.
[41] Dnyaneshwar Nadkarni, *op. cit.*, pp. 36, 49, 57.
[42] Govindrao Tembe, cited in *ibid.*, p. 34.

and Bal Gandharva, rather than bearing any stigma, became national icons and recipients of the Padma Bhushan. The position of their audiences within the burgeoning consumer economy introduced opportunities for the commodification of their images. Just as textile companies advertised cloth using Sundari's lyrics, Bal Gandharva's photograph appeared on products such as medicinal tonic, soap, toilet powder and even key chains. A particular kind of cap, the Gandharva *topi*, was widely sold among male admirers, as were the Gandharva turban, coat and trousers. Bal Gandharva also popularised particular styles of wearing the sari and adornments such as the weaving of garlands of flowers in the hair. He brought the bun into vogue, introduced the nose-pin (*nath*), and promoted the carrying of handkerchiefs. His image radiated such a sense of fashion and prestige that framed photographs of him playing female roles adorned the drawing rooms of elite homes, appearing on mantels and sideboards throughout Maharashtra. Through the extra-theatrical circulation of his image, Bal Gandharva developed a cult following that reinforced his career on stage. His particular transvestite style was completely assimilated within visual culture. To our benefit, more photographs of Bal Gandharva exist than of any other female impersonator, including both studio portraits and recreations of staged scenes.

Beyond the visual, Bal Gandharva made a tremendous impact as an actor who could also sing. Like other female impersonators, but probably to a unique degree, his voice communicated the complex yearnings of the heroines he played and added a significant layer of erotic power to his performances. His voice production was not falsetto but midway between today's male and female registers, a kind of androgynous timbre that was fairly typical of both male and female vocalists at that time. His spoken voice is said to have been a stylised version of what was presumably the speech of upper caste women. Bal Gandharva sang in the classical *natya sangit* style, and many of his recordings survive in private collections. It is beyond the scope of this article to examine in full the topics of vocal style and voice production, and their role in the creation of gendered subjectivities. I simply wish to underscore the role of the voice in projecting affect (the power to move the listener), agency (the attribution of volition to a characterisation) and authority (the display of musical virtuosity).

Outstanding vocal artistry immeasurably enriched the performances of actors like Bal Gandharva, adding as well to the allure
of countless lesser-known female impersonators.

Sexuality and Subculture

When consideration of the voice is combined with the more
readily accessed external look of the transvestite performer and
the gaze that links the hero and male heroine on stage, an enlarged
expressive space comes into play. In the variety of responses
evoked, between spectators and actors, among actors, and among
spectators and even those outside the theatre, could such a collective zone of interaction be said to constitute a transgender or
homosexual subculture? Robertson in her discussion of the all-
male Kabuki and all-female Takarazuka argues that theatrical
transvestism in Japan has long been linked to alternative subcul-
tures. These practices, in her treatment, have both reproduced
dominant gender ideology and subverted it. While the *onnagata*
in Kabuki, like the female impersonator of western India, constructed the ideal standard of femininity for Japanese women to
follow, specific *onnagata* were known to prefer homosexual relations. As early as 1652, boy actors were banned because of their
off stage homosexual activity. In the case of the twentieth century
Takarazuka, 'The revue continues both to uphold the dominant
ideal of heterosexuality and to inform a lesbian subcultural style.'[43]

Significantly, Robertson highlights the importation of European
sexological discourse into Japan that began in the early twentieth
century. The works of Freud, Krafft-Ebing, Carpenter, Ellis and
Hirschfeld were translated into Japanese and employed in the
identification of 'social problems'.[44] The naming of homosexual
practices, even though it stigmatised them, enabled public debates
and rhetorics to develop around theatrical practices involving
transvestism. In the South Asian context, such naming and specificity are missing. The wives and mistresses of Jayshankar Sundari
and Bal Gandharva are mentioned in the record, as are the special

---

[43] Jennifer Robertson, *Takarazuka: Sexual Politics and Popular Culture in Modern
Japan* (Berkeley, University of California Press, 1998), p. 73.
[44] *Ibid.*, p. 20.

friendships between leading hero and heroine actor pairs: Bal Gandharva's long-lived relationship with Balasaheb Pandit and Jayshankar Sundari's with Bapulal Nayak. But what does this tell us? The celebratory character of the biographical literature makes it nearly impossible to get beyond the public persona. Indeed, so little is known about how the 'private' and the 'public' subject were constructed in India at this time, especially in terms of an alternate sexuality, that one baulks to interpret the silence of the biographer as innocence, evasion, or erasure.

A few scattered accounts confirm the general impression that, in India as in China and Japan, the theatrical subculture afforded a space for homosexual inclinations and practices. Madhavacharya, the author of a Hindi commentary on the *Kamasutra*, asserts that theatre personnel were known for their proclivity for oral sex with other men. He obliquely recounts a knife fight that once broke out between M.A. and B.A. students 'on this account'.[45] Theatre histories also report that actor–managers had their favourite 'boys'. Female impersonators were called by female kinship terms as well as by proper and pet female names. In a report of the first performances of the *Indar Sabha* in Lucknow, Nasir describes 'thousands of people [who] became captivated and went mad over these beautiful beardless youths.' Elaborating, he attributes the production of homosexual lust to this popular performance. 'Just as having read Mir Hasan's poetic romance (*masnavi*), thousands of women became debauched, similarly from this romance *Indar Sabha*, thousands of men became sodomites and pederasts.'[46]

As a project in the recovery of alternative sexual histories, it may be important to claim the urban theatrical environment of western India as a site that enabled transgender or homosexual activity. The evidence I have presented may well be sufficient to prove the case. However, it needs to be added that the theatrical milieu was (and for some, still is) associated with excessive sexuality in general. Actors and actresses, regardless of their

---

[45] Madhavacharya (ed.), Vatsyayana, *Kamasutra* (Bombay, Khemraj Shrikrishna Das Prakashan, 1995), Vol. 1, p. 522; 'The Kamasutra in the Twentieth Century', in Ruth Vanita and Saleem Kidwai (eds), *Same-Sex Love in India: Readings from Literature and History* (New York, St Martins Press, 2000), p. 239.

[46] Trans. by the author, aided by Carla Petievich, Sa'adat Ali Khan Nasir, *Tazkirah Khush Ma'arika-i Ziba* [An Elegant Encounter: An Anecdotal Literary Biography] (Lahore, Majlis-i Taraqqi-i adab, 1970), p. 231.

sexual orientation, were deemed suspect as moral agents from the days of the *Natyasastra*, and invariably placed in inferior social and caste categories because of their allegedly unrestrained sexual behaviour. The transgressive energies that spilled out from the playhouse into the surrounding neighbourhoods were controlled and kept at a distance in nineteenth century Bombay by establishing the red light district on Grant Road, far from the residences of the elite in the Fort district on the southern part of the island. The problem for the modern South Asian theatre has been primarily that of defusing or denying heteronormative sexuality, in contrast with which concern about homosexuality fades into insignificance.

Even if it be argued that the simultaneous attraction and aversion that characterises the societal attitude toward theatre does not prevent the useability of the theatrical space for diverse ends, the difficulty remains of identifying the boundaries around such a space. Were the transformations of gender effected by the female impersonator part of a fluid system of role play available to certain males (but not to females) in this period? Was the lower class male excluded when the urban middle class indulged in play with transgender identity? How did men whose gender and sexual identities were in formation—college students for example—move in and out of this expressive arena? Where did the specificity of homosexual preference fit in?

Even as the ambiguities surrounding gender and its representation opened outward toward the end of the nineteenth century in a public embrace of transvestism, a more rigid system of binary difference was being implanted, in part by the same theatrical culture. The eclipse of theatrical transvestism has been heralded as a triumph for the female performer and therefore for women in general, but it also marked the end of an era of gender ambiguity. A binary sex/gender regime allied to differences of class and caste has displaced the transvestite performer and distanced urban spectators from the circulation of homoerotic imagery. This sea change makes it difficult to recover the nuances of meaning that envelop a bygone practice. For clues to interpretation, we must continue to scour the historical evidence within South Asia as well as bring forward comparative data from other cultures.

5

Rekhti

Impersonating the Feminine in Urdu Poetry

◆ Carla Petievich

Teri faryad karun kis se zanaakhi tu ne
Yih meri jaan jalaayi kih Ilahi taubah
To whom can I complain of you, my dear?
God, but hasn't your harshness scorched my soul!

Insha' Allah Khan 'Insha'

Tis pairu men uthi uhi miri jaan gayi
Mat sitaa mujh ko dogaana, tire qurbaan gayi
This throb in my nether regions has nearly killed me
Dear One, don't tease me, you've already done me in!

Sa'adat Yar Khan 'Rangin'

For nearly three hundred years the Urdu *ghazal* has figured among the most popular art forms of South Asia. Deriving from the Perso–Arabic literary tradition, the ghazal's highly conventionalised aesthetics can tend toward the complex, the metaphysical and the philosophical while also satisfying less arcane romantic impulses. As a result, this poetic genre enjoys great prestige and is also highly popular, being claimed and consumed by diverse audiences. Although Urdu as a language has become increasingly associated with Muslim culture in the past decades, the ghazal's popularity and prestige extend well beyond the language community of South Asian Muslims and the territorial bounds of Hindustan, Urdu's historic heartland. The ubiquitous and extraordinarily popular Hindi film song, for example, is clearly inspired by the ghazal, and many of the most successful songwriters in the Bombay film industry have been Urdu poets.

Yet, in spite of how mainstream the ghazal is in contemporary South Asia, aficionados as well as scholars remain largely unaware of its gender politics. Because so much of 'culture' is so profoundly and ubiquitously gendered, hegemonic reading and reception conventions associated with the ghazal actually work to render its gender politics invisible to huge audiences. Feminist scholarship has, over the past few decades, exposed this cultural and social invisibility, and the result has been a sea change in standard critical thinking in many fields. Unhappily, scholars of Urdu have not made such changes in their own ways of thinking about their subject. When directly confronted with the challenge of gender's relevance to the ghazal genre, for instance, one expert has gone so far as to summarily dismiss the issue as a concern of foreigners, suggesting that these intellectual concerns are driven by the desire to judge the 'political correctness' or 'moral soundness' of a culture's literary output.[1] Rather, it should be argued that the time has come for lay and expert enthusiasts, for cultural historians and for social science audiences alike to reread the Urdu ghazal in a similarly critical fashion. A discussion of its poetics and a sketch of its reception history should convince most sceptics that more, rather than less, gendered analysis is needed. A look at even marginalised Urdu poetic genres illuminates the infrastructure of gender in the mainstream ghazal, and the focus here will be on one such genre. First, normative ghazal poetics.

Classical Urdu ghazal (called *rekhta*)[2] is a literature narrated in the masculine voice (the narrator/lover is called the *'ashiq*).

---

[1] See also, S. R. Faruqi, 'Conventions of Love, Love of Conventions: Urdu Love Poetry in the Eighteenth Century', *Annual of Urdu Studies*, Vol. 14 (1999), pp. 1–30. The above remarks occur on p. 16.

[2] *Rekhta* means 'that which is scattered', it was a term commonly used to refer to poetry in Urdu during the nineteenth century. 'Unscattered' poetry would have

Idealised love (*'ishq*) is its main subject, and the idealised Beloved
is referred to as grammatically masculine even though s/he may
be female. What follows is an example:

> *Un ke dekhe se jo aa jati hai munh par raunaq*
> *Voh samajhte hain kih bimaar ka hal acchha hai*
> The flush that suffuses my face when I look at [her/him]
> [S/he] interprets as a sign of my return to good health.

The first layer of indirection in this verse must be unpacked through
interpretation. The flush on [my], the 'ashiq's, face comes from
excessive emotion, an indication of his lovesickness. But the Beloved, conventionally cruel, deliberately chooses to see the flush as
good health, thus allowing her/him to ignore her/his own implication in the 'ashiq's distress. The indirection that is more germane
to the present argument, however, is brought centre stage through
the process of translating this verse into English. In English, unlike
in Urdu, third person pronouns are necessarily gender-marked.
Another way of understanding this grammatical dilemma, for the
translator, would be to point out that the only way of retaining
gender neutrality in English would be to translate third person
pronouns, such as *un* and *voh*, incorrectly as an inanimate 'it'. Most
of this verse's audience would automatically translate the *voh* and
un into 'she' and 'her', but that is a completely arbitrary convention, not required grammatically. It would be grammatically correct to translate this verse in either of the two following ways:

(i) From the flush that suffuses my face when I look at him
     He understands, 'the patient's condition is good'.

(ii) Looking at them, the face turns red;
     They take it to mean that the sick one has recovered.

Indeed, the only grammatically *incorrect* way of translating this
verse would be to do what most people do: to indicate that the
person being looked at—and misunderstanding the flush—is a
'she'.

The remarkable invention to be discussed here, on the other
hand, is a poetic genre called *rekhti* (literally the grammatical
feminine counterpart of the word rekhta). Not considered at all

---

been written in Persian, which had been the established, prestige language for
Indo-Islamic poetry for several centuries.

normative—though it observes a number of classical conventions—rekhti is the name by which all premodern Urdu poetry narrated in the *feminine voice* has come to be called.[3] Rekhti is associated with the domestic sphere of the socially elite, secluded women of the late eighteenth and nineteenth centuries, and alleges to speak in the particular idiom of their milieu. Its reputed creator was one Sa'adat Yar Khan 'Rangin' (the Colourful) (1755/56–1834/35), a famous poet associated with Lucknow.[4] Other authors of rekhti include Insha' Allah Khan 'Insha' (God Willing) (1756–1817/18), Qalandar Bakhsh 'Jur'at' (the Audacious) (d. 1810) and Mir Yar Ali Khan 'Jan Sahib' (1818?–1897?).

Two things that are important to know at the outset, and to remember, are: first, Rangin is said to have adapted rekhti from the idiom of the women of ill-repute with whom he spent his youth consorting; and, second, that Jan Sahib is said to have dressed himself 'like women and recited verses in the accent and gestures peculiar to them, much to the amusement of his audience'.[5] This sort of 'biographical' information has done much to determine the shape of rekhti's place in Urdu literature, an issue to be expanded upon below.

Culture and Poetry in Lucknow and *Rekhti's* Early Reception

To Rangin and his contemporaries rekhti doubtless represented an exciting innovation in a talent-glutted cultural marketplace. By

---

[3] See also, *Firozul Lughat (Urdu Jadid)*, (FerozeSons, Lahore, n.d.), p. 388: '*Voh nazm jo auraton ki boli men kaha ja'e*' (that verse which is spoken in women's idiom); J. T. Platts, *A Dictionary of Urdu, Classical Hindi, and English* (London, Oxford University Press, 1960), p. 611: 'Hindustani verse written in the language of women, and expressing the sentiments, etc. peculiar to them. (The two principal writers in this idiom are the poets Rangin and Jan Sahib)'.

[4] '*Lakhnavi*' means 'of Lucknow', a northern city in modern India and a major cultural centre for Urdu during the eighteenth–nineteenth centuries. Andalib Shadani, however, discusses the rival claims for Insha'Allah Khan 'Insha' as the creator of rekhti in 'Rekhti ka Mujid [Rekhti's Creator]', in *Tahqiq ki Roshni Men* (In Light of Investigation) (Lahore, Shaikh Ghulam Ali and Sons, 1963), pp. 91–104. Ironically, Shadani quotes Insha's treatise on poetics, *Darya-i Latafat* [*Ocean of Delicacy*] (1807), which seems to support Rangin as the creator of rekhti.

[5] M. Sadiq, *A History of Urdu Literature* (London, New Delhi, Oxford University Press, 1964/1984), p. 197.

the end of the eighteenth century the city of Lucknow had established itself firmly as a major cultural centre (*markaz*). Indeed, it was second in status only to Delhi, the Mughal capital. Delhi had seen hard times through much of the eighteenth century in the guise of invasions by the Persians, Afghans, Marathas and Europeans. As the seat of Avadh, the largest spin-off state from a decentralising Mughal empire, Lucknow was home to legions of refugee nobility and artists from Delhi and its environs, including Mirza Suleiman Shikoh, the Mughal heir apparent. The Mughal prince and the ruling Nawabs of Avadh, offered lavish patronage to scores of poets and other artists from all over northern India and made Lucknow 'the place to be'.[6] Featured prominently in Lucknow's cultural life were such literary luminaries as Sirajuddin Khan-i 'Arzu' (1689–1756), Mirza Muhammad Rafi 'Sauda' (d. 1781), Mir Taqi 'Mir' (d. 1810) and Shaikh Ghulam Hamdani 'Mushafi' (1750–1824), in addition to the rekhti poets about to be discussed. Great monuments were being built; schools and centres of Islamic learning were thriving; and literature was in a ferment. Some of Delhi's erstwhile elite were actively engaged in the process of 'perfecting' Urdu in Lucknow as an indigenous literary language to rival Persian.[7] The standard literary genres of the Perso–Arabic tradition were flourishing under the Urdu masters, and the sense of rivalry among them for patronage drove cultural production to new heights.

It was into this milieu that rekhti was introduced by Sa'adat Yar Khan 'Rangin', the son of a Persian nobleman who had migrated to Lucknow around the turn of the nineteenth century. By way of introduction to his literary innovation, Rangin explains that, in the course of a wild and misspent youth he consorted

---

[6] See C. Petievich, 'The Feminine Voice in the Urdu Ghazal', *Indian Horizons*, Vols. 1–2, No. 39 (1992), pp. 25–41; and C. M. Naim and C. Petievich, 'Urdu in Lucknow, Lucknow in Urdu', in Violette Graff (ed.), *Lucknow: Memories of a City* (New Delhi, Oxford University Press, 1997), pp. 165–80, for a fuller discussion of Lucknow's milieu.

[7] This aspect of Lucknow's history has been widely celebrated in Urdu and in English. See also Abdul Halim Sharar, *Guzishta Lakhna'o* (Bygone Lucknow), trans. by E. S. Harcourt and Husain Fakhr as, *Lucknow: The Last Phase of an Oriental Culture* (Boulder, Westview Press, 1976). See also Insha'Allah Khan 'Insha's', *Darya-i Latafat* (1807), purportedly the first linguistic and literary treatise on Urdu.

extensively with the famous courtesans of the day.[8] In their company he developed familiarity with, and an appreciation of, their particular idiom. The pithiness of their expression and their wit so impressed him that he decided to compose poetry in this 'ladies language' (*begumati zaban*) and to call his collected poems 'rekhti'. The combination of its feminine narrator and its begumati idiom made rekhti a distinct genre. Indications are that this immediately-popular style of poetry was accepted quite unproblematically into Lucknow's thriving milieu. Anecdotal sources indicate that Rangin recited his rekhti for the general delight and delectation of the Lakhnavi elite.[9] No less a literary master than Rangin's bosom buddy, Insha' Allah Khan 'Insha' composed a collection (*divan*) of such poems;[10] and the poet Jan Sahib composed at least two full divans of rekhti, on which his literary reputation largely rests.[11] The few extant scholarly sources offer numerous other names which are identified as versifiers in rekhti,[12] though few of them are still known today. The very fact that so many names can be found, and so little poetic output can be connected with them, speaks volumes about how attitudes toward this poetry have changed.

Rekhti's Reception by Modern Critics

In contrast to the apparently unproblematic early reception of rekhti, twentieth century critical writing on the subject has been characterised by moralistic judgments and a great deal of

---

[8] While the histories associate courtesan culture especially with Lucknow, it actually flourished all over India. Rangin speaks of himself as a poet of Shahjahanabad (Delhi), though later histories associate him with Lucknow. See also his *Majalis-i Rangin* (Lucknow, Naval Kishore, 1929).

[9] Sabir Ali Khan, *Sa'adat Yar Khan Rangin* (Karachi, Anjuman-i Taraqqi-i Urdu [Pakistan], 1956), p. 95.

[10] See his *Divan-i Rekhti* in the *Kulliyat-i Insha* (Lucknow, Naval Kishore, 1876), pp. 185–219.

[11] Dr Mubin Naqvi, *Tarikh-i Rekhti ma'a Divan-i Jan Sahib* (Allahabad, n.d.).

[12] See especially Irfan Abbasi, *Tazkirah-i Sho'ara-i Rekhti* (Lucknow, Nasim Book Depot, 1989); Dr Mubin Naqvi, *op. cit.*; Sibt-i Md. Naqvi, *Intikhab-i Rekhti* (Lucknow, Urdu Akademi, 1983); and Khalilur Rahman Siddiqi, *Rekhti ka Tanqidi Mutala'ah* (A Critical Study of Rekhti) (Lucknow, Nasim Book Depot, 1974).

evasion.[13] It has received very little scholarly attention in a literary culture obsessed with its own past and present, and does not appear on the syllabi of university level degree programmes.[14] The following is a fair representation of Urdu criticism's more benign conventional wisdom on the subject:

> *Rekhti* is a *badnam* (disreputable) genre of Urdu poetry which is thought to serve especially for the expression of women's particular emotions and generic concerns in women's idiom...[15]

a slightly less benign, yet also representative, pronouncement has been:

> *Rekhti* is mostly a woman speaking to another about her delusions and anxieties, the infidelity of husbands or the daring of her companions who ventured into social taboos.... *Rekhti* never attained respectability and often sunk [*sic*] into vulgarity, catering for those who sought decadent pleasure. It is, however, useful for a study of the miserable life the womenfolk led under the feudal order, and the resultant discontent and the evil it bred. Linguistically, it provides a convenient collection of the idioms of the women of the time.[16]

The discrepancy between early enthusiasm, and later distaste, for rekhti may seem at first glance to be anomalous. But a judicious probe into the cultural constructions of gender resolves much of that anomaly, especially shedding light on the logic of its rejection by Urdu literature's modern custodians.

Recall that not only was rekhti's narrator gendered feminine, but the idiomatic expressions which make up a significant part of its poetic corpus are said to be particular to secluded women and

---

[13] This is evident in all the standard literary histories and in lesser-known critical works as well. See also T. Grahame Bailey, *A History of Urdu Literature* (Calcutta, Associated Press, 1927/1932); Sadiq, *op. cit.*; A. Schimmel, *A History of Classical Urdu Literature from the Beginning to Iqbal* (Wiesbaden, Otto Harassowitz, 1976); A. J. Zaidi, *A History of Urdu Literature* (New Delhi, Sahitya Akademi, 1993); R. Russell, 'The Pursuit of the Urdu Ghazal', *Journal of Asian Studies*, Vol. 29 (1969), No. 1, pp. 107–24.

[14] A perusal of personally-held copies shows that rekhti is omitted from current M.A. syllabi for both Delhi University and Punjab University, Lahore.

[15] Hafeez Qateel, *Dakan Men Rekhti ka Irtiqa* [The Rise of *Rekhti* in the Deccan] (Hyderabad, Majalla-i Usmaniya, Dakani Adab Nambar, 1964), pp. 139–48.

[16] A. J. Zaidi, *op. cit.*, p. 137.

distinct from standard, polite discourse. The following is an example from Rangin, and takes the form of a *sarapa* (literally head-to-foot), in which the beloved's beauty is delineated by the lover/narrator, the 'ashiq:

Hai gi meri dogaana ki sajaavat khaasi
Chunpa'i rang ghazab tis pe khichaavat khaasi
All decked out, my other half is something special:
Her complexion's golden, her figure splendid to match!

Sar ke ta'viz sitam aur fateh pech 'ajib
Baal mehke hu'e choti ki gandhaavat khaasi
That forehead gem's a killer! The braided coiffure a wonder:
Her perfumed hair and fragrant forelock choice.

Sab se guftaar khudi sab se niraali nik-suk
Daant tasvir hain missi ki jamaavat khaasi
In speech she's like no other, from toenails to hair-plait
   unique:
Those powdered-black teeth, complete the picture!

Kurti jaali ki pari sar pe dupattah achha
Qahr pajama aur angiyaaa ki kasaavat khaasi
How lovely on her body lies her lace chemise!
Her headscarf's really super—
Those tight pajamas and bodice torment me!

Naaz zebindah hayaa aafat-o 'ishvah jaadu
Ghamza voh zulm-ada aur rukhaavat khaasi
Even her blandishments enchant me;
Her side-glances cast calamity
The winks are cruel, her coolness, private torture.

Kyun na aise se phanse dil Aji insaaf karo
Guftagu sahr kamar khub lagaavat khaasi
How could the heart not be ensnared?
Dear One, have mercy!
Your discourse casts a spell, your waist is gorgeous,
Our intimacy exquisite.

Pa'on men kafish bhabhuka voh magharraq naadir
Sar-o qad aur hai raanon ki dhulaavat khaasi

Those foot slippers are gilded a rare, brilliant red;
Tall and willowy is her build but deliciously curvy
   her thighs!

Sab se sab baat khudi sab se anokhi guftaar
Sab se poshaak alag sab se sajaavat khaasi
She's unlike all others in all things,
Her speech strange and marvellous!
Her costume distinct from all others, her adornments
   exquisite.

Is ka azhaar karun tujh se main kya kya Rangin?
Dast-o paa zor men mehndi ki rachaavat khaasi
How might I ever convey her to you, Rangin?
From hand to foot she's formidable, hued in henna!

As the poem suggests, this poetry in 'women's idiom' (*auraton ki boli*) is generally light and racy in tone, often suggestive, occasionally salacious or even obscene. All these characteristics seem to be understood by the critics as defects that are part and parcel of what it means for women to express themselves. Whether or not they are correct, that is what rekhti is all about; raciness and salaciousness would seem to compromise the idealised and ennobled construction of the Urdu lyric's standard diction (rekhta). On the other hand, suggestiveness is no stranger to rekhta (nor, to be perfectly candid, is occasional lewdness)—the discussion below of ambiguity in the ghazal demonstrates that suggestiveness of various kinds is absolutely central to rekhta's aesthetic. So the feminine voice of its narrator both is and is not, simply, what distinguishes rekhti from rekhta.

   Critics who dismiss rekhti as decadent may be alluding possibly to generally informal/immodest speech; or to flirtations with servant boys; or to fantasies about males from outside the household espied across the rooftops—all of which do find a place in rekhti poetry. More than its casual tone and (heterosexual) naughtiness, the problem with rekhti probably lies in the open secret among the pitifully few cognoscenti that a certain amount of its content is not only erotic, but female-to-female. The previously-quoted 'particular emotions' and 'decadent pleasure' of 'venturing into social taboos' must surely be allusions to the obvious but implicitly indicated erotic relationship between rekhti's feminine 'ashiq and 'her' Beloved such as is manifest in this sarapa. Is this the 'logical extension' of women expressing emotion? My reading is that the critics draw no meaningful distinction between 'lesbianism' and the 'particular emotions of women'; to them, these emotions constitute 'decadent pleasure' and are necessarily socially taboo, rendering rekhti illegitimate poetry.

By deductive reasoning, polite discourse and legitimate poetry are rendered the domain of men. So, it should come as no surprise that in our time rekhti has become a thoroughly marginalised body of literature. One of the great ironies in all this is that, though narrated by one 'woman' who usually addresses another in intimate terms, existing records indicate that rekhti was recited by *male* poets (sometimes in female dress) to a *male* audience.[17] Women were, as one writer has observed, quite incidental to this 'women's' poetry.[18] Not only that, but none of the scholars that have mentioned, let alone analysed, rekhti in Urdu critical literature have been women. This would not have been particularly remarkable during the late eighteenth and nineteenth centuries, since formal Urdu has been, and remains, a male arena. What does seem remarkable is that two centuries ago, during an expansive period in Urdu culture, men were open to exploring the notion of a distinct female experience; and, during the past century, that openness has been replaced by an anxiety so deep as to lead Urdu's (male) elite to condemn all poetic expression—of women's experience—real or imagined—in the feminine voice as delusional, decadent, even evil.

Does the existence of rekhti as a literary phenomenon mean that, within the culture which produced it, lesbian desire was accepted as an inevitable product of a life lived in seclusion? Can this ex-pression be seen as a site of resistance, as at least one scholar has suggested, based on interviews with courtesans of Lucknow in the 1970s?[19] How did we get from Rangin's adoption

---

[17] Perhaps the best known example of this comes in Farhatullah Beg's depiction of a poetic assembly (*musha'irah*) in *Dilli ki Akhiri Shama* (Delhi's Last Candle). Reprinted and edited by Dr Salahuddin (Delhi, Urdu Akademi, 1986), trans. by Akhter Qamber as *The Last Musha'irah of Delhi* (Delhi, Orient Longman, 1979).

[18] Adrienne Copithorne, 'Poet in Drag: the Phenomenon of Rekhti', unpublished paper, 1998.

[19] Veena Oldenburg, 'Lifestyles of Resistance: the Courtesans of Lucknow' *Feminist Studies*, Vol. 16 (Summer 1990), No. 2, pp. 259–88.

of idiomatic expression of the courtesans to the experience of the *sharif* (respectable) married women? Despite the obsessions with honour and respectability that govern the seclusion of women, how do courtesans and socially elite women come to be conflated in rekhti? Unfortunately only the first of these questions can be taken up here.[20]

How 'Lesbian' is Rekhti?

Na batole mujhe do yahaan se arancuo ho ja'e
Kis ko kahte hain muhabbat Aji kaisa ikhlaas
Don't try to talk me into 'it': scram! get outta here!
What are you calling 'love'?
What kind of affection is this?

Hain yih dulhaa dulhan ikhlaas o muhabbat Insha
Jaise jal-bakht yih kam-bakht voh taisa ikhlaas
This affection and love are bride and groom, Insha:
One's ill-fated, the other fated for hell!

Even the erudite among Urdu readers have supposed that the scholarly value of this poetry lay in the catalogue it constituted of female dress, adornments, household furnishings, or particular idiomatic expressions of an emergent dialect—that of the secluded (*pardah-nashin*) women.[21] One is tempted to deduce that these readers and commentators reduce rekhti to catalogue value out of reluctance to take on the subtext of its (lesbian) reputation. To venture into the 'problems' indicated in the following statement by Dr Sabir Ali Khan, in a book on rekhti's alleged 'inventor', Rangin:[22]

According to [Urdu poets] what is meant by *rekhti* is poetry in which, in women's idiom, are versified the depravity, affairs and emotions of women who are sinful or have gone astray.

---

[20] The other questions posed above are among those I address in 'Dakaini's Radha–Krishna Imagery and Canon Formation in Urdu', in Mariola Offredi (ed.), *The Banyan Tree: Essays on Early Literature in New Indo-Aryan Languages* (New Delhi, Manohar Publishers, 2000).

[21] '*Pardah-nashin*' is the expression in Urdu referring to women who observe *pardah* or gender seclusion.

[22] Sabir Ali Khan, *op. cit.*, p. 406.

Or, as we saw earlier:

> *Rekhti* never attained respectability and often sunk into vulgarity,
> catering for those who sought decadent pleasure. It is, however,
> useful for a study of the miserable life the womenfolk led under
> the feudal order, and the resultant social discontent and the evil
> it bred....[23]

Actually, much of rekhti does not paint a 'miserable' picture at all
of the secluded life. And while racy, while charming and idiomatic,
while clearly set in the *zanana*, much of it is hardly obscene. Indeed,
the following poem is in the form of *Hamd*, an offering of devotional praise (usually to God or the Prophet or Ali):

Vaari tire ja'un main khaaliq hai tu khalqat ka
Kab mujh se bayaan zarrah hu'e tiri qudrat ka
I'm your slave, you're Creation's Creator
When could I offer even an atom of insight into your
    Nature?

Kuchh mujh ko gunaahon ka khatrah nahin mahshar men
Chhorungi na main daaman khaatun-i qayaamat ka
My sins pose no threat on Judgement Day:
I'll hang on tight to the skirt of Lady Judgement.

Tu voh hai jawaan jis ne phir kar ke Zulaikha ko
Yusuf ko kiya mufton us chaand-si surat ka
You're the one who, making Zulaikha young again
Caused Joseph to be tried by that moon-like face.

Jo Nuh ki beti thi tha Da'ilah naam us ka
Tufaan men kiya tu ne murid use la'nat ka
The daughter of Noah—Da'ilah by name—
You cursed her to drown in the tempest.

Aur Hazrat 'Isa ko bin baap kiya paida
Maryam ka mire vaali shaahid hai tu 'ismat ka
And you caused Lord Jesus to be born fatherless
My master, you're witness to Mary's purity.

[23] A. J. Zaidi, *op. cit.*, p. 137.

Ab aath pahr tujh se maangun hun du'a yih main
Bandi ko pare hauka Rangin ki na chaahat ka
All hours do I now beg for your blessed protection:
May this slave never fall captive to Rangin's avaricious
    desire!

What makes this ghazal 'rekhti' are several linguistic cues indicating that the speaker is female. To address oneself as a bondswoman or slave (*bandi*), grammatically marked feminine versus a *banda*, or male slave or *'vaari'* (devoted, sacrificed for) and someone else as *'vaali'* (master, guardian, ruler, protector) constitutes one such cue. And in the second verse there is a verb conjugated in the feminine: *'chhorungi na'*—'I won't let go'. But I am afraid I see no particular lesbian desire here, though the poem is clearly designated as rekhti. Indeed, that absence is not particularly surprising since the Hamd is conventionally a poem of devotional praise rather than one of erotic expression; there is not the overlap of devotion with the erotic in non-Sufi Islamic poetry that one finds so commonly in Bhakti (Indic devotional) literature.[24] True, references to venerated women in Islamic tradition might be less surprising coming from a woman devotee than a man, and there is certainly the open possibility that the 'you' addressed here could be a woman, though the opening verse declares that 'she' is 'Creation's Creator', and we are not operating in a conceptual universe of feminised divinity. So while there may be awe expressed here, and this can certainly be seen as poetry in the feminine voice, no particular erotic desire communicates itself to me. The use of a feminine narrator is what to designates this poem as 'rekhti'; but is it disreputable, delusional or 'lesbian'?

Nor do we see eroticism expressed in the poem below:

Kal 'Ali Kiblain zaraa, jaaiyo Bi Saiyidaani
Hauz ko dudh se bharaaiyo Bi Saiyidaani
Noble Lady, just go to the tomb of Ali Kiblain
And fill up the tank there with milk, Noble Lady.

---

[24] A Hamd can also mention other revered figures in Islamic mythology, for example, Noah's daughter Da'ilah, Muhammad's daughter Fatima, Jesus, Mary and Joseph and Zulaikha (the name given in Islam for Potiphar's wife).

Aaj Nauchandi hai sauda miri sahnak ka tamaam
Chowk se jaa ke tumhin laaiyo Bi Saiyidaani
Today's the new moon—go bring from the market
All the ingredients to make an offering to Fatima.

Laa ke saude ko mujhe peeto agar jaa'un kahin
Ru ba ru baith ke pakvaaiyo Bi Saiyidaani
Beat me if, when you bring them back, I've budged:
Sit face to face and have me cook, Noble Lady.

Pak chuken sab to vahin BiBi Zanon ko bulwaa
Saamen apne voh khilvaaiyo Bi Saiyidanni
When everything's cooked go call the married women
See to it that they are fed, Noble Lady.

Khaa chuken voh to lagaa haath men sab ke mehndi
Phir du'aa un se yih mangvaaiyo Bi Saiyidaani
When they've finished eating, decorate their hands with
    henna—then ask them to pray for this:

Ya'ni is bandi ko jo jo kih sataataa hai 'abas
Apni aoni voh sazaa paaiyo Bi Saiyidaani.
That whoever has tormented this poor servant unduly
Shall each get what they've got coming, Noble Lady!

Here the content does indicate 'women's culture' in the rituals
described and the terms of address employed, not to mention in
the idiomatic expression of the poem. It could also be said that
ultimately, the concerns of the narrator are frivolous rather than
noble, since they come down to revenge. But if critics applaud the
catalogue which rekhti represents of feminine expressions and
rituals, as we saw in remarks quoted above, then what can be
objectionable in this poem?

In other poems there is some suggestiveness, and some more
of the kind of subculture reflected in the 'Noble Lady' poem:

Mere ghar men Zanaakhi aayi kab?
Main nagori bhalaa nahaayi kab?
When did my Zanaakhi last come to my house?
Poor me, when's the last time I had a bath?

Larki muddat se voh gayii hai ruth
Meri us ki hu'i safaa'i kab

That girl's been angry for a long time:
When have we ever cleared up matters between us?

Voh na-bakhti to apne ghar men na thi
Paas us ke gayi thi daayi kab
When I sent the nurse round to her place
The wretch wasn't at home.

Hargiz aati nahin hai saanch ko aanch
Pesh jaavegi yih baraayi kab
Truth is never scorched by fire:
When will this great truth be emblazoned?

Gundh kar haath paa'un men Rangin
Us ne mehndi mire lagaayi kab
When did she last apply henna, Rangin,
Kneading my hands and feet?

The relationship depicted here (though currently on the outs) is clearly one of intimacy, yet not explicitly either sexual or platonic. Even so, the term '*zanaakhi*' used in the first verse to indicate the absent friend, is one which we see only in rekhti and indicates a relationship of intimacy extending to eroticism. While there is little explicit lesbian content in rekhti, erotic relationships between the narrator and her beloved 'other' are overwhelmingly alluded to by employing the terms '*zanaakhi*' and '*dogaana*'. They are not found in standard dictionaries and are nearly untranslatable. Here is how Rangin is said to have explained these terms of address (in the glossary he provided by way of introducing his rekhti collection, the *Divan-i Angekhta*):[25]

Dogaana—having ordered almonds from the bazaar, they (f.pl.) shell them. Those almonds from which twin, or double, nuts are extracted, usually are formed in such a way that one is implanted

---

[25] According to Sabir Ali Khan the source is the Introduction (*Dibacha*) to Rangin's *Divan-i Angekhta*, the fourth and final section of his *Nau-Ratan-i Rangin*, no published edition of which I have either uncovered or seen referenced in the critical literature. The only published source for these definitions of which I am aware is Sabir, who seems to have worked from this manuscript in London during the 1940s. The microfilm copy in my possession does not include this *Dibacha* and/or glossary.

within the other. This implanted nut is called 'masculine' (*nar*) and the one in which it is embedded is called 'feminine' (*maadah*). Then an unknown person (*shakhs*) is summoned and, giving him the two almond fruits, one of them tells him, 'Give me one of the fruits and give her the other.' The one in whose hand he places the *nar* fruit then thinks of herself as the 'man' (*mard*) and the one in whose hand the 'feminine' fruit is placed becomes the 'feminine' and they call each other '*dogaana*' or 'twin'.

Zanaakhi—After slaughtering a chicken and having it cooked, they (f.pl.) sit down to eat together. In this chicken's breast is a bifurcated bone (the wishbone) which they refer to as the '*zanaakh*'. Simultaneously, each of them takes one branch of the bone and pulls it toward herself. The one whose end snaps is the feminine and the one whose end remains whole is called the masculine, and if the wishbone snaps in the middle, then they order another chicken to be slaughtered and repeat the exercise *so that it may be fully determined who is masculine and who feminine.*'[26]

Ironically, Rangin and Sabir 'Ali Khan confirm stereotyped views about men viewing lesbian acts—or purporting to—insofar as their voyeurism concerns itself with how to gender the interactions. It does not seem to occur to them that sexual acts are not inherently gender-marked. How else do we understand the explained principle behind the definitions above, viz., 'to fully determine who is masculine and who feminine', when the terms 'dogaana' and 'zanaakhi' themselves do not imply gender differentiation within the relationship?

Perhaps of greater interest than why we need to know who does what to whom, and what that means in terms of gender, is that the Urdu critics' dismissive explanations of 'lesbian' sexuality as a 'depraved' by-product of 'the feudal order' deflect the reader's attention away from the critique of patriarchy crying out to be made here.[27] It seems to this reader that *rekhti* is better explained

---

[26] Cited in Sabir Ali Khan, *op. cit.*, pp. 215–16, emphasis added.

[27] One might also note that blaming 'lesbianism' on feudalism is quite consistent with the analytical terms of the Progressive Writers Movement, which simultaneously rebelled against the suppression/sublimation of sexuality and repudiated the gender oppression of the old social order. See also Krishan Chander's analysis of Ismat Chughtai's 'lesbian' short story, '*Lihaaf*' (Quilt) in the Introduction to her collection of short stories, entitled *Choten* (Aligarh, Educational Book House, 1982/1961). However, as in Zaidi's remarks given earlier, the critique of feudalism

as a by-product of patriarchy's cultural constructions than as a by-product of feudalism's gender oppression. After all, the gender oppression of patriarchy is alive and well in post-feudal South Asia and the rest of the world, and continues to be amply documented and witnessed.

To offer the promised critique of patriarchy we need to return to a discussion of standard ghazal convention.

Rekhti, 'Ishq and Ambiguity

Perhaps ultimately the crucial problem posed by rekhti is this: when a 'woman' addresses an unambiguously feminine beloved, she challenges *the* central axiom of Urdu love poetry, viz., that the Beloved be of ambiguous identity, both in terms of gender and in human versus divine terms (in other words, the beloved might, theoretically, be human or divine). Ironically, this ambiguity, while ostensibly gender-neutral, proves to be less than benign. It creates an expressive environment quite receptive to male homoeroticism, as some scholars have discussed,[28] but tends to close the door on the expression of female homoeroticism.

The point has been made that conventionally and in material fact Urdu poetry has been the provenance of men and its domain masculine: the poets are men, the narrator–lover/hero is male, and the beloved is referred to in the masculine gender. Even when physical attributes are described, and strongly suggest a female person, the Beloved is referred to as 'he'.[29] Here are two examples of ambiguous desire commonly expressed in rekhta, one more

---

remains profoundly homophobic, because, it attributes homoeroticism to feudal decadence, and assumes that the *zenana* was the last recourse for the assuage of sexual frustration in (presumably) otherwise heterosexual women.

[28] C. M. Naim, 'The Theme of Pederastic Love in Premodern Urdu Poetry', in M. V. Menon (ed.), *Studies in the Urdu Ghazal and Prose Fiction* (Madison, University of Wisconsin South Asian Studies Publication Series, Publication No. 5, 1979), pp. 120–42; Frances Pritchett, 'Convention in the Classical Urdu Ghazal: The Case of Mir', *Journal of South Asian and Middle Eastern Studies*, Vol. 3 (Fall 1979), No. 1, pp. 60–77; Tariq Rahman, 'Boy-Love in the Urdu Ghazal', *Annual of Urdu Studies*, Vol. 7 (1990), pp. 1–20; and S. R. Kidwai (unpublished).

[29] This problem is discussed in some detail in C. Petievich, 'The Feminine Voice in the Urdu Ghazal', *Indian Horizons*, Vol. 39 (1990), Nos. 1 & 2, pp. 25–41.

abstract and one less so. Both were written by the great Mirza Ghalib (1797–1869):

Yih na thi hamaari qismat kih visaal-i yaar hota
Agar aur jite rahte yahi intizaar hota
It was not my destiny to unite with the Beloved; yet
Had I gone on living, I would still have kept on waiting

Nind us ki hai dimaagh us ka hai raaten us ki hain
Teri zulfen jis ke baazu par pareshaan ho ga'in
Sleep is [his], peace of mind is [his], the very nights are [his]
Upon whose shoulder lie strewn your scattered tresses/
    rumpled locks.

Neither of these verses compromise the ambiguity of gender or humanity (divinity) in the lover or the beloved. Anyone can claim them and identify with the desire they both express,[30] be the lover male or female, human or divine.

With (masculine) humans in search of the divine (probably conceived of as genderless but referred to in the masculine) there is little place left for female humans, or even for the feminine principle. Rekhta has served for centuries as a central icon of cultural identity and self-esteem among South Asian Muslims. Its elevated value hinges on the aesthetic of love ('ishq) as the most noble of human endeavours, and this aesthetic was developed over several centuries in the context of Sufism, a rich mystical tradition. Perfecting oneself as a lover ('ashiq) is seen as the only true path toward unity with the divine; and the presumption that the ultimate beloved is the divine has been Urdu love poetry's best defence against the austere and conservative forces of religious authority who might otherwise have tried to squelch it, along with other arts manifesting an extravagance of passion. Such a defence has been augmented by conventions which insist that the physical aspects of passion remain sublimated. Claiming the human–divine divide as the ultimate reality, and its ultimate subject,[31] rekhta is love poetry on the exquisite pain of separation.

---

[30] This is also somewhat the case in the *Hamd* above, though references to female figures and knowledge that the poem is considered *rekhti* might incline the reader to assume that the narrator is female.
[31] *'Ishq* expressed toward the divine beloved is known as 'true love' ['*ishq-i haqiqi*],

Not so rekhti, neither sublimated passion, nor love in separation—let alone gender ambiguity—are its forte. The emotions
expressed are understood as arising from the social reality of
women being thrown together, which is exactly the opposite of the
separation on which 'true love' is predicated.

Even so, we must be careful in our analysis. It may be tempting
for the feminist reader of rekhti to see in it a private world where
women, obliged to live in seclusion, resist the misery of gender
oppression by discovering rich emotional and erotic possibilities
with one another. And if the authors of this poetry were secluded
women such an interpretation of rekhti would be far more per-
suasive. Alas, this is not so. We cannot look to rekhti for an insight
into what it means for women, living together, to develop a
literature of same-sex eroticism. Intellectual honesty requires that
we look too for an insight into what it means for men, who keep
women secluded and socialise with other men, to invent a parody
of their own idealised love literature, and to perform it for other
men while impersonating women. This critique of patriarchy need
not presuppose malice on the part of the male poets and their
audience, because the way patriarchy works, in this case, is
structural rather than strategically-deployed.

Sabir Ali Khan is only one of a number of scholars to slide over
rekhti without taking it on as a literary product reflective of how
culture is profoundly gendered.[32] As is too often the case when
it comes to Urdu poetry, rekhti seems to have been mentioned
much more than read (and it is mentioned relatively little in the
first place), so statements of conventional wisdom tend to reinforce this poetry's obscurity and our ignorance. My own readings
in the genre yield much suggestion and innuendo through the use
of particular terms of address, but exactly two poems are explicitly
lesbian in content. Ironically, some of the raciest rekhti I have read
was written not by its 'inventor,' Sa'adat Yar Khan 'Rangin', but
by two other poets of Lucknow, Insha' Allah Khan 'Insha' and
Qalandar Bakhsh 'Jur'at'.

---

while love for a human, being only an approximation of divine love, is called
'metaphorical love' ['*ishq-i majazi*].

[32] Others include M. A. R. Barker, *Naqsh-I Dilpazir: Classical Urdu Poetry*, 3 Vols.
(Ithaca, Spoken Language Press, 1977); T. Grahame Bailey, *op. cit.*; Naim, *op. cit.*;
Sadiq, *op. cit.*; Schimmel, *op. cit.*; and Zaidi, *op. cit.*.

Teri faryaad karun kis se, Zanaakhi tune
Yih meri jaan jalaa'i kih Ilahi taubah!
To whom can I complain about you, Zanaakhi?
God, but how your harshness has burned my heart!

The Suppression of *Rekhti* and Its Lesbianism

As mentioned earlier, rekhti's employment of the terms 'dogaana' and 'zanaakhi' has resulted in its content being designated 'lesbian'. While the content of some verses does imply a lesbian relationship between the narrator and 'her' dogaana or zanaakhi, the use of even these unglossed terms of address seems to have been enough to 'spook' the Urdu literati; certainly examples of rekhti in historical surveys of Urdu literature are all but absent.

One way to understand why rekhti is such an extremely difficult body of poetry to lay hands on involves consideration of gender segregation in the linguistic realm. The institution of pardah removes women not only from public space but also from the sphere of literature and the expression of ideas. In other words, in addition to the obsessions with honour that continue to symbolically rationalise the practice of gender segregation, actual physical segregation of women from the public sphere has worked to remove them from the imagined community of Urdu speakers.[33] Thus a body of poetry purporting to be about women must necessarily be segregated from the more public, normative world of Urdu poetry. Ergo its subsequent suppression.

A corollary condition to the bodily seclusion of women is the absence of female authorship in pre-modern Urdu poetry.[34] There have been no female poets canonised in Urdu. Indeed, there have

---

[33] Cf. David Lelyveld, 'Zuban-e Urdu-e Mu'alla and the Idol of Linguistic Origins', *Annual of Urdu Studies*, Vol. 9 (1994), pp. 107–17.

[34] No female poet is ever mentioned in standard anthologies of the Urdu canon. There are a few anthologies of woman poets housed in archives, but, they are clearly defined as 'female poets in Urdu' rather than 'Urdu poets'. The first pre-modern 'poetess' to have been anthologised, Mahtaqa Bai Chanda, a courtesan of eighteenth century Hyderabad, was presented in published form in an English language collection only recently. See S. Tharu and K. Lalitha, *Women Writing in India: 600 B.C. to the Present*, Vol. 1 (New York, The Feminist Press at the City University of New York, 1990).

been no women writers of repute until well into the twentieth century. Even these authors tend overwhelmingly to write prose[35]— in a tradition which favours poetry over any other form of literature, and over most other art forms as well.[36] There are fewer than a handful of reputed women scholars of Urdu even today. This absence of female writing also characterises the Perso–Arabic tradition from which Urdu consciously draws its lineage. Thus, any poetry authored by 'women' represents a novelty.

The novelty is exacerbated into high camp[37] by the fact that rekhti was reportedly authored and performed by men in drag. It is by no means novel, the world over, for men to speak for women no matter what persona they adopt,[38] but drag is one of the few realms where it is suggested that femininity is best expressed by men, although that could be seen as the logical expression of men speaking for women altogether. In any case, this particular case of men speaking for women announces firmly that feminine erotic or emotional expression is not poetically 'normal'.

We can also see a mirror image of this same logical trajectory in silencing. Rekhti is, as we have noted, a highly expurgated body of poetry. Whatever has been made available to the interested reader is almost solely available in the truncated format known as 'selected' (*muntakhab*). Few of those editors who have prepared

[35] The earliest such writers to gain acclaim would include, but not necessarily be limited to, Rashid Jehan, Khadija Mastoor and Hajira Masroor, Ismat Chugtai and Qurratulain Hyder. This rule has begun to erode during the last quarter of the twentieth century, with the modern canon now including such famous female poets as Parveen Shakir, Zehra Nigah and the overtly feminist poets Kishwar Naheed (b. 1940) and Fahmida Riyaz (b. 1945). These exceptions do not, however, alter the norm of Urdu poetry and scholarship being an overwhelmingly male domain.
[36] In a recent essay, Shoaib Hashmi made a succinct allusion to this phenomenon during the course of a review of women in drama. 'Muslim civilization', he says, 'was not interested in the drama, one way or another, and the dramatic conflict was worked out instead in poetry', thus rendering other literary forms irrelevant. See S. Hashmi, 'Women in Drama', in Kishwar Naheed (ed.), *Women: Myth and Realities* (Lahore, Sang-e Meel, 1994), pp. 299–324.
[37] This argument has been advanced by S. R. Kidwai in a recent review of the book by Violette Graff, *Lucknow: Memories of a City* (New Delhi, Oxford University Press, 1997) which appeared in the journal *Biblio*, Vol. 4 (March–April 1998), Nos. 3 & 4.
[38] One of the more familiar essays on the subject is Gayatri Spivak's 'Can the Subaltern Speak?', in *In Other Worlds* (New York, Methuen, 1987).

these selections have worked from early manuscripts, and none of these editors has translated any rekhti into another language. Indeed, their standard practice is to replace verse they deem 'objectionable' with dots in the texts of the poems![39] Furthermore, biographical and other potentially illuminating information from rekhti poets and their contemporaries have been preserved not in Urdu but in Persian, with one partial exception.[40] While Persian was indeed the language of literary criticism used for Urdu until the end of the nineteenth century, it is not nearly so widely taught today, and the decision to keep primary information in Persian further excludes potential readers, mediating between them and the text.

Are we being protected from literature like Rangin's sarapa (presented above)? This playful poem hardly seems depraved to us; nor does it seem particularly reverent, lofty or noble. Its appeal lies in the entertainment value of a lusty description through the gaze of the admirer, as in any sarapa; but it must be acknowledged here that the sarapa itself, even as a genre of rekhta, is marginalised. The reason, again, is that its concreteness of imagery in describing the beloved militates against the ghazal's cherished ambiguity. Its elaborate description encourages us to visualise the beloved as female. Not only is this inconsistent with normative Islam's understanding of the divine, it echoes rather uncomfortably with the idolatry of Hinduism.[41]

Lesbian Erotic Desire

Desire is a complex concept, and there is voluminous literature addressed to its complexity, so let us accept, for the purposes of argument, that desire is either being expressed or alluded to in the verses cited above. But, it would be difficult to argue that its representation here compares very favourably with the 'male'

---

[39] Perhaps the most egregious example of this can be found in Askari and Fazl (eds), *Kalam-i Insha* (Allahabad, Hindustani Akademi, 1952).
[40] Sabir Ali Khan occasionally presents parallel translation from Persian into Urdu.
[41] Adorning the deity (*shringaar*) is a common Hindu ritual; and the head-to-toe description of the beloved would seem to echo such poetic motifs from Sanskrit as *keshadipadavamana* in which a beautiful woman (or a deity) is described in elaborate, iconographic detail, fashioning a verbal sculpture.

homoeroticism of rekhta poetry, some of which is explicit and some of which thrives on the conventionalised gender ambiguity central to the Urdu ghazal. The sarapa above, for example, suggests a rather carnal sort of desire of one woman for another— the gender identity of neither is ambiguous. Rekhti, by definition, precludes this. It is hard to say, therefore, whether rekhti would be the chosen voice in which a woman would have expressed desire or erotic feeling of a more abstract, less carnal kind, toward another. Why would she not, indeed, make use of the complex, layered and nuanced expression of such rekhta verses as has just been cited? How much more limited (if camp and amusing) is the desire expressed in rekhti! It can only reinforce the culturally constructed feminine domain as trivial, depraved and ignoble, even if amusing, and therefore unsuitable for Urdu love poetry in which the erotic is built upon allusion and suggestion, and broken by explicit description.

The rekhti of Rangin or Insha or Jur'at is sometimes quite explicit. Sometimes it relies for its effect on allusion, but the allusions are salacious. Of such rekhti[42] C. M. Naim has this to say in support of the current argument:

> *Rekhti* ... was about women, for the entertainment and titillation of men ... it was not a 'feminised' form of *rekhta*; if anything, it was a kind of misogynistic verse 'that aimed to entertain its male audience by making gross fun of women, its enhanced appeal lying in the fact that it also pretended to be a view from the inside....[43]

While Naim also claims that some later Lakhnavi rekhti reflects a 'genuine concern for women's lives in domestic confinement', that has not been demonstrated sufficiently to save the genre from the axeman's block. Urdu poets once found a place for the suggestion of eroticism between 'women' but created in it a poor counterpart

---

[42] I deliberately limit my stated reservations above to the Lakhnavi rekhti discussed herein. A consideration of Dakani 'rekhti' from the sixteenth and seventeenth century Muslim courts in central India yields a somewhat different argument. C. Petievich, 'The Feminine Voice in the Urdu Ghazal', *Indian Horizons*, Vol. 39 (1990), Nos. 1 & 2, pp. 25–41, C. Petievich, 'Dakani's Radha–Krishna Imagery and Canon Formation in Urdu', in Mariola Offredi (ed.), *The Banyan Tree: Essays on Early Literature in New Indo–Aryan Languages*, Vol. 1 (New Delhi, Manohar Publishers, 2000), pp. 113–28.

[43] Naim and Petievich, *op. cit.*, p. 171.

to their literary tradition's celebration of male beauty by male poets in the masculine gender. The narrator of this male–male poetry is an 'ashiq, a lover, a human being striving toward transcendence, the narrator of this Lakhnavi rekhti is not.

What is left the reader after the depredatioñs and mediations of editors and other scholars is not a body of poetry celebrating serious, erotic love between women, nor even a body of poetry which could be easily subverted, as rekhta can be, by homoerotically-inclined male poets. That, of course, would be tremendously threatening to patriarchy. What is left, rather, is a body of verse featuring frivolous 'women' concerned with petty and mundane things, meanwhile reiterating patriarchy's gendered status quo. In times like these, with Muslim culture under threat in India from Hindu chauvinism, and with secularity and the realm of an idealised erotic under threat from orthodox Muslim ideologues in Pakistan, that status quo would seem to offer a sufficient palliative to the beleaguered male elite that willingly sacrifices rekhti in order to hold on to the self-esteem derived from the perpetuation of rekhta. To do so is not so very difficult. It only requires that they divest this literature of the 'feminine' garb it had earlier donned, and end the episode of impersonation which rekhti represented in the life of Urdu poetry.

6

Crossing 'Lines' of Subjectivity

The Negotiation of Sexual Identity in Hyderabad, India[1]

◆ Gayatri Reddy

It was early evening in Hyderabad, and the Public Gardens—a centrally located, popular meeting-point for many young couples—was gradually coming to life. I was sitting on a low wall adjoining the tea-stall, having a cup of *chai* with Suresh,[2] a young, self-identified 'gay' man, when we had the following conversation. 'Is it true that in America there is a book that tells you specific locations across the country where you can find other gays?' Suresh asked me eagerly. 'Where did you hear that?' I asked in turn. 'This friend of mine went for a homo-sex party in Bombay, and there was a gay man who had just come from abroad. He told my friend,' Suresh replied. 'It would be so great if there was one like that for India also, because then easily, we could go enjoy with other people in this line,' he added wistfully.

---

[1] This essay was originally presented as a paper at the conference on 'Sexualities, Masculinities and Culture in South Asia: Knowledges, Practices, Popular Culture, and the State', 6–8 July 1999, Melbourne, Australia. The current essay retains much of the conference presentation format and reflects an argument that the author has since developed considerably.

[2] All names used in this essay are pseudonyms.

In this article, I want to focus on the two somewhat related images or notions circulating within this modern Indian 'gay' narrative: the first is the construction of sexual subjectivity implied by the usage of the 'gay' label in Hyderabad. Despite the differences between the nineteenth century episteme of 'homosexuality' uncovered by Foucault, and the newer twentieth century episteme of 'gay' identity, both tend to elide the receptive/ penetrative sexual distinction so common in parts of Latin America and Asia.[3] This elision appears to be in marked contrast to the accounts of other commonly encountered figures in the narrative linking India with sexual difference, the best-known being the quintessential 'third-sexed' *hijras*.[4] The second image

---

[3] P. Jackson, *Male Homosexuality in Thailand: An Interpretation of Contemporary Thai Sources* (New York, Global Academic Publishers, 1989) and 'Kathoey><Gay><Man: The Historical Emergence of Gay Male Identity in Thailand', in Manderson and Jolly (eds), *Sites of Desire, Economies of Pleasure* (Chicago, University of Chicago Press, 1997); D. Kulik, 'The Gender of Brazilian Transgendered Prostitutes', *American Anthropologist*, Vol. 99, No. 3 (1997) and *Travesti: Sex, Gender and Culture among Brazilian Transgendered Prostitutes* (Chicago, University of Chicago Press, 1998); R. Lancaster, 'Subject Honor and Object Shame', *Ethnology*, Vol. 27 (1988), No. 2 and 'That We Should All Turn Queer?: Homosexual Stigma in the Making of Manhood and the Breaking of a Revolution in Nicaragua', in Gagnon and Parker (eds), *Conceiving Sexuality: Approaches to Sex Research in a Postmodern World* (London, Routledge, 1995); R. Parker, 'Acquired Immunodeficiency Syndrome in Brazil', *Medical Anthropology Quarterly*, Vol. 1, No. 2 (1987) and *Bodies, Pleasures and Passions: Sexual Culture in Contemporary Brazil* (Boston, Beacon Press, 1991); J. Seabrook, *Love in a Different Climate: Men Who Have Sex with Men in India* (London, Verso, 1999).

[4] See also S. Nanda, *Neither Man Nor Woman: The Hijras of India* (Belmont, Wadsworth, 1990). I want to make two caveats here: first, I realise that a vast body of literature explicitly addresses the differences between 'homosexuality as we know it today', (E. Sedgwick, *Epistemology of the Closet* [Berkeley, University of California Press, 1990]), and previous arrangements of same-sex relations (*loc. cit.*); D. Halperin, *One Hundred Years of Homosexuality* [New York, Routledge, 1990]); J. Weeks, *Sex, Politics and Society* (London, Longman, 1981). Although recognising that the terms 'homosexual' and 'gay' may refer to distinct periods in the history of this phenomenon, I use the terms interchangeably, drawing primarily on my informants' articulations. Second, I realise that the axes of subjectivity and behaviour respectively, as the basis for a differentiation between Foucault's nineteenth century 'homosexual' and contemporary 'third sex' categories is a flat, simplistic and perhaps even overly crude characterisation. Nevertheless, I retain this distinction on the basis of my informants' repeated differentiation between homosexual or 'gay' and *hijra/kothi* identities.

refers to the transnational links invoked by Suresh and the people he referred to as being 'in this line,' and the particulars of their narratives and subject-positionings stemming from these perceived connections. Importantly, I want to highlight the apparent difference in the dynamics of this self-construction in urban India vis-à-vis the protracted, internal process of disciplining and dividing that produced Foucault's 'modern' homosexual in the 'West'.

In this article, I highlight these images by addressing the relationship between two apparently different models or archetypes of same-sex sexuality that are currently deployed in the South Indian city of Hyderabad. Following a brief theoretical overview, I sketch the ideal-type outlines of these two models— what one of my informants referred to as a 'modern gay' model and the 'traditional *kothi*' model—before problematising their depiction either as coherent definitional fields, or as mutually exclusive markers of 'tradition' and 'modernity'. In particular, I point to two problematics: first, the mutually coexisting nature of these sexual paradigms, and the potentially diverse manner of their production. I argue that the simultaneous presence of these 'different' models and the potential interaction between them question Foucaultian understandings of modern homosexuality in terms of a 'unidirectional narrative of supersession'.[5] And second, the trans-local nature of 'gay' subjectivities in India that argues against a coherent, universal 'global gay identity',[6] as well as an explicitly non-universal, local particularity. Ultimately, what I hope to emphasise is the complexity of the cultural production of homo/sexual identity in the interactions of 'west' and 'non-west', local cultural systems and global politico-economic forces.

---

[5] Sedgwick, *op. cit.*. As Foucault notes, 'Particularly from the eighteenth century onwards, Western societies created and deployed a new apparatus which was *superimposed* on the previous one', namely the 'deployment of sexuality', which, like the 'deployment of alliance … connects up with the circuit of sexual partners, but in a different way'. M. Foucault, *The History of Sexuality*, Vol. 1 (New York, Vintage, 1980), p. 106.

[6] D. Altman, 'Global Gaze/Global Gays', *GLQ: A Journal of Lesbian and Gay Studies*, Vol. 3 (1997); see also M. Warner, *Fear of a Queer Planet: Queer Politics and Social Theory* (Minneapolis, University of Minnesota Press, 1993).

Exploring the Contemporary Terrain of (Homo) Sexualities

In the now famous passage from *The History of Sexuality*, Foucault states:

> .... As defined by the ancient civil or canonical codes, sodomy was a category of forbidden acts; their perpetrator was nothing more than the juridical subject of them. The nineteenth century homosexual became a personage, a past, a case history, and a childhood, in addition to being a type of life, a life form, and a morphology, with an indiscreet anatomy and possibly a mysterious physiology.... The sodomite had been a temporary aberration; the homosexual was now a species....[7]

According to Foucault, this instance of subjectification in the 'west', resulted from an epistemic disjuncture in the nineteenth century in which sexual identity was produced by the disciplining knowledge of the sexual sciences, and the dividing practices of modern states. Foucault's historical method focuses on unearthing epistemic ruptures that occur across the passage of time in one spatial unit, namely the 'west'. But what happens if we take into account the genealogy of knowledge/subjectivity across *space* as well as time, as Donham asks in a recent article.[8] Quite apart from the fact that Foucault did not take into account the potential importance of the colonial relationship in the *production* of current western notions of homosexuality—a point Stoler eloquently makes[9]—he also did not address the potential impact of the rapid transnational flow of knowledge, commodities, persons and narratives, and their role in the formation of notions of sexuality in parts not 'in the western part of the world'.[10]

---

[7] Foucault, *op. cit.*, p. 43.

[8] D. Donham, 'Freeing South Africa: The "Modernization" of Male–Male Sexuality in Soweto', *Cultural Anthropology*, Vol. 13, No. 1 (1998).

[9] A. Stoler, *Race and The Education of Desire: Foucault's History of Sexuality and The Colonial Order of Things* (Durham, Duke University Press, 1995) and 'Educating Desire in Colonial Southeast Asia: Foucault, Freud and Imperial Sexualities', in Manderson and Jolly (eds), *op. cit.*.

[10] Foucault, *op. cit.*, p. 11.

Further, as Sedgwick points out,[11] recent historical work in gay/ lesbian studies, following Foucault's initiative and pointing out ever more precise datings/narratives of the development of homosexuality as we know it today, implicitly 'underwrite[s] the notion that homosexuality as we conceive of it today itself comprises a coherent definitional field rather than a space of overlapping, contradictory, and conflictual definitional forces.'[12] Rather, contemporary notions of 'homosexuality' can be effectively denaturalised and better understood only by exploring the 'gaps between minoritising and universalising ... gender-transitive and gender-intransitive understandings of same-sex relations',[13] especially in varied 'sites of desire'[14] in today's transnational world.

A recent body of literature that appears to address these transnational flows of sex/gender signs and commodities is one which advocates what I shall refer to as the 'global gay' narrative.[15] The premise of this narrative is the 'emergence of a "western" style homosexuality' in 'non-western' regions of the world, characterised by a 'modern invention, namely, the creation of an identity and a sense of community based on (homo) sexuality.'[16] With the increased transnational traffic in signs and narratives, this 'modern invention', which developed as a result of particular historical specificities in the 'west', has apparently diffused to emerge as a variant of a universal, 'global gay' identity in 'non-western' regions, including Asia. Although proponents of this view obviously recognise that this pattern is not a simple diffusion from west to east, replacing 'traditional' or 'indigenous' sex/ gender formations in a 'linear genealogy',[17] such formulations perhaps inadvertently perpetuate the somewhat sterile and culturally marked binarisms of gay/west/modern versus indigenous/non-west/traditional. For instance, Altman states:

---

[11] 'Axiom 5: The historical search for a Great Paradigm Shift may obscure the present conditions of sexual identity'. (Sedgwick, *op. cit.*, p. 44).

[12] *Ibid.*, p. 45.

[13] *Ibid.*, p. 47.

[14] Manderson and Jolly, *op. cit.*.

[15] See also D. Altman, 'Rupture or Continuity? The Internationalization of Gay Identities', *Social Text*, Vol. 14, No. 3 (1996); Altman, 'Global Gaze/Global Gays', among other essays.

[16] Altman, 'Global Gaze/Global Gays', p. 423.

[17] Altman, 'Rupture or Continuity?', p. 79.

> On the one hand, Asian gay men, by stressing a universal gay identity, underline a similarity with westerners. Against this, on the other hand, the desire to assert an 'Asian' identity...may undermine a similarity with westerners.[18]

In another section, he states that the 'claiming of lesbian/gay identities in Asia...is as much about being western as about sexuality.'[19]

Clearly, the 'gay' identities and practices of 1990's Asia are, in certain recognisable terms, different from earlier sex/gender configurations. The construction of a 'gay' identity primarily around homoerotic sexuality does in fact appear to be a recent development. And, while this is to a large extent tied to the emergence of global networks of communication between gays and lesbians worldwide, this is by no means a simple instance of a coherent, universal 'gay' identity. What I want to point to in this article is the complexity of these transactions and the subsequent productions of identity. Based on fieldwork in the South Indian city of Hyderabad, I hope to provide some understanding of this 'local' terrain of (homo)sexuality by juxtaposing the sex/gender 'dichotomies' of 'traditional kothi' and 'modern gay' identity. My ultimate goal is to highlight the complex, negotiated nature of contemporary sexual identity in Hyderabad, interrogating in this process notions of sexuality, identity, culture and modernity.

'Traditional' Subjectivities: The *Kothi* Sexual Archetype

I will first sketch the outlines of the kothi model of same-sex sexuality—the classificatory grid against which the 'gay' model is seemingly crafted. This model was described to me primarily by the hijras—a fact that perhaps needs to be kept in mind. For those unfamiliar with these South Asian so-called 'third sexed' figures, hijras are those individuals often described in the literature as 'eunuch transvestites'[20] or the 'third sex' of India. In the context

---

[18] Altman, 'Global Gaze/Global Gays', p. 418.
[19] *Ibid.*, p. 430.
[20] M. Vyas and Y. Shingala, *The Lifestyle of the Eunuchs* (New Delhi, Anmol Publications, 1987).

of this essay, hijras are one of the various categories of kothi I encountered in the field. For the most part, they are men who wear female clothing and enact a 'transgendered' role. A 'real' hijra is said to be like a *sannyasi* or ascetic, having renounced sexual desire and practice. Most, if not all hijras undergo complete emasculation—what they refer to as the *nirvan* operation in which the penis and testes are excised—and are subsequently believed to be endowed with the power to confer fertility on newly weds or new-born children. They see this as their 'traditional' ritual role, although at least half the current hijra population engages in sex for money, or otherwise engages in sexual activity with their lovers or husbands.

Over the course of my fieldwork with the hijras, I gradually learned about the existence of a broader homosocial universe of individuals in Hyderabad, of which the hijras were a part, with their own social categories, idiomatic terminology and rules of membership. For the purposes of this paper, I shall briefly summarise these as follows:

- First, all sexually active or adult individuals are categorised into three identities, *kothis* being one of these, with the other two being *narans* and *panthis*. While narans are women— an undifferentiated category based primarily on anatomy and gendered practice, kothis are those men who 'like to do women's work' and desire the passive/receptive position in same-sex encounters with other men. Panthis, in this sex/gender system, are the active partners of kothis and/or narans, bounded not merely by the form of their penetrative sexuality, but also *against* the constellation of 'female' practices and desires embodied by these other identities.
- Second, there are a range of kothi identities—of which the hijras are just one group—differentially positioned along a hierarchy of authenticity and respect. In the eyes of the hijras, the most important criteria that garner this respect are kinship, sexual desire (or its lack) and the degree of visibility and respect in the public sphere.

Perhaps the single most important of these criteria, repeatedly mentioned by the hijras in their definitions of authenticity, is kinship. Very briefly, kinship is defined in this context as affiliation and social obligation to one of the hijra houses or lineages in the community.[21] By deploying the marker of kinship—or the *rith* as they refer to it—individuals signify their membership in that house as well as within the wider community of hijras and kothis. The rith not only denotes membership in the wider community, but also hierarchises the kothis along this axis of kinship. There are kothis who are 'officially' kin—those who 'have a rith in the *haveli* (house)'—and those who are not—*bina rithwale* or those without a rith. While this does not prevent the latter from identifying as kothis, it clearly places them lower in the kothi prestige hierarchy. Over the course of my fieldwork, I encountered repeated references to this hierarchy as exemplified by the following incident.

It was about two o'clock in the afternoon and most of the hijra prostitutes were either sleeping or had gone out for a movie. All of a sudden, Kishori, one of the more senior hijra prostitutes walked up to where Sunila, another hijra, was sleeping and started hurling abuses at her. Kishori was obviously very upset about something, and from what I understood, the issue centred on her hijra disciple, Meenakshi. Kishori was accusing Sunila of negatively influencing Meenakshi and instigating the latter to run away from her. That morning, Meenakshi had apparently decided that Kishori was too abusive, physically and emotionally, and had left for her natal village in Warangal. According to Kishori, it was Sunila who was responsible for Meenakshi's change of heart, and she proceeded to abuse Sunila verbally, using extremely harsh and crude language. 'You are an *andoli* (orphan) hijra, and you think you can make trouble for us real hijras! We—me and my sisters—are real hijras, not you. Remember that! We have a rith, unlike you,' Kishori screamed at Sunila. Almost the first questions asked of any visiting hijra are either 'which house do you have

---

[21] According to the published literature and some of the Hyderabadi *hijras'* accounts, there are seven *hijra* houses in the country namely, Poonavala, Lashkarvala, Lallanvala, Bullakhvala, Dhongrivala, Mandirvala and Chaatlavala (Vyas and Shingala, *op. cit*..); S. Nanda, *Neither Man Nor Woman* (Belmont, Wadsworth, 1990); Z. Jaffrey, *The Invisibles* (New York, Pantheon, 1996). Only two of these houses are currently represented in Hyderabad–Poonavala and Lashkarvala. According to the *hijras*, currently Mumbai is the only city that has all seven houses.

the rith in?' or, 'who is your *guru*?' Most importantly, 'if there is no guru…and no rith in the hijra community, that person does not have *izzat* (honour/respect), and is not recognised as a hijra,' Munira told me in no uncertain terms.

In addition to the rith, all hijras define themselves in opposition to the, overly licentious and much disparaged, *khada-chatla kothis* or *gandus*, as they more commonly (and pejoratively) refer to these individuals. According to the hijras, gandus, or men who enjoy anal sex, are defined not only by the *form* of their sexual desire, but, more importantly, by its *excess*. As such, the gandus are disparaged by all hijras, both the supposedly asexual hijras as well as by the sexually active. These hijra 'prostitutes' not only employ a life-cycle rhetoric of sexual prostitution progressing to asexual ritual practice, but also profess a dislike of indiscriminate sexual desire/practice. According to the hijras, excessive sexual desire is a marker of inauthenticity that both defines the gandus and, by that token, separates them from the supposedly asexual hijras. An active symbol of the hijras' essential asexuality that is deployed for this purpose is the physical emasculation of their genitalia that all hijras are ideally meant to undergo—a process that they refer to as a rebirth or nirvan.

Apparently, according to the hijras, having had the nirvan operation not only signals respect within the kothi community and indicates the possession of *himmat* or strength necessary to acquire seniority, but it also provides a measure of izzat in the outside world. One becomes resolutely and irrevocably a 'real hijra' following this operation. One of my hijra friends, Sakila, said her motivation for her nirvan operation followed just such an incident when she lost her respect in public. This is her story as she recounted it to me:

> I went to the shopkeepers to ask for money.… When I walked up to one shopkeeper though, maybe because he didn't recognize me, he said 'show me that you are a real hijra'. I was still *akkuva* (not operated) then. Having completely lost respect and feeling ashamed, I quietly came back. After that, I decided to become a *nirvan sultan* and after a few months I went for my nirvan.

In hijra constructions, this corporeal symbol instantiates their greater authenticity and respect, serving simultaneously as an indictment of their more libidinous fellow-kothis.

'Modern' Subjectivities: The 'Gay' Sexual Archetype

Against this kothi model of same-sex desire and identity is the model delineated by the self-identified 'gay' individuals such as Suresh in the opening vignette. The classificatory grid that these 'gay' individuals outline not only creates an identity based primarily on sexual object choice, but, in addition, this reconfiguration of identity apparently involves different criteria from those employed by the kothi sexual paradigm. Although this model of same-sex sexuality was clearly not beyond contestation, by and large, the contours of this grid conform to certain rules.

For one thing, much like the production of the homosexual as a distinct species of person in the nineteenth century west, the 'gay' men of Hyderabad see themselves in opposition to the heterosexual population, the boundary defined explicitly by their sexual orientation, rather than anatomical sex or gendered practice. In Suresh's wistful fantasies, 'this line' of homosex/sociality was squarely opposed to 'that line' of heterosexuality. In this 'modern' sensibility, sexual identity is construed in the idiom of consumption—as a function of object choice and of practice defined in those terms. Rather than accept the penetrative/receptive kothi/panthi model described above, both partners in this 'modern' same-sex relationship are reconfigured as 'gay'.

A case in point is Pramod, a handsome middle class man who prided himself on straddling both worlds—that of the 'gay' men as well as the khada-chatla kothis. During my fieldwork in Hyderabad, I heard frequent rumours that Pramod was the partner or panthi of at least one khada-chatla kothi. In fact, Bharat, the khada-chatla kothi who had recently joined the hijra prostitutes claimed that Pramod was her panthi, before he abandoned her. Given the kothis' sex/gender differentiated world, wherein panthis are clearly separate from kothis, how is Pramod's dual identity reconciled within this domain? When I asked Pramod about the rigidity of the division, he answered, 'Not like that. It is not fixed like that. It is not that panthis cannot become kothis and vice versa. After all, we are all gays.' Other 'gay' men I spoke to articulated similar beliefs even if they did not use the kothi terminology. 'You know like top/bottom, bottom/top as some people say? The same way the active partner can sometimes be the passive partner and sometimes be the active. It depends on various things you know,'

Rajeev told me in a conspiratorial whisper, not wanting to be caught divulging these embarrassing details to a woman. Given the classificatory grid I outlined earlier, this is not a notion that appears to sit easily with other kothis. For them, kothis are defined by their desire to be the passive partners, and panthis, who included heterosexual men, are the active, penetrating partners. However, as Kishore, a self-styled 'gay' spokesman stated:

> those are all different… old-fashioned ideas—this kothi, panthi and all this business. It is not fixed like that. Some like to do this way, some like to do another way. But we all like to go with another man. That is the difference. Only those hijras and people talk in that kothi/panthi language like that. Here… we are all just homosexuals or gays, you know.

In this scenario, 'this line' of homosexuality, marked by its modernity as compared to the 'old-fashioned' subject-positions of the hijras and other kothis, is defined in opposition to 'that line' of heterosexuality.

Further, the criteria of membership for this subject-position requires neither official kinship in the manner prescribed for the hijras nor any rhetoric of asexuality. Identifying the pattern of desire—that is, occupying the 'gay' public space of gardens and bus stations in Hyderabad—and acknowledging a desire for other men makes all such individuals *equally* gay, as Kumar implied, without the hierarchical positionings that are so vital to hijra community structure. In addition, within this sexual paradigm the very definition of the players seemingly centres explicitly on their *sexuality* or sexual object choice rather than other aspects of identity such as gendered practice, ritual performance, hierarchical kinship or asexuality, as with the hijras.

A new 'class' of individuals appears to have been created, for whom sexuality indeed seems to have replaced gendered practice as a marker of self-identification.[22] Perhaps two events, more than others, hastened the creation and acceptance of this sexual paradigm. One was the establishment in 1990 of the first magazine for

---

[22] See also Altman, 'Global Gaze/Global Gays'; Balachandran, 'Pink Triangle, Red Lotus or the Bow of the Love-God? Field Data on Emerging Gay Geographies in India', paper presented at the conference on 'Sexualities, Masculinities and Culture in South Asia: Knowledge, Practices, Popular Cultural and the State', 6–8 July 1999, Melbourne, Australia.

'alternative sexualities' titled *Bombay Dost*, and the public 'gay' persona of its chief editor, Ashok Row Kavi. This in turn inspired the establishment of several gay advocacy groups in India—at least sixteen at last count, including two in Hyderabad.

The second facilitating condition was the liberalisation and globalisation of the economy that was initiated in the early 1990s in India. This move not only heralded the entry of multinational companies, greatly increasing the transnational traffic in persons, signs and images, but also reformed import policies and introduced foreign-based satellite television such as the Rupert Murdoch-owned Star TV network with its accompanying baggage of soaps, sitcoms and Hollywood movies into India. These changes facilitated the emergence of an increasingly wealthy upper middle and middle class populace who not only had access to these previously out-of-reach objects and narratives, but, who could, for the first time, also afford them. As Edward Gargan noted in a *New York Times* article that was written shortly after the first 'legal' issue of *Bombay Dost* was printed for circulation, 'most of the homosexuals [in Bombay] are young professionals who work in this city's expanding private sector and whose standard of living is well above the national average.' This point is key to the 'evolving gay culture' according to Ashok Row Kavi. 'There have always been opportunities for gay sex,' he stated to the reporter, 'but the point is that it is now a movement, that it is an evolving gay culture.'[23] Clearly, as I noted earlier, this commitment to gay identification and the political liberation premised on a notion of 'gay culture' does appear to be somewhat different from earlier conceptualisations of sex/gender difference and identity. But, as I argue in the following section, these differences are far more complex, and cannot be neatly dichotomised along the axes of modernity and geography, as some theorists of the 'global gay' school of thought appear to advocate.

The Fluidity of Archetypes

While the simultaneous coexistence of these two somewhat different sexual paradigms was immediately apparent to me, clearly,

---

[23] Edward Gargan, 'Coming Out in India, With a Nod From the Press', *New York Times*, 11 Aug. 1990.

the picture was far more complex. These 'traditional' and 'modern' models were *not* consistently or evenly adopted. Neither, as I gradually realised, were they entirely mutually exclusive. For one thing, the evolution of this 'gay culture' in urban India, despite its transnational origins and ongoing connections, is clearly not isomorphous with its international label. Not only do some of the casual partners of these 'gay' individuals *not* acknowledge themselves as 'gay', being more comfortable with 'traditional' labels such as panthi or khada-chatla kothi; but in addition, it is polysemic images of the *yaar* or the *dost* (very loosely translated as friend) that condition many 'gay' individuals' quest for, and subsequent relationships with, other men. In February of 1999, for instance, a 'conference of gays in the country'[24] was held in Hyderabad entitled 'Yaarian 1999'.[25] One of the self-conscious agendas of this conference was to 'try and identify an indigenous or *desi* terminology for the concept of gay.' As one of the participants quipped, future conferences should be referred to as 'Yaarian–Sari/an', to include a broader spectrum of gender identities and practices specific to India. The Yaarian 1999 conference also occasioned the creation of a national collective named 'LGBT India'—Lesbian, Gay, Bisexual and Transgender Support Groups of India—until such time as a 'more creative, more inspiring...more *desi* (native to the country) name could be determined.'

For, every transnationally received symbol of gayness in India is one that self-consciously emphasises the Indian aspect of identity. While this is most evident in the concerns of the Indian diasporic gay community, it is also apparent in the resident 'gay' population of urban India.[26] In the 1998 anniversary issue of

---

[24] This was the second national 'conference of gays in the country', the first being in Bombay in 1994.

[25] For the plural of *yaar*.

[26] Given the limitations of space, the potential differences/identifications between the gay men and women of the 'diaspora' and those in Hyderabad cannot be explored in this article. For thoughtful analyses related to this issue see G. Gopinath, 'Funny Boys and Girls: Notes on a Queer South Asian Planet', in Leong (ed.), *Asian American Sexualities* (New York, Routledge, 1996); N. Shah, 'Sexuality, Identity, and the Uses of History', in Eng (ed.), *Q&A: Queer in America* (Philadelphia, Temple University Press, 1998); J. Puar, 'Transnational Sexualities: South Asian (Trans)nation(alism)s and Queer Diasporas', *ibid.*. See also issues of *Trikone*.

Bombay Dost, for instance, juxtaposed against articles such as 'A Stonewall Inn Collection,' an exhibit of photographs of white, male actors by 'renowned photographers' such as Costa and Bianchi, are articles that attempt to self-consciously reclaim 'our thousand-year heritage of homoeroticism', as one author maintains.[27]

On the one hand, there are individuals attempting to carve out a unique space on the transnational 'gay' platform by claiming 'local' self-referential labels and invoking culturally-inflected images of the *dost* (friend) in their self-fashioning as gay *Indians*. On the other hand, there are those like Suresh in the opening vignette, who are given tantalising glimpses of this 'modern' sexuality, but do not embrace this 'alternative sexuality' in its upper middle class form. This 'class' of people who refer to themselves as both 'gay' and 'khada-chatla kothi', draw on globally circulating narratives of gayness while simultaneously constructing themselves within local networks of meaning and 'traditional' subject-positions within the hijra/kothi model. Suresh has friends who frequent the 'homo-sex' New Year bashes in Bombay, apparently attended by 'gay men from [various cities across India], as well as those from San Francisco, New York and London', as he informed me, at the same time that his other friends are 'adopted' into the hijra kinship network as daughters and disciples in their hierarchical community structure. Bhabi, for instance, was 'officially' Malathi's daughter in the hijra kinship network, while simultaneously constructing himself both as a khada-chatla kothi and 'gay' in the Public Gardens of Hyderabad. Likewise, Vimal, although now a 'full-time hijra' in Bombay, considered himself a khada-chatla kothi in Hyderabad, actively cruising for male partners with his '"homosex" friends', as he stated it, in the Public Gardens.[28] Similarly, his friend and fellow

---

[27] *Bombay Dost*, Vols. 2 and 3 (1998).

[28] The politics of location and space in the construction of (sexual) identity is a topic of obvious significance in this context. See also R. Bleys, *The Geography of Perversion* (London, Cassell, 1996); B. Colomina, *Sexuality and Space* (New York, Princeton Architectural Press, 1992); Trans. by Donald Nicholson-Smith, H. Lefebvre, *The Production of Space* (Oxford, Blackwell, 1991); E. Soja, *Postmodern Geographies* (London, Verso, 1989); J. N. Brown, 'Black Liverpool, Black America, and the Gendering of Diasporic Space', *Cultural Anthropology*, Vol. 13 (1998), pp. 291–325.

Bombay hijra, Sushil, hosted parties for self-identified 'gay' men, in addition to *jogins*, *zanana* and *khada-chatla kothis*—his 'previous forms', as he stated, or 'other' identities—every time he returned to Hyderabad for a visit.

To further complicate the discursive production of a stable and coherent 'global gay identity,' one can point to the differences apparent within the so-called 'modern gay' community in India. As a recent vituperative exchange on the lgbt_india list-serve between two South Asian self-identified 'gay' activists revealed, not only were there radical differences in their respective constructions of what it means to be 'gay' in India, whether one should 'come out' and confront one's family, and how one should go about doing so, but also differential investments in a 'globalising' rhetoric and 'need for recognition' by the international 'gay' community. As one of the participants in this debate disparagingly stated, possessing even 'a modicum of nationalism' would obviate the necessity for global recognition, a priority for the gay community in India according to the other activist. Likewise, the ideological differences between the two 'gay' advocacy groups in Hyderabad in their constructions of 'gay' identity, and the meanings of Indian 'tradition' and modernity, quite apart from the politics and practice of activism, militate against the emergence of a universal 'western-style…homosexuality in Asia.'[29] 'To see oneself as "gay" is to adhere to a distinctly modern invention, namely the creation of an identity and a sense of community based on (homo)sexuality', Altman states.[30] But clearly, identifications and differences between similarly positioned actors are not as coherent or stable as a global gay identity would presume.

Conversely, on my last visit to Hyderabad, I was entrusted with the task of finding out more about the medical clinic that was apparently established by 'one of our kothis [living] in [a] foreign [country]', as the hijras described a well-known London-based gay activist. 'Last month, one of my "customers" from Saudi [Arabia] told me about it. I believe this clinic is only for us—the kothis here and in the Garden,' Shanti, my hijra friend explained to me, including in her lexical label both her fellow-hijras living in Secunderbad, as well as the 'gay'-identified men frequenting

---

[29] Altman, 'Global Gaze/Global Gays', p. 421.
[30] *Ibid.*, p. 423.

the Public Garden, perhaps the best-known Hyderabadi male, same-sex cruising area. Later that week, when I spoke to some of these self-identified 'gay' men in the Garden, I was reassured that indeed, the clinic was for 'all gays...but please tell the hijras to come only on Sundays.' On further inquiry, I was told that this was because their *izzat* (respect) was at stake: 'If the hijras come during the day, what will people think? Everyone will know this is a "homosex" clinic then, and our izzat will go. You can understand how this will look.... So you tell them,' Rakesh said, somewhat apologetically. In the same discursive move, the hijras are being included as a recognisable 'gay'-identified subjectivity/ community on the one hand, while on the other hand simultaneously being differentiated by the apparently 'traditional' kothi criterion of izzat and sartorial visibility. Interestingly, this differentiation is posited as one that someone like me, perceived by Rakesh as a straight woman '[outside] this line', could easily appreciate and thereby convey to others 'in this line'. Clearly, 'lines' of identification/difference are not merely sexual, but can shift along local frames of reference, revealing varying alignments of sociality.

Finally, not only are the particular articulations of the Indian 'gay' male refracted through different lenses, but so-called 'traditional' subject-positions such as the hijras also construct themselves creatively within this apparently 'modern' matrix. For instance, when an Indian cosmonaut went into space along with a Soviet crew in the 1980s, the president of a hijra organisation in Delhi wrote to the Indian and Soviet leaders, requesting that in the interests of parity, the 'sexually underprivileged' such as themselves be sent into space in future ventures.[31] Likewise, a hijra making a bid for Parliament in 1996 ran under the slogan 'You don't need genitals for politics. You need brains and integrity', explicitly highlighting the hijras' inability to produce children, thereby making them perfect antidotes to the rampant corruption and nepotism of modern Indian politics. In the past year alone, at least two hijras have run for local office and won their elections on this platform. Interestingly, the mainstream political parties including the Congress and BJP are now actively courting hijras

---

[31] 'Clapping Demand,' *The Hindustan Times*, 10 Apr. 1984.

as the new 'sexual' minority. For instance, in a recent interview, Uma Bharati, the controversial spokesperson for the BJP has apparently indicated that her party is extremely open to the idea of fielding hijras as candidates in future elections.[32]

Disjuncture and Difference: Notes Toward a Conclusion

Sedgwick and others have criticised Foucault's early work on the formation of sexual identity as a 'unidirectional narrative of supersession'.[33] As Sedgwick contends, we need to relinquish the narrative of rupture that has sustained the discourse on sexuality in the wake of Foucault. As she states:

> ...issues of modern homo/heterosexual definition are structured, not by the supercession of one model and the consequent withering away of another, but instead by the relations enabled by the unrationalised coexistence of different models during the times that they do coexist.[34]

The present appears to be one of those times in India when apparently different systems cohabit in a single social field. The simultaneous presence of these 'different' sexual classificatory grids in India and their varying emphases on modernity, illustrates the fluid constructions of sexual subjectivity in this region.

Further, as I argue in this essay, the 'unrationalised coexistence' of these so-called 'traditional' and 'modern' models—the 'paradoxical unity ... of disunity' as Berman describes it in a different context[35]—not only questions the facile dichotomies between these very discursive terms, but also blurs the boundaries that define 'gay' identity, both in India, as this article chronicles, as well as

---

[32] 'Voting in a Gender-Bender,' *Indian Express*, 28 Feb. 2000.

[33] Sedgwick, *op. cit.*, p. 46; see also. J. Butler, *Bodies That Matter: On the Discursive Limits of 'Sex'* (New York, Routledge, 1993); R. Morris, 'Three Genders and Four Sexualities: Redressing the Discourses on Gender and Sexuality in Contemporary Thailand', *Positions*, Vol. 2, No. 1 (1994).

[34] Sedgwick, *op. cit.*, p. 47.

[35] M. Berman, *All That Is Solid Melts Into Air: The Experience of Modernity* (New York, Simon and Schuster, 1982).

in the imaginary location of the 'west'. Clearly, the refraction of 'this line' in Hyderabad to reveal several competing paradigms of homosociality, with the concurrent deployment of 'sexuality', 'alliance', corporeality and respect, among other bases of identification, militates against an epistemic disjuncture of any one 'line' or model in favour of another.

7

A Preliminary Report on Emerging Gay Geographies in Bangalore, India[1]

◆ Chandra S. Balachandran

In the higher-order urban centers of India, the concepts of 'gay' and 'lesbian' are recently gaining visibility. These are often new—sometimes confining, sometimes liberating—labels for older patterns of same-gender sexuality. Popular discourse and the Internet are making a considerable contribution to the development of new spaces where sexuality-identities, particularly those of gay men, are being developed and expressed. Transnational movements of people, commodities and consumption patterns are contributing to the increased visibility of a nascent gay population

[1] An earlier version of this essay was presented at the conference on 'Sexualities, Masculinities and Culture in South Asia: Knowledges, Practices, Popular Culture and the State', held at Deakin University, 6–8 July 1999, Melbourne, Australia. The very nature of the development of non-heterosexual spaces renders any data obsolete (usually within a month or two). Data presented in this essay is to be read in this context.

My fieldwork in Bangalore was supported by a Senior Research fellowship from the American Institute of Indian Studies, 1998. Deakin University supported part of the presentation at the conference in 1999. Respondents for the project shared so many details of their personal lives freely and cheerfully. I remain indebted to all of the above for the invaluable assistance which has made this project possible.

in India. However, few empirical studies examine male homo-sexualities in South Asian countries, particularly India, outside the context of public health (HIV/AIDS, STDs and so forth).

This paper, based on a 1998 field project on emerging gay geographies presents a case study of Bangalore. Socio-economic, linguistic and ideological patterns, agendas and other variations were examined using ethnographic interviews and participant observation. The history and process of the formation of gay men's 'safe spaces' explicate tensions (*a*) between the categorical notion of 'gay' and the attempts to accommodate it in an essentially continuous spectrum of traditionally tolerated (even accepted) male-male sexualities, and (*b*) between a tacit social triad (recognition, tolerance, acceptance) and an overt discourse about male–male sexualities in Indian society. At the personal (micro) level, the data informs issues such as individuals' self-identity construction, the struggle with the traditional procreative preoccupation, and the traversal of boundaries between the self-constructed identity-space and heteronormative spaces. At a macro level, new coalitions and networks are forming and the beginnings of a gay polity are being seen.

Indian Gay Spaces and Discourses

The existence of a spectrum of sexualities has always been known in India. Indian culture has even accorded non-heteronormative sexualities some space (albeit limited and marginal) in its rich cultural tapestry. Owing to complex processes of cultural change including (but not limited to) colonial influences, modern India struggles with notions of 'other' (non-hetero) sexualities as aberrations of some kind—often as imports from a decadent West.

Procreative responsibility is very important in the Indian ethos. The community-oriented locus of the individual in Indian society is an important component of his/her identity. The *dharma* (duty) of a man addresses many scales of the realm of action (*karma*)—he must continue the lineage by procreating within wedlock, and conform to the group's normative elements (i.e., he must lead a 'family life'). In this manner, he must also ensure the family's good standing in the larger community (within the immediate geographic space), clan (immediate family space) and larger ethnic/religious/caste-group space. As long as a man shoulders these responsibilities, he might generally consider his sexual intimacies with other men as allowable. Such a man identifies himself not as 'gay' or 'bisexual', but as a 'heterosexual' man or simply a 'man'.[2]

Though *patterns* of same-gender sexualities are not new, *notions* (categorical labels and sexuality-identities) such as 'gay' and their empirical study are relatively new to the Indian landscape.[3] Of late, more or less formalised 'gay' spaces are emerging, which go much further than merely homosocial spaces, in many Indian cities such as New Delhi, Lucknow, Kolkata, Mumbai, Pune, Bangalore, Hyderabad and Chennai. The nascent gay spaces in India form part of a nested hierarchy of cultural spaces. The visible, pervasive and socially approved hetero-normative space (Figure 7.1, A) surrounds all the others.

This space—through its many ideologies, institutions and technologies[4]—places many constraints on the other spaces,

---

[2] D. Dasgupta and D. Purkayastha, 'Being in the Game: Perspectives of Married Indian Men who have Sex with Men', *Trikone*, Vol. 11 (1996), No. 2, p. 10; S. Essajee, 'Rocking the Boat: Anjali Gopalan's Work with Men who have Sex with Men', *Trikone*, Vol. 11 (1996), No. 4, pp. 6–8; S. Khan, *Making Visible the Invisible* (London, UK, The Naz Foundation, 1997); Mahesh, 'On the Verge of Out', *Trikone*, Vol. 11 (1996), No. 1, p. 51; Ramakrishnan, Global Theorisations and Local Contexts—A Study of LesBiGay Rights Movement in the Indian Context, Unpublished dissertation, The University of Warwick, UK; T. Muraleedharan, 'The Writing on Absent (Stone) Walls', *Thamyris*, Vol. 3 (1998), No. 1, pp. 41–57.

[3] J. Holley, 'The Pleasures of Ambiguity', *Trikone*, Vol. 13 (October 1998), No. 4, pp. 14–15; S. Kakar, *Intimate Relations: Exploring Indian Sexuality* (Chicago, The University of Chicago Press, 1990); A. Kala, *Invisible Minority: The Unknown World of the Indian Homosexual* (New Delhi, Dynamic Books, 1991); C. Balachandran, Cultural Geography of KHUSH—A Cybernetic Place for South Asian LesBiGay Interactions, Paper presented at the 24th Annual Conference on South Asia held at the University of Wisconsin, Madison, WI, 20–23 October 1995; C. Balachandran, Geographies of Gay India at Home and in the Diaspora: Some Thoughts, Paper presented at the Annual Meeting of The Association of American Geographers, Charlotte, NC, April 1996; V. Balasubrahmanyam, 'Gay Rights in India', *Economic and Political Weekly*, Vol. 31 (1996), No. 5, pp. 257–58; S. Joseph, 'Gay and Lesbian Movement in India', *Economic and Political Weekly*, Vol. 41, No. 33, pp. 2228–33; G. Reddy, 'Crossing Lines of Subjectivity: The Negotiation of Sexual Identity in Hyderabad, India', this book.

[4] The ideologies, institutions and technologies together constitute a cultural complex, cf. W. Zelinsky, *The Cultural Geography of the United States* (Englewood Cliffs, New Jersey, Prentice-Hall, 1973).

Figure 7.1 Nested Indian male–male sexuality spaces and their relative scales.

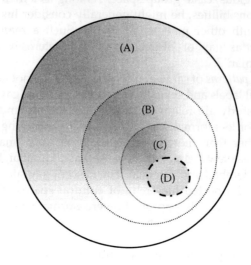

(A) Heteronormative Indian cultural space
(B) Visible male homosocial space
(C) Underground male homosexual space
(D) Nascent gay spaces

marginalising them to a certain extent (note that the spaces in the lower orders of this hierarchy are increasingly marginal in location). Within the context of this larger space, a homosocial space (B) is visibly present and enjoys a certain sanction (largely due to restricted public male-female sexual contact). Further down in the hierarchy is the underground homosexual space (C), which is largely the realm of transitory, situational, as well as long-term male homosexual intimacy. Many publicly heterosexual men express their homosexuality here forming the transitory, situational component of the space. Self-identified, but non-public, homosexual men, who are not publicly heterosexual also, occupy this space (ranging from the transitory to permanent/long-term components of the space depending on the nature of the relationships entered into).

Out of this, a number of men who not only identify themselves as gay, but are also public about it (to varying degrees) are emerging, forming the nascent gay spaces (D). These spaces are less transient and are more strongly identified using constructs going beyond merely physical desires, into the realms of social support structures, and even political activity. At this stage, Indian gay spaces do not show any tendency towards 'ghettoisation' as is common in many Western locales.

Reddy[5] organizes gay spaces thus:

1. Real space—the public and social contexts of interactions.
2. Discursive space—the medium of language to construct identity/space.
3. Cyber space—a uniquely dislocated medium accessed through Internet.

The discursive space is strongly aided by trends in popular discourse, which are slowly, but surely, becoming more open to the topic of sexualities in general and to non-heteronormative sexualities in particular. As generational shifts in culture occur, partly resulting from the globalisation process, urban India is witnessing greater discussion of the concepts of 'gay', 'lesbian', 'bisexual' etc. The popular media is also increasingly covering such topics in a variety of ways ranging from the scandalous to the issues-oriented.[6] As the discursive space achieves greater visibility, and internal clarity, the boundaries it shares with the real and cyber spaces becomes more malleable and porous. Each aspect of this organisation modifies the others in continuous, complex, feedback loops. The boundaries among these spaces are very malleable and are also tense. I will be addressing the traversal of these boundaries, the currency of negotiation, the modalities of access etc. elsewhere. Here, suffice to say that traversals do occur and men have multiple locational identities.

The Cybernetic Frontier

A graduate student who started KHUSH, an e-mail discussion list for gays and lesbians of South Asian origin, in 1993 pioneered the

---

[5] G. Reddy, Unpublished personal communication, 1999.
[6] Altindia.net,1999,http://www.altindia.net/altsex/OUTINGS%20THE%20MEDIA.html.

first cybernetic space for them.[7] Since then, the Internet and increased access to it has led to a significant growth in the number of people accessing the KHUSH list. This access, for many, is a new route to a possible future public self-identification. To those who are already publicly self-identified as gay, this is a medium for pooling activist energies across distance and time. To those who are not sure, or are afraid of going public, this medium offers a degree of anonymity while still allowing contact with others. The cybernetic frontier thus offers a newly ordered space for Indian gays.

What started out in 1993 as a text-based medium accessible to a small number of (largely diasporic) South Asians, is now a medium rich with textual communications (including instantaneous real-time communication using Internet chat facilities such as chat rooms) and also graphics (in the many web pages set up for various interest groups ranging from activism and outreach to pornography). This growth is evident in the number and the distribution of LesBiGay[8] discussion lists and web sites (Table 7.1). At present, KHUSH has been 'reincarnated' as KHUSH-LIST and has a worldwide membership of nearly 600, spanning about eleven countries (Table 7.2).

The cybernetic component is an increasingly important medium of communication, and is leading to greater malleability of the boundaries between the spaces discussed earlier (Figure 7.1). Of the small, but growing, nascent gay population, the subset that accesses and traverses the cybernetic gay Indian space is even smaller (but it is also growing).

It is in the context of the foregoing discussion that India's, particularly Bangalore's, emerging gay geographies are situated.

Cultural Geographic Framework

From a geographic standpoint, we may seek to understand the nascent gay spaces, starting with two fundamental concepts of

---

[7] C. Balachandran, *op. cit.*, 1995.
[8] LesBiGay is a term commonly used to denote lesbians, bisexuals and gays. GLBT (Gay/Lesbian/Bisexual/Transgendered) is also used and is considered more inclusive.

Table 7.1 Selected cities with named LesBiGay lists hosted on egroups.com. Data are as of 8 December 1999

Group	URL	Members
Gay Bombay (gaybombay)	http://www.egroups.com/group/gaybombay/info.html	830
Gay India (gayindia)	http://www.egroups.com/group/gayindia/info.html	369
Gay Delhi (gaydelhi)	http://www.egroups.com/group/gaydelhi/info.html	159
les-gay-bi-trans-mumbai (lgbt-mumbai)	http://www.egroups.com/group/lgbt-mumbai/info.html	127
Gay Bombay WebSite (gaybombayweb)	http://www.egroups.com/group/gaybombayweb/info.html	97
Gay Calcutta (gaycalcutta)	http://www.egroups.com/group/gaycalcutta/info.html	93
Gay Bangalore (gaybangalore)	http://www.egroups.com/group/gaybangalore/info.html	91
Gay Chennai (gaychennai)	http://www.egroups.com/group/gaychennai/info.html	86
Gay Pune (gaypune)	http://www.egroups.com/group/gaypune/info.html	71
Gay Goa (gaygoa)	http://www.egroups.com/group/gaygoa/info.html	65
Gays Resident in India (khushindia)	http://www.egroups.com/group/khushindia/info.html	56
Gay Hyderabad (gayhyderabad)	http://www.egroups.com/group/gayhyderabad/info.html	50
BiIndia—Indian Bisexual Forum (bi-india)	http://www.egroups.com/group/biindia/info.html	41
Gay Cochin (gaycochin)	Http://www.egroups.com/group/gaycochin/info.html	38
Lesbians resident in India (lesbianindia)	Http://www.egroups.com/group/lesbianindia/info.html	29

Table 7.2 Domain information for KHUSH-LIST as of 8 December 1999

Total domain types	526	(most are located in U.S.A.)
Total country domains	36	(U.S.A. does not use a country identifier)
Other (overlaps, etc.)	17	
Total membership	**579**	

Domain types	Description	Number of members
.com	Commercial company (may be an Internet service provider)	402
.edu	Educational institution	66
.net	Network (commercially owned, may be an Internet service provider)	51
.org	Organisation (usually non-profit)	7
Total		**526**

Country domains	Country	Number of members
.au	Australia	4
.fr	France	2
.hk	Hong Kong	1
.id	Indonesia	3
.in	India	12
.nl	Netherlands	1
.nz	New Zealand	3
.sg	Singapore	2
.uk	United Kingdom	7
.za	Zambia	1
Total		**36**

geography: (*a*) *site*, and (*b*) *situation*. *Site* refers to the individual space's location and its internal content, while *situation* refers to the external relationships of this space with other spaces. Despite some work in this direction,[9] there has not been a systematic, in-depth and across-scale empirical study of the spatial characteristics of these populations: HIV/AIDS-related work has touched upon these to some extent but some of the questions that still need to be addressed are:

1. How are these spaces being conceptualised, articulated, enacted, traversed and sustained?
2. What are the characteristics of the boundaries of these spaces, where are they located, how are they defined and what do they represent?
3. Who are the people who populate these spaces?
4. What is the 'gay' identity in the minds of these people? How does their conceptualisation of this identity influence (1) above?
5. How do the extant spaces of the Indian cultural ethos (e.g., gender, caste, religion, socio-economic status, language, location, mobilities) intersect with the emerging gay spaces?
6. Where are the 'formalised gay spaces' emerging, under what cultural geographic circumstances, and what form are they taking?
7. How do the occupants of this space organise themselves?
8. How are these 'gay' spaces situated in relation to the larger cultural geographic space of India and that of the Indian diaspora of the West?

Details of the Project

Aim

My project aimed to explore some broad issues of the spatial production processes (i.e., their creation, maintenance, occupancy and traversal), and the characteristics of emerging gay spaces in

---

[9] L. Cohen, 'The Pleasures of Castration: The Postoperative Status of *Hijras, Jhankas,* and Academics', in S. Pinkerton and P. Abrahamson (ed.), *Sexual Nature, Sexual Culture* (Chicago, the University of Chicago Press, 1995); S. Joseph, *op. cit.*, 1996.

India. Given the short time span of the project, and the nature of the issues involved, I could not realistically aim at anything more than a preliminary study to identify certain issues that would bear further inquiry.

The Target Population of the Study

The gay space of Bangalore is comprised of four broad types of populations (Figure 7.2):

1. Anonymity-seekers who are also group-avoiders:
   This population consists of the informal ('invisible' or 'underground') networks of men who:
   i. Don't identify themselves as gay, but do feel attracted towards other men. A fact which is to be hidden for various reasons. This group also consists of those whom some would call 'MSM' or 'men-who-have-sex-with-men'.
   ii. Do identify themselves as gay, but prefer to keep it carefully hidden except for their involvement with each other in the networks—'forming groups attracts unwanted attention and therefore, groups are to be avoided'.
2. Anonymity-seekers who are also group-formers:
   These men, though in groups, prefer to remain anonymous (many use pseudonyms) for a variety of (readily imaginable) reasons. This population includes a few men who are married and are trying to cope with the issues of their marital status and sexuality. This population is a 'transition' between the first and last types of men—both in terms of typology and also the 'coming out' process.
3. Anonymity-indifferent who are also group-formers:
   These are men who are either deliberately open about their gay sexuality (i.e., 'out') or who are indifferent to the question of anonymity.
4. Anonymity-indifferent who are also group-avoiders:
   I met only a very small number of these individuals. Their location in my scheme is still not clear to me and will require further investigation.

The target population of my study included elements from (2) and (3), the common trait between them being group-formation—i.e.,

Figure 7.2 The progression of urban gay population organisation, group formation and spatial production over time in Bangalore. Note the absence of data for rural areas.

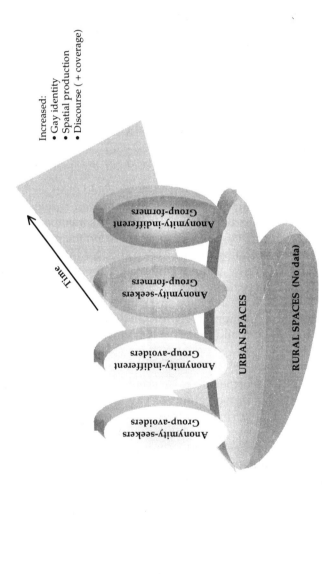

Increased:
• Gay identity
• Spatial production
• Discourse (+ coverage)

Time

Anonymity-seekers Group-avoiders

Anonymity-indifferent Group-avoiders

Anonymity-seekers Group-formers

Anonymity-indifferent Group-formers

URBAN SPACES

RURAL SPACES (No data)

gay men who are members of groups which have as their goal the creation of a safe social space for gays.

I am most familiar with Bangalore and its main languages, and also had had some preliminary in-person contact with the group in Bangalore, so I chose G.A.Y., in Bangalore, as my reference group. This paper is largely based on my Bangalore work, even though the Humsafar Center group in Mumbai was used as a secondary group (eventually) to compare with the reference group.

The History of Bangalore's Gay Spaces

Good As You (G.A.Y.)

In 1994 , a small group of self-identified gay men happened to talk about the need for a safe space where they could meet socially and offer each other support. They initially started meeting at the house of one of the members of the group. As membership grew by word of mouth, the need for more space led the group to meet at the premises of an NGO. This group adopted the name 'GOOD AS YOU' (G.A.Y.), a group for 'anyone who is not exclusively heterosexual.' Since its inception, according to the founders, more than 500 people have availed of the support activities it provides. The group now includes a few lesbians[10] and also conducts outreach work via e-mail (goodas/ou@hotmail.com).

Yavanika-Panchavati Group

Soon after G.A.Y. came into existence, and partly because of this, there emerged a similar group of gay men who also formed a network of their own to address issues common to them and provide a safe space for themselves. There are, however, some cultural differences between this group and G.A.Y.. This particular network or community of gay men has not identified themselves by any particular name. They provide mutual support to a large number of men who are not only self-identified as gay, but also to those who do not clearly place themselves in any category.

---

[10] Mahesh, 'Good as You', *Sangha-Mitra*, Vol. 1 (1998), No. 1, p. 6. This author is different from the one mentioned in Note 2.

Gaybangalore Discussion List

This is one of the lists identified in Table 7.1. At the time of writing, the list appeard to have a largely social networking, not activist, function. The traffic on it is still sporadic, however, crossovers from this list to the other cybnernetic spaces and real spaces (e.g., groups) is increasing.

In addition, of course, there are the non-organised networks among gay men in Bangalore.

The Emerging Visibility of Bangalore's Gay Spaces

For some time, these groups had been functioning very quietly, and any discourse on gay issues had largely been confined to the safe spaces they had created. It has been known for a long time, and in varying degrees, that gay men did exist in Bangalore. But the general public was largely unaware of even the existence of these networks and groups, much less about the issues faced by gay men.

In late 1997, a few students from the National Law School University of India, organised a seminar on gay rights with funding, and other support, from G.A.Y. and other sources. Despite initial resistance from the School authorities, they persisted and the same authorities soon recognised the importance of the event and cooperated with their efforts. Academic discourse spawned social action and, soon, a well-attended and well-received seminar occurred. This suddenly opened up new spaces for discourse on gay issues. Professionals from many fields, activists, and others participated in the proceedings and contributed to the deliberations on a wide variety of topics pertaining to gay issues. Out of the larger effort of the seminar, a diverse group of individuals came together to form a group devoted to the fostering of open discourse on sexualities in general, including all forms of sexuality (hence naming itself SABRANG—meaning 'all colors').[11]

In 1998, the students who had organised the 1997 Law School seminar organised a three-part workshop on gay issues for

---

[11] A. Narain and S. Bavikatte, 'National Law University Seminar on Gay Rights', *Sangha-Mitra,* Vol. 1 (1998), No. 1, p. 18.

first-year law students. I was invited to lead the second part (a screening of 'Wedding Banquet') and the third (a discussion forum). The organisers, noted that the workshop represented a remarkable progress in general openness to discourse, and understanding, on campus as compared to the previous year (1997). Not only were students willing and eager to confront the issues involved and to ask difficult questions, they were also willing to listen carefully to answers given, during the discussions. The professor in charge of a sociology course at the National Law School has since provided for the discussion of these issues as part of the curriculum, so that students are able to see them in their larger social context.

Of late, the popular media in Bangalore has also been covering gay issues. Both the local and national media covered the National Law School Seminar. A few days before I left Bangalore in 1998, I delivered a public lecture on emerging gay spaces in Bangalore which was covered by the local media.[12] Further, a local magazine carried a detailed article on being 'Gay in the Garden City'.

Method

Participant-Observation

Initial contact with G.A.Y. was made through e-mail and followed up with a formal letter addressed to the group as a whole, providing a broad outline of the project. Subsequent to my arrival in Bangalore, after the first few meetings, I was allowed time at several meetings (January–March) to describe my research project in both English and Kannada, and to answer any questions that members might have. G.A.Y. has no roster and members are free to keep their identities confidential if they so prefer. Therefore, suitable assurances to address issues of confidentiality were also given. The project description was printed in Kannada and English and was posted on the bulletin board with takeaway copies being available.

---

[12] C. Balachandran, 'Emerging Gay Spaces of Bangalore', Public lecture, 29 Aug. 1998. http://www.crosswinds.net/~balachandran/lbg/plect.htm>.

In the announcement, I stated that members would not be approached for an interview so as not to put a pressure on them to speak with me. Rather, if a member volunteered to grant me an interview, I would greatly appreciate it. Those interested in volunteering were requested to talk to me personally (confidentially via telephone or by otherwise meeting me if necessary) to schedule an interview. Thereafter, my questionnaire (that had been revised) was ready in both English and Kannada.

The Survey Questionnaire

The survey questionnaire consisted of the following broad themes:

1. Socio-economic status;
2. kinship ties;
3. geographic characteristics; and
4. sexuality characteristics.

Each respondent was given a copy of a detailed consent statement for his personal record. The respondent was given time to read the form and ask any questions he felt necessary. At the outset, the respondent was told about the structure of the questionnaire. After this, the survey questions were read out and the responses were written down. This usually took fifty to sixty minutes. At the end of this, I solicited a follow-up interview with the respondent at a later date.

The survey questionnaire was not used with key actors in the group, but only with the general membership. Ten members responded. Since the total strength of the group was not known, it is hard to estimate what percentage this represents.

The Follow-up Interview

Follow-up interviews were audiotaped if the respondent and the interview location permitted it. Again, before the tape recorder was switched on, the respondent was reminded of his rights and asked if he had any questions before the taping began. After explicit permission from the respondent, the tape recorder was turned on. These interviews were unstructured and picked on themes or points made by the respondent during the questionnaire interview. Of the respondent pool, four kept their appointments for the follow-up interview. Of these, three were audiotaped.

General Findings

The congregational gay spaces of Bangalore are ephemeral but recurrent. The meetings of the groups occur at the same location, but the space is defined by the shared goals for the period of the meeting alone. The three broad locales for congregation are: (a) G.A.Y.'s meeting which takes place at its premises on Thursdays, (b) Yavanika's meeting place in the open area in front of a state government facility on Fridays, and (c) a group that meets in a public park on Sundays. This last-named being older than the other two. (Figure 7.3).

Figure 7.3   The gay spaces of Bangalore and their linkages.

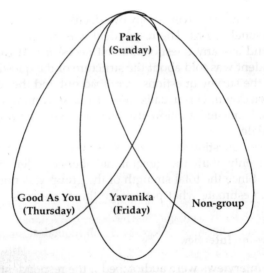

Key actor interviews reveal that the boundary between G.A.Y. and Yavanika has been growing more and more defined in recent times. This boundary is defined not only by personality-differences among the leaders of the two groups, but also by (real or perceived) class differences. The language of discourse used by the two groups is different and is a signification of the class differences that exist between their membership: G.A.Y. is decidedly English-speaking, while Yavanika is more multi-lingual with English as a marginal language of discourse. This sort of division is evident in other urban areas as well[13] where the distinction is often cast in terms of 'posh' and 'vernaculars' (or 'vernacs'). However, class distinctions do not follow neat lines of economic status, because, in both groups there appear to be significant number of people who are at least middle class. Yavanika has a larger number of members of a 'lower' economic status than G.A.Y. However, circumstances did not permit me to conduct interviews with members of Yavanika.

The congregational space of 'The Park' has been reported in the popular media and is fairly common knowledge among gays and non-gays alike. In this space, there is a greater propensity for members of the two groups to mix with each other and also with the non-group (i.e., the group-avoider) populations.

Members of G.A.Y. are generally well connected to western sources of gay images and information. Reading patterns (books, magazines, newspapers), television viewing patterns (types of programs, frequency of viewing), language abilities and contact with friends/relatives abroad (particularly in the West) tend to favor access to external information sources. Also evident is the impact of the recent globalisation process, which has given group members access to information about Indian gays and gay issues in India and in the West.

Participant observation of G.A.Y., and to a limited extent of Yavanika, supports the core-periphery model of information flow (Figure 7.4) even within the groups. The flow of information between the Indian space and the diasporic space directly connects the gay spaces of both. The diasporic space's boundaries are also porous and allow non-Indians, even non-South Asians, access and input. The Indian immigrant in the West is increasingly gaining access to the diasporic gay spaces. The migration streams are restricted to people of a small socio-economic stratum— employed in high-tech industries, affluent, etc. In the Indian space, there is a classic 'core-to-periphery' social stratification—

---

[13] J. Holley, 'The Pleasures of Ambiguity', *Trikone*, Vol. 13, No. 4 (1998), pp. 14–15.

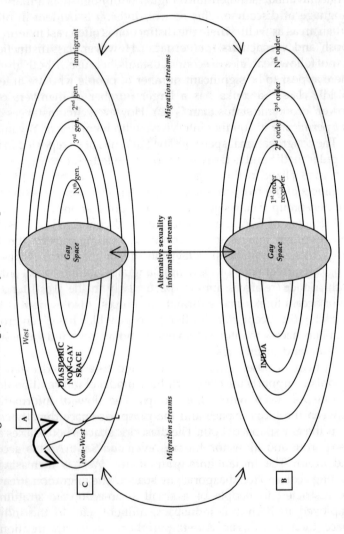

Figure 7.4 Transnational linkages and flows of gay sexuality identities, persons and consumption.

Immigrant

2nd gen.

3rd gen.

Nth gen.

Gay
Space

Migration streams

West

DIASPORIC
NON-GAY
SPACE

Non-West

A

C

Alternative sexuality
information streams

Nth order

3rd order

2nd order

1st order
receiver

Gay
Space

INDIA

Migration streams

B

the first order receivers, located in urban areas, with the closest direct access to incoming information, are also important filters to the flow of information towards the socio-economic and geographic periphery. Increased access to the Internet modifies this stratification only minimally, that too among those already predisposed to being first order receivers.

Two examples illustrate this model. In G.A.Y., those who travel abroad (especially to the West), those who have direct contact with people in the West, and those who access the Internet tend to be higher in the order of receivers (Figure 7.4). In Yavanika, the leadership consists of men who have powerful political connections and are polyglots (English being one of the languages they know). At present, there is hardly any published information for non-English-speakers (except pictorial pornographic material, if at all). Direct non-traditional (i.e., anything other than postal or personal contact) access to networks and information sources outside of the immediate group or the city is largely confined to these first order receivers.

The age range in the groups is usually 18–mid-30s. Those outside that age range tend to be group-avoiders (either due to ignorance about the existence of groups or a lack of interest in joining a group). This lack of interest increases with age. The reasons range from the 'immaturity of people in groups' to their current marital/social status which precludes group membership. Thus, the boundaries between group-seekers and group-avoiders become more rigid with increasing age.

Access to sources of information shows a distinct pattern of gay images more rooted in western-based media than Indian-based media when it comes to films/videos. In the print media, most gay books cited are in English and are Western in origin while the television more or less evenly covers Indian and non-Indian sources. All are, however, in English. Though respondents were familiar with more than one language, none mentioned any non-English (i.e., mother tongue or local language) media as a source of information on gay issues. This is not surprising, as there has really not been any serious coverage of gay issues in the local languages at least in Bangalore.

Most respondents lived with their biological family which included their parents. None reported living with extended families. Their economic status was never less than middle class.

Family relationships showed a wide range from the fairly harmonious to the conflict-laden. In no case was a respondent fully 'out' to his whole family.

Invariably, respondents described themselves as gay and their notion of 'gay' as an 'attraction between two males'. While respondents spoke of attractions, desires, safety and increased understanding of their own sexuality, none spoke of a 'gay lifestyle' per se. Yet, the images they cited as supporting their search were largely from western sources and involve the corresponding notion of a 'gay lifestyle'. The evolution of the category 'gay' and its meaning, and the relation of this to the evolution of a 'gay lifestyle' are at present unclear.

Their understanding of the goals of the group and their personal goals (with which they joined the group) were, of course, closely correlated. In general, the respondents claimed significant fulfilment of the goals with which they had joined the group. The group's political dynamics did not seem to figure in this assessment.

The lives of the respondents suggest, over time, a spatial production model as shown in Figure 7.5. Invisible and discursive

Figure 7.5   Progression of gay spatial production along three axes over time.

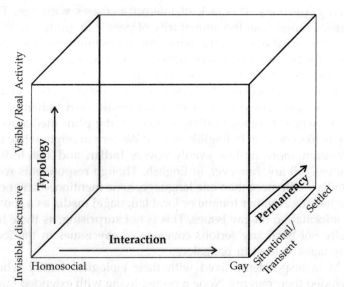

Also follows Reddy (2004)

spaces lead to increasingly visible spaces of identity enactment and assertion. The proliferation of both traditional and newer communication networks facilitates this. As these networks and visibility increase, the potential for the progression of spaces from homosocial to gay spaces also increases. Even those who may not be 'fully' public about their self-identification as gay men may still benefit from the increasing visibility. As the spatial production progresses along the axes of typology and interaction, the potential for longer-lasting interconnections (monogamous or otherwise) increases because the site and situation features of the nascent gay spaces (Figure 7.1, D) are likely to be more conducive to permanency.

In summary, the following general observations may be made:

1. The notion of 'gay' as a category is still nascent even among self-identified gay men who are members of the group.
2. Though this notion is largely connected to western images of gays and a 'gay lifestyles', there is as yet no autochthonous concept of either the category or a lifestyle.
3. Groups are divided along class lines (not just economic) and their language of discourse is an important factor in the division.
4. Boundaries separating the various gay spaces are quite tense.
5. Increasingly open discourses on gays in the local and national media are leading to greater visibility of the groups and their membership is also increasing as a result.

Directions for Future Research

Data from this study still needs considerable analysis—particularly content analysis of the audiotaped parts of the interviews. This study lacks statistical rigor. Rapid changes in the membership of the groups compounds the problem. This appears to be the case in most other groups in India also. Qualitative data poses fewer problems related to its collection, but presents other attendant problems. The nature and quality of information a researcher obtains from (a) casual conversations, (b) during group meetings, (c) during a formalised tape-recorded interview session and (d) the secondary-information networks within a group may vary considerably. Combined with the attrition rates among members, the time-tested build-up of this information is quite a challenge. More time is therefore needed.

My notion of the category and lifestyle termed 'gay' was largely shaped in the United States of America (U.S.A.). My exposure to the intersection of South Asian (a problematic concept for me), Indian and gay spaces occurred fairly late in the U.S.A. beginning only in 1994. When I returned to Bangalore to work on this project, I had already participated in G.A.Y. meetings and several of the long-time ('core') members were personally known to me. I had left home a physical science student and was now returning as a social scientist whose disciplinary exposure to cultural geography was in the West but under an Indian mentor. I was an NRI (Non-Resident Indian). Thus, I was at once an insider, an outsider, an observer, a participant and an agent for change in the group by my mere presence. Any vestigial delusions of '100 per cent objectivity' I might have entertained earlier were quickly dispelled. Despite the extent to which my location was advantageous, it took considerable amount of time before members started volunteering for interviews. This waiting period involved their observation of my interactions and also second-hand reports about me from the other 'core' members. Finally, my fluency and comfort with the Kannada language in interactions with members of the group had a significant impact on reducing what might otherwise have been a longer waiting period. I will be writing about these locational issues elsewhere.

During my work with the group, I found myself coining some Kannada words for use in formal discourse on gay issues (most extant terms are pejorative, and there is no word that really captures the English word 'gay'). I also employed some words used by one or two others who had written in non-pejorative terms. The former introduced new terms, the latter gave greater currency to other words. The evolution of the local language for use in the nascent gay discourse is extremely important.

The evolution of a culture, or a part of it, involves three important groups of traits: (a) mentifacts, (b) sociofacts and (c) artifacts.[14] Language is a very important connecting thread between these

---

[14] W. Zelinsky, op. cit., 1973.

three components of culture. In this case, the gay cultural spaces are emerging amidst a lot of pressure from all sides. Yet, the larger cultural ethos *has* had a history of accommodating new motifs. Part of the struggle will be to reconnect with the ability of the larger culture to accommodate so that the process is made smoother. At the moment, this is not being sought or accessed with much clarity.

The study of gay spaces needs to occur across *class categories* and *place categories* in India. Class is an extremely important issue that pervades the dynamics of gay spatial production but is generally kept in the background. It is brought up only when contentious differences are encountered. Here again, language plays a very crucial role—at the moment, it is divisive, but it has the potential to help find a common ground for the various types of groups mentioned earlier.

Intersecting with language and class is the issue of location in the spatial hierarchy. At the moment, most access to information and discourse is in the higher-order urban places but next to nothing is known about the lower-order urban and rural places.

Any researcher who wishes to gain such a comprehensive understanding needs to spend a long time, *continuously* and *visibly*, among these groups. Many of these men still have a lot to fear and they are not likely to open up freely and honestly to any fly-by researcher. Short-term project data also needs to be treated with considerable caution.

8

Emancipated Bodies/ Embodying Liberation

Debating through Fire[1]

◆ Vikash N. Pandey

> The body is at once the most solid, the most elusive, illusory, concrete, metaphorical, ever present and ever distant thing—a site, an instrument, an environment, a singularity and a multiplicity.[2]

The film *Fire* by Deepa Mehta had evoked considerable public and academic debate. Subsequent to its screening in India, there have been some excellent reviews. In addition, much has been written and debated about the contextual dimensions of the

---

[1] I have benefited a great deal from discussions with Himika Bhattacharya, Priyanka Pandey, S. K. Ravi, Sharit Bhowmik, R. N. Sharma, R. C. Dutta and Ranu Jain. Neena Singh and Premila D'Cruz not only intensely discussed the issues and the film but also constantly commented on (and corrected) earlier drafts. Without Neena's help, the essay would have been almost a non-starter. An earlier version was presented at the National Seminar on Social Identity in the Mass Media in India, held at the Department of Sociology, University of Hyderabad, India. I am thankful to the participants in the Seminar, whose comments and criticism have helped revision. Alpana Thadani and Aruna Chavan took much care in preparing the typescript. My sincere thanks to all of them. However, the usual disclaimer applies.
[2] B. S. Turner, *The Body and Society: Explorations in Social Theory* (London, Sage, 1996), p. 43.

film.[3] I do not intend to repeat all of this. In this essay, I discuss certain elements in Mehta's film in the context of the particular concerns that engage my thoughts. The specific aim is to reflect upon the resurrection of the body—female body, the dilemma of desire–identity and the im/possibilities of emancipatory discourse through the film, Fire. As Zygmunt Bauman has written, 'reflexivity, like rationality, is a double-edged sword. [It is] servant as much as a master, healer as much as a hangman.'[4]

Tilting from structure to agency, certain poststructuralist debates move towards emancipatory possibilities through the primacy of uncoded desire, purposelessness and disorder. The erasure of meaning/purpose and the abolition of referentiality are seen as the rehabilitation of the free play of the body against the enclosure of the normal/the social/order. Deepa Mehta's Fire is related to one such turn: the liberation of the body, particularly the female body. Within this paradigm, the film is an artistic articulation of the politics where, in our day-to-day existence, we are struggling against the boundaries that produce normality. There is a desperate search for locating the struggle—the identity of the agency that would dismantle the organising technologies (a priori moral–social norms and values, the home, the family, etc.) and herald a new era of the play of desire and body. The film offers a solution in the recovery of an emancipated, coherent personhood—the identification of the feminine essence. In sum, the narrative offers an anxiety-ridden spiritual resolution of the dilemma of desire and identity.

From Inscription to Free Play

It is the threat to male ownership of women. It is fear of Fire—what if women really begin to claim their own bodies as their own?[5]

---

[3] Such as S. Ghosh, 'From the Frying Pan to the Fire', Communalism Combat (Jan. 1996), pp. 16–19; M. E. John and T. Niranjana, 'Minor Politics: Fire, Hindutva and Indian Culture', Economic and Political Weekly, Vol. 34, Nos. 10 and 11 (1999), pp. 581–84; and C. M. Naim, 'A Dissent on Fire', Economic and Political Weekly, Vol. 34, Nos. 16 and 17 (1999), pp. 955–57.

[4] Z. Bauman cited in U. Beck, 'Risk, Societies and the Provident State', in S. Lash, B. Szerzynski and W. Wynne (eds), Risk, Environment and Modernity (London, Sage, 1996), p. 39.

[5] M. S. Kapur, 'Fear of Fire', Communalism Combat, Jan. 1999, p. 20.

In *Fire* we see that the desirous body of the woman necessitates social and self-regulation. She is required to be a body, an object for her master's physical needs, and also a laboratory for his spiritual salvation. She is supposed to just 'be there', as and when required, for pleasure, for reproduction and for the purposes of her husband's experiments in abstinence. When she is not available in these ways, male-hood is threatened and the whole facade of the good-natured husband and his 'innocent' religiosity and dharmic orientation collapses. Similarly, the taken-for-granted ownership of the female body, contemptuously looked down upon because of its dependence, evaporates. This resurrection results in violent attempts to regain female bodies through the hopeless, and quite late, assertion of male-hood. However, male bodies are not *desired* any more. Besides, the moral and social hypocrisy of the home, marriage and the husband–wife relationship is exposed. In the horror of the fire, Radha is left alone and Ashok chooses to take care of Biji (the old mother-in-law: the immobilised and mute carrier of patriarchal values and norms). After illuminating the bankruptcy of the home, the fire completes its double performance of destruction and creation by dismantling the home and facilitating the emergence of the emancipated female self and sisterhood. The fire is caused by the assertion of living through desire. Initially suppressed, then hesitant and ultimately unapologetic, the female body (Radha) proclaims: 'without desire there is no point in living.... I desire to live. I desire Sita. I desire her warmth, her compassion and her body. I desire to live again.'

What *Fire* articulates is the deep split between eroticism and emotional attachment in the heterosexual relationship: when wives threaten to become unavailable, the men of the house are erotically charged; and when the women are caring, they are perceived as sexually unstimulating, by the husbands, as they are already the conquered ones. On the contrary, however, the symbiosis of the erotic and the emotional in the female is because of equality and similarity, making 'women-loving-women' a more authentic, emancipatory fulfilment of desire. For women, sexuality is developed not with reference to the husbands who are unavailable for caring relationships, but in relation to the person (Radha–Sita) with whom the deepest attachment is formed. This is the promise of the lesbian relationship.

Such interrogation of masculinist norms and images exposes the regulation of desire and sexuality, and the subjugation of the female body, through which the home and the social order are achieved and maintained. Against this, *Fire* posits an autonomous, positive femininity and a portrayal of the emancipatory potential of desirous female bodies.

Fire seems to have worked on the following premise. Subordinations are inscribed on the female body, and there are no pre-given natural sexual differences; there are marked bodily differences, but neither is it immutable, nor biologically pre-ordained. One needs to see through the privilege accorded within two binary nomenclatures: reason over passion and male over female. These pairs are marked as sexed bodies of man and woman, where mind and reason are associated with men and masculinity, and body and passion are associated with women and femininity. As a result, the control of women by men is warranted.

One such inscription is through *karwa chauth*, which produces the ritualised female body. This is an annual ritual when dutiful wives fast an entire day for the long lives of their husbands. The fast is broken after the sighting of the moon and after they receive their husbands' blessings. It attempts to tame and formalise libidinal intensities, regimenting 'the body's movements into "behaviours", which then have interpersonally and socially identifiable meanings and functions within the social system.'[6]

However, the desiring bodies are also sites of struggle and resistance against such fantasies of coherent and ordered body images. There is always a gap, a discontinuity, between the unified, totalised body image and the lived body that is largely fragmentary—a gap between identity fixation and libidinal fluidity. Through libidinal free-play, psychic energy is discharged, desire is fulfilled through the 'unhindered mobility of cathexis'.[7] According to Lyotard 'the flow of libido...foster[s] the decoding...effects of the unconscious...[in a] highly political battle over the structuration of the unconscious in the everyday world.'[8]

---

[6] E. Grosz, 'Bodies and Knowledges: Feminism and the Crisis of Reason', in L. Alcoff and E. Potter (eds), *Feminist Epistemologies* (New York, Routledge, 1993), p. 196.

[7] S. Lash, *Sociology of Postmodernism* (London, Routledge, 1990), pp. 99–100.

[8] J. F. Lyotard, *The Postmodern Condition: A Report on Knowledge* (Manchester, Manchester University Press, 1984), p. 58.

Emancipatory hope lies in the release of this movement: in the transgression of referentiality into the aesthetics of desire and disorder. This, in short, is the journey from referentiality to passion.

Such is the resurgence of the desirous body against inscriptions. In *Fire*, this metamorphosis occurs on the tyrannical day of *karwa chauth* which is the high tide of the textual incorporation of the female body. The metamorphosis denotes the micro-politics of unleashing libidinal flow which collapses the closure of the unconscious, desire, sexuality and the body. Now let us turn to the politics of desire in *Fire* that constitute my proposals for debate.

From Revolt to Retreat?

> (D)esire does not desire satisfaction. To the contrary desire desires desire.[9]

Fire stands at the crossroads, being against the facade of masculinist identity-marking, and at the same time, offering a metaphysical destination for the feminine self. In the last scene:

> Radha and Sita are reunited at the shrine of Hazrat Nizamuddin famed for his intense and homoerotic bonds with the legendary poet Amir Khusro. The film ends with the women in embrace within this symbolic space.[10]

'And they lived happily ever after!' I am not very sure whether in *Fire*, the lesbian relation/desire is already present (if suppressed) or it is a potential to be realised in a golden land of the emancipated female self. Either way, it is a 'romantic naturalisation of female bonds'[11] producing the illusion of an inner sexual essence or psychic gender core. Such an image of a monolithic and homogenous femininity subordinates the lived particularities to an

---

[9] M. C. Taylor and E. Saarinan, cited in Z. Bauman, *Work, Consumerism and the New Poor* (Buckingham, Open University Press, 1998), p. 25.

[10] Ghosh, *op. cit.*, p. 19.

[11] J. Weeks, 'Sexual Identification is a Strange Thing', in C. Lemert (ed.), *Social Theory: The Multicultural and Classical Readings* (Boulder, Westview Press, 1993), p. 636.

imagined universal.[12] Moreover, such a universal carries the potential to repress and regiment diverse desires.

This leads me to raise once again the problem of the governance of the human body—the link between the policing of sexuality and the production of forms of sexuality. I am drawing attention to the two-fold imageries in the film: differential treatment of the 'peripheral' sexualities—masturbation and fantasising by the male servant, and the lesbian (sensuous) sexuality between the two ladies of the house. Both are the effects of the policing, suppression and inequalities to which male and female bodies are subjected in a given middle class household, and which in their counter-insurgencies become productive of pleasure and of the second hand gratification of desire.

For the moment, let us concentrate on the lesbian relationship (I will discuss the issues related to the servant in the next section). In *Fire* the lesbian relationship seems to be only a proxy relation caused by the unavailability of the husbands. Such a rational explanation of emergent 'other' sexual desires makes desire secondary, a derivative of the social. There are few (including Deepa Mehta) who have argued that the film is not about lesbianism. If so, then, one of the possible suggestions of this articulation may be that good/erotic husbands will produce good wives. This comes closer to the form of pop psychology and rational calculation of sexual desire: an image which, if men chose to adopt it, would rectify the malfunctioning of the family system. It constitutes a sort of therapeutic dose for the conversion of desire and emotions into rational communication.

I am not suggesting that the idea of the suppression of lesbian desire, ascribed to the masculinist hierarchy, is not a valid one to a great extent. Also, the film's celebration of the desirous female body and of lesbian sexuality does not lapse into another affective intensification of the family space. However, it recodes sexual desire and bodies. The patriarchal denial of the female body is refilled by the recovery of the feminine core—a Self and Home beyond home. Through this process, the flow of sexual desire collapses into an achieved destiny—'and they lived happily ever after'. An ambivalent and uneven libido is tamed into a hyper-real

---

[12] J. Bulter, 'Imitation and Gender Insubordination', in Diana Fuss (ed.), *Inside/Out: Lesbian Theories, Gay Theories* (New York, Routledge, 1991), p. 30.

liberation of spiritual merging at Nizamuddin Auliah's *dargah*, where there can be no failure of normality. Homelessness and an open-ended play of desire get bounded to the holism of another ideal 'couple'. Behind this 'new desiring asceticism'[13] seems to be the idea that as a playful creature in search of personal satisfaction, I can contact my Higher Self and then everything else will take care of itself.[14] Such regularised sexuality and constricted desire seems to suggest that a particular desire can be eliminated and replaced by another coherent, monogamous desire embodied in a female couple. This marks sexuality as rational, 'subject to quite a degree of conscious (explanation) and control'.[15] But, is desire so bounded, closed or rational? Does this emancipated spiritual merging 'forever' coincide with the forms of lived sexuality?

Desire points to the excess of meaning, an excess that eludes its codification. The uncertainty of desire does not allow closure into the categories of male/female or a coherent sexual identity and behaviour. After destabilising the norm of heterosexuality, we cannot bind sexuality to alternate norms. Sexual desire is 'fluid, not fixed, a narrative that changes over time ...'.[16] It raises the difference to the level of the deferral of closure, beyond its resolution in any metaphysical destination. In other words, it is the non-fixity of desire that destabilises the sexual boundaries and defers the marking of sexual differences into identity. Thereafter, there is no metaphysical 'Self' (male or female) which can be recovered. Seen from this perspective, naming the endless play of desire will always be a deliberate imposition of certain kinds of closure—a re-enactment of metaphysical authority. 'The experience of the politics of feminism demonstrates that it is simply too easy to speak of changing images.... Sexuality is stubborn and excessive.'[17]

In trying to find a new harmonious marriage between the desirous body and the coherent self, Mehta relocates emancipatory struggles into the spiritual Self, Home and Destiny. Binding sexuality and its ambivalence to the eternal, authentic love of a couple

---

[13] Turner, *op. cit.*.

[14] See K. Wilber, *A Brief History of Everything* (Boston, Shambhala, 1996), p. 315.

[15] J. Ryan, 'Psychoanalysis and Women Loving Women', in T. Lovell (ed.), *British Feminist Thought: A Reader* (Oxford, Basil Blackwell, 1990), p. 245.

[16] M. Garber cited in K. Manral, 'Bi, bi, love', *Saturday Times*, 6 Mar. 1999, p. 1.

[17] P. Adams, 'Family Affairs' in Lovell (ed.), *op. cit.*, p. 267.

(Radha–Sita) is almost a spiritual solace/justification for the desirous bodies. Instead of facing the polymorphous, protean existence of decentred bodies and concurrent homelessness, a hyper-real eternal Home/Self is contrived. Hence, *Fire* betrays our contemporary anxiety: a desire for a non-disciplinary, free-floating body/sexuality and an urge to get 'true' love, faith and eternal companionship.

By celebrating the romantic twist of the body against the corrupting suppression of passion, *Fire* vocalises the contemporary repulsion against gendered hierarchies. At the same time, it projects love and passion as essential feminine qualities. Passion is re-formulated into a transcendental gendered identity, even as the critique of the general patriarchal fear of the non-rational and the unconscious disrupts the masculine home.

As mentioned earlier, the film exposes the marking of the female body and normalising devices which manufacture female distinctiveness and confinement. This normality is the technology which constitutes 'home' as an enclosed space and the dichotomy of inside–outside. The normal space of the home-inside is the comfortable, safe surrounding walls of family affairs. It means closed-ness, for the 'interns'—ladies, servant and the masters of the house. It is because of these markers that it is clear that Sita looks like someone who would commit the crime 'Sita madam is too modern'. She falls out of the range of normality and, therefore, the 'normal ones' are likely to be anxious about her presence.

Radha and Sita both find the circumstances of the home oppressive, and move towards questioning the territorialisation of life/body. But for Radha, it is not easy, because the call of freedom, against the enclosures within which minds/bodies are locked, implies moving out of the home. The transgression of the home-boundary also means dissolving her own (hitherto) self-understanding and giving up the comforts/consolation of a safe enclosure.

As M. Schoolman argues:

> Are the homeless not seeking...fields that circumscribe modern experience and fix our identities? Do the homeless articulate a desire in each of us to disappear, to become anonymous and thus escape the new enclosures?...The homeless would remind us of the freedom missing from our lives, make us aware of the enclosures

within which we live, suggest what distances we must travel in order to step outside our identities'.[18]

Precisely because of such connections between the home and oppression, homelessness is the open space which denies any enclosures. At the same time, this incites homesickness, a longing for a new enclosure, identity, sense of purpose, place and security. Desperately searching for a ground to stand on and a home to rest in, we threaten to revert back to new enclosures, new normalisation and new boundaries: 'Home ... as a private place ... a place of fixed meaning where one is protected from disorientation ...'.[19]

And that takes us back home; if not to a patriarchal home, then to a spiritual home; if not to the ideals of heterosexual love, then to a homosexual one; if not to the lanes of Lajpat Nagar, then to Nizamuddin Auliya's Dargah. This double move dismantles the first home and, then, goes on to dream the second one as the Normal, Solid, Natural, Final—where the contingent character of the desirous body is settled forever. It is used as an instrument for the transgression of established structures and then for the reorientation of the life/body to be at home and at rest in another destination. This quest to achieve coherence and clarity for our lives, bodies and selves further confines alternate governing principles of gender, sexuality and identity. Difference claims lie in questioning universal claims and, despite this, some universalistic assumptions make a backdoor entry. The creation of the female as the 'other' becomes the ground from which emerges the transcendental female self.

Fire constructs women's emancipation as released from the reservoirs of human desire. But will desire allow its fluidity to get submerged into another bondage, that is, the singularity of a body/sex? Ultimately, for those of us anxious to find a place of peace, living out ambivalent desires and inconsistencies would still be undesirable, perhaps even unimaginable. Hence the security of the female Self—a pure, compassionate lesbian pair! To what extent is such a state not (*a*) a repetition of the endless hero–heroine, now heroine–heroine, meeting in their heavenly

---

[18] M. Schoolman, 'Series Editor's Introduction' in T. Dumm, *Michel Foucault and the Politics of Freedom* (Thousand Oaks, Sage, 1996), p. 17.

[19] T. L. Dumm, *United States* (Ithaca, NY, Cornell University Press, 1994), p. 153.

abode; and (h) an encoding of the free libido? Are we then not talking about female emancipation on this promise of a return to that pre-social identity, namely, the unitary-absolute female Self?

Such aesthetics of *Fire*, with its proposal of self-realising personalities, faces a violent outburst—the protest against *Fire* in the larger social context—and against Sita and Radha in the film. Because 'self-realisation is independence, resistance to enculturation', it is a cause of worry for the forces of order and civilisation. At the same time, there are traces of such anxiety in *Fire* as well: self-realisation is a dangerous game for its inherent 'excessive independence or downright eccentricity'. '[I]t would be a fluke if such a character were to remain completely monogamous … the self-realiser is usually ill-mated.'[20] Germaine Greer notes:

> A woman who decides to become a lover without conditions might discover that her relationships broke up relatively easily because of her degree of resistance to efforts to 'tame' her … as a figure of protean existence … not the lifelong, coherence of a mutually bound couple, but the principle of love that is reaffirmed in the relationship of the narcissistic self to the world of which it is a part. It is not the fantasy of annihilation of the self in another's identity …[21]

I wonder how self-realising Radhas–Sitas would respond? They seem to be in the company of many desirants eager to consume New Age spiritual packages.[22]

---

[20] G. Greer, 'The Ideal', in Lovell (ed.), *op. cit.*, pp. 15, 16.

[21] *Ibid.*, pp. 16–17. Greer goes on to quote S. E. Gay, '… who are the most part brought together through attraction of passion … would be as far asunder as the poles'.

[22] For a discussion on societal and philosophical context and the interlinkages between the New Age Movement and Postmodernist politics of desire, see my 'In the Midst of Anxious Times' in S. Menon, *et al.* (eds), *Scientific and Philosophical Studies on Consciousness* (Bangalore, National Institute of Advanced Studies, 2000). *Fire* also ends up with the similar desperate dreaming of soul–body merger, harmony, fusion and overcoming the contemporary human state of self-alienation: 'the two lovers met in the rain at Nizamuddin's tomb. Their tears and the rain dousing out the fire. Radha comes through this final *agni-pariksha* unharmed. Her love for Nita (Sita in the original version but changed to Nita when the film was screened for Indian audiences) hasn't made her impure, thus providing with an elaborate directorial flourish that love, hetero, homo or sapphic conquers all. See what I mean about the symbolism?' J. Banerji, 'Fire and Fury', *Biblio*, Vol. 3, Nos. 11 and 12 (1998), p. 22.

Difference or Essence?

The poststructuralist proposition that meanings are not natural or neutral has intensified the challenges to the masculinist idea that women's subordination is rooted in a pre-cultural, biologically ordained, unequal sexual difference.[23] The body is in dispute and there is large question mark about sexual essence. Now the postmodernist distrust of metaphysical absolutes implicates sexual dualism and the very idea of a sexual identity. As Lyotard points out, 'sexual difference is a paradigm of an incompleteness of not just bodies, but minds too. Of course, there is masculinity in women, as well as femininity in men.'[24]

Consequently, instead of a unified presence, there is a lack of unity or oneness of being, and an incompleteness of identity. Sexual identity is always fractured through an unconscious desire, something which always exceeds meaning and representation. Rose has argued that the unconscious 'reveals...the failure of identity...there is a resistance to identity at the very heart of psychic life.'[25] Extra-libidinal forces organise us to live as sexed males/females and as encoded sexualities. However, the point is to question it; in other words, to counter the fixity of the body and the ideas of sexual essence and identity. After all, a critique of an 'original sexual identity' is the initial point of departure from the patriarchal knowledge–power nexus. An assertion of a distinct female identity would be a repetition of the presumption of a singular reality, pre-existent representational categories and an unambiguous identity. It would be a retreat into biological/ psychic determinism.

What we see in *Fire* are certain initial unsettling gestures: giving back to men what they feared most—an irrational, natural female body. Such 'weakness' is turned into the very reason for any 'pure', 'uncontaminated' living of the female body (desiring life

---

[23] Earlier, Freud's idea of bisexuality, trans. by J. Strachey, Freud, 'Femininity', in *New Introductory Lectures on Psychoanalysis*, Vol. II (London, Penguin, 1991), pp. 145–69 and Simone de Beauvoir's critique of the notion of a fixed female essence had already broached this issue. See, trans. by H. M. Parshley, Simone de Beauvoir, *The Second Sex* (London, Penguin, 1949).

[24] Trans. by G. Bennington and R. Bowlby, J. F. Lyotard, 'Can Thought Go on Without a Body?', in *The Inhuman* (Cambridge, Polity, 1991), p. 20.

[25] J. Rose, 'Femininity and Its Discontents', *Feminist Review*, Vol. 14 (1983), p. 91.

and not negating it in favour of death). But then, it works the other way around as well: accepting the construction of the female body as a mirror-image of the masculine. In *Fire*, the lesbian challenge, therefore, has worked from the marginalised position, a working which is both within and beyond the bounds of that marginality. No doubt, it subverts the existing boundaries. By exposing such operations, the anxiety-ridden, homophobic disciplinary regime is challenged. Yet, presuppositions of the 'feminine' are also harnessed. In this sense, identity politics is an erasure of difference. And yet, in the game, identity politics re-articulates otherness— that is, it questions identity and reasserts it, and erases the codification of female and then re-codifies it. Interestingly, such a gesture not only negates a fractured, non-unitary, undecidable human subject and desire, but also compromises the very politics of female emancipation by erecting it as the mirror-image of the unitary-absolute male self.

This is not to naively advocate throwing out the baby with the bathwater, where lesbian desire is the baby and the construction of the female body as an embodiment of the irrational and the natural, the bathwater. And, lest we forget: 'men are able to dominate ... because women take on the function of representing the *body*, the *irrational*, the *natural*, or other epistemologically devalued binary terms.'[26] In spite of participating in the discourse of female emancipation by challenging masculinist metaphysics, Mehta's politics of identity chooses to carry on the burden of the unitary, primary, universal feminine essence associated with women.

Let me turn to another instance of revolt and retreat. We know that the domestic and familial activities ascribed to women facilitate the idea of a fundamental and *a priori* gender difference. Nancy Chodorow's famous work used one such representation— mothering—to construct gender identities and to argue for overturning the masculinist hierarchy and dominance.[27] For her, this monocausality becomes the foundation of two selves: male

---

[26] E. Grosz, 'Bodies and Knowledges: Feminism and the Crisis of Reason', in L. Alcoff and E. Potter (eds), *Feminist Epistemologies* (New York, Routledge, 1993), p. 209.

[27] N. Chodorow, *The Reproduction of Mothering: Psychoanalysis and the Sociology of Gender* (Berkeley, University of California Press, 1978).

and female. This view has been criticised because it assumes that:

(i)   everyone has a deep sense of self which is unitary and constant throughout life;
(ii) this 'Self' is singular and unified with a gender, and is different between male–female bodies, irrespective of class, race and ethnicity variations; and
(iii) everything else is a derivative of this Self: that is, everybody bears traces of their masculine or feminine gender identity.[28]

Now, this view is supposed to facilitate ideas of a female identity, of sisterhood and ties between women. However, such a construction of the female self around motherhood (and, therefore, caring, authentic intimacy and love) is at the cost of marginalising many women and repressing differences. For example, those who cannot be 'mothers', or choose not to be, get excluded.[29] We know how oppressive it has been for real women. In *Fire*, this 'identity' of women is challenged by Radha and Sita: Radha, who has 'failed' to deliver offspring to the family; and Sita, who revolts against being put into place as a reproductive machine, and against performing her divine duty of mothering.

Radha's revolt culminates in retreat: the recovery of the true female self and sisterhood between Radha and Sita. So an 'original' idea still prevails, or rather, it is reinvented through the essential feminine qualities of authentic intimacy and love; this time caring without the burden of motherhood. Through the emergence of lesbian rights and desires in *Fire*, the very idea of a female essence in terms of motherhood is questioned as the patriarchal technology of power. Paradoxically, this female essence gets reinscribed through the recovery of the authentic female self. Vestiges of meta-narratives continue to haunt *Fire's* 'gynocentric' alternatives to mainstream androcentric perspectives.'[30] For those 'who have not fully abandoned the universalist

---

[28] N. Fraser and L. Nicholson, 'Social Criticism with Philosophy: An Encounter between Feminism and Postmodernism', in S. Seidman (ed.), *The Postmodern Turn: New Perspectives on Social Theory* (Cambridge, Cambridge University Press, 1994), p. 253.

[29] *Ibid.*, pp. 254–55.

[30] *Ibid.*, p. 256. Various feminist scholars have spoken against such universalised pretensions of 'gendered' identity with reference to working-class women, women of colour and diverse sexual preferences (including lesbian ones).

pretensions of the latter... this represents the continuing subterranean influence of those very mainstream modes of thought and
inquiry with which feminists have wished to break.'[31]

Let us turn to the scene where we see the younger brother
Jatin's mechanical, insensitive sexual act performed on his wife,
Sita. From the beginning, till he 'finishes the job', the act is carried
out without any tenderness or concern for Sita's feelings; upon
completion, he simply turns his back on her and goes to sleep. The
violence and brutality of the act is made apparent by the way in
which Sita gets up and finds the bedsheet soaked with blood. She
cleans up the 'mess' alone, and simultaneously another mess gets
cleaned up in her mind, the next time Jatin is refused.

Thus far, it is a sensitive and symbolic portrayal of existing
oppressions and the struggle to follow. That Sita had 'preserved'
her body for her husband indicates the psychic inscription: women's
desire and gratification are supposed to be expressed only in
relation to their marriage and husbands. In addition, one may
argue (I am referring here to various personal discussions) that
Mehta has used the timeless imagery of the 'virgin wife' in order
to highlight the trauma and brutality of women's experiences.

Nonetheless, I cannot help but see the other side of this reproduction of the myth of the virgin bride. It again reinforces the idea
that 'woman-loving-woman' emerges only when her desire is not
met through her (uncaring) husband and (unhappy) marriage.
One is left wondering about the compulsion to portray victimhood
through the imagery of a virgin bride. Would the brutality of the
sexual act, performed by an insensitive, 'pompous fool', be less
without this portrayal? Would the intensity of the oppression and
trauma faced by Sita over her body and psyche become lighter?
This is a Bollywood type picturisation of trauma and oppression;
but, the point is not that simple, it is also, an encoding of female
pain in blatant Hindutva masculinist imagery.

Seen from this angle, *Fire* shows conflicting traces of dissent
against the mechanisation of female bodies on the patriarchal
track, with a concomitant essentialist structuring of gender identity. To use Fraser and Nicholson's expression, *Fire* propositionally
decries essentialism even whilst performatively enacting it.[32] There

---

[31] *Loc. cit.*.
[32] N. Fraser and L. Nicholson, *op. cit.*.

is a vocalisation of a variety of bodily desires and then an imposition of a monotonous similarity on the 'female' body: women
being 'drowned in the great tide of womanliness'.[33] To repeat the
earlier point, *Fire* depicts a desperate search for Self and Identity
after deconstructing them. Seen this way, I feel, the film undercuts
hierarchies in the 'family' but does not go far enough. In terms
of the lesbian relationship, it undercuts sexual polarity and
gendered inscriptions (including women such as Biji spitting on
Radha's face) but once again, not enough.

Other Differences

Difference is the lack of identity or sameness. A term derives its
primacy through the suppression of difference. However, replacing the 'higher' term with the 'lower' term would still be a
'hierarchy with a higher' term and, therefore, ripe for further
overturning. To keep the process/flow from degrading into another structure/hierarchy, difference has to proceed to a second
moment. Thus, it is a perpetual double moment against the
metaphysics of presence: identity.[34] The differential nature of the
wor(l)d cannot be bounded into a singular identity. Thereby, there
is no simple location of the female Self, body or identity. Joan Scott
argues that:

> ... there needs to be at once attention to the operations of difference
> and an insistence on differences but not a simple substitution....
> The resolution of the 'difference dilemma' comes neither from
> ignoring nor embracing difference as it is normatively constituted.
> Instead, it seems to me that the critical feminist position must
> always involve *two* moves. The first is the systematic criticism of
> the operations of categorical difference, the exposure of the kinds
> of exclusions and inclusions—the hierarchies—it constructs, and
> a refusal of their ultimate 'truth'. A refusal, however, not in the
> name of an equality that implies sameness or identity, but rather
> (and this is the second move) in the name of an equality that rests
> on differences—differences that confound, disrupt, and render
> ambiguous the meaning of any fixed binary opposition. To do

---

[33] E. Wilson, 'Forbidden Love' in Lovell (ed.), *op. cit.*, p. 178.
[34] J. Derrida, *Writing and Difference* (Chicago, The University of Chicago Press,
1978).

anything else is to buy into the political argument that sameness is a requirement for equality....[35]

In *Fire,* a break in the deconstruction of inscribed bodies leads to a new formalism, where both nature and fundamental sexual differences are reinstated in the ideal of the unisex, self-realising female personality. It is a form of psychic essentialism which may be 'almost as debilitating...as the biological essentialism it displaces.'[36] This is starkly apparent in one move: there are only middle class women in *Fire,* not even a maidservant. There is only a male servant, Mundu.[37]

This raises the issue of social hierarchy and female identity. If we are arguing against a totalised, static femininity and the masculine body, then we cannot ignore the systems of hierarchy other than the sexual, 'or they too will produce no more than an anti-humanist *avant garde* version of romance.'[38] That is exactly what seems to have happened in *Fire.* The other social hierarchy is represented by Mundu, the servant. His uneasy presence had to be deferred in the imagination of the feminist identity. In fact, the facilitation of the pure feminine world gets triggered as an open revolt following the perverted male servant's actions of peeping into the bedroom and reporting to the male master of the house. This ultimately leads to the recovery of the female 'Home beyond Home', and the servant becomes homeless, being thrown out by the male master. This expulsion protects the female protagonists from any humanitarian guilt. A relational-compassionate, non-violent, egalitarian feminine essence is engendered. The ladies' hands are not soaked in the blood of other social hierarchies. At the same time, this narration helps to intensify the brutality of malehood.

---

[35] J. W. Scott, 'Deconstructing Equality-Versus-Difference: Or, the Uses of Poststructuralist Theory for Feminism', in Seidman (ed.), *op. cit.,* p. 298.

[36] T. Lovell, 'Introduction' , in Lovell (ed.), *op. cit.,* p. 190.

[37] Regarding the silence surrounding other hierarchies (including 'other' women, as mentioned earlier), do we conclude from this that the subjectivity of women of other classes, and with other sexual orientations/desire, cannot be authentically talked about in a fictional narrative by a middle class woman narrator, however sympathetic s/he may be to such differences?

[38] C. Kaplan, 'Pandora's Box: Subjectivity, Class and Sexuality in Socialist— Feminist Criticism', in Lovell (ed.), *op. cit.,* p. 346.

The new category of a feminine self is marked from the beginning by a two-fold exclusion—masculinity and class. The autonomy of the female inner self, body and psyche and the moral triumph in its resurgence is projected as progressive political thought. Is exclusion such an essential element of the emancipatory struggle that it must choose either gender or class? Probably not so, at least if the self itself is a *protean* existence devoid of any essence or foundation.

But these social contestations are superfluously referred to in *Fire*: Radha gets disturbed for a while after her angry outburst (when she finds Mundu watching blue films and masturbating). Mundu reacts: 'What to do, madam? Work, work and work throughout the day!'. He then, plays his threatening trump card— that he will talk about whatever is going on between Radha and Sita. Radha's moral dilemma is that she is, herself, engaged in 'morally degrading' sexual gratification. Sita helps her to resolve this dilemma. 'Finally, it is Radha's unapologetic acceptance of her own desires that reconciles her to her relationship with Sita and provides the impetus to leave Ashok.'[39]

Interestingly, from this resolution onwards, Mundu's position as the servant recedes into the background. His male egocentric fantasy and reactions only provide a fillip to the dismantling of the patriarchal home. In fact, Mundu is an anxious presence which has to be faded, ousted and silenced, in order to reduce the question of discipline and hierarchy of diverse bodies into a static, unproblematic feminine psychic space and liberation. This is the closing of the split and a looking away from differences towards the dualism of sense and sensuality. Sense (male) is negative, oppressive and destructive and denies life for power and control; whereas sensuality (woman) is positive, creative, egalitarian, liberating and loving, life beyond oppression/control.

The possible implication of such a critique of identity politics is the erasure of women. However, the material reality of women's lived experiences calls for reasserting the sexual difference between men and women. A political project of female emancipation—that changes the social conditions of women's lives—is

---

[39] Ghosh, *op. cit.*, p. 18.

possible only through female identity reclamation. Otherwise, the politics of difference is only politically incapacitating:[40]

> Why is it that just at the moment when so many of us who have been silenced begin to demand the right to name ourselves, to act as subjects rather than objects of history, that just then the concept of subjecthood becomes problematic? Just when we are framing our own theories about the world, uncertainty emerges about whether the world can be theorized. Just when we are talking about the changes we want, ideas of progress and the possibility of systematically and rationally organizing human society becomes dubious and suspect.[41]

This argument would imply that we have to necessarily halt the interrogation of metaphysical absolutes and fixed categories and return to biological/psychic determinism and closures of identity for a political change. That would, probably, also be the argument from those who uncritically celebrate *Fire*.

Writing against the fundamentalist fear psychosis and ban on *Fire*, Ghosh makes a very valid point. She suggests that 'the Hindutva imaginary of Hindu culture as *homogeneous, pure* and *originary is threatened by any hint of diversity*'.[42] Let us suppose I add the words: 'imaginary of feminine identity'. And, then I wonder: why is there so much apprehension about apprehensions? Why silence apprehensions as we claim to start the resistance against the act of silencing? What is wrong with being vigilant about the violence of naming? After all, naming is part of an oppressive regime's technology—creating others/women. Are we doomed in this circle? Do we, then, concede that here we exhaust our emancipatory possibilities and imaginations?

Caught between desire and identity, we are in a dilemma. We struggle to release women from pre-cultural determinism. Yet, we cannot lose sight of the material or the bodily marking of sexual difference. We want to open the spaces which have been coded

---

[40] A. Jardine, *Gynesis: Configurations of Woman and Modernity* (Ithaca, NY, Cornell University Press, 1985), p. 61. Also see, R. Braidotti, 'The Politics of Ontological Difference', in T. Brennan (ed.), *In Between Feminism and Psychoanalysis* (London, Routledge, 1989), pp. 85–105.

[41] Nancy Hartsock, 'Foucault on Power: A Theory for Women?' in L. J. Nicholson (ed.), *Feminism/Postmodernism* (New York, Routledge, 1990), pp. 163–64.

[42] Ghosh, *op. cit.*, p. 17, emphasis added.

as male and female to free women from 'man's truth'.[43] This task sits at odds with the masculinist certainty of sexual difference and also cautions against the possible slip into a sexual essence as a backdoor repeat of the metaphysical sexual dualism on which masculinity sustains itself. Overall, *Fire* walks on this double edged terrain. On the one hand, it suggests scepticism towards the existence of an extra-discursive sexual essence; on the other hand, it insists on the political necessity of recognising gender identity.

The Dilemma

Let us turn to the trajectory of emancipatory discourses with specific reference to alienation and the vision of a human future.

Classical modernism/liberalism pinned its hope upon the Individual Self. One can variously name it as the bourgeois, the entrepreneur and the rational calculating subject. Then emerged its antidote: the revolutionary subject, and the proletariat which was to replace the asocial rational agent. The bourgeois self might have been a revolutionary agent of history at a particular juncture (in the transition from feudalism to capitalism). Now, it has simply remained the oppressive engine of the capitalist order. It was suggested that the capitalist order not only alienates labour from the world and from itself but also alienates the bourgeoisie from the world and from itself. The uni-dimensionality of bourgeois existence strips one from her/his own humanity and human potentiality. It reduces life to a mono-activity of 'profit-earning' trapped into the circuit of capital—from capital to capital. In theory, the revolutionary proletariat erases this capitalist order, and in liberating itself eventually liberates the bourgeoisie and, in this process, the whole of humanity. However, the Marxian hope of emancipation has waned in the face of the oppressive universal ideals of liberal individualism and scientific communism. Emancipatory discourses have also taken various turns.

Interestingly, there are parallels with this shift in *Fire*. One such turn has shifted the focus towards the body, and within the body, towards the female body. Here, the wor(l)ds of the bourgeois and capital get replaced by the male and patriarchy, labour and the

---

[43] Jardine, *op. cit.*, p. 61.

proletariat, and the revolutionary self by the desirous body and the female self. Thus, in *Fire*, '[Sita] proves to be the catalyst in Radha's life, the one who conjures change, and brings back the sun into her dreary landscape.'[44]

This has certainly led to the culturist cry that westernisation (with its collateral concepts of marriage, sex and self-indulgent individualism) is corrupting our *dharmic* order and compassionate duties toward the family and others; that the passion of the modern, western debased personality is threatening to cause both social and family breakdown and decay. However, this imagery of the 'catalyst' is well shared across the board—for erasing the debased polluter, and for celebrating the coming of the enlightened liberator into the lives of static, passive, tortured yet silent natives/women. In *Fire*, it is no more a male labour leader, but the 'modern' girl, Sita. Nonetheless, while protesting against the ban on *Fire*, and in defence of lesbian sexual desire, Saraf says, 'Go and talk to your *nanis* and *dadis* (grandparents) and they will tell you lesbianism is not new to our culture. The massage-*waalis* know it is there, the folk songs tell you it's there.'[45] So much for the 'captive' Radha being educated by the 'modern' Sita.

Another parallel is related to the vision of the future. The emancipated future of humanity is where order/the normal is not imposed through (and organised by) capital/patriarchy; and, liberated humanity resides in its pure, voluntary and free living of life/the body/desire. The hope and the ideal of the Marxist struggle against the capitalist order are superseded by the post-Marxist struggle against the ordering of desire and the body.

Fire is an aesthetic articulation of this journey where, in day-to-day existence, we are confronted with the erosion of the blissful boundary/identity of a coherent personhood/self. On this slippery ground, *Fire* imagines the shift from social romanticism to a romance of the female body/desire. And here lies the tension between the two, namely, identity and uncoded libidinal flow. The former is rooted in boundary (re)creation, groundedness, commonality and *difference marking*. The latter denotes escape from boundaries and a movement towards ground/homelessness and a celebration of chaotic libidinal impulses. Set in paradoxical

---

[44] Banerji, *op. cit.*, p. 21.
[45] Babli Moitra Saraf quoted in *Communalism Combat* (Jan. 1999), p. 42.

terms, identity is the politics of differences, whilst libidinal flow is the politics of desire. One stands for *purpose,* and the other for *passion.*

To become a part of a movement is the call of identity, and to struggle against the various forms of regimentation/homogeni-sation that stifle movements into instruments of domination is the call of desire—continued gestures against all boundary-marking of our bodies and everyday behaviour. This is the struggle of the im/possibilities of the desirous body and gendered identity as manifested in the debate around *Fire.* Having located its propo-sitions regarding oppression and dissenting voices, the discourse invites us to look into the possibilities and limits of this micro-politics of identity and desire. Seduced in this reflection, we face the deadlock: on the one hand, libidinal free play gets bounded through the metaphysics of presence, i.e., gender identity (read female essence); and on the other hand, unhindered and de-differentiating desire (another pure existence!) sabotages the emancipatory possibilities of identity, that is, the struggle against the oppressed female body. This tension remains hanging over our heads. For these are the questions so integral to our everyday existence that they will always elude the dictates of film studios, and the judgements delivered in courtrooms and universities.

9

Redrawing the *Lakshman Rekha*

Gender Differences and Cultural Constructions in Youth Sexuality in Urban India

◆ Leena Abraham

Introduction

This essay examines gender asymmetry in youth sexuality in India through an analysis of young people's sexual experiences and their perceptions and views on marriage, virginity and premarital sex. Through this analysis the cultural constructions of male and female sexualities are explored and an attempt is made to delineate the core social and ideological forces that shape and reshape gender asymmetry. The essay is based on a larger study that explored youth sexuality in its several dimensions—individual beliefs and practices, sexual socialisation, access to information on sex, exposure to erotic materials and sexual experience.

Since the concept of sexuality includes, sexual identities, sexual norms, sexual practices and behaviour and also the subjective dimensions of the experience of sexuality it becomes an important tool in understanding social relations, particularly gender relations.[1] As sexuality is culturally defined within specific socio-

---

[1] For instance, see R. Dixon–Muller, 'The Sexuality Connection in Reproductive Health', *Studies in Family Planning*, Vol. 24, No. 5 (1993), pp. 269–83; and J. Holland,

historical contexts, its meanings and forms differ across communities, societies and groups.[2] Further, the meanings differ across
age groups, social classes, ethnic groups and gender.[3] Thus, one
may speak meaningfully of youth sexuality and adult sexuality,
of male, female and mixed-gender sexualities and of sexualities
that are rooted in class and caste divisions and kinship relations.

Our study focussed on sexuality among a specific segment of
Indian youth: the low-income, college going, urban youth.[4] The
study was conducted in the city of Mumbai (Bombay) in India.
Mumbai embodies cosmopolitan India with its trend towards
sexual liberalism, it also has the largest commercial sex industry
in India and perhaps the largest number of female bars, male and
female strip shows, gay bars and video parlours in the country.

The Context

In urban India, particularly in the metropolitan areas, we are
witnessing a growing trend towards liberal views with regard to
sexuality. A few recently published studies and other media
reports, indicate that the attitude towards premarital sex is no
longer as conservative as it is believed to be; and, that, premarital
sex among young people is on the rise resulting in unwanted
pregnancies and sexually transmitted diseases.[5] Sexual behaviour

---

C. Ramazonoglu, S. Sharpe and R. Thomson, 'Pleasure, Pressure and Power: Some
Contradictions of Gendered Sexuality', *The Sociological Review*, Vol. 40, No. 4
(1992), pp. 645–74.

[2] J. Weeks, *Sexuality* (London, Tavistock Publications, 1986); P. Caplan, *The Cultural Construction of Sexuality* (London & New York, Routledge, 1987).

[3] C. S.Vance, *Pleasure and Danger: Exploring Female Sexuality* (Boston, Routledge and Kegan Paul, 1984).

[4] The choice of low-income students was deliberate, as the existing studies on sexual behaviour or attitudes to sexuality, although few, have focussed mainly on English speaking, upper class students from 'elite' colleges.

[5] For instance see A. Rakesh, *Premarital Sexual Attitudes and Behaviour among Adolescent Girls* (Jaipur, Printwell, 1992); Family Planning Association of India (FPAI), *Youth Sexuality: A Study of Knowledge, Attitudes, Beliefs and Practices among Urban Educated Indian Youth 1993–94* (Mumbai: Sex Education, Counselling, Research and Training/Therapy (SECRT), Family Planning Association of India, n.d.); M. Savara and C. R. Sridhar, 'Sexual Behaviour Patterns amongst Men and Women in Maharashtra: Results of a Survey', paper presented at the workshop on Sexual Aspects of AIDS/STD Prevention in India, Tata Institute of Social

studies, although few in number also indicate that the incidence of extramarital liaisons and commercial sex among married men is not rare.[6] Yet, there is a general reluctance to discuss sexuality, both in public and in private, as sex continues to be a taboo subject.

Sexual liberalism appears to have received a boost under the recent impact of economic liberalisation and globalisation. These economic processes have had a major influence in the cultural arena. In the context of an unprecedented expansion of worldwide television channels and consumer goods, erotic literature and films are widely available. New cultural and material products with modern values and meanings have brought different dimensions of sexuality into the open.

Sexuality not only figures as a central theme in the consumption of these products but also is increasingly used in the promotion and sale of various consumables. These draw upon the dominant norms of gender-asymmetric heterosexuality; male sexuality as aggressive and uncontrollable and female sexuality as passive and compromising, and male sexuality extending beyond the family boundaries and female sexuality as centered around the marriage and spouse. Alongside this however, there are newer themes and representations that increasingly find expression and emphasis in the print and visual media—the objectification of the male body, the unabated pursuit of pleasure and desire and multiple sexual relationships. Sexuality becomes a crucial marker of identity, image

Sciences, Bombay, 1993; L. Goparaju, 'Unplanned, Unsafe : Male Student's Sexual Behaviour' (Paper presented at the Workshop on Sexual Aspects of AIDS/STD Prevention in India, Tata Institute of Social Sciences, Bombay, 1993); G. Rangaiyan, 'Sexuality and Sexual Behaviour in the Age of AIDS: A Study among College Youth in Mumbai', Ph.D, dissertation (unpulished) (Mumbai, International Institute for Population Sciences, 1996); M. C. Watsa, 'Premarital Sexual Behaviour of Urban Educated Youth in India', (Paper presented at the Workshop on Sexual Aspects of AIDS/STD prevention in India, Tata Institute of Social Sciences, Bombay, 1993); R. Ramasubban, 'Sexual Behaviour and Conditions of Health Care: Potential Risks for HIV Transmission in India', in Tim Dyson (ed.), *Sexual Behaviour and Networking: Anthropological and Socio-Cultural Studies on Transmission of HIV* (Belgium, Deronaux—Ordina, 1992), pp. 75–81; A. C. Urmil et al., 'Medico-Social Profile of Male Teenager STD Patients Attending a Clinic in Pune', *Indian Journal of Public Health*, Vol. 33, No. 4 (1989), pp. 176–82.

[6] For a review of some of these studies see M. Nag, *Sexual Behaviour and AIDS in India* (New Delhi, Vikas Publishing House, 1996); S. Jejeebhoy, *Adolescent Sexual and Reproductive Behaviour: A Review of the Evidence from India*. International Center for Research on Women (ICRW) Working Paper No. 3, Washington, 1996.

and success. The body has emerged as the signifier of both traditional and modern social norms. It has become a site for the expression and realisation of modernity, as reflected increasingly in television programmes, films, advertisements and events such as fashion shows, beauty pageants, and so forth.

Within the traditional cultural ethos, male sexuality in India is viewed in liberal terms, in the sense that, it is neither defined by nor confined to the social institutions of marriage and monogamy. On the other, female sexuality in the Indian tradition is confined within the institution of marriage and is subordinated to male (the husband's) sexuality through rigid norms that insist on the maintenance of virginity before marriage and chastity after marriage.[7] The traditional practices of child marriage and the prohibition on widow re-marriage are reflections of the above subordination.

At the same time female sexuality in Indian culture is seen as being ambivalent in the sense that women are regarded in myth and popular culture as being both 'goddesses' as well as in the possession of dangerous power, 'both pure and impure in their embodiment'.[8] However, the belief in everyday life is that if not controlled through direct regulation, female sexuality takes a dangerous and destructive form.

Further, control of female sexuality is at the core of both patriarchal relations and caste relations.[9] The primary means of maintaining caste boundaries is through the regulation of the marriages and sexual relations entered into by the members of the group. Female sexuality then becomes the factor most crucial to the maintenance of caste boundaries. Family, marriage and kinship

---

[7] The control of female sexuality among the tribals and some of the 'lower' caste communities is considerably different from the dominant cultural practices.

[8] M. Thapan, Embodiment; Essays on Gender and Identity (Delhi, Oxford University Press, 1997); V. Das, 'Masks and Faces: An Essay on Punjabi Kinship', Contributions to Indian Sociology, Vol. 10, No. 1 (1976), pp. 1–30; L. Gatwood; Devi and the Spouse Goddess. Women, Sexuality and Marriage in India (New Delhi, Manohar, 1985); and R. Kumari, Female Sexuality in Hinduism (Delhi, The Indian Society for Promoting Christian Knowledge (ISPCK), 1988).

[9] P. Chowdhary, 'Enforcing Cultural Codes: Gender and Violence in Northern India', in M. E. John and J. Nair (eds), A Question of Silence? The Sexual Economies of Modern India (New Delhi, Kali for Women, 1998); P. Velaskar, 'Caste-Patriarchy and the Dalit Woman's Subordination: Towards a Theoretical Framework', Sugava, Dr Ambedkar Special Issue, Vol. 4, (1998), pp. 54–67.

structures form the primary institutions through which female sexuality gets defined and controlled.

In the dominant cultural discourse, the concept of *pativrata* embodies the confinement of female sexuality through the complete devotion of a woman to her husband regardless of how he treats her. Sita, the heroine of the Ramayana, is the most cherished symbol of *pativrata* as she is seen as the 'quintessence of wifely devotion'.[10]

The Ramayana, one of the two great Hindu epics, continues to have a powerful hold over the imagination of all Indians, male and female.[11] In a pivotal scene in the epic, Lakshman, the brother of Ram, draws a line (*Lakshman Rekha*) on the ground around Sita with an arrow—the line is intended to protect Sita from the dangers of the forest. For Indians, the line symbolises the limits of Sita's confinement and also the idealised confinement of the chaste Indian woman who must cast herself in the Sita mould.

It is in this context of the foreboding cultural tensions between the traditional and modern constructions of sexuality that our study on youth sexuality is situated. The youth are major consumers of the modern cultural expression of sexuality while being located within and circumscribed by the traditional familial, caste and community boundaries. For an understanding of the social impact of a changing cultural climate, one may focus on the construction of sexuality among this group of the population. Such constructions may possibly shape gender relations in contemporary Indian society.

Anthropological studies and feminist analyses in India have shown the structural and cultural pathways of the gender socialisation of girls and have analysed the core ideological elements in the construction of gender in Indian society.[12] These studies analyse the

---

[10] S. Kakar, 'Feminine Identity in India', in R. Ghadially (ed.), *Women in Indian Society* (New Delhi, Sage, 1988); also see U. Chakravarti, 'The Development of the Sita Myth: A Case Study of Women in Myth and Literature', in Kumkum Sangari & Suresh Vaid (eds), *Women and Culture* (Mumbai, Research Centre for Women's Studies, SNDT Women's University, 1994).

[11] The story of the 'Ramayana' has been made into a television serial and has been one of the most popular television programmes ever made. It has been telecast and viewed repeatedly.

[12] For details, see L. Dube, 'Socialisation of Hindu Girls in Patrilineal India', in Karuna Chanana (ed.), *Socialisation, Education and Women* (New Delhi, Orient Longman, 1988); L. Dube, *Women and Kinship: Comparative Perspectives on Gender*

construction of male and female sexuality as based on diverse gender roles, division of labour and kinship arrangements, which are in turn constructions of a patriarchal social structure.

However between the socialisation of young girls, and the regulation by institutions and power structures of the lives of adult women, lies an important formative period when ideologies are absorbed and norms are internalised. What elements of the patriarchal ideology are active during adolescence? How do different constructions of sexuality get inscribed on the psyche and body of young girls and boys? What social arrangements support such constructions? The present paper attempts to address some of these issues.

The paper first provides a descriptive analysis of the asymmetry in the sexual experiences of boys and girls.[13] It examines the broad range of sexual experience and the different relationships through which these are realised. The subsequent sections attempt to identify the ideological and structural elements that support and reinforce gender asymmetry in the construction of sexuality. The sense of shame in relation to the body and the control of information constitute the ideological elements in our analysis while the norms relating to marriage and sexual expression constitute the structural elements.

Data

The empirical findings for this paper have been drawn from a general study conducted among the students of four colleges during 1996–98. These four colleges were selected as they catered

---

in *South and South-East Asia* (New York, United Nations University Press, 1997); V. Das, 'Feminity and the Orientations to the Body', Karuna Chanana (ed.), *ibid.*; G. Dietrich, 'On the Construction of Gender: Hindu Girls in Patrilineal India', Karuna Chanana (ed.), *ibid.*; G. Dietrich, 'Discussing Sexuality', in G. Dietrich, *Reflections on the Women's Movement; Religion, Ecology, Development* (New Delhi, Horizon, 1992).

[13] The use of the terms 'boys' and 'girls' is not in any hierarchical sense or should not be seen as being paternalistic. Their usage is strictly contextual. In India, young men and women are commonly referred to as 'boys' and 'girls' until they are married or cross the marriageable age. With marriage they attain the social status of man and woman. Hence, the usage of girl and boy throughout the paper although they are in their late adolescence or early adulthood.

mainly to students from low-income families. The students were in the age group of 16–22 years, both boys and girls and both juniors (first year of higher secondary—Standard IX) and seniors (final year undergraduates—Third Year students). Data was gathered using Focus Group Discussions (FGDs) (10 groups), in-depth interviews (87 students) and a survey using a self-administered questionnaire (977 students). The discussion here is primarily based on qualitative data, but some of the findings from the survey have also been included.

To briefly describe the background of the students involved, while they shared a low-income status, they belonged to different religious and ethnic backgrounds, Hindus (both lower and upper caste) and Muslims. Students did not consider themselves 'religious' while they viewed their families as 'religious'. Many however observed some religious rituals. A majority of the students who participated in the study belonged to families with low parental education and lower strata occupations. Fathers' were employed as mill workers, taxi drivers, watchmen, police constables, peons, small traders and so forth, and their income was correspondingly low. Many mothers were illiterate or with only a primary education. The majority were housewives while some of them were engaged in small scale, home-based businesses. The students lived in crowded homes, often in single room tenements, some located in the slums.

Girls lived closer to their colleges, while boys came from different parts of the city and the suburbs. Some of the students, mainly boys, took up jobs along with their studies. There was considerable segregation of boys and girls in these colleges as compared to the 'elite' colleges. However, there were several opportunities to interact with the opposite sex through curricular and extra-curricular activities. Although the medium of instruction in all the four colleges was English, students conversed mainly in Marathi and Hindi.

The Experience of Sexuality

The sexual experiences of youth, for boys and girls, showed a marked difference in terms of the type of experiences that they had had and the avenues available to them for the exploration of their sexuality. The early exploration of sexuality among the boys included masturbation and 'touching' women, and in later years it ranged from kissing to sexual intercourse. Accessing erotic sources was another dimension in the exploration of male sexuality. In contrast, girls' experiences included being 'touched' by men, experiences of kissing and hugging and in a few cases sexual intercourse.

From early adolescence, the sexual experiences of boys and girls followed distinct trajectories. Boys' experiences in most cases began with masturbation followed by 'touching' women. Masturbation, (*halwayache* or 'hand practice') which was almost universal among the boys who were interviewed, caused guilt, a feeling of weakness in many and a fear, in a few others, that it minght hinder the normal growth of the body. However, such notions did not deter boys from engaging in it. The overall findings showed that boys did not demonstrate a negative attitude towards masturbation.[14] Findings showed that only a fourth of the boys believed that 'masturbation is unhealthy', and disagreed with the statement that, 'It is alright for boys to masturbate.' An equal number of boys believed that 'girls should not masturbate.'

Heterosexuality being the societal norm, boys were early to extend their explorations to include the opposite sex. They begin by 'touching' and 'pushing' girls in crowded places, often in an aggressive manner.[15] Accounts of any resistance on the part of girls/women towards such acts were completely absent in the boys' narratives, although some of them found themselves in embarrassing situations.[16] As they had not encountered any resistance from girls, boys took this as their approval and some even believed that girls liked such advances. Further, boys did not consider their behaviour 'offensive' or 'indecent' in any way, rather, they described it as 'normal male behaviour' and a part of 'growing up'.

In contrast, a majority of the girls interviewed showed no awareness of the sexual act of masturbation, neither did they know that masturbation was common among boys. When explained to

---

[14] A few boys considered masturbation the safest mode of dealing with sexual desires until they were married.

[15] A few of them reported such behaviour at the age of 12.

[16] For example, sudden erections in public places.

them, they not only expressed surprise but considered such an act 'shameful', 'abnormal' and 'dirty'. Only two of the senior college girls mentioned hearing of it from friends.

Girls reported being 'touched' by the opposite sex very early on. They expressed anger at unwanted male advances, and felt both humiliated and helpless. According to the girls, they did not protest when such incidents occurred as they felt it would attract public attention towards themselves and particularly towards their body. Some of them even thought that they might have unknowingly touched the boys and provoked such advances, thus shifting the blame onto themselves. For most girls, there was also the fear that the men would 'take revenge' if they resisted.

In later adolescence, particularly after leaving school, the exploration of sexuality was directed towards heterosexual experience of greater physical intimacy. This included kissing, hugging, 'touching' genitals and sexual intercourse. Once again there were marked gender differences in the experiences of physical intimacy with the opposite sex,[17] in terms of the type of sexual experience, its frequency and partners. For instance, a greater number of boys, in comparison to the girls, reported experiencing various sexual acts. Most of the boys who had experienced kissing had experienced it more than once. Of course, unlike in a Western context, most of the students in the study did not consider kissing and hugging to be sexual acts. It was found that kissing rarely meant deep kissing, and was often on the cheeks or the forehead. The qualitative data showed that the sexual history of boys was marked by multiple partnerships, which included long and short-term partnerships with peers, older women and commercial sex workers. Girls' partnerships were limited mainly to their peers.

Sexual partnerships among boys and girls were mainly of two types: these were popularly referred to as 'time-pass' and 'true-love' friendships. 'Time-pass' was a transitory relationship with a partner of their age, characterised by sexual intimacy leading to sexual intercourse. The second type called 'true-love', was also with a partner of similar age, and was pursued with the implicit or explicit intention of marriage. In general, these heterosexual

---

[17] The survey showed that 26 per cent of the boys had experienced sexual intercourse while only a small number, 3 per cent, of the girls reported experiencing sexual intercourse.

relationships are far more complex than what is typically under-stood in terms of 'boyfriend–girlfriend' relationships. It becomes particularly complex when the two partners perceive the same relationship differently. It was seen that while boys tended to see their relationships as `time-pass', girls described it as 'true-love'.[18]

Boys' sexual partnerships extended beyond peers and included commercial sex workers and older women referred to as 'aunties'. A boys' first experience of sexual intercourse was often with a commercial sex worker and occurred under peer influence. Sex with older women was initiated by the woman herself and in some cases peers played a role in liaising with her. Through these channels of sexual partnership, boys explored oral sex and anal sex, sexual acts they considered unconventional or 'not normal'.

A third dimension in the exploration of sexuality was the gratification of curiosity and sexual desire by accessing erotic materials. In this regard boys had greater opportunities of availing such material. Most of the boys had seen erotic films (BPs or blue pictures as they are called) and drawings. Reading as a general habit was poor among these students and reading erotic books was not popular among them. Boys accessed erotic films through video parlours that are quite common in the slums and other low-income localities. Since they lacked privacy in their crowded homes, they rarely watched these films at home. It was found that watching erotic films was a common peer activity among the boys. Girls, however, lacked physical access to video parlours and their home environment prevented them from watching these films. More than the lack of access, it was their attitude to erotic mate-rials that prevented girls from seeing such films. Although girls were aware that boys watched erotic films, they felt it was shame-ful for them to see it as they had heard that 'dirty things' or 'sex' was shown 'openly' in these films. Boys on the other hand felt that girls could not be shown these films. Except for a few senior girls, most girls did not have any exposure to erotic films.

Despite greater exposure to the media, and greater opportuni-ties for interaction between boys and girls, in a cosmopolitan city

---

[18] These relationships are discussed in detail in Leena Abraham, 'Understanding Youth Sexuality: A Study of College Students in Mumbai', (Mumbai, Tata Institute of Social Sciences, 1998).

like Mumbai, the experience and attitudes of boys and girls from the same social, economic and educational backgrounds was radically different. With a common denominator of background variables, what factors have led to such divergent constructions of sexuality for boys and girls? The gender asymmetric sexual experiences can be understood and explained only through an analysis of the societal arrangements that differentially allocate access to opportunities on the one hand, and the cultural and ideological constructs that legitimise such arrangements on the other hand.

Sexual Socialisation: Growing Up in Ignorance and Shame

The formation of male and female sexual identities begins early in life with very striking gender differences in the socialisation of boys and girls. As Veena Das, Leela Dube and others have shown, sexual segregation and the internalisation of what constitutes feminine and masculine behaviour begins early in childhood.[19] Family socialisation plays a key role in shaping male and female sexualities.

Boys and girls learn about sex and sexuality through indirect inferences from, as they said, 'here and there'. The family (especially the parents) is rarely a source of information on sex for young people. Girls learn very early on that questions relating to sexuality could not be addressed to their parents or elders. Even when some of them broke this rule and asked questions, they were either reprimanded or at best given vague answers. For instance, one young girl (Standard XI) who asked her mother what the difference between girls and boys was, was told that, 'in girls, the *"bathroom ki jagah"* (genitals) is different.' Another girl (Standard XI) was told that *'stree baherchi hote'*, an expression that refers to menstruation and also implies its polluting nature.

The onset of puberty brings about dramatic changes in the life of a girl as menstruation is seen as the marker of female sexuality. The girl and her family become actively involved in the management of her sexuality. As a result her physical mobility is curtailed,

---

[19] L. Dube, *op. cit.*, 1988; V. Das, *op. cit.*, 1976.

her interaction with male members of the family becomes restricted and monitored and she is often escorted:

(Third Year girl)
When I was in 7th standard mother used to say that, 'Don't talk
much with boys, girls shouldn't dance and laugh like that.'

(Standard XI girl)
At home they used to tell that, 'Stay away from boys, don't go
much close to them.' Then playing with boys got stopped. Then
they used to tell that, 'Don't talk much with boys.' Then talking
also became less.

(Third Year girl)
Yes, they know I have friends in college, but they don't like me
talking too much or going out with boys.
Did they tell you so?
No, they never told this to me, but they don't like it. I know.

(Third Year girl)
When I used to come home from school he would be standing at
his balcony... I would look up... he would smile. I would smile
back. Then my family came to know.
About what?
That I liked him and he liked me too—[pause]—when my family
came to know this, my father started accompanying me whenever
I went out... always... everything stopped.... Now I rarely get to
go out alone.

On reaching puberty, girls experienced sudden control by parents
and others over their behaviour. Several of the narratives refer to
the control explicitly and subtly exercised to curtail social relations
between boys and girls. With a few exceptions, boys were never
told to keep away from girls. Almost all girls irrespective of their
age were cautioned about keeping a distance from boys:

(Standard XI girl: whose parents lived in a village)
Do you talk to boys?
No. Don't talk much with boys.
Why?
Feel afraid to talk to them.
Why?
My uncle scolds. He doesn't like it. If my uncle comes to know,
he will scold.

Why?
Because, he doesn't like girls talking much with boys.

She lived with her uncle; and often such arrangements can be more restrictive for the girls as the relatives assume the responsibility of 'protecting' her sexuality and her family's 'honour'. Girls' interaction with boys was not only controlled by the family elders, in addition teachers, relatives, neighbours and family friends often acted as agencies of control:

(Third Year girl)
When I was in school, from 1st standard, there used to be competition between me and one boy. I used to be first among girls and he used to be first among boys in our class. We used to always talk, discuss about studies. Our teacher noticed this, and one day (in the 7th standard) she scolded both of us.... She said that now you are not small.... Why do you always stay together? So we stopped talking to each other. Since then, I never spoke to him. Even now, when I come across him, we don't talk.
You liked him?
I never felt any such thing, but my neighbour used to say that something is going on between us.

The practices of segregation are underlined by the ideological construct that perceives women as being simultaneously dangerous and in danger. Women are dangerous because, their sexuality is seen as uncontrollable. If uncontrolled, their sexuality poses a threat to the social order. They are in danger because, the violation of their sexuality brings dishonour and shame not only on themselves but also to their families and the extended kin group.[20] In everyday life the former governs the sexuality of adult women while the latter governs the sexuality of pubertal girls. The double-edged ideology, then, neatly confines women to the spaces socially prescribed for them.

---

[20] K. Ganesh, 'Seclusion of Women and the Structure of Caste', M. Krishnaraj and K. Chanana (eds), *Gender and the Household Domain*, (New Delhi, Sage, 1989); K. Ram, *Mukkuvar Women: Gender, Hegemony and Capitalist Transformation in a South Indian Fishing Community* (New Delhi, Kali for Women, 1992); K. Viswanath, 'Shame and Control: Sexuality and Power in Feminist Discourse in India', in *Embodiment; Essays on Gender and Identity* edited by M. Thapan (New Delhi, Oxford University Press, 1997), pp. 313–33.

The woman's social confinement is complete when she perceives the socially prescribed spaces as her rightful place. The girls who took part in the study, found their family environment 'comfortable'. In spite of the restrictions imposed, by the family, on their movements and interaction with boys, they did not perceive their families as 'restrictive'. This was in striking contrast with the boys, who perceived their general family atmosphere as 'uncomfortable' and 'restrictive' in spite of the fact that there was little control over their mobility and social interactions. Very few boys reported being constrained by the family in their interaction with girls as boys were never told 'not to talk' to girls. The boys who were employed, had much more freedom vis-à-vis their family, yet their perception of their families as restrictive did not differ significantly. One can infer that, unlike boys, girls are socialised to accept the constraints and confinement, and to be comfortable with it.

In some instances, restrictions on the movement of girls and their communication with boys began prior to the onset of puberty, in anticipation of post-pubertal control. However, with the onset of menstruation, those restrictions that acted as reminders become not only normative but circumscribed most of the girls activities. During this period, a girl's consciousness of her own sexuality was also suddenly enhanced. As she was seen to be bodily mature, maturity of behaviour was expected of her as well.

Girls were rarely prepared for menstruation, despite it being perceived as an important event in their lives. Girls were not told anything about menstruation prior to its onset. Only few were informed about why it occurs and others were told about general restrictions to be followed with respect to food, worship, domestic work and play.

The first menstruation was sudden, it often occurred outside the home and caused anxiety, fear, shame and embarrassment, and was accompanied by physical pain. Although there was no celebration to mark the first event, it drew attention from others much to the dislike of the girls. As has been pointed out in other studies this may be due to the fact that, as marriages are delayed, families nowadays prefer not to announce their daughter's coming of age in order to avoid any threat to her sexuality.[21] In addition,

---

[21] A. George, 'It Happens to Us: Menstruation as Perceived by Poor Women in Bombay' in J. Gittelsohn, M. E. Bentley, P. J. Pelto, M. Nag, S. Pachauri,

the difficulty faced in following the various rituals of purity and pollution due to crowded urban living conditions, and girl's disapproval of such attention owing to their education, may have contributed to the 'silence' now associated with menstruation.

In our study, most girls were made to follow some rituals or restrictions. Menstrual blood is seen as polluting, and a sense of shame is associated with menstruation. Since menstruation drew attention to the female body, managing menstruation without drawing the attention of the male members of the household was difficult. Thus cultural practices, compounded by the physical living conditions of lower class households made management of menstruation difficult for girls, thus adversely affecting menstrual hygiene.

The restrictions imposed on girls included those directed at the self—restrictions on cooking, dietary restrictions and restrictions related to religious practices. There were also restrictions with regard to others, especially restrictions on interactions with male members of the family. Religious restrictions were common across communities. Muslim girls did not say *namaz* or touch the *Quran* during menstruation. Similarly, Hindu girls abstained from performing *puja* and touching pictures of the gods. On the positive side, girls did get some respite from household work such as cooking and the washing of utensils during menstruation.

Many of the girls believed that menstruation was the expelling of 'impure blood' or 'waste' from the body. Only a few senior girls knew the significance of menstruation and its link with fertility. Some of the girls had heard of the absence of menstruation during pregnancy but did not know the reason for this.

In the absence of other sources of information, girls relied mainly on their own or others' experiences. They also did not, themselves, make any serious effort to gather information about menstruation. Wherever girls queried the why and how of menstruation, they were told 'it happens to all women', 'it is part of being a woman', 'now you are young, you will come to know when you grow up' and so on.[22] Such experiences during early

---

A. D. Harrison and L. T. Landman (eds), *Listening to Women Talk about Their Health: Issues and Evidence from India* (New Delhi, Har-Anand Publications, 1994), pp. 168–83.

[22] In many cases, the mothers themselves may not know enough to inform their daughters.

adolescence are effective socialisers into the practice of 'silence' especially with regard to matters concerning their body and sexuality.[23]

The poor level of information among girls about their bodies acts in consonance with cultural practices reinforcing the notion that menstruation is polluting. Their lack of knowledge becomes convenient while imposing other means of control over their sexuality such as instilling the fear of pregnancy in them.

(Third Year girl)
Mother told me about M.C. [menstrual cycle]
When? ....What did she tell you?
Periods came, after that she told me now you have grown up, you shouldn't sleep near anyone. Not even near your brother. If you sleep like that you will get children.
I used to feel afraid. My stomach used to pain a lot and I used to feel afraid to sleep near anyone.
Do you know how children are born?
No.
Have you ever asked anyone?
No. She [mother] will tell that you are in a hurry, is it your age for marriage now?

The general lack of information was not limited to menstruation, girls knew little about their own bodies. Almost all the girls who were a part of the study did not know about the existence of the hymen, a majority believed that there was a single passage for urine and menstrual blood, there was a lack of awareness of the association between menstruation and fertility. Although boys were better informed than girls, the overall level of knowledge regarding conception and childbirth, contraception and STDs among both boys and girls was partial or incorrect and was inadequate to prevent unwanted pregnancies and sexually transmitted infections.[24]

As our study shows, despite the similarity in socio-economic and educational status, girls gathered much less information in

[23] Recent studies on women's reproductive health have shown that women delay seeking health care in the case of reproductive tract infections and sexually transmitted infections causing much suffering and misery. The socialisation of young girls has much to do with this neglect of the self.
[24] L. Abraham, *op. cit.*, 1998.

comparison to boys. Two factors were responsible for the disparity: lack of physical access to information, and more importantly, the girls' reluctance to actively seek information. The latter was related to the internalisation of the notions of 'shame' attached to the female body and sex on the one hand, and the belief that seeking information on sex related topics was unfeminine on the other. `Good girls should not be interested in such things', said many younger girls. As 'sex' was perceived to be 'dirty', and 'shameful', it was better to keep away from it. Another response was, `when you get married, you will come to know' implying that experience would provide the necessary knowledge. Far worse was the feeling among many girls that they knew enough and there was no need for more knowledge. Their existing knowledge being obtained from hushed discussions with close friends and sisters, who were, perhaps, as ill informed as they themselves were.

Girls' narratives were punctuated with expressions such as 'chee', 'dirty' and with long pauses:

(Third Year girl)
Do you have any sexual experience?
Chee! No.

(Third Year girl)
When girl and boy meet what happens?
[Long pause]—Kiss, will hug and something more must be happening, I do not know. On TV only that much is shown.
Do you have any type of sexual experience?
Chee [shyly looking down] *nahi* [No].

In contrast, boys discussed sex more openly, actively sought information from various sources, and experienced and experimented with sex. There was no 'shame' associated with the male body, and sex was viewed in terms of desire and pleasure.

Much of the boys' information came from erotic sources, which were inaccessible to girls. More than half of the male students had seen pornographic drawings or films and more than one third had read pornographic literature. A fairly large percentage of boys from the study reported exposure to erotic material. Third Year students reported much higher rates of erotic exposure as compared to Standard XI students. In contrast, more than half of the girls said that they had never seen erotic drawings, about 90 per cent had not read such books and most of them had never seen such films. For girls, moving from Standard XI to the Third Year, did not increase their exposure. Qualitative data confirmed that boys had greater exposure to erotic materials, blue films being the most popular form. Watching blue films was an important peer activity among the boys, and peer influence is quite significant in initiating exposure to erotic films and commercial sex.[25]

The main source of information for many boys on matters concerning sex were pornographic films. Information about the female body, sexual intercourse, types of sex: vaginal, oral, anal, group sex, sex with animals and so forth, came mainly from these films.

(Third Year boy)
At first, did not have any information. Had got some information only from friends. When saw BP—understood what intercourse 'originally' [actually] is.
What is shown in BP?
In BP, how intercourse is done is shown. Different types of intercourse, different positions, 'dog-shot' ... 'original intercourse', dog-shot, from rear side, taking in mouth.

(Third Year boy)
Only different -different types of '*shots kase lawle jatat te.*' It is shown [how to engage in different types of intercourse] in detail, animal BP is also there, homo type is also shown.

As mentioned earlier girls had not only not seen blue films but were strongly against seeing them. The girls' sources of information were Hindi films, television, including the cable network, friends and magazines.

Another related factor that contributed to the girls' inability to access and process information was their poor vocabulary and language skills in matters relating to sexuality. In everyday communication, boys were well-equipped with a wide vocabulary which enabled them to express themselves on such matters. Their vocabulary included terms for body parts, 'type' of girls, sexual partners, intercourse, commercial sex and type of sex. Boys used

---

[25] L. Abraham, *op. cit.*, 1998.

complex sets of terminology: one set consisted of terminology that belonged to dominant languages such as English or Hindi or was culled from medical literature (for example, intercourse, condom, *'pardah'* for hymen). A second set consisted of commonly used English terms with their meanings changed. (for example, oral sex for talking about sex and/or kissing). Other sets consisted of terms used by men in general (such as `hand practice' for masturbation) and terms whose meanings were shared exclusively by specific groups of boys. Boys not only communicated using different sets of terminology, they were at ease using them. Even the younger boys were comfortable using slang:

> (Standard XI boy)
> To ball [breast] we call ball only, *'gole'*—circles, 'football'.
> *'Pimpalaache pan'* that is, peepal leaf for the backside.
> **For boys?**
> *'Lund'* to penis, *'shemana'*, 'tubelight and two bulbs'.

> (Standard XI boy)
> *'Maal'*, *'chavi'*, *'samaan'*, for girl in 'time-pass'.

> (Third year boy)
> [For 'premature ejaculation'] code words are there, means *'shai lavkar galli, kinwa shai sampli'* [The ink leaked out soon, or the ink is over].

Boys spoke about sex mostly using slang, which was strikingly different from the language used in sex education or from the normatively prescribed language of sex. It was highly eroticised and often seemed 'obscene'. The language used by them may have a direct association with their high degree of exposure to erotic materials.

In contrast with the boys' command over the terminology to describe sex, the girls' possessed a severely limited vocabulary for describing body parts or sex. Except for terms such as *'chavi'*, *'maal'*, 'ball' (breasts), girls were not only unfamiliar with the terminology used by boys but were unaware that boys possessed such a vocabulary. Girls were shy to use words describing body parts and sex. Some of these factors made eliciting information on sexual behaviour from girls difficult. Girls neither possessed technical terminology to describe sex, nor were they comfortable using slang.

The level of information and means of communication also determined the perception of what constitutes sexual behaviour or sexual acts, among the boys and girls. It was found that while the majority of the boys did not view kissing and hugging as sexual acts, some of the girls did. Boys used the term 'sex' to refer to the specific sexual acts of 'touching sex organs', sexual intercourse, oral sex and anal sex:

(Standard XI girl)
What is sex according to you?
What is seen on the TV.
What have you seen on the TV?
———— [Pause] ————
How will you describe?
Chee, —[pause]—It should not happen.
Why?
[Pause]—[hesitantly] I don't know that much.

(Third Year girl)
Physical relationship means what?
[Laughing, feeling shy] They sleep together and then what happens I don't know.

(Third Year girl)
[Sex] Means physical relationship, *'hamnastri'* [intercourse].
What is intercourse?
Male and female come close together.
Then...
[Feeling shy] Bodies of both unite—[long pause]—and heat spreads in the body—[pause]—and male's water enters into female.
How?
Because of heat it [water] is released.
How does this water enter?
From place of urination.

(Third Year girl)
[Sex is] What happens after marriage.
What happens after marriage?
Baccha [child].
How?
It is heard that if periods do not come child is born.
And before marriage is child born?'
Ha [Yes].
Then how does it happen?
This I don't know properly. Boys know all this.

(Third Year girl)
[Sex is] 'Private parts' of boys and girls.

(Third Year girl)
[Sex is] What happens on the first night.
What happens on the first night?
'Honeymoon'.
Means?
[—Pause—feeling shy] Kiss and come closer.
And ...?
And then do sex.

In contrast, even younger boys were more direct and had no difficulty in describing sexual intercourse:

(Standard XI boy)
Boy puts his *chot* [penis] into the girl's *yonit* [vagina] and *chotatun dravya yete* [fluid comes out from the penis].

(Standard XI boy)
It is one of the inner hunger of a person. It is a need.

Boys' narratives also revealed the cultural constructions of male and female sexuality. As the following excerpt shows, the female body is seen as an object of male sexual pleasure, and to view it as such is seen as natural:

(Third Year boy)
Firstly sex means, '*Stree chya shariracha upbhog ghene*' [taking pleasure from a woman's body]; and such things happen naturally.

While almost all the boys, irrespective of their age, knew what sexual intercourse was, several girls, especially the younger ones were unaware of the penetrative aspect of intercourse. From their expressions of surprise and doubt and from their descriptions we believe that they were not feigning ignorance.[26] Boys knew about oral sex and anal sex while only a few girls had any information about it.

---

[26] Other studies have also pointed out that a woman's first experience of intercourse is often traumatic, as she does not expect penetration to be a part of it. For instance, see A. George, *Sexual Behaviour and Sexual Negotiation among Poor Women and Men in Mumbai—An Exploratory Study* (Baroda, SAHAJ Society for Health Alternatives, 1997).

The experience of sexuality during adolescence followed dia-
metrically opposite trajectories for the girls and boys. This was
mainly the outcome of the differential socialisation of boys and
girls in Indian society. The urban, metropolitan environment of
Mumbai city has not significantly altered the sexual socialisation
of girls as it has for boys.

In addition to the general discriminatory socialisation of girls
such as restrictions on mobility, gender segregation practices,
allocation of space and so on, female sexuality was controlled
essentially in three ways: by the withholding of information, by
instilling fear (of pregnancy and of men in general) and by
creating a sense of shame attached to the female body. Women are
socialised to feel a sense of shame with regard to their bodies and
their sexuality. Keeping women ignorant about their bodies and
sexuality is one of the ways through which the ideology of shame
is perpetuated.

The Centrality of Marriage

The social norms and cultural practices that govern male and
female sexuality are distinct and are imposed and internalised
early in life. These differential norms are also reflected in the views
and attitudes of young boys and girls towards marriage, partner/
spouse, sex in general and premarital sex in particular.

On the one hand, girls viewed sex and the body as shameful,
polluting and 'dirty', on the other hand, both were to be preserved
for marriage and the husband, the most important event and
person in their lives. Girls viewed marriage as inevitable, although
marital relationships within their families or those of their
neighbours and relatives were far from ideal, and were often
characterised by drunkenness, wife battering and lack of romance.
Yet, for them, marriage had a special significance as it symbolised
social security and the only legitimate relationship for the realisation
and expression of their sexuality. Girls' narratives reflected both
the hope of the ideal and the inevitability of subjugation.

The dominant discourse legitimises sexuality only as heterosexuality and within the context of marriage. The cultural beliefs
and social arrangements tend to confine female sexuality within
the institution of marriage while male sexuality often extends

beyond the marital relationship. As a result, in their conversations, girls associated sex only with marriage:

(Third Year girl)
[Sex] It is very bad thing...it should be after marriage only. Otherwise there is no meaning in marriage.... [embarrassed, feeling shy]. These [kissing, hugging and touching] all should happen only after marriage.

(Third Year girl)
[Sex is] Relationship between girls and boys.
What type of relationship?
Relation after marriage [laughing].
What type of relation is there after marriage?
After marriage—[long pause]—physical relationship *(jismani talukat)*.

(Third Year girl)
[Sex is] What happens after marriage.

(Third Year girl)
Do you have any sexual experience?
No.... I just told you... because I am not yet married.

Girls looked forward to marriage. In girls' narratives the life of an unmarried girl and that of the deserted woman are reminders of a woman's social insecurity and the threat to her sexuality. Some of the girl respondents reported following ritual practices meant to ensure a long, stable married life and a good husband. Thus, the centrality of marriage in a woman's life continues to have a strong hold over the girls. Their location in a metropolis, in modern times, does not seem to decenter it.

Studies have shown how the patriarchal structuring of unequal social relationships within marriage subordinates women through marital violence. Marital violence acts as a means of controlling female sexuality.[27] Girls' narratives brought out the fact that they see violence as a common aspect of the marital relationship. They hoped that their husbands would not be violent. According to them one of the main reasons for violence is 'suspicion' about the wife's chastity or her premarital relationships.

---

[27] A. George, *op. cit.*, 1997.

In the families to which the students in the study belonged, marriages were almost exclusively arranged. Girls had little freedom in the selection of their marriage partners and they seldom got to know the partner before they married. Under such circumstances girls had to follow the prescribed social norms and in fact be as close to the societal norm as possible so as to be chosen by a 'good' groom. As marriage is seen more in terms of an arrangement that provides security, girls especially liked to ensure this. Girls preferred 'arranged marriages' to 'love marriages' as the latter was seen as an arrangement beset with enormous insecurity.

The majority of boys and girls thought that 'love marriages' were unsuccessful while 'arranged marriages' were successful, but they gave different reasons in support of their views. According to the girls, parents generally opposed 'love marriages'. If the couple married against the wishes of family, they were likely to face hurdles and in the end the girl is tortured by her husband, *'Ladki ki dhulai hothi hai'* (FGD, Third Year girls). 'Love marriages', did not, thus, ensure an escape from violence. They visualised the future of a girl in a 'love marriage' as being worse than that of a girl in an 'arranged marriage' as she had neither the support of her husband and his family that of her natal family. Students, especially girls, preferred an 'arranged marriage' for its stability and security—*'isme bharosa hota hai'*—as 'it is the family's responsibility' (FGD, Third Year girls). In 'love marriages', the responsibility for their decision rested entirely with the couple and all the consequences had to be faced alone. Although some of the students did favour 'love marriage', the general opinion was against it:

(Third Year girl)
[I will] Marry the boy uncle decides.
Why?
When people at home have arranged the marriage, then even if in-laws ill-treat, then family can be blamed for arranging it. When parents arrange the marriage, then much of the responsibility is on them.

(Standard XI girl)
I will never do it [marry] with my own choice, I will do with my parents' choice only.

(Standard XI girl)
Only arranged marriage…because it is like that only in our

culture. If we do love marriage and husband leaves us then daddy will say, 'you had done it, so now you only suffer', that's why arranged marriage is only good ... [In arranged marriage] parents do not become unhappy or else those parents who have brought us up they will get a bad name in society.

As caste considerations continue to dictate marriage and kinship arrangements, girls were particularly warned against violating caste norms:

(Standard XI girl)
Love marriage or arranged marriage?
Arranged.
Why?
At home [they] will not give permission. They don't like all these.
Did they say anything like that?
Yes. Before coming to college [they warned me]. Even now they say, 'If any boy teases you, you tell us. If I come to know that you have an affair with any boy (*Challa aahe*) then I will kill him and kill you too.'
Why so? Any love marriage in your family?
Yes. Cousin brother.
Then for him is there no problem?
No. He is a boy and I am a girl.

(Third Year girl)
Do you like any boy?
Yes.
Have you told [your family] about it?
No.
Why not?
It [marriage] will not happen only, then why tell [anyone]?
Why will it not happen? Is he of another caste?
Yes.
Where does he stay?
Near my house.

Boys had different reasons for voting against 'love marriage'. For them, since 'love marriages' were often outside of one's caste and community it led to problems of adjustment with each other's families and customs. This led to conflicts within the family. Under such circumstances, 'boy is in a dilemma whether to listen to his mother or to his wife' (FGD, Third Year boys).

There seemed to be consensus among boys and girls that they would consider marrying for love if the religion, caste and community of the partners matched and if their parents and family members had no objection to the marriage.[28] Some of the boys saw an advantage in a 'love marriage', as they would know the girl's past but in the case of a mariage that was arranged, this was difficult. Further, boys stated that 'love' and 'marriage' do not go together as 'love is only with the opposite sex and marriage is with the whole family' (FGD, Third Year boys). Such distinctions were also reflected in the differential qualities that they sought in a lover and wife. Girls made no such distinction between lover and husband.

With regard to partners, boys and girls had different expectations. Boys emphasised the 'good character' and virginity of the girls they were to marry. In addition, they considered 'looks' important, but more important were other considerations; 'the girl should be simple but not an *agdich kakubai*' (a very traditional woman), 'should be '*ghareloo*' (homely), 'of understanding and compromising nature', 'should respect elders', and 'of over all good character'. Further, the girl should be educated but not more educated than the boy. With regard to partners in temporary relationships such as 'time-pass', boys preferred partners with good 'looks' and a 'carefree' (*bindaas*) nature.

Girls desired partners more educated than themselves, with a steady job and who were by nature loving and caring. There was an emphasis on his character too, 'he should not look at any other girl after marriage', 'should not have any addiction', 'should not be suspicious' and 'should treat wife with respect'. Good looks were not as important as these qualities.

The theme of virginity was discussed at length during FGDs and was emphasised directly or indirectly in the interviews. Girls used terms such as 'pure', '*paripakwa*', 'untouched', '*kaumaryata*', to refer to virginity, which reflected the cultural connotations

---

[28] The girls who had a boyfriend preferred what some of them referred to as 'love-cum-arranged' marriage, that is, to route the proposal through the parents who would then arrange the marriage. Those who had boyfriends from another religion, caste or community did not expect parental consent and were aware that the relationship may be temporary. The awareness that the relationship was temporary prevented girls from establishing physical intimacy with their male partners.

embodied within them.[29] Boys used English terms such as 'virginity', 'hymen' or the Hindi term, 'pardah' or terms such as 'seal', 'seal pack', 'curtain', and so forth. It was found that although girls lacked anatomical knowledge of the hymen/pardah in the female body, the cultural meanings of virginity as embodied in terms such as 'pure' and 'untouched' were well known to them.

The high premium placed on a girls' virginity may be seen from the fact that more than half the girls and boys from the survey considered 'virginity as a girl's most valuable possession'. Similar views were expressed during the FGDs and interviews. Emphasising the importance of a wife's virginity, boys stated that '*Aadmi to* fresh *phal hi khayega na!*' (man will consume only fresh fruit. Isn't it!) (FGD, Third Year boys). The test of virginity was that the girl should bleed at the time of first intercourse.

(Third Year boy)
In married women, first time, blood comes, it is painful.
Why?
Because the 'seal' breaks.
What is it?
It is a curtain [pardah] on the vagina. It tears while doing intercourse.... The penis pains while breaking the 'seal'.

(Third Year boy)
Girl with whom 'game' [intercourse] is done she is called a non-virgin, and the girl who has never come in contact, not had intercourse, she is called a virgin female.
In virgin girl, the 'seal', means one curtain [pardah] is there. If it is not there this can be known during intercourse.

(Third Year boy)
Can come to know if there is 'seal pack' during first intercourse experience. It is not necessary, if she is sports woman, or goes to gym., then in them it is not there.... And if that thing [sex] is not done then during first intercourse there is heavy bleeding.

(Third Year boy)
[Virgin means] Whether lady is '*paripakawa*' or not.
'*Paripakawa*' means.
Has any man used her before.

---

[29] Many girls who participated in the FGDs and interviews were unfamiliar with the English terms, 'virgin' and 'virginity'.

Contrast the above narratives of the boys with that of the girls:

(Third Year girl)
Paripakwa means?
Means 'pure'. That girl who has not been involved in any sexual affairs before marriage.
How do you come to know?
That I don't know, you tell me please.

(Third Year girl: The only girl among the girl participants who had some information about the hymen and who had reported sexual experience.)
If a girl does not bleed after doing sex, that means she has experienced sex before ... so he comes to know that she had already experienced sex before. I think, when a boy does sex forcefully, then if the girl is doing sex for the first time, then there are some tissues in her private parts, they get torn, and bleeding takes place.

Girls, in the hope of preventing violence in their lives, controlled their sexuality prior to marriage by preserving their virginity. Loss of virginity and premarital pregnancy not only jeopardises the prospects of marriage for these girls, but also brings 'shame' on them and their families. As some of them during the FGDs, stated, 'anything can happen' and 'it is better not to get into these things' (relationships and sex) as 'our family will get a bad name in society':

(Third Year girl)
This is not good, at least not before marriage.
With the person whom you are going to get married?
No, not even with that person. There was a couple near our place, in their case this [sex] had happened ... that their marriage was fixed and the boy died in an accident just eight days before marriage; and the girl is pregnant now. Now, who will marry her?

(Third Year girl)
What is your opinion about having sexual relations with some-one before marriage?
Chee—[pause]—It should not happen only.

(Third Year girl)
Chee—[keeping her hand on her face] should not do only.

Thus since virginity in girls was highly valued, for girls pre-marital sex was taboo. Girls themselves believed that it was all right for boys to engage in premarital sex but certainly not all right for girls. As premarital sex was seen as a major cause of marital discord, some of the girls had stated that even if girls had engaged in premarital sex, they should not reveal it to their husbands as it may lead to domestic discord, violence and even desertion. Boys stated that if their wife had previous friendships with boys it would be tolerated but not any sexual relations thus confirming the fears that girls expressed. The double standards in sexuality were obvious, as boys felt it was permissible for them to have had premarital sex but not so for their wives:

> (Standard XI boy: He has a girl friend and plans to marry her yet the notion of virginity was strong).
> If she isn't like this (virgin) then I won't marry her... [I will] tell her to go—kissing is okay, nowadays it has become common.

> (Standard XI boy)
> **If you come to know that your wife had an affair before marriage?**
> Will divorce her.
> **But how will you come to know?**
> She will have a 'seal'.
> **Where?**
> In vagina.
> **What is it like?**
> *Te mahiti nahi pan pahilyanda thokeyavar raktat yete asa mahiti aahe* (That I don't know, but first time when fucked blood comes—that I know).
> **Every woman has the seal?**
> Yes, it is there and if not, then she is called *bhikarchot*.

As far as the extramarital relations of their future spouse were concerned, girls were more tolerant. For instance, the common responses were: 'will try to find out if it is true', 'will try to understand', or 'will try to make him understand'. Some of the boys saw the possibility of extramarital relations for themselves, however, divorce was the answer if their wives engaged in such relationships. There were a few boys who felt less strongly about their wives having premarital or extramarital relationships.

Many boys believed that the pardah (hymen) is thick and therefore has to be forcefully penetrated which leads to bleeding. Some of them also thought that the seal completely covers the vagina. The misconceptions regarding virginity were not limited to the thickness of the pardah, bleeding as a sure test of virginity and how much bleeding occurred, it extended to other physical features as well.[30]

Preserving one's virginity for one's future husband figured prominently in the narratives of girls as a reason for abstaining from premarital sex.

(Third Year girl)
I would allow to touch my hand and all, but no kissing and all.
Why....
I don't want all these before marriage.
Why is it so?
I want to be a virgin ... true and loyal to the person whom I am going to marry.

Other important reasons for girls abstaining from premarital sex were its undesired consequences such as pregnancy, shame for self and family and marital conflicts. Boys too expressed concern over a girl's virginity:

(Standard XI boy)
[girls] should not do all this.
Why?
If marriage doesn't take place then she will feel very bad *na*—that some boy had touched her.

(Standard XI boy)
If they are not married then it is not at all worth because this ruins a girl's life.
How?
They will do kissing, smooching, take hand in hand, then who will marry her and who will accept her?

Contrast the above responses of the boys with that of the girls:

(Standard XI girl)
Because children can be conceived.... Everywhere girl gets bad

---

[30] Beliefs such as 'the breasts of a non-virgin are loose' and so on.

name and boy remains aside [he is not in the picture, no body blames him].
If boy does such a thing then is it alright?
People will not say anything to the boy but to a girl they will say that she was like that only.

(Standard XI girl)
After marriage if the husband comes to know then there will be unnecessary fights and parents will also get a bad name.

(Third Year girl)
Before marriage it is wrong but after marriage it is not wrong.
Why is it wrong?
The society we all live in, considers all these things to be wrong.

Some of the girls felt boys could not be trusted.

(Third Year girl)
Because after keeping such relationship, the boy can betray the girl. Nowadays many such incidents are heard of. Can't trust anyone, and the woman is so weak [helpless], On top of this, our society blames only the woman for this.

Thus, attitudes towards premarital sex are closely linked to the notion of virginity, the fear of desertion by the boy and family honour. Gender differences and double standards in sex are reflected in their attitudes.

For girls, the focal point around which sexual discourse takes place is marriage. While premarital and extramarital sex was perceived to be 'all right' for boys, it was a taboo for girls. For most girls sex and marriage were synonymous and therefore premarital sex was 'bad' or 'wrong'. Preserving one's virginity was perceived as crucial in the context of marriage. But for boys sex and marriage were not synonymous and therefore premarital and extramarital sex were viewed as being different from sex within the confines of marriage. As far as boys were concerned, male sexuality could not be confined to the institution of marriage.

The degree of gender difference and the nature of double standards seen in young people's attitudes to sex, specifically premarital and extramarital sex, reflect the social and cultural constructions that control and subordinate female sexuality. Both men and women are agents involved in the construction and maintenance of patriarchal ideology; embodied in virginity, in the centrality of marriage, as well as in the potential use of violence in the subjugation of female sexuality.

Conclusion

Our study on youth sexuality in an Indian metropolitan city shows that gender relations among the youth from lower middle class, nuclear households, continues to be asymmetric and all pervasive. The differences are most significant in the differential opportunities that boys and girls have in terms of access to information, and in the exploration of their sexuality. The narratives of boys and girls, in the context of a patriarchal sexual culture reflect distinct early sexual experiences. These early experiences manifest in the development of male sexuality as assertive/aggressive, and in the cultivation of sexual passivity, timidity and a sense of shame in females. Thus, sexual identities are formed and gender roles are internalised by boys and girls, during early adolescence. These are reflected in their social interactions, attitudes and views regarding marriage and sex and in the nature and extent of their sexual experiences.

The family continues to play a significant role in the sexual socialisation of young people but particularly so in the case of girls. The socialisation of girls and the management of their sexuality are effected through various cultural practices and religious rituals. Other studies have shown that girls are socialised from birth to believe that they do not belong to the natal family. As the saying goes 'bringing up a daughter is like watering a plant in someone else's courtyard'.[31] The idea of the centrality of marriage in a woman's life is imbibed by girls in childhood and is strengthened during their adolescence.

Life, however, does not take a significant turn for a girl until she attains puberty. There is considerable difference in the life of pre-pubertal and post-pubertal girls. After puberty is attained, elders, by chaperoning and policing them, impose restrictions on girls. Religious rituals and practices that are expected to enhance fertility, to ensure a good husband and motherhood and to control sexual feelings, are initiated. The overall content of a girl's

---

[31] L. Dube, *op. cit.*, 1988.

socialisation during this period is to groom her mind and body for the future husband, who is to be worshipped. In the formation of female sexuality, the onset of menstruation is the most significant event as it embodies all the elements that constitute female sexuality: the female body as polluting, the body as the signifier of family honour, shame attached to the female body, female sexuality as dangerous and in danger and the linking of fertility with sexuality.

Although in premarital relationships girls do not feel pressurised to have sex with their boyfriends and they exercise their choice not to do so, this choice is often made as a security measure 'just in case the relationship did not end in marriage' or to protect themselves from undesired consequences. A closer look reveals that the girls' abstinence from sex is guided by the patriarchal ideology of preserving one's virginity for one's future husband. The notion of virginity embodied in the cultural construct of *pativrata* expressed as being 'pure' and 'untouched' continues to be strongly held both by girls as well as boys. Boys expect their brides to be virgins even though they themselves have had premarital sexual relations with more than one partner. The views of boys and the behaviour of girls, are mutually reinforcing, simultaneously reinforcing the dominant, gendered sexual ideology.

Our study shows that liberalism with regard to sexuality is male oriented and preserves the traditional notions of male and female sexuality. This is evident from the internalisation and perpetuation of the ideology of 'shame' and 'honour' linked to female sexuality, and the social arrangements that continue to keep girls ignorant about their own bodies and sexualities while enhancing avenues for information and exploration of male sexuality, through easy access to erotic sources, commercial sex and sexual liaisons with 'aunties'. The modern trends in sexual liberalism of the metropolises promoted by forces of globalisation are by themselves inadequate to question this ideology and the cultural significance of the *Lakshman Rekha*, confining female sexuality, continues. It neither protects the woman nor does crossing it liberate her.

10

'Cheli-Beti' Discourses of Trafficking and Constructions of Gender, Citizenship and Nation in Modern Nepal

◆ Sushma Joshi

Trafficking, as a cultural construct, national myth, media enter-prise and social issue, has generated discourses around it from multiple locations. Engaging with these discourses means interrogating notions of gendered bodies and sexuality, migration and work, transnational boundaries and capital and the virtual circulation of media representations. By looking at the sites from which these discourses originate, and are reproduced and dis-seminated, I hope to chart a rough guide that allows us to traverse the fault-lines of power in modern Nepal.

Within Nepal and in other parts of the subcontinent, trafficking has come to symbolise a process through which women and girls are taken across borders and sold in mass numbers into brothels and into sex-work without their knowledge, acquiescence or con-sent. This concept has been taken up as an issue by actors from diverse locations: activists, non-governmental organisations, international organisations, the media and the state have all started to act, write and represent the issue within their own frameworks and capacities. The term has elicited donor funding from a wide variety of sources, shaping the contours of the discussion.

This is an attempt to interrogate some of the main discourses that have arisen and gained prominence around the concept of trafficking. I am especially interested in the effects they have on different imaginative terrains, state policies and, eventually, on constructions of gender, citizenship and nation. I have chosen to focus mainly on discourses generated in and around Nepal; specifically around Nepali women and girls in India.

In the first section, I look at the main processes of gender formation within the Nepali nation, including the notion of women-as-kin and the concept of the nation as the natal home. I go on to analyse some of the assumptions behind rehabilitation, and the trope of genderised purity that exists within Nepal, and their value in maintaining existing power relations and hierarchies within the family and the nation state.

I then go on to look at the main disjunction within the activist movement: the sex-as-slavery versus the sex-as-work issue, and how hegemonic formations of gender and sexuality are reconstructed and reified around this debate. I end by highlighting the role of the media and the symbolic violence that occurs with Orientalist representations, and the ways in which these representations help to reify concepts of a poor, backward and dependent nation, thereby allowing existing power relations to continue.

Cheli-Beti

Nepal, a nation state ruled by a feudal aristocracy until the 1950s, has notions of female citizenship that are still based on ideas of kinship. In a world of feudal relations, power circulated within kinship networks and systems of patronage. The family was the linchpin of the social network, and people were organised according to their kinship relations. Within this cosmology, kinship still plays a very strong role in access to any government or private institution. The concept of a citizen as it exists in other democratic states, imbued with 'rights' that give them automatic access to certain privileges, has yet to be thought out within Nepal.

Because of this, women's identities within the nation are still very much as kin: as mothers, daughters, sisters and in-laws. Although the constitution guarantees the equality of men and women, discriminatory provisions in the National Civil Code still exist.[1] Women, for instance, still do not have the legal right to inherit parental property unless they stay unmarried until the age of 35, since sons are still regarded as carrying on the family line. In the aftermath of the Democracy Movement, feminist activists were still struggling to carve out a gendered space where female citizenship could be articulated and defined. This indeterminate period was filled up very quickly with conceptualisations of a very strong and articulate anti-trafficking movement. The movement, dominated by urban, middle class, Brahmin–Chettri women, was very successful in using the language of kinship to push forward its women-as-victims narrative of trafficking. *Cheli-beti* (literally, daughters) is used as a blanket term to refer to all Nepali women living and working in India, regardless of their age. The notion of women as cheli-beti has been so successfully disseminated that trafficking in the Nepali language is known as *cheli-beti bech bikhan* (the sale of daughters). This phraseology has consolidated and reified the status of women-as-dependent-kin within the nation, blurring attempts to restructure women as citizen–subjects.

I have used a number of eclectic sources of information, including publications by non-governmental organisations (NGOs), conference narratives and personal experiences, to talk about the discourses of trafficking and their impact inside Nepal. While personal experience is never indicative of the larger framework, I would like to use one to illustrate a number of pertinent points about the trafficking discourse and its impact on gender roles, female citizenship and female mobility within Nepal.

In 1997, I was going on a professional trip to Dhaka when I was stopped at the airport by immigration officials. I had all my papers with me, including documentation from the organisation that I worked for that corroborated why I was making the trip. I had a male colleague with me from my office. The border official who stopped me started to interrogate me about my activities in Dhaka. 'Timi', the form of address that he used to speak to me, is usually used in informal situations between younger family members or very close friends, or as a patronising form of address to a stranger.

---

[1] Shadow Report on the Initial Report of the Government of Nepal on the Convention on Elimination of All Forms of Discrimination against Women (CEDAW).

After ten minutes of this, I started to get angry and raised my voice. The man told me flatly that he was not going to allow me to get through immigration.

After I complained, I was approached by the head official who explained to me that he was only doing this for my own protection, because '*hamro cheli-beti haru lai hamilay hayrnu parcha* (we have to take care of our daughters and sisters).' He also explained to me that I might be trafficked in Bangladesh, and that I needed a male guardian to take responsibility and vouch that I would not get sold (*bechinu*) in Bangladesh. He told me that if I was travelling to the Gulf I would never be allowed to go, but since I was only going to Bangladesh I could leave the next day if I came back with a guardian who would vouch for my safety.

The next day, when I came back with my brother, I was met by a more important immigration official who told me that he was only letting me go because he knew my brother personally. Then he said: 'I heard you used all these foul words yesterday. *Aimai bhayara pani testo garne kasto laj nabhayako* (how could you, as a woman, use such words without shame?)' Only after I was properly chastised was I allowed to take my delayed flight.

Due to this articulation of women-as-kin, it was perfectly acceptable for an immigration official to address me as 'timi' (younger female kin), to use quasi-legal authority to stop me from making any moves to defile my sexual purity, and to chastise me for the use of language inappropriate for a sister or daughter. Within this framework, it was also completely acceptable to ask for a male guardian to guarantee my safety, implying that I could cross the home boundaries only with the full cognisance of my (male) guardian. As a woman, any work that I did outside the home did not have the same legitimacy that a man's would have had: while men can and are expected to work outside the home/nation, within the frameworks of a middle class gender formation, women still stay at home and do not go travelling alone into dangerous terrain without their family's permission. To this day, a Nepali woman, cannot apply for a passport without her guardian's permission. An official form signed by the guardian and attested by a 'gazetted' officer of His Majesty's Government is a prerequisite for making the application. Any woman who steps outside the familial territory and reproductive role is, therefore, automatically under suspicion of breaking moral and social codes of appropriate behaviour.

Perhaps more pertinently, as a woman, I was seen to be incapable of stopping myself from being sold without my knowledge—even when I was 25 years old, was working for the Harvard School of Public Health and had spent six years living, by myself, abroad. Women, within this conceptualisation, are viewed as dependent on men for their safety, their knowledge of the world, and the parameters of their activities. It was also acknowledged that I could 'sell myself' (*afailai bechnu sakhuhuncha*), but while it was acknowledged that a woman would have the agency to 'sell herself', it could never be a voluntary act. By the very nature of the transaction, one cannot sell oneself. By consolidating the multi-faceted nature of people's mobility and reducing multiple and complex economic, social and political transactions under one mythical signifier, 'selling' (*bech-bikhan*), the discourse of trafficking within Nepal has managed to co-opt and reduce all issues of migration and labour to a single homogeneous event.

To summarise, the anti-trafficking discourse voiced mostly by a middle class, Brahmin–Chettri group of female activists, has been very influential in creating a myth of trafficking that has been instrumental in shaping the relationship of women to the state and nation. Most of this discourse has been influential in reifying the notion of women-as-kin, while obfuscating the need to define women as citizens of the nation.

Maiti

Maiti, in Nepali, means the natal home. Before I go on to elaborate on the concept of maiti, I would briefly like to mention that the most influential, and visible, non-governmental organisation in the anti-trafficking movement in Nepal in the last few years has been 'Maiti Nepal'. This organisation received international attention after Prince Charles initiated a fund-raising campaign by sending an open letter to the *Sun* appealing for funds by selling his limited edition of watercolours. The readers of the *Sun* collected a total of £67,000, and *You* magazine another £20,000 for this organisation. Since then, an enormous amount of attention has been showered on the organisation, including funding from all over the world, citations in media productions on trafficking, fund-raising dinners in wealthy areas of the West Coast of the

United States, and even oil painting exhibitions. The founder, Anuradha Koirala, has recently appeared on none other than *The Oprah Winfrey Show*, the globally syndicated American talk show. This attention has recreated Maiti Nepal as a virtual icon of all that symbolises Nepali trafficking in the global imagination. In this section, I would like to tease out some of the implications of the concept of maiti, rehabilitation, and the way this discourse has impacted on policy and gender formations within Nepal.

The term maiti, in Brahmin–Chettri culture within Nepal, refers to the natal home, the home territory that girls grow up in before they get married and go off to their husband's homes. In Nepal, the term is imbued with certain connotations: a space where women will always be treated with love, but also a space where they do not have any rights vis-à-vis their brothers. It is a space that evokes sadness, since it is the space that women live and grow up in, all too briefly, before they have to leave; it is also a place of joy since it is there that they are able to see their families again. While the maiti offers women special privileges, like love, care and limited financial support, it is also clearly defined as a space where daughters have no formal inheritance or economic rights. It is a space restricted to a woman once she formally leaves it— the 'leaving' imbued with the assumption that girls only leave the home on the occasion of their marriage.

Once a woman is married, she cannot come back to the maiti at all times. The times when she can come back are carefully controlled and regulated from both sides of the family. Visits are restricted to certain festivals and days. Even today, women in very orthodox Hindu families visit their natal home only on these days. These formalised visits apply social pressure on reluctant in-laws, who control women's mobility to the extent of not allowing daughters-in-law to visit their parents. On the other hand, women are also discouraged by their maiti if they try to stay for long periods of time, since that space formally belongs to their brothers and, by extension, to their sisters-in-law. Within this framework, the women are loved members of the maiti, but still outside the family parameters, and can come only as visitors. It is a space where women can return in situations of extreme desperation, for example, in cases of desertion or the death of a husband, but this coming back is never a right: it is always a favour bestowed on the woman by her natal family. The woman and her children, if she has any, are always treated as family members with limited rights. Within the hierarchy of the family, where gender and age privileges are paramount, a woman who returns to the maiti is usually a social outcast.

I would like to take up this trope of the maiti as a defining feature of the anti-trafficking and rehabilitation discourse within Nepal, and its implications for national policy. After the Bombay raid in 1996 when the police 'rescued' hundreds of girls and women from brothels, the Nepali government refused to take responsibility for rehabilitating underage girls from Bombay, citing the spread of AIDS in Nepal as a reason. Bombay care organisations finally approached a number of Nepali NGOs and the girls were formally divided between them. Among these organisations were CWIN, WOREC, ABC Nepal, Maiti Nepal and a few others. These organisations are not unified in their political positions: while half of them belong to the National Alliance against Trafficking, which views women as kin, who have been victimised by poverty and evil criminals, and prostitution as sexual slavery, the other half belong to the Alliance Against Trafficking in Women and Children in Nepal (AATWIN), with members who take into account questions of labour and migration. Most of the organisations have gained prominence through individual leaders who have appeared in print publications, on radio and on the television and in other forums citing a discourse of kinship, sacrifice and service to the cause of the helpless. Anuradha Koirala, the founder of Maiti Nepal, has been referred to as an 'Angel of Mercy' by Prince Charles, and although this title, also used to refer to Mother Teresa of Calcutta, has not gained currency in Nepal, it has been picked up and circulated through a variety of media in the West.

The history of professional social work in Nepal is very brief. There are no institutions that train people in providing care in a professional setting. With the exception of a few classes in social work at some colleges, most people who work in non-governmental organisations have come from other professional backgrounds. In the case of organisations run by women, many have been started by women who had no particular work experience but were personally committed to saving oppressed women. Anuradha Koirala has been depicted as a committed housewife who started taking destitute women into her home and who overcame enormous odds to help them. An Internet brochure[2] says that Maiti Nepal started by facilitating an initial project at Gaushala, Kathmandu, which was:

> aimed at providing a safe shelter to the poor and destitute women living in the Pashupatinath area. A majority of these women had, at one time or the other, been forced to submit to the numerous social injustices so common in our society, and whose only means of a sustainable life was to beg for alms or indulge in prostitution.

Pashupatinath, one of the main Hindu temples of the Kathmandu Valley, has always attracted women who have fallen out of the social net, and it has always been a long-standing tradition that bourgeois women rendered service by providing for the poor, the destitute, the sick and the ailing. This tradition of charity means that the relationship between the women being saved and the women doing the saving has always been conceptualised along the familiar lines of family and kin. The organisational head is conceptualised as the mother or mother-in-law, with the authority and the power to control the other women's desires, movements and morality. The victims are often portrayed, as in the trafficking discourse, as daughters or daughters-in-law—as younger female kin who are to be protected, but also to be disciplined, regulated and brought within the confines of normal social behaviour.

This model of social work becomes particularly problematic when one begins to question ethnic dynamics: Nepal, a country of diverse ethnic cultures, also has many different acceptable models of marriage, sexuality and sexual behaviour. However, orthodox, Bhrahmin–Chettri, mores of sexuality have come to define the hegemonic form of 'Nepali culture', with virginity seen as a valued social concept, and premarital sex, multiple marriages and separations seen as unacceptable social practices. Nonetheless, it is well documented that polygamy, premarital sex, divorce and other social practices unacceptable outside of the mainstream 'Nepali culture' exist and flourish in the diverse ethnic groups of the nation.

In the trafficking discourse, however, girls are still conceived of as pure virgins, without knowledge and without sexual desire, waiting for their monogamous arranged marriages when they are

---

[2] http://www.captive.org/maiti.htm#MAITI NEPAL.

spirited, duped and sold off by criminals, including 'lazy and parasitic'[3] men belonging to their own community. This model brings up a few intriguing questions, including the sheer logistical impossibility of taking a supposed 200,000 women across the borders against their will.

A revealing document that illustrates this mode of thought, is a report titled *Girls Trafficking in Sindhupalchowk*, brought out by ABC Nepal, one of the organisations involved in anti-trafficking activism. The document goes on to note that: 'In Nepalese society, women are respected and considered an important part of the society, but in these village committees they were not only disrespected but even harassed by their own brothers, fathers and boyfriends.' The report further goes on to note that:

> Tamangs comprise about seventy per cent of the total population.... Tamangs send their daughters and daughter-in-laws to the brothels in India to supplement their income....In a place where most of the people are illiterate, one can see signs of relative prosperity....Further, when questioned, they seemed to prevent each other from disclosing facts.... Information given to the interviewers showed that the trading of girls was in fact an open affair among Tamang households...when questioned, they were rather aggressive and arrogant about any sort of discussion about the issue and thus made the survey impossible.[4]

This report not only brings up questions about the exact nature of the power relations between the interviewers and the interviewees, including ethnic, class and religious dynamics, but also raises some pertinent points about the influx of wealth and how this is viewed by groups from outside the community. The exact nature of the relationships between the procurers, the brothels, the girls, the women and their families, the symbolic market of expectations, the nuances of negotiations are also subsumed and erased in this hegemonic representation.

This representation also assumes that women, once they have gone off to Bombay, become defiled and cannot come back without special symbolic purification rites. While ethnic communities might accept girls who have left their homes to work, have earned

---

[3] *Girls Trafficking in Sindhupalchowk*, ABC Nepal.
[4] *Loc. cit.*.

money, have had sexual relationships outside of marriage, and might even accord them status; mainstream 'Nepali culture' demands that women who have stepped outside their reproductive roles only come back as victims, because only then can they be embraced back into the home territory. As people without agency, their experiences can be blamed on evil criminals. As victimised bodies, they have had no hand in the experiences that they have undergone, therefore exempting them from taking responsibility for their overstepping of social and sexual boundaries. As suffering, destitute victims, women have a right to the nation's sympathy and compassion, and a moral right to return to the maiti.

While translating an interview, for two British journalists, with one of girls rescued from Bombay, at Maiti Nepal, I asked a 16 year old girl, 'Did you know the man that you were going to Bombay with? Did you like him?' While the girl smiled and acknowledged that she had liked him, one of the Maiti guards who had been present throughout the interview, even when we had requested privacy, reacted angrily and answered, 'She did not know him well. He was a stranger.'

While the discourse of victimisation allows the girls to come back to the acceptable sphere of morality, and be suitably rehabilitated, it also eradicates any need to think about the opportunities for knowledge, work and mobility that make young women leave in the first place. Within this mainstream trafficking discourse, individual desires to travel, to be with a man, to get married, to cross borders, to look for work are eradicated. The woman is presented as a pure victim who was entirely unaware of the designs of the evil trafficker, who then sold her body into sex-slavery.

I am not disputing the fact that there is deceit and misinformation, that women suffer under tremendously difficult working conditions, that they contract diseases and often become destitute. My concerns are simply with the erasure of the woman/girl as a subject within this discourse, as a subject within social and community networks with her own thoughts, desires and experiences, and the impact of this on how 'Nepali women' get created in the national imagination. I am concerned also about the reconstruction of the female subject as a body vulnerable to the whims of other people, a body that can be used and thrown away. Issues of adolescent sexuality and the need for sexual education are also erased within this framework.

Without agency, women are immobilised. They are bound to the roles given them: familial roles of dutiful wives and daughters, subject to the whims of domestic violence, to the powers of a state that defines them as kin and does not allows them the legitimacy to demand any other rights. The discourse of maiti, in this way, consolidates the familial gender roles of women within the nation. It also manages to co-opt younger and ethnic women's overstepping of gender roles by bringing them back within the hegemonic framework of what Nepali women are supposed to be like.

By redefining girls once again as younger family members, vulnerable and in need of paternalistic protection, grateful to be back in the maiti, the discourse allows the state to evade the responsibility of providing women certain rights: rights to inheritance; to land and property; to education and health care; to non-discriminatory laws regarding labour and migration; rights that could potentially transform cheli-beti into women who, voluntarily or involuntarily, would not have to get 'trafficked' again.

Rehabilitation

After the cheli-beti are trafficked, they are rehabilitated. What does this entail? A police raid ordered by the Bombay High Court in 1996 upon the brothels of Kamathipura led to the 'rescue' of approximately 400 to 450 women and girls. The figures vary as widely as 408, 437, 456 and 473 in various news accounts. These women were then put in ten children's homes and schools, like St. Catherine's Home and Nirmala Niketan, which are institutions for 'orphans and destitute children', some of them against their will. Problems quickly arose, with the women demanding food in excess of the meagre rations allocated by the government, and threatening to get violent if they were not released. A percentage of the women managed to escape this confinement by running away. Finally, the Bombay High Court was forced to segregate the 'prostitutes from the destitutes'.[5] After negotiation with the

---

[5] *Daily*, 17 Feb. 1996.

Nepal government, which refused to take the women back on the grounds that they would spread AIDS in Nepal, a number of non-governmental organisations were approached and given the task of rehabilitating the girls and women. About a hundred of them refused to go back to Nepal. In 1998, two years after the raid, 124 women and 4 children were sent back to their 'homeland'.[6]

The discourse of 'rehabilitation' within Nepal has focused on 'an education, counselling and safe home'.[7] Rehabilitation has also focused on 'encouraging women to be financially self-sustaining by teaching them income-generating skills, and providing women with information about personal health care and disease prevention.'

An education in most cases is basic literacy, and basic literacy in most cases mean adult literacy classes of limited scope where women learn, at the most, to write their names. The education that they receive often does not provide them with the skills needed to get higher-paying jobs. Income-generating skills like embroidering tablecloths, while admirable in intention, also often do not provide them with any long term, sustainable skills or institutions through which they can make a living. As women who have been living for a long time in the city are unlikely to choose to go back to the village and farm, this means that many have to find alternative, low-paying jobs in the urban sector.

While there are no clear statistics on women who have been 'rehabilitated', there are questions, and often speculative answers, since there has been no research done on the efficacy of the programmes that women go through, or their likely progression in the urban workforce. Do women go back to working in environments like the carpet and garment factories, which are the main sites of recruitment by procurers? In one of my interviews with a 25 year old Nepali in Falkland Road, the woman told me that many of the girls/women who had been 'rescued' in the raid of 1996 were back in Bombay living under assumed names and in disguise to evade further raids and to avoid being sent back to Nepal.

---

[6] John Stackhouse, 'Bangladeshi and Nepali Girls are in the Indian Brothels', *Toronto Globe and Mail*, reprinted in *combat*, Vol. 1, No. 3.

[7] *Maiti* Nepal's brochure.

Counselling, within the framework of bourgeois women's organisations, is counselling to return back to the family institution and back to a 'good life'. Durga Ghimire, President of ABC Nepal, 'an agency caring for twenty eight of the repatriated prostitutes', is quoted in a news article as saying: 'They are full of diseases but we can accept that. It is their right to return to Nepal, and if they return, we can give them good lives.'[8] Women are also counselled out of their bad habits. An interview with Maiti Nepal revealed that 'the girls' are often 'very rough when they come back, and speaking foul language....We re-educate them. It takes time but eventually they stop swearing and start behaving decently.' In other words, women are normalised back into bourgeois behaviour.

Another interesting aspect of the rehabilitation homes is the notion of the 'safe home'. A safe home for bourgeois Nepali women is one that is not easily accessible to outsiders, one where women can stay behind enough boundaries so that they are protected from any unwanted sexual, casual encounters, random violence, or force. A safe home creates women who are always under protection from the outside; women who, after a while, start requiring protection. A safe home entails setting up a certain number of boundaries so that undesirable people cannot easily locate or enter the space. Most domestic violence shelters in other countries are also not easily locatable for the sake of security and for protecting the women from intrusive media. The rehabilitation homes in Nepal, on the other hand, have a certain criteria for acceptable visitors. The houses are not off limits to foreign journalists, donors or visitors, no matter what their reason for visiting. Journalists from Nepal are also allowed to enter, but all Nepali visitors are discouraged, even barred. This raises the question of how many of the 'outside', specifically the Nepali outside, are seen to be undesirable and restricted from contact with the girls. Are family members allowed to visit the girls if they are under suspicion of having sold them? Are men, boyfriends or lovers, allowed to visit, or are these unacceptable relationships? Do the girls/women want these visitors? Are their wishes overridden by the authorities? Is there a fear that women will want to go back

---

[8] 'Indian, Nepali Prostitutes Rounded Up, Detained in AIDS Raids', Scripps Howard News Service by John Stackhouse, *Toronto Globe and Mail*.

to Bombay, in which case, they must be saved from themselves by sheer physical boundaries?

Barred doors, grilles and omnipresent guards watch every movement of the girls and visitors: one might expect this in the brothels of Kamathipura. There is a sense of psychic disjunction when one encounters this degree of surveillance in the rehabilitation homes. Perhaps the most alarming aspect of the 'safe space' of the' rehabilitative homes is their similarity to the brothels: institutions where women's mobility and access to the outside world is tightly controlled, where they are confined within a social system that provides them with very few opportunities to move on and do anything different, and where their behaviour, bodies and speech are regulated to fit the social norm. Women are not allowed to leave the institution because it is believed that the outside world is unsafe, and that they can only be safe within the confines, and the protection, of the home.

During my interviews with Nepali women in the red-light district of Bombay, I asked them if they knew the women in the other streets. Their answer was that they never left their area, and did not really know the other women even if they were living only a few rooms down the road. They were afraid to leave their area because it was 'unsafe out there, one did not know what would happen or what people would do to you.' The brothel was safe because it was bounded and familiar, with people to take care of any outside danger. This sense of women who were immobilised in a bounded space by fear was reconfirmed by my interviews with a pimp who also had his own laundry shop, who reiterated that I should not to leave his little cubby-hole while I was there: 'This is Kamathipura. You never know what will happen out there. Don't go out. Stay here and only then will you be safe.' He said this enough times and with enough conviction to make me uneasy about the street, even though I had been walking around it for many days without any sense of danger.

The tools used by rehabilitative homes and bourgeois family institutions to control the women's sexuality and to keep them within their gender roles, ends up paralleling the brothel's restriction of women's mobility through fear, and the psychological paralysis created in women. Women in North America do not get trafficked or sold without their knowledge because they learn to walk down the street, take a bus, go to school, go to the market, get a job and navigate a whole range of physical spaces without the notion that it is unsafe for them to do so. Bourgeois women in Nepal, on the other hand, are always being told of the dangers of 'the outside': stepping outside the safe *lakshman rekha*[9] of the home is always fraught with uncertainty.

This kind of fear, implanted in women at an early age, allows for the debilitating sense of paralysis and immobility that allows hard trafficking to exist in South Asia. Women in the brothels of Bombay, who might not have come there voluntarily and who would like to leave, are unable to conceive of other options because they do not have the knowledge, or the skills, to navigate beyond the bounded space that has been given them. The rehabilitation homes, by creating the very same limiting environment for returnees, do not give them additional skills to navigate the social, cultural and physical spaces that exist once they leave the safe home, making them vulnerable once again to control through fear.

More importantly, by reinforcing the notion that the only way to keep women safe/controlled is by putting them behind locks and bars, the rehabilitation homes continue to replicate the logic, and the conditions, that make trafficking possible. The 'safe home', ironically, is the very model that creates women who are vulnerable and need protection, who are not equipped with the skills to navigate any space beyond a very limited one, and who, once trapped into a condition from which they can see no other alternatives, can be very easily controlled with the spectre of outside dangers.

Purity

In a conference against sex trafficking in Dhaka, a 13 year old Nepali girl who had been rehabilitated in one of the homes told us her story in one of the panels for the survivors of prostitution.

---

[9] In the Ramayana, Laxman, the brother of Ram, is left by his brother to guard Sita. Sita sees a golden deer and demands that Laxman get it for her. Laxman is reluctant to leave his sister-in-law to the dangers of the forest but eventually, at her insistence, goes, but only after drawing a line with his bow across the threshold. This line, known as the *lakshman rekha*, would protect her from harm as long as she did not step across it.

In the beginning, the girl was unable to speak, and only did so after the head of the organisation in which she was being looked after encouraged her. Then she burst into tears and went on to say that she was going to share her tale of suffering so that other sisters might not have to go through the same experiences. Her story, which was told in Nepali and translated, was long and complex, and involved many incidents and sub-narratives. At the end of her testimony, one of the participants remarked, 'I did not know that Nepal was such a barbaric place.' Perhaps what struck me most about this narrative was the emotional resonance of the details in Nepali, details and themes that, to me, rang familiar bells from childhood fables: getting lost in forests, being found by millers, being adopted by a kind person, being treated unkindly and driven out of the home by a stepmother.

I am not disputing the nature of her suffering or the exploitative conditions of her childhood. What I found striking was the form of narrative that she chose to represent herself publicly, and the number of cultural themes of oppression, and parables of suffering, she had to include in a story that was being presented to the world. Compared to the stories of other survivors from the USA and the Philippines, which were straightforward, personal, autobiographical accounts of economic deprivation and familial abandonment that led to a slow slide into prostitution, I found the narrative of the 13 year old Nepali girl different in two fundamental ways: her story was not just her story, it was a parable of suffering and oppression of all destitute and abandoned girls. Secondly, she was very aware of it being a 'Nepali' story.

Let me elaborate on these two themes. A Nepali girl who returns from Bombay is tainted in many ways: physically, sexually, socially, morally. Nepal as a bounded, ritual realm of unadulterated Hinduism, with an inner moral world separated from the outer immoral world, leads to a situation where crossing the border of the nation taints all Nepalis with the outside, and they become adulterated by their foreign experiences. The notion of people defiled by crossing the borders is symbolised by the *pani patiya*:[10] the 'complicated and time-consuming rites of ritual

[10] Mark Liechty, 'Selective Exclusion', *Studies in Nepali History and Society*, Vol. 2, No. 1 (1997).

purification' mandated by Prithvi Narayan Shah, and later the Gorkhali rulers, for any Nepali returning from outside the Hindu world.[11] It does not matter, therefore, that a woman left because she was destitute or abandoned, she still has to prove that her leaving of the inner, moral space was justified. The only way for her to regain a space in a society whose framework is built upon norms of sexual purity is to prove that she suffered from circumstances beyond her control. This, then, can only be done by including every single cultural trope of women's suffering in the oral tradition.

Putting all these parables together also creates a narrative that acts as a warning for other girls who might also be contemplating crossing boundaries. The woman who ran the organisation that the girl came from had, in fact, produced a tape of songs that warned women about what would happen to them if they went to Bombay. A narrative with such resonance acts as a public expiation: only somebody who has suffered so much, and who has come back to warn others about her experiences, one who, in other words, has redeemed herself by her suffering, can come back over the sacred threshold of the home.

Moreover, the concept of 'cheli-beti bech-bikhan', appropriated by many actors, in many locations, for their own purposes, has also been appropriated by the state as a Nepali 'national' story. It encapsulates all the elements of Nepali national identity: poverty, destitution, forced migration for the sake of labour opportunities, long separations from family members. All these elements come together to create a public image of Nepal in the eyes of the world that reinforces what we have always known: bad things happen to women in Nepal because it is a poor country. This myth side-tracks other issues, including questions of political commitment to changing gender discriminatory laws, nationwide efforts to make education accessible to girls, and provisions in the constitution that still treat women as kin rather than citizens.

In other words, trafficking has become a narrative that binds the nation together in certain fundamental ways: it keeps Nepal secure in the knowledge of its poverty, and the inevitability of the exploitation of its people outside the nation. It also keeps Nepal united against India and Indians, the Other, who exploit and use

---

[11] *Ibid.*.

the bodies of its women: its sisters and daughters. This anti-India feeling, I suggest, is fundamental to the consolidation of a national identity that keeps the boundaries of the two nations separate. Nepal, fundamentally dependent on India and the open border for the free flow of goods, capital and labour, has to actively recreate the border at all times in order to maintain the separation of the two nations. This permeability of the border, and the free flow of men and women into India looking for jobs, upsets the equilibrium of sovereignty. By making the flow of women into India forced, and never voluntary, Nepal manages to recreate the inviolability of its borders. By casting the clients as evil, exploitative Indian men, it reconsolidates the barrier against what is most threatening to Nepali national identity: the violation of purity.

Kumari: The Virgin Goddess

The myth of the virgin goddess is indisputably one of the biggest national myths of Nepal. The Kumari, the Living Virgin Goddess, extensively photographed, painted, filmed and written about in many languages, used as an icon for every single project representing Nepal, is a familiar symbol. The millions of tourists who come to Nepal every year are greeted by her image at the threshold between the airport and immigration. The Kumari, as a national trope of purity, reinforces certain gender norms within Nepal that I will expand on in this section.

One of the criteria for a 5 year old girl to be chosen as the Kumari, the Living Goddess, is that she should not have bled from any part of her body, so that even a girl who has cut herself is not acceptable as a candidate. The girl is cloistered in the old Kumari Ghar, a safe home where she looks out of the window and occasionally receives the king. She is also watched anxiously to make sure that she never cries while she is applying *tika*[12] the kings forehead, since a crying Kumari is an inauspicious event, and a sure sign that the present king is going to die. When she is around nine, before she reaches puberty, has her period and

---

[12] A sticky preparation of vermilion, rice and yogurt applied to the forehead as a blessing.

starts bleeding, she is replaced by another little girl. The Virgin Goddess, once she is symbolically defiled by her period and the permeability of her body, loses her divine status and can no longer represent the nation. Instead, she must go back to being an ordinary little girl. She is not, however, any ordinary girl: once fallen from the status of divinity, she is feared and thought to bring death to any man that she may marry. Her fall from divinity imbues her with the power to cause men's death.

The trafficking myth of Nepal cannot be analysed without taking this national myth into account. The Kumari is integral in consolidating and holding together the authority and legitimacy of another human divine: the king. The traditional power structure of the present Shah monarchy has always hinged on the notion of the Virgin Goddess, and the two institutions have always supported and legitimised each other. The king, regarded as an incarnation of Vishnu, is present at every Indra Jatra and at Dashain[13] to watch the procession and to receive the blessings of the Living Goddess. With the advent of the Democracy Movement, and voices of dissent and treason that might do away with the monarchy altogether, the monarchy is now on shaky ground and may have to define itself in more secular terms.

The political authority of the monarchy, while still derived from and tied to divine authority, has had to readjust to changes in power structures. Most people who support the king do so because they believe he is the one institution that keeps Nepal from being completely merged with India. With the historically friendly ties between the Nepali Congress Party and the Indian Congress Party generating no security or confidence in people that the party will not completely 'sell and eat Nepal',[14] many people see the king as the last remaining bulwark between Indian intervention and encroachment, and eventual takeover, of Nepali territory and affairs. It is of interest to note here that the notion of 'selling' the country has the same cultural resonance and generates the same outrage as 'cheli-beti bech-bikhan'.

---

[13] The 'National Festival' of Nepal, a fifteen-day harvest festival that takes place around Sept.–Oct., which celebrates the nine incarnations of the goddess Durga and also brings together the family as a social unit of meaning.

[14] 'bechara khai dincha', literally, 'they'll sell and eat Nepal.'

Nepal, as a nation, since the time of Prithvi Narayan Shah down to the Rana regime, has always constructed itself as geographically inaccessible, secluded and closed. National ideology has always stated that Nepal's seclusion is the reason for the non-interference of both its big neighbours in its internal affairs. Nepal's impermeability, in a way, has ensured its existence as a separate nation: unlike Sikkim, which was absorbed into the Indian state, Nepal sees itself as having managed to maintain its existence by being geographically and politically inaccessible.[15]

After the Democracy Movement in 1991, the new political leaders have been more amenable to the opening up of the borders, and allowing a better flow of trade between India and Nepal. This transitional time of national reinterpretation, where a closed, feudal political system starts renegotiating with its neighbours, has been fraught with anxieties. The anxieties revolve around two themes: the need to maintain sovereignty, and the need to maintain Nepal's boundaries.

With the advent of the change in political systems, there has been a high rate of migration both to and from India. This free mixing of migrant labour has blurred sharply maintained notions of an impermeable nation, sealed from the outside world. Another intrusion has been the free availability of Indian media and cultural productions in Nepal. India and Indian cultural influences are easily available and consumed at all levels: through Bollywood movies, through Doordarshan, through goods, through education, through travel and pilgrimages and through shared cultural notions. Prominent voices in Nepal have been raised about the need to maintain Nepal's own cultural and linguistic heritage against the onslaught of India. Nepal has at present felt a great need to create boundaries that cannot be breached. Women, the last frontier, add another blow to a carefully maintained sovereignty and purity by being publicly infiltrated by Indian men.

The reaction of the Nepali police illustrates this with more specificity. The police, having been involved by women's NGOs

---

[15] Liechty, in his article, 'Selective Exclusion', in *Studies in Nepali History and Society*, Vol. 2, No. 1, on the selective exclusion of foreigners from the Kathmandu Valley, discusses some of the historical reasons for 'isolation' and the efforts to 'hold back time', and how this became 'State policies and increasingly state myths'.

and International NGOs (INGOs) in their anti-trafficking activism, have taken up the issue with enthusiasm and have been active in promoting their anti-trafficking activities through the mainstream media, especially radio and television. Their involvement has meant that the nuances of trafficking have been reduced to a simple crime: an operation where women are drugged, duped or deceived into going to India. The television programmes, which are dramatised versions of police operations, are simple narratives of women who are intercepted at the borders and brought back to their homes.

One television programme, called *Beyond the Mountains*, warned women that if they did not see mountains any more, they could be in danger of being trafficked, and should therefore get off the bus and run away. The mountains, the omniscient symbol of Nepal, are used here as barriers between the women and their eventual destruction in India. In another television programme the issue was portrayed with flowcharts, with the police sitting around the table and talking about how to stop the flow of women, reminiscent of a military operation. The process, while envisioning and re-envisioning national boundaries through the mythic female body, also plays out the national anxieties of attack, adulteration and inundation by India.

To reorder the inaccessible nation again, it is necessary to recreate the myth of involuntary desecration. These anxieties of cultural and national disintegration, when reinscribed on female bodies, reinforce the notion of India as an encroachment. The discourse of trafficking in Nepal, then, always looks at trafficking as a 'Nepali' problem—never as a phenomena shared with Bangladesh, or the poorer states within India. Within the framework of the Nepali nation, trafficking is an event that only happens to Nepali girls. The thought of young cheli-beti, who are by extension Virgin Goddesses, being violated and desecrated by Indian men is intolerable and morally unjustifiable. The trafficking myth, in this way, gives a moral shape to Nepal as a sovereign nation and reinforces its separateness from India.

Legal Strategies

Women, as naive and guileless *cheli-beti*, can be rescued from the borders. They can be brought back from Bombay and put in rehabilitation homes. But what happens if they have never crossed a border in their life, if they are still living at home and are defiling themselves by working voluntarily as sex workers? This fundamental paradox of prostitution as work has been a major challenge to the anti-trafficking movement. For many people, the idea of prostitution is fundamentally unacceptable. Influential lobbies in the West, including the Coalition for Trafficking Against Women (CATW), which has consultative status with the UN, have written strong rebuttals of the idea of sex as work.

In Nepal, the anti-trafficking movement is starting to work towards tying the trafficking issue to prostitution. Presently, the laws regarding prostitution criminalise the woman. Brothels and organised prostitution are illegal. While there are no clearly defined red-light areas in Nepal, there are plenty of areas where women run tea-houses and small restaurants and have women who work as prostitutes as a side business.

Legal strategies to control prostitution have been suggested as part of the increasingly vocal activism of the anti-trafficking movement, which sees the market and demand for prostitution as the reason for trafficking. In a talk given at the British Council Library in Kathmandu by a prominent lawyer working with SNV, a Dutch INGO, on strategies to control trafficking, he discussed the need to control prostitution, including voluntary prostitution, in order to stop trafficking. If trafficking is the phenomena of taking women across borders through misinformation and against their will, why is it so imperative that in order to stop trafficking, we also need to stop women from voluntarily working as sex workers within Nepal? What is the linkage between the crime of involuntary trafficking and the crime of voluntary prostitution?

Prostitution, by removing women from the bourgeois reproductive order, acts to destabilise the moral framework in fundamentally the same way as trafficking: it removes young women from their homes, makes them cross moral and social boundaries, takes them beyond the control of the institutions of marriage and sometimes, the family. In other words, the phenomena of 'voluntary prostitution'—even though 'voluntary' is a laden word and the voluntary/involuntary binary too simple a dichotomy—makes us revise our ideas about trafficking. If women can and do 'choose', even outside of direct coercion and duping, through whatever economic, social and cultural factors, to work as sex workers, does this mean that there might be an element of 'choice' in the phenomena of girls/women leaving in mass numbers across the borders? In order to maintain the present narrative of trafficking, then, the anti-trafficking lobby has to suppress the idea that women could ever choose to practice sex as a profession, an income augmenting activity, a family business, or in exchange for favours. They have to be defined as the victims of a crime, otherwise the entire framework based on the ideology of women as dependent kin/victim would collapse.

In 1980, a revised law against human trafficking and control was passed establishing trafficking as a crime against the state—punishable with up to 20 years incarceration. The 1980 law also made the state responsible for proving guilt beyond reasonable doubt. Surveillance funding and programmes have also increased. The lawyer who gave the British Council talk was involved in a programme providing non-formal education to 2,400 girls between the age of 12–14 from the untouchable castes who are seen to be at risk of being trafficked. This programme seeks to register these adolescents with the authorities if they want to leave their guardians' house.[16]

In 1991, the Labour Department also framed a law which made it illegal for single women to travel to the Gulf. While men also suffer from unregulated and dangerous working conditions in the Gulf, this law is not in force for men. This forced women to travel through other exit points like airports in India, adding to their expenses. The government, after much criticism from activists, finally lifted the ban in January 2003.

These legal provisions and changes, while allowing for stricter control and regulation of women's and girls' mobility and for their surveillance, do not let go of the two fundamental frameworks that structure gender within Nepal: first, that women need guardians in order to be protected; and second, that they need to be put under surveillance so that they will not do anything that will put them in danger. In other words, women are still wards of more responsible powers, be it the family, the state or the police, and they are also objects who can be acted upon by other forces without their knowledge.

---

[16] Tal Halpern, *Report on Bol.* Mailing list about talk given by Yubraj Sangroula at the British Council Library, Kathmandu, Nepal.

Working from these ideological assumptions, the state structures gender in a way that limits the roles that women can take: women can only be wards of the family and community, dependent kin and reproductive beings within monogamous marriages. As J. Ann Tickner observes:

> Building on the notions of hegemonic masculinity, the notion of the citizen–warrior depends on a devalued femininity for its construction. In international relations, this devalued femininity is bound up with myths about women as victims in need of protection; the protector/protected myth contributes to the legitimation of a militarized version of citizenship that results in unequal gender relations that can precipitate violence against women.[17]

By restricting women's rights to cross borders and to look for work, in addition to criminalising an activity through which many women make a living, the state reinforces and legitimises the conditions of trafficking.

Orientalist Representations

I would like to end by looking at the way the issue of trafficking has been actively embraced, recreated and reified by a media apparatus that spans print publications, radio, television and independent documentary and the Internet, in both South Asia and outside. In this section, I argue that a neo-colonial apparatus of representation has been active in creating and supporting Orientalist constructions of trafficking. These constructions have combined with the representations circulating within Nepal, and the two have merged to create a specifically virtual image of the 'trafficked woman'. This process, in what Escobar has called an 'objectifying regime of visuality', is one where 'the panoptic gaze moves beyond its function of control to encompass the production of the social.'[18]

---

[17] J. Ann Tickner, *Gender in International Relations* (New York, Columbia University Press, 1992).
[18] Arturo Escobar, 'Power and Visibility: Tales of Peasants, Women and the Environment', in *Encountering Development: the Making and Unmaking of the Third World* (Princeton, Princeton University Press, 1994).

In spite of, or perhaps because of, the proportions this issue has assumed, the predominant narrative about trafficking has remained a journalistic one: evil traffickers lure naive village girls and sell them wholesale to brothels in the big city, where they are kept in slave-like conditions and eventually die of a fatal disease. This hegemonic narrative is created out of a combination of the discourses present and actively created in Nepal: from the press, the state, the women activists, the non-governmental organisations, which all have a stake in maintaining the narrative, which is then taken up and reified outside Nepal.

The international media has been very active in this hegemonic representation. While a few articles written by Indian journalists on sex workers' rights, on the nuances of the anti-trafficking movement, and on the poor rehabilitative measures of the government after the 1996 raid have appeared in newspapers and on the Internet, most articles have appeared in big US or British dailies or magazines, all of which reiterate and compound the dominant myth of trafficking. A few samples include: *Prince Charles Appeals to Save Sex Slave Children* (Reuters, London, 15 July 1998); *They Come Out of the Shadows* (*Hindu Online*, 3 March 1998); *Prince brings Hope to Nepal's Sex Slaves*, and so forth. Questions of migration and labour are never touched upon. Depictions of living and working conditions, the women's state of health, often depicted in horrific terms, fail to mention that working conditions are similarly horrific for many other men and women engaged in low-paid, low-skilled wage labour in poorer parts of the continent.

I would like to elaborate on this symbolic repression of representation by looking at the British media as a case study. Discourses cannot be separated from the means of cultural production that created them, and I have been especially interested in looking at how mainstream media has been instrumental in portraying and creating this story. No analysis of this journalism is complete without also looking into the imperatives of photography that accompany it, and the urge to virtually possess and capture the corporeal bodies that embody the fantasies of readers back home, and the visual violence, enabled by technological power, that can accompany this process.

The process of image-creation is tied to preconceived notions of what trafficked women *should* be like. With the exception of a few photographers who have done photojournalist work in the realist tradition, most photographic representations of trafficked Nepali women focus their panoptic gaze on young and beautiful women, most of them with Tibeto–Burman features, which fit notions of what Oriental women look like. Although there are enough Nepali women in areas like Kamathipura from the Chettri, Sarki and Kami castes, whose features look more like their southern neighbours from India, these women are never seen in photographs of 'trafficked Nepali women' in the mainstream media. Ironically, it is possible that these women might in many ways fit the definition of 'trafficked women' more than the women from the other ethnic groups. Women from Tamang and Gurung communities often seem to come to India in family or community groups, whereas the Chettri, Kami and Sarki women often live in isolation, an indication that they might have been brought to India and sold there individually.

But the vicarious gaze already has expectations: Nepali women without Mongoloid features would ruin the careful constructions of a story that the audience knows already. The process of creating art also requires that bothersome details like children, men, families and other nagging reminders of social relations be eradicated, presenting a pure space where 'the trafficked woman' is the only object.

The trafficking story is inescapably tied to the politics of representation that creates it. The British media's interest in the sex-trafficking issue has soared in the last few years, with big dailies competing for their very own trafficking exposé. The colonial imagination has also always found Nepal to be of special interest, with its colonial links via the Gurkhas. But the catalytic point seems to have been Prince Charles' involvement in the issue. While the motives of the royal personages and stars who get involved in various social issues are always matters for speculation, it is interesting to note that Prince Charles' popularity was at a low ebb after the death of Diana, and the sex-trafficking exposure managed to boost his popularity ratings. Sex and death have always been hot-sellers for the media, easily commodified and packaged for the mass market. This is particularly obvious when tied to children, who are vulnerable and therefore a perfect target for the moral activism of the socially conscious.

Mainstream journalism creates stories through processes which erase the nuances, the subtleties and the contradictions in search of a simple, black and white, saleable story. The story has to mirror the public's expectations. Complications ruin interest and lose readers who require digestible chunks of news. Moreover, in some cases the story has already been written in the head office by editors. This makes for an interesting working method: we basically have journalists who fly down for a week to 10 days, who must then make all the connections, find an interpreter, and in the case of a child trafficking story, find a trafficked child within a limited span of time. This process becomes quite difficult if 'the child' is already reified in the editor's mind in some specific way: a child who is shut up in the brothels, who is being held against her will, who has AIDS, or who is dying. So when journalists find themselves in brothels that are apparently being run by women, with girls and boys of all ages present, apparently not held in terrible slave-like conditions, the imagined story flounders. This is not the groundbreaking exposé the journalists were sent to discover.

The real story is one that legitimises a perceived dichotomy: a moral and ethical West, with a civilised culture, where women can be safe; and the immoral and unethical space of the East, where women and children are brutalised by their men. This construction engenders several possibilities: it allows for the supposed superiority of Western civilisation over the Eastern to continue; it allows for a rescue mission where people can go in, record and expose and then rectify, rescue and save; and it allows an elision of questions of global inequality, the effects of globalisation and liberalisation, and the history of colonialism. All of these difficult issues can be glossed over in the stark myth of Oriental brutality.

As a temporary translator of this process of mythic creation, I was especially struck by the disjunction between the questions asked by journalists and the responses of the girls who had been rescued from the brothels. The journalist wanted to know: Was the girl beaten? Raped? How many times did she have sex with the clients everyday? The girl laughed at the estimates, which she found ridiculous, and said that was not how it was at all.

Another aspect of the way the trafficking narrative has been constructed is its strange parallel with narratives of sexual titillation involving Asian women in virtual spaces, especially the Internet. The trafficking story, with its narratives of young, beautiful and caged girls, the physical details of bars and grilles, the images of forced sex, holds out a promise of a virtual reliving of captivity and bondage that has drawn a huge audience and participants within chat rooms, websites and other virtual spaces on the Internet. This point becomes particularly salient when we realise that most of the information about trafficking has been circulated through mailing lists, websites and other Internet channels.

Keeping within the theme of exotic, faraway, captured sexualities, a Los Angeles-based group against trafficking has chosen to call itself 'Captive Daughters', neatly encapsulating all the issues of titillation and exoticism. This group, with a website on the Internet, held a fund-raising dinner called 'Flavors of Nepal: An evening of authentic food and fun to raise funds for Maiti Nepal and Captive Daughters'. The event was covered by the *Los Angeles Times* as: 'One Night in Nepal—A famous chef recreates the royal cuisine of Kathmandu'. The report describes how Preeti Singh, 'of an aristocratic family in Kathmandu … specialising in subtle, refined royal cuisine … served the flavours of Nepal, in silver dishes, and desserts with costly garnish of edible gold leaf, saffron, pistachios and almonds.' It is perfectly appropriate that this event was held to benefit captive women: after all, the Orient as a constructed idea where women are brutalised by men cannot exist outside of a vacuum. It has to be visualised, tasted, experienced.

By being recreated in Los Angeles, complete with gold leaf and silver plates, the Orient is partaken of by the Captive Daughters (the line is not so clear here: one assumes that members of an organisation called Captive Daughters are using the term as a signifier for both their cause as well as themselves, in a perfect mirroring of desire and identity). Participating in an event derived from the many fantasies of what 'the Orient' is supposed to be like, filled with the smells, the sounds and the taste of the lavish display of royalty, reinforces notions of the difference of the Other, while, at the same time becoming a tangible, consumable event of difference. By consuming the Orient, the Captive Daughters turn it into an edible creation: a corporeally absorbed reality. By making no clear distinctions between the captive daughters of the brothels of Kamathipura and the Captive Daughters of Los Angeles, the organisation also leaves us with room to visualise, vicariously, all the imagined brutalities imposed on trafficked women being visited on middle class American Captive Daughters. In this sense, the Captive Daughters take on the virtual identities of the trafficked women, and like characters in chat rooms and other virtually created spaces, fleetingly turn into their referents. It is perhaps logical that the money raised from this night of decadence would go to an institution that reinforces the notion that women, once trafficked corporeally and virtually, are only safe within spaces that can protect them.

This critique of the reduction of a complex social phenomenon to a single homogeneous event can also be applied to a whole host of cultural productions that have recently sprung up around the issue of trafficking, including, among others: *Tara, A Fleshtrade Odyssey*, a novel by a former USAID employee, *Selling of Innocents*, the Emmy award winning video by Ruchira Gupta and *All our Daughters*, an oil painting exhibition by Jan Salter held in Kathmandu.

By fixing and freezing notions of what the 'trafficked woman' is like, cultural productions are active in creating and disseminating, sometimes long distance, a homogeneous representation of a fractured, multi-faceted and diverse group of women. By appropriating the fragments and broken strands of discourses floating around the subcontinent and reifying them, media productions also help legitimise mythical discourses that are actively being used to control women within very specific gender roles.

11

Knowledge, Attitudes, Beliefs and Practices

The Social Shadow of AIDS and STD Prevention in Nepal

◆ Stacy Leigh Pigg / Linnet Pike

In 1997, when we undertook the task of tracing the recent history of aids intervention efforts in Nepal, planners and programmers frequently warned us that we would find that very few people had 'even heard of AIDS'. From the perspective of the people in charge of raising public awareness, ignorance was a huge problem—a problem that could only be solved by more information campaigns supplemented by outreach work and training programs for health workers. However, our interviews and observations made it evident to us that the term 'AIDS' was operating as a powerful social signifier. In this essay, we look at the particular ways that AIDS may be 'heard of' in Nepal. Although educational efforts measure knowledge about AIDS according to a biomedical understanding of transmission, in the process of publicising facts about HIV/AIDS and STDs they also convey messages that structure and limit understandings of personal risk and social responsibility. Moreover, by turning a new kind of public attention to sexuality, they also weave HIV risk and sexual behaviour into a discourse of citizenship and social difference that strengthens existing patterns of exclusion.

The formal activities of prevention-oriented AIDS and STD education communicate and reinforce informal knowledge about social boundaries. Research on social responses to AIDS within a number of national settings shows that, on both individual and collective levels, AIDS is made meaningful through a process that transmutes medical and epidemiological facts into social knowledge.[1] For instance, Kielman, commenting on a group of Kenyan sex workers who were the target of an AIDS education campaign, points out that 'the idea of risk, even in the context of AIDS, is socialised, rather than medicalised, and informal knowledge about AIDS reflects concerns with social boundaries of gender, social status and community.'[2] In Nepal, too, through the often subtle processes involved in the production and reception of AIDS prevention initiatives, AIDS and HIV risk are 'socialised' into concerns about social boundaries.

The title of our essay raises a question about the Knowledge, Attitudes, Beliefs and Practices (KABP) surveys that have been used by health planners to gauge knowledge about AIDS.[3] KABP surveys attempt to gauge people's belief in the sexual transmission of HIV versus their belief in casual transmission, their awareness of condoms as a preventive measure, the degree to which they perceive AIDS as a problem, and their perceptions of personal vulnerability. In Nepal, simple tests are used to measure the 'success' of workshops, training sessions and informational campaigns. These bureaucratic practices reflect an instrumentalist view of AIDS and STD prevention, a view that measures

---

[1] C. Waldby, S. Kippax and J. Crawford, 'Cordon Sanitaire: "clean" and "unclean" women in the AIDS discourse of young men', in P. Aggleton, P. Davies and G. Hart (eds), *AIDS: Facing the Second Decade* (London, Falmer Press, 1993); P. Setel, 'AIDS as a Paradox of Manhood and Development in Kilimanjaro, *Social Science and Medicine*, Vol. 43, No. 8 (1996), pp. 1169–78.

[2] K. Kielmann, '"Prostitution", "Risk" and "Responsibility": Paradigms of AIDS Prevention and Women's Identities in Thika, Kenya', in M. C. Inhorn and P. J. Brown (eds), *The Anthropology of Infectious Disease: International Health Perspectives* (Amsterdam, Gordon and Breach, 1997), p. 403.

[3] See J. Cleland and B. Ferry (eds), *Sexual Behaviour and AIDS in the Developing World* (London, Taylor and Francis and the World Health Organization, 1995).

knowledge about AIDS solely according to whether respondents can correctly parrot back a set of authoritatively determined 'facts' about HIV transmission. The methodological criticisms of such surveys are well known, and we do not want to rehearse them here;[4] rather, we want to show that another set of attitudes, beliefs and practices also forms Nepali understandings of AIDS.

In Nepal, as a result of a huge influx of donor funds made available to local NGOs, basic information about AIDS began appearing on posters, pamphlets and billboards, as well as in radio jingles, street theatre performances and video dramas in the early 1990s. The incidence of HIV infection in Nepal remained extremely low throughout the 1990s and, thus, for most Nepalis the danger of AIDS was determined and delineated by awareness campaigns and media reports. Within a few years, these types of informational messages were widespread in urban areas and among targeted sub-populations throughout the country. How did these context-neutral public health initiatives become imbricated in the social dynamics of Nepal? How have these efforts shaped Nepali understandings of AIDS? Our discussion

---

[4] See C. Vance, 'Gender Systems, Ideology and Sex Research', in A. Snitow, C. Stansell and S. Thompson (eds), *Desire: the Politics of Sexuality* (London, Virago, 1984), on the salience of the 'normative' in sex research in general; L. Manderson, 'Researching Risk: Prevention Research on Substance Abuse, Sexual Behavior, and HIV/AIDS in Asia and Australia', in P. L. Marshall, M. Singer, and M. Clatts (eds), *Integrating Cultural, Observational, and Epidemiological Approaches in the Prevention of Drug Abuse and HIV/AIDS* (Bethesda, U. S. Department of Health and Human Services, National Institutes of Health, National Institute on Drug Abuse, 1999), on the methodological problems of these surveys; L. Stone and J. G. Campbell, 'The Use and Misuse of Surveys in International Development: An Experiment from Nepal', *Human Organization*, Vol. 43 (1984), pp. 27–37, on non-sampling errors arising from the social context of survey implementation in Nepal; and L. Manderson, C. T. Lee and K. Rajanayagam, 'Condom Use in Heterosexual Sex: A Review of Research, 1985–94', in J. Catalan, L. Sherr, and B. Hedge (eds), *The Impact of AIDS: Psychological and Social Aspects of HIV Infection* (Amsterdam, Harwood, 1997); R. Parker, 'Sexual Diversity, Cultural Analysis, and AIDS Education in Brazil', in G. Herdt and S. Lindenbaum (eds), *The Time of AIDS: Social Analysis, Theory and Method* (Newbury Park, Sage, 1992); and H. L. Smith, 'On the Limited Utility of KAP-style Survey Data in the Practical Epidemiology of AIDS, with Reference to the AIDS Epidemic in Chile', *Health Transition Review*, Vol. 3, No. 1 (1993), on the inability of such approaches to provide an understanding of the meaning of sexual practice.

mirrors the two separate research projects upon which this paper draws.[5]

Stacy Pigg's research focused on the production of public knowledge about AIDS, with particular attention given to NGO educational efforts, while Linnet Pike's research focussed on sex workers, with particular attention given to the Badi (a caste in mid and western Nepal that, during the era of AIDS prevention, became notorious as exemplars of the 'social evil' of 'traditional prostitution'). By moving between the viewpoint of the urban middle class elites who are largely responsible for running AIDS awareness programmes and the viewpoint of those to whom these programmes are addressed, we tell the story of emergent understandings of AIDS. Of particular note is the way that a social logic of respectability intertwines with a social logic of development. AIDS has played an important role in establishing sexuality as a matter of public debate and national concern in Nepal, and what we will show is that messages about sexual deviance related through AIDS education tend to converge with a development discourse about 'ignorant' or 'backward' villagers in a way that aligns HIV/AIDS with social marginalisation.

[5] Linnet Pike's fieldwork was conducted in Nepal (in Kathmandu, Nepalgunj, and in Badi communities of Kailali and Bardiya Districts) from 1996–98 with support from a University of Queensland Postgraduate Research Scholarship and assistance from the Australian Centre for International and Tropical Health and Nutrition. Enormous assistance was offered by SAFE (Social Awareness for Education), an NGO based in Nepalgunj that works primarily with Badi communities in the Western districts of Nepal. SAFE Director Dilip Pariyar and members Kamal Nepali, Suklal Nepali, Sunil Pariyar, Asok Nepali, as well as many residents of Badi communities all offered friendship and guidance throughout and beyond the period of fieldwork. Stacy Leigh Pigg's research was conducted in Kathmandu for 8 months in 1997 with support from a grant from the Joint Committee on South Asia of the Social Science Research Council and the American Council of Learned Societies with funds provided by the National Endowment for the Humanities and the Ford Foundation. The Social Sciences and Humanities Research Council Small Grants Program administered by Simon Fraser University supported background research on public representations of AIDS in newspapers and educational materials. Dr Rajendra Bhadra, Dr B. K. Suvedi, Mrs Renu Wagle and numerous people in various NGOs and offices, including B. P. Memorial Health Foundation, WICOM, LALS, Save the Children-US and the National Centre for AIDS and STC Control, generously shared insights and expertise. The interpretations presented here do not necessarily reflect the views of the agencies that funded the research or that assisted the researchers.

HIV/AIDS Intervention in its Historical Moment

The explosion of interest in HIV/AIDS and STD intervention in Nepal occurred at a historical juncture during which, globally, donor funding shifted from the public sector toward the private sector, particularly toward non-profit, non-governmental organisations (NGOs).[6] Since the early 1990s, in Nepal, as in the rest of the world, there has developed what could be described as an NGO/AIDS industry.[7] During this period there was an 'explosive' increase in both NGOs and the flow of funds to them, in part because local organisations were 'associated with the advantages of a community oriented "people to people" approach' to AIDS prevention. NGOs were perceived to be politically independent, cost-effective, flexible, able to gain access to the poor and able to encourage local participation. The flurry of NGO activity related to AIDS in Nepal has been a response to donor-led initiatives that focused on having NGOs serve as the main agents of AIDS prevention.[8] This is part of a more general shift away from channelling donor funds through the state toward a system of subcontracting development projects—a system that involves linking international non-governmental organisations (INGOs) and international development non-profits to nationally and locally based NGOs. Moreover, in Nepal the expansion of NGOs has been a direct result of the local introduction of a multi-party system and various attempts to open civil society.[9]

---

[6] C. A. Meyer, 'A Step Back as Donors Shift Institution Building from the Public Sector to the "Private" Sector', *World Development*, Vol. 20 (1992), p. 1118.

[7] D. Altman, 'Change, Co-option and the Community Sector', *AIDS*, Vol. 9 (suppl. A) (1995), pp. S239–S243.

[8] Funding has come from a range of sources, such as USAID, the European Union, the American Foundation for AIDS Research (AmFAR), the United Nations Development Programme (UNDP) and various INGOs and governments. P. Janssen, *The Role of NGOs in the Implementation of the National AIDS Program in Nepal: A Study into Factors Affecting Conditions* (London, Unpublished manuscript, 1994), p. 15.

[9] The *Jana Andolan*, or People's Movement, of 1990 led to the introduction of a multi-party system and attempts to open civil society. Prior to 1990, all NGOs were strictly regulated and monitored by a national council controlled by the royal palace. Now, while NGOs still need to be registered, there has been a dramatic increase in their number—from approximately 200 in 1990 to an estimated 25,000 by late 1997. As has been suggested, many were created for the purpose of

In Nepal, the influx of capital and technical support for AIDS prevention has resulted in a range of medium and small Nepali NGOs and local community-based organisations (CBOs) becoming involved in a global effort to combat AIDS. And this has brought with it standardised approaches to prevention and their concomitant universalising paradigms.[10] As Dennis Altman has noted, AIDS:

> ...is also a cause of one particular form of globalization, namely the dissemination of western-derived discourses to other societies. Global mobilization around the demands of a bio-medical emergency inevitably means the further entrenchment of western concepts of disease, treatments and the body.[11]

The increasingly bureaucratised international response to AIDS involves viewing HIV/AIDS and STDs within a biomedical framework, and it entails an implicitly medicalised view of sex and sexuality in general. Prevention strategies involving 'peer education'—strategies derived almost entirely from Western experiences of the AIDS epidemic—have become routinised within institutional dogma.[12] The reification of such categories as 'sex worker' and 'men-who-have-sex-with-men' targets these groups, effectively eliding locally specific social forms. For example, Porter, who writes about INGO involvement in HIV/AIDS prevention in Myanmar, has noted the 'singularity' with which a complex, messy and fluid situation is rendered stable through the repetition of techniques for identifying target populations.[13] In Nepal, AIDS

attracting foreign funding. See L. Brown, *The Challenge to Democracy in Nepal: A Political History* (London and New York, Routledge, 1996), p. 68; J. Hannum, *AIDS in Nepal: Communities Confronting an Emerging Epidemic* (New York, AMFAR/ Seven Stories Press, 1997), p. 59; Janssen *op. cit.* (1994); *Kathmandu Post*, 'Make NGOs Accountable' (editorial), 21 Oct. 1997, p. 4.

[10] Stacy Pigg, 'Languages of Sex and AIDS in Nepal: Notes on the Social Production of Commensurability', *Cultural Anthropology*, Vol. 16, No. 4.

[11] D. Altman, 'Globalization and the "AIDS Industry"', *Contemporary Politics* Vol. 4, No. 3 (1998).

[12] See A. Murray and T. Robinson, 'Minding Your Peers and Queers: Female Sex Workers in the AIDS Discourse in Australia and South East Asia', *Gender, Place and Culture*, Vol. 3, No. 1 (1996), pp. 43–59.

[13] D. Porter, 'A Plague on the Borders: HIV, Development, and Travelling Identities in the Golden Triangle', in L. Manderson and M. Jolly (eds), *Sites of Desire/ Economies of Pleasure: Sexualities in Asia and the Pacific* (Chicago and London, University of Chicago Press, 1997).

intervention emerged in tandem with the increasing standardisation and professionalisation of AIDS prevention techniques—techniques whose orthodoxy increased in direct proportion to NGO accountability. What has this meant for the public understanding of AIDS in Nepal? In the 1980s, AIDS appeared as a tidbit of foreign news, an item in the newspaper or on the radio about a mysterious medical crisis unfolding in distant lands among people thought to be very different from Nepalis. When the first reports of AIDS deaths and HIV-infected individuals were registered by public health authorities, they stressed the foreigness of AIDS. For example, a report written during the first Mid Term Plan (1990–92) stressed the number of foreigners who had been found to be HIV positive after the testing of blood samples taken from hospital patients, antenatal clinic attendees, drug addicts and jail inmates. This report noted that the majority of infected nationals had been sex workers abroad.[14] An early educational pamphlet (1988) put out by what was then called the AIDS Prevention and Control Programme of the Ministry of Health explains that the groups most likely to contract AIDS are:

- people who travel abroad frequently who have had sexual contacts
- people who cross the border frequently…who have had sexual contacts
- people who live in single-sex institutions where homosexuality exists (for example, hostels, prisons, and so forth.)
- tourists in the high-risk groups listed above (homosexuals, IDUs, recipients of blood transfusions and 'heterosexuals who have had many sex partners')

---

[14] Of 3,682 samples tested in 1988, four foreigners were found to be HIV positive. Of 22,815 samples tested in 1990, eleven people were found to be HIV positive— seven 'STD clinic attendees' (four Nepali citizens and three foreigners), one 'drug addict' (foreigner), one 'blood donor' (Nepali) and two 'prisoners' (foreigners). Of the five Nepalis who tested positive, it was noted that four were 'girls involved in prostitution outside the country'. The report did not specify the nationalities of the 'foreigners', V. L. Gurubacharya and S. Pradhan, *Profile on HIV/AIDS Prevalence and Control Activities, Nepal* (Kathmandu, National AIDS Prevention and Control Project, n.d.).

After 1993 (the year in which donor funding dramatically boosted AIDS awareness activities), in official discourse AIDS was gradually transformed from a disease linked to 'travel' to a problem linked to specific 'risk groups' within Nepali society. The assumptions underlying these early efforts to deal with AIDS concern social boundaries and social stratification. For example, the fact that boot-shine boys and rickshaw wallahs were also seen as potential risk groups says much about the fears and assumptions of those charged with determining how HIV was entering Nepali society.

Over the same period (roughly 1988 to 1999), public AIDS awareness messages gradually changed: the initial fear-based messages were replaced by terse information about modes of transmission, and these eventually gave rise to references to 'safe sexual behaviour', 'prompt treatment of sexually transmitted diseases', and 'compassion for people with AIDS'. For instance, the covers for a series of pamphlets, produced by the Ministry of Health and first printed in 1988 (then reprinted in 1990), feature a ghoulish rendering of a skeleton, its skull surrounded by a spider web, enveloped in the flames emanating from the lotus flower upon which it appears to rest. Across this image is a banner that read: 'AIDS—a new fatal disease' (ek naya ghaatak rog).

Issued in Nepali and English versions, these early pamphlets, which contain sections entitled 'epidemiology', 'etiology', 'asymptomatic carrier state', 'criteria for diagnosis of AIDS in adults', and 'what a sero-positive person must not do', appear to have been based on technical pamphlets aimed at Western professionals such as doctors and journalists. It is unclear for whom these pamphlets were intended, or who actually read them (never mind understood them), but they give us an idea of what Nepali officials first believed constituted information relevant to 'AIDS awareness'. The 1993 influx of support for AIDS programmes resulted in more streamlined and better designed information campaigns. Technical advisers for donors instructed NGOs to define their target audience, to avoid ambiguous messages, and to pre-test materials to ensure their intelligibility. It was during this period that the standard approach to AIDS awareness—an approach that presents AIDS as a biomedical phenomenon—was set in place. Of central importance was 'how HIV is transmitted'.

The standard AIDS information package includes guidelines for AIDS prevention and risk reduction. Although these boil down to a few established principles—use condoms, reduce your number of sexual partners, use clean needles—their rendering into Nepali has been uneven and controversial. Most donors are committed to the basic precept of public health communication—the presentation of accurate and non-judgmental information. The intense and ongoing Western critique of the politics of AIDS messages ¹as internationalised a set of 'red-flag' concerns pertaining to the dangers of stereotyping and moralising, and the result of this is that technical advisers have instructed Nepali NGOs to avoid making certain kinds of statements. However, most NGO leaders, outreach workers and government officials place AIDS prevention within an implicit socio–moral framework. Consequently there is a persistent tension between how donors want to present AIDS prevention messages (i.e., in the form of seemingly self-evident public health precepts) and how Nepali officials want to present them (i.e., in the form of seemingly self-evident socio–moral precepts). Some Nepali officials and outreach workers, for example, reject the message 'use a condom every time' because they believe that it promotes illicit sexuality.

Messages such as 'only have sexual contact between husband and wife' are problematic in Nepal because available evidence suggests a rising number of sexually monogamous women are being infected by their husbands. People are warned 'not to have sexual contact with unknown persons', a point sometimes rendered more explicitly as 'avoid sexual relations with prostitutes'. In their efforts to avoid ambiguity, NGOs have produced numerous versions of these messages. However, one of the difficulties is that the guidelines they receive from international sources contain much that is itself ambiguous or difficult to render in Nepali terms. For instance, these materials sometimes refer to transmission of HIV through 'homosexual' contact. The concept of a sexual identity—a sexual orientation that defines the nature of a person—makes very little sense to Nepalis; it is, after all, a notion that emerged in the West in the late nineteenth century.[15]

---

[15] J. D'Emilio, 'Capitalism and Gay Identity', in R. N. Lancaster and Miceala di Leonardo (eds), *The Gender/Sexuality Reader* (London, Routledge, 1997), pp. 169–78; Trans. by Robert Hurley, M. Foucault, *History of Sexuality, Vol. 1: An Introduction* (New York, Vintage Books, 1978), p. 230; J. Weeks, *Sex, Politics, and Society: The Regulation of Sexuality Since 1800* (London, New York, Longman, 1989).

It has been difficult for AIDS workers to make a connection between these references to homosexuality, which most find baffling, and real forms of male-to-male sexual relations that they might recognise in Nepal. The potential for male-to-male sexual transmission of HIV receives almost no attention in Nepali AIDS prevention efforts, but the categories 'heterosexual', 'homosexual' and 'bisexual' are taught in many of the sex education modules as irrefutable medico–scientific truths about human sexuality. The effect (it seemed to us) was to make this 'homosexuality' seem very alien to Nepal and to reinforce a sense that AIDS is the result of distinctively Western sexual perversions that have no Nepali equivalent.

In the past, safe sex messages directed at Nepali sex workers have assumed the existence of a universal set of behaviours. For example, field workers and peer educators in the Badi community reported that they were amazed to hear of anal and oral sex in an HIV 'awareness' training session conducted by an NGO. The notion of 'multiple sexual partners' has also had a strange life in Nepal, conjuring up images of orgies rather than a series of sexual encounters with different partners. Promiscuity is treated as an abstraction ('multiple sexual partners'), not linked to locally well-recognised patterns of male sexual behaviour, thus creating a lingering impression that HIV transmission occurs through very unusual, foreign, or especially perverse sexual acts. Two ways of looking at sexuality clash at the juncture where AIDS prevention messages are rendered in Nepali. In late nineteenth and early twentieth century Europe and North America, sexuality became objectified and sexual acts and inclinations were minutely catalogued and this way of thinking about sexuality pervades the common sense assumptions of international public health.[16] The reification of carefully labelled sexual acts sits awkwardly with the existing socio–moral understanding of sexuality in Nepal. Through health promotion activities linked to national development, HIV/AIDS has brought Nepali sexuality into the public spotlight and has introduced medicalised ways of talking about sexual acts.

---

[16] See Foucault *op. cit.*; R. Porter and L. Hall, *The Facts of Life: The Creation of Sexual Knowledge in Britain, 1650–1950* (New York, Yale University Press, 1995); Weeks, *op. cit..*

International support augmented AIDS information campaigns in Nepal and led to expanded information-gathering activities. The first Medium Term Plan (1990–92) was 'inclusive of all the globally recognised strategies for AIDS prevention and control',[17] including World Health Organization (WHO) technical support on the protocol and methodology for KABP surveys.[18] The Social and Behavioural Research Unit of WHO's Global Programme on AIDS had identified a need for country-specific baseline data on 'psychosocial information' on risk-behaviours, explanatory frameworks and coping responses.[19] During this early period of AIDS prevention, baseline KABP studies on sexual behaviour in Nepal were conducted but there was little in-depth qualitative research. Furthermore, much of the work was based on questionnaires and centred on issues derived from biomedicine and epidemiology— STDs, number and type of sexual contacts, HIV/AIDS knowledge, and so on.[20] Generally the focus of this flurry of KAP studies fell

[17] V. L. Gurubacharya, B. K. Subedi, S. Prasad, H. B. Kshatri and S. Acharya, *Activities of National AIDS Prevention and Control Project* (Kathmandu, National AIDS Prevention and Control Project, 1993), p. 2.

[18] *Ibid.*, p. 4.

[19] Cleland and Ferry, *op. cit.*; Smith, *op. cit.*, pp. 1–16.

[20] P. Bhatta, V. L. Gurubacharya and G. Vadies, 'A Unique Community of Family-Oriented Prostitutes in Nepal Uninfected by HIV-1', *International Journal of STD and AIDS*, Vol. 4 (1993), pp. 280–83; P. S. Bhatta, S. Neupone, S. Thapa, J. Baker and M. Friedman, *Commercial Sex Workers in the Kathmandu Valley: Their Profile and Health Status* (Kathmandu, AIDS and STDs Prevention Network/Valley Research Group, 1993); P. S. Bhatta, S. Thapa, S. Neupone, J. Baker and M. Friedman, 'Commercial Sex Workers in Kathmandu Valley: Profile and Prevalence of Sexually Transmitted Diseases', *Journal of the Nepal Medical Association*, Vol. 32, No. 111 (1994), pp. 191–203; T. Cox and B. K. Suvedi, *Sexual Networking in Five Urban Areas in the Nepal Terai* (Kathmandu, Valley Research Group, 1994), and V. L. Gurubacharya and B. K. Subedi, *Sexual Behaviour Pattern in Nepal* (Kathmandu, National AIDS Prevention and Control Project, 1992); New Era: *A Baseline Study of Commercial Sex Workers and Sex Clients on the Land Transportation Routes from Naubise to Janakpur and Birgunj* (Kathmandu, Report submitted to AIDS Control and Prevention Project [AIDSCAP]/Family Heath International, 1995); New Era: *Rapid Qualitative Assessment of AIDSCAP Effects on Behaviour Change Among Commercial Sex Workers and Their Clients* (Kathmandu, Report submitted to AIDS Control and Prevention Project [AIDSCAP]/Family Health International, 1996); New Era: *An Evaluation of Interventions Targeted at Commercial Sex Workers and Sex Clients on the Land Transportation Routes from Janakpur and Birunj to Naubise* (Kathmandu, Report submitted to AIDS Control and Prevention Project [AIDSCAP]/Family Health International, 1997).

upon those believed to be 'vulnerable to exposure to these diseases...because of their sexual behaviour, the commercial sex workers (CSWs) as well as their clients, [who] represent a reservoir for the rapid transmission of STDs and AIDS throughout the general population.'[21] In both research efforts and program development, the focus has been on 'risk groups'—CSWs and the men assumed to be most involved with them (migrant workers, truck drivers, the police, soldiers, and so forth).

A primary emphasis on CSWs is inevitable as, worldwide, research on these people has proven elusive: 'The [client] population is diffuse, the tasks of sampling onerous, and men's privacy represented as sacrosanct. There appears also to be personal reluctance to explore too closely a population that in other ways is no different from the general population of men.'[22]

According to the National Centre for AIDS and STD Control (NCASC), HIV has affected two categories of Nepali women— 'housewives' and 'commercial sex workers'. If 'the housewife' is the product of high caste Hindu expectations of virginal marriage and lifelong female fidelity, then any woman who has had sex with more than one man is, effectively, a 'sex worker'. This distinction is enshrined in the categories NCASC uses to track the incidence of HIV infection in Nepal.[23] NCASC breaks these numbers down according to sex, age and risk group: *(i)* sex workers; *(ii)* clients of sex workers/STD clinic attendees; *(iii)* housewives; *(iv)* recipients of blood transfusions;*(v)* injecting drug users (IDUs); and *(vi)* victims of perinatal transmission.[24] When, in 1997, NCASC

---

[21] Bhatta, *et al., op. cit.* (1994), pp. 192, 200.

[22] Manderson and Jolly, *op. cit.* (1997); see also B. O. de Zalduondo, 'Prostitution Viewed Cross-culturally: Towards Re-contextualizing Sex Work in AIDS Intervention', *Journal of Sex Research,* Vol. 28 (1991), pp. 223–48.

[23] These statistics are known to be inaccurate, as they rely on a crude count of HIV positive test results reported to the centre. It is widely believed that the results of the majority of HIV tests conducted in private clinics are not reported to NCASC. A sentinel surveillance system, using sampling to monitor emerging patterns of HIV infection, was established with GPA support but lapsed due to logistical difficulties with regard to carrying out the sampling.

[24] NCASC actually presents the first three categories as types of people and the last three as modes of transmission. Sexual transmission is thus rendered as social categories. In comparison, UNAIDS uses the following sub-populations to track epidemic patterns: pregnant women, sex workers, IDUs, prisoners and STD patients. See UNAIDS (Joint United Nations Program on HIV/AIDS), *Nepal:*

officials presented lecture modules entitled 'the HIV situation in Nepal' in various forums, they pointed with alarm to the increase in the number of 'innocent housewives' infected with HIV. (Ironically, the preferred prevention message continued to be 'avoid sex with unknown persons/only have sexual contact with husband or wife.') The risk of HIV infection was personified by *types* of women. At the same time, various NGOs were using the term 'sex worker' to tease out different categories of prostitution.[25] As outreach workers continue to ask which women are 'sex workers' or are 'at risk of becoming...sex worker[s]' more and more such people are found. Providing information tends to be linked to collecting information through AIDS intervention programmes, and the awkward, morally fraught, issue of addressing sexual behaviours in the name of health education is linked to increased official attention to the sexual behaviour of Nepali citizens.

Moral Crisis

Health development activities in Nepal intersected with a moral crisis. A few years before AIDS awareness activities burst onto the scene, newspapers commonly ran sensationalist stories dealing with prostitution and girl-trafficking. The recognition of AIDS as a serious problem fed this sensationalism, magnifying the attention given to these issues both in the form of journalists' reports and in the form of widespread urban rumours. It became increasingly likely that a literate urban person would hear of AIDS within the context of a (usually lurid) newspaper article. As prostitution appeared to become more widespread (and certainly more visible), AIDS was conjoined with it as yet another form of 'social evil'.

The upsurge in concentrated AIDS awareness activities also coincided with rapid economic privatisation—a trend that saturated ordinary people, particularly those living in urban areas,

---

Epidemiological Fact Sheet on HIV/AIDS and Sexually Transmitted Diseases, 1998. Electronic document: http://www.unaids.org/hivaidsinfo/statistics/june98/fact_sheets/pdfs/nepal.pdf.

[25] Whatever term is chosen, the category itself is problematic because, through it, women are identified solely by their sexual behaviour and/or work.

with seductive advertisements for a consumption-oriented lifestyle. That such a lifestyle is out of the reach of most Nepalis appears to be besides the point: advertisements for it are everywhere. Advertising took a distinctly sexualised turn during this period, as such foreign conventions as selling car oil using the image of a bikini-clad woman became more common. Privatisation, also fuelled new forms of popular culture that focused on the urban elite, and that promulgated international pop culture through newly available satellite television and FM radio stations. These revolved around mostly youth-oriented fashion and music interests, and they affected dating patterns. Nepali parents worried more and more openly about the corrupting influences of Western culture, and people in their thirties spoke of the differences between their own experiences and those of people not ten years their junior.

One of the most prominent public symbols of this form of popular culture is the fashion show/beauty contest. In 1994 the very first 'model search and beauty contest' was held in Nepal, and in 1997 the 'The Hidden Treasure's Miss World Nepal' (sponsored by Mount Everest Brewery, producer of San Miguel and Tiger Beer, and affiliated to the Miss World Beauty Pageant) offered a window onto the 'glitz...and glamour of the West'.[26] This beauty pageant received extensive coverage in both Nepali and English newspapers and was broadcast live and in full on prime time television. Articles glamourised contestants while simultaneously asking the unspoken question, 'What kind of Nepali girl would do this?' Other newspaper accounts directly associated fashion models and actresses with loose morals, prostitution and 'the dreaded AIDS'.[27] An excessive interest in fashion was commonly depicted as leading to prostitution among middle class women.[28] These associations, which concern what happens

---

[26] S. Pradhan, 'Working Hard in Unison for the Crown', *Kathmandu Post*, 4 July 1997; see also S. Pradhan, 'Time to Guess Lucky One for Crown' *Kathmandu Post*, 31 July 1997; A. Ranjit, 'Miss Talent Show: An Art and Glamour', *Rising Nepal*, 20 July 1997.

[27] S. Pradhan. 'Nepali Models in Need of Professionalism', *Kathmandu Post*, 23 July 1997; G. Rajbhandari, 'Puberty, Virginity and Fidelity', *Sunday Post*, 1 June 1997.

[28] One strategy document from NCASC, for instance, avers that young women students should be targeted for prevention programmes because 'with the freedom of school life, limited parental supervision, the urge to maintain a certain

when one deviates from middle class, Brahmanic models of feminine behaviour, have the self-evident quality of cultural common sense. In both official and popular accounts, negative changes in Nepali society were attributed to increasing access to foreign commodities and values, and this provoked anxiety about changing norms of sexual behaviour.

Into this milieu, in which shop windows, television screens and the pages of mainstream magazines and newspapers were becoming increasingly sexualised spaces devoted to stoking fantasies of consumption, came AIDS prevention messages. In the name of public health, made-for-television films, posters, pamphlets, bumper stickers and billboards spoke of condoms and various modes of sexual contact. For example, the NCASC created a poster detailing ways that HIV is transmitted and how people can protect themselves. The simple colour drawing illustrating the statement '[HIV can be transmitted by] sexual contact with someone other than husband or wife' shows a man and woman (apparently naked) in bed together; viewers can recognise this as an encounter with a prostitute by the girlie poster on the wall and the liquor and cigarettes on the table. '[You can protect yourself from HIV by] only having sex with husband or wife' is illustrated by showing a husband, sari-clad wife and child eating together on the floor of their village home. At the same time that these AIDS prevention messages were in circulation, the strikingly sensual, glossy, high-production advertisements for Indian-made Kamasutra condoms, with their explicit photographs of a nearly undressed couple in the throes of passion, were also appearing in magazines and posters. Condom promotion (to which we will

---

standard of living coupled with peer pressures, female college students could be targets of sexual exploitation'. (National Centre for AIDS and STD Control [NCASC], with the assistance of WHO and UNDP. *National Information, Education and Communication [IEC] Strategy*, Kathmandu, unpublished document, 1995), p. 9. In the same vein, newspaper articles criticise the pursuit of fashion by young middle class women: 'It's OK for those with strong financial support', Pradhan wrote, but for those without 'it's not an exaggeration but a bitter fact that has made many young girls sell their bodies in lieu of money for fashion.' ('Of Women, Fashion and Society', *Kathmandu Post*, 5 Feb. 1997). See also M. Liechty, 'Paying for Modernity: Women and the Discourse of Freedom in Kathmandu', *Studies in Nepali History and Society*, Vol. 1, No. 1 (1996), pp. 201–30 on moral discourses around middle class women and modernity.

return below) had become an arena simultaneously occupied by official didacticism, slick public health-oriented social marketing and international high-intensity commercial advertising.

These new forms of public attention to sexuality constitute an ambiguous territory cross-cut by contesting narratives. Claims that sexuality is being addressed for the public good exist side-by-side with a general eroticisation of consumption patterns, and both these phenomena are the target of a series of counter-claims about Nepali norms of acceptability. An FM radio show that was launched in 1997 as part of an AIDS prevention initiative pro-voked debates that clearly show the sorts of tensions that occur when public attention is drawn to new forms of sexuality. Called the CRS Hotline (after Contraceptive Retail Services, the semi-private company that sponsored it), the show featured a DJ and a guest expert who fielded questions about AIDS and STDs, contraception and sexuality (broadly defined to include puberty, sexual technique, sexual relationships and sexual identity). Simul-taneously advertised as HIV/AIDS public health education and as an 'exciting' and 'hot' program, the show's attempt to appeal both to urban youth culture and to those concerned with health education fascinated its audience and horrified many official broadcasting and public health gatekeepers. FM radio, newly launched in Kathmandu, had become a symbol of the emerging youth-oriented, international pop culture and its distinctive pat-terns of consumption and self-presentation.[29] The sexual innuendo that pervades FM broadcasting (for example, in the lyrics of international pop music; in the flirtatious banter of the DJs; in the advertisements for dance parties, fashion shows and restaurants) was widely seen as different from—and more morally dangerous than—the sexual innuendo that pervades, say, traditional Nepali folk songs. The Hotline openly and purposefully made sexuality its prime topic. It did so in the name of health education and the public good; its programmers argued that it was merely 'teaching people about their bodies'. But listeners—both fans and critics—responded to the tantalisingly *risque* possibilities of even this

---

[29] See M. Liechty, 'Media, Markets and Modernization: Youth Identities and the Experience of Modernity in Kathmandu, Nepal', in V. Amit-Talal and H. Wulff (eds), *Youth Cultures: A Cross-Cultural Perspective* (New York and London, Routledge, 1995).

hygienic approach to sexuality. The show not only invited questions on 'anything' related to sex, but it also directly addressed such topics as same-sex relationships, female orgasm and masturbation. So, although the show focused on health education and discussed issues within a medical framework, the fact that real, local, Nepalis were asking questions and talking about their sexual concerns was itself erotic.

The show thus became the focus of a debate about the scope, form and intent of sex education. The most vocal critics felt that the show was not didactic enough, and that it did not inculcate the proper mode of discourse about sexual health. As one broadcasting official put it, people are 'getting sexual feeling out of it'. The show was, he argued, 'whetting people's curiosity'. In his view, a show that intends to provide STD and AIDS prevention information should be modelled on government-sponsored radio programmes that present the advantages and disadvantages of different contraceptive methods without allowing listeners to stray off track. According to this point of view, the moral crisis facing the urban middle class was to be dealt with by policing the boundaries of official public discourse about sexuality. At the same time, officials, parents and the youth sometimes saw sex education as increasingly necessary to protect the young from the new temptations of middle class urban life.

The ambiguity of the Hotline, which represented both a moral crisis and its solution, encapsulated the cultural predicament of the urban middle class. The discussion about whether the Hotline was 'acceptable' to 'Nepali society' echoed the discussions of planners and health workers, concerning whether, given the values of Nepali society, it was possible to communicate information about HIV/AIDS and STD prevention The Hotline was seen as 'bold'—and often 'too bold'. 'We are not ready for that yet', a number of people commented; 'no matter how developed, we are still embarrassed by this kind of discussion; we are just not that *free* yet.' These comments implicitly contrast Nepali society with the West, the latter being seen as open and, by implication, perverse, and the former being seen as restrained and, by implication, respectable. Indeed, for some it was easy to see the Hotline's 'bold' and 'free' talk as symptomatic of the very sexual immorality that they believed led to problems like AIDS in the first place.

Not surprisingly, the foregoing characterisation of Nepali society is inflected with urban, middle class, and largely upper caste concerns and values. This is, quite simply, because the majority of NGO leaders, programme officers, and health workers come from this background and have had little sustained contact with rural or lower-class Nepalis or with those of other caste/ethnic backgrounds. Although, as individuals, these workers hold a range of views on the importance of sex education, condom promotion, and so on, their notions of how things are in their culture reflect the sense of moral contrast between the West and Nepal described above. This, in turn, makes it difficult to recognise variations *within* Nepali society in terms other than those that compare degrees of 'frankness' and 'freedom', which are already coded as not typically 'Nepali' and as indicative of risk group status. Within this discourse, to talk about conditions that foster sexual patterns that diverge from high caste ideals is to insinuate that a group of people are promiscuous and morally inferior.

Respectability in Practice: Implementing Social Distinction

AIDS workers must mediate between donor expectations regarding the correct way to carry out AIDS prevention and a grassroots reality that is often not amenable to those expectations. They use claims about the way things are in Nepali society both to resist pressure to carry out programmes that seem dangerous or offensive and to attempt to make donors and expatriate consultants aware of the conditions in Nepal. AIDS workers must attempt to balance both the need to address sexual behaviours and the social implications of doing so. As public health agents, their work consists of helping to frame sexuality in terms of health and hygiene. However, at the time of our research, attempting to speak of sexual matters even within this medicalised frame posed difficulties. For example, workers faced embarrassment and shame (*laaj*) because they were forced to appear to be 'too bold' and 'frank'. They ran the risk of having others think that their health education efforts were indicative of personal immorality; women field workers had to be especially concerned about this and, as a result, few revealed to their families the precise nature of their employment.

This problem of a cross-over between professional and personal worlds came to the fore at a workshop launching a new training manual for workers involved in sexual/reproductive health issues. One middle-aged woman voiced widely shared objections to the manual's inclusion of certain exercises and illustrations, arguing that the INGO that expected them to use it had to understand that they would have to take it home with them at night and that their family members would invariably see it. When AIDS workers spoke about the 'acceptability' of certain topics, they were not only gauging possible public reactions but also stating what they, as relatively high-status, middle class workers, were not prepared to do.

Worker self-consciousness and Nepali attitudes toward target groups are two sides of the same coin. Despite being skewed by a moral crisis around sexuality, AIDS intervention efforts operate, *de facto*, within the lowest common denominator of shared Nepali social knowledge. The key element of these efforts is a deeply internalised sense of the relation between restraint and respect. The way one shows respect toward those of high-status is to exercise restraint in their presence—to control one's speech, defer gratification and subordinate one's desires. In Nepal, the regulation of speech is one of the most important manifestations of propriety. Discussing sexual matters within such public domains as schools, training sessions, and so on is problematic because the status markers associated with them demand the exercise of restraint. AIDS workers, therefore, have had to come up with respectful ways of raising topics that inherently violate the Nepali sense of propriety. And this sense of propriety influences how workers view those whom they are attempting to help. They assume, for example, that members of target groups who do not seem appropriately embarrassed by AIDS education are promiscuous.

One of the most blatant representations of the self-image desired by the middle class AIDS worker appears on the 1997 NCASC calendar. This calendar features a colour photograph of a tall, elegantly coiffed and bejewelled woman in a purple silk sari, forefinger held didactically aloft as she addresses a crowd of mostly dark-skinned villagers dressed in worn homespun. The caption reads: 'Safe sexual behaviour is the basis for a healthy life'. This image leaves no doubt as to who is in a position to teach whom about 'safe sexual behaviour'.

At a mid-west region orientation session for middle class, high caste people who were to conduct interviews with sex workers and other high-risk groups as part of a follow-up to a baseline KABP survey, men and women shifted uncomfortably when asked to name the wooden dildo held aloft by the facilitator. Finally, someone called out that it was a 'penis' (indeed, NGO workers generally preferred using English when discussing sex).[30] Pushed by the facilitator to offer a Nepali word, participants finally settled on the Sanskritic and religiously sanctioned word *linga* rather than on any of the more common words (which they consider 'vulgar'). The preferred English and Sanskritic terms, which have become increasingly standardised in AIDS and reproductive health efforts, are perceived by most Nepalis as formal and stiff. To some they are incomprehensible.

In the absence of any serious empirical research, the identification of risk groups is based on the impressions of NGO and government planners. For instance, the majority of NGOs working directly or indirectly with CSWs (particularly those operating in the Kathmandu area) are primarily operated and staffed by high caste, middle class men and women. With few exceptions, their class positioning both informs and determines their institutional assumptions, focus and programme content. For example, one NGO that was running an innovative needle exchange in Kathmandu initially assumed that its target population of IDUs would 'naturally' include hidden CSWs; consequently, it attempted to approach women who had been so identified on the basis of the personal evaluations of its field workers. To their dismay they found that the women thus approached were extremely offended: the behaviour and dress that had underpinned staff evaluations were signs of class distance that had become embedded within a moral framework.[31]

As early as 1994, many NGOs concerned with HIV/AIDS issues focused their energies on the rehabilitation of CSWs.[32] NGO fieldwork observations throughout the period between 1996 and 1998 revealed a continued emphasis on painting tablecloths and

---

[30] See Pigg, *op. cit.*.

[31] Personal communication from an employee of the NGO LALS.

[32] CSWs are assumed to be women and all programmes targeting sex workers have restricted themselves to women, despite the existence of male CSWs.

knitting as ways to escape from a life of prostitution; possibly some NGO workers found it reassuring to see former CSWs engaged in such innocuous tasks. For many NGO workers, their first encounters with CSWs filled them with nervousness and fear. One woman recounted how surprised she was upon meeting some of the CSWs who had been returned to Nepal from Bombay brothels under the auspices of a 1996 coalition of NGOs. She had never met a CSW and had been uncertain as to how to talk to them. However, apart from their heavy make-up, she reported that she had found CSWs to be no different from 'normal' women.

Elite assumptions regarding appropriate female behaviour underpin depictions of CSWs both in popular accounts and in NGO programmes. Prostitution, even when characterised by such neutral public health jargon as 'sex work', is regarded as a low and profane occupation that no woman would undertake by choice. Thus, although NGO workers have learned to use the internationally acceptable, purportedly neutral term 'sex worker' when talking about this category of woman, the derogatory implications of the Nepali terms for which it substitutes (*beshya, randi* or, more vulgarly, *bhalu*) nonetheless infuse it with a deep moral ambivalence. Both NGOs and the media portray prostitution through generic images of the exploitation of innocent, naive women; however, these images are cross-cut by other, more ambiguous assumptions. Poor and 'traditional' women (assumed to be of certain ethnic groups and castes and, therefore, already 'other' in relation to the elite norm) are portrayed as either being duped into prostitution or resorting to it to escape from poverty; yet these portrayals also insinuate that these women engage in sex work because of their 'bad characters', laziness, or moral failings. In addition to poverty, 'lack of awareness' is one of the core characteristics of the women thus stereotyped. They are said to be victims of tradition and ignorance. In contrast, women from high castes are said to be seduced into prostitution by a 'modern' desire for 'fashion'.

Coincident with the intensification of AIDS education campaigns is a widening of the cultural gap between the elite and the majority of the Nepali population. Although economic disparities have always been large, the recent commercialisation of middle class life has qualitatively intensified them. The differential marketing of condoms reflects these disparities and shows how AIDS prevention efforts subtly replicate their apparent inevitability. For example, the Nepal Contraceptive Retail Sales (CRS) Company was established in 1978 under the Ministry of Health within the Family Planning and Child Health Section. In 1983 it became an autonomous private company. Its initial objective was to make contraceptives readily available at a reasonable price. From its inception the CRS was funded by USAID, and it received contraceptives free of cost; it also received financial assistance for marketing and distribution, as well as technical support. With the advent of AIDS, the company's focus expanded and, since 1994, under an AIDSCAP-funded project, condoms have been available from non-traditional outlets, with eleven thousand establishments (such as *paan pasal* and tea shops) selling condoms.[33]

As with commodities such as alcohol and cigarettes, condoms are marketed with particular target populations in mind. These target populations have specific social, class and geographic locations and embody the cleavages of the wider social world. The marketing strategies for commodities such as contraceptive pills and condoms reflect, to quote a management figure at CRS, such attributes as 'social status', 'value' and 'image' and so segment the market along class lines. In terms of intent, contraceptive pills and condoms are identical products, but they are marketed and priced differently. The contraceptive pill, a 'premium product' for urban women, is marketed on Kathmandu FM radio, while the condom, produced primarily for rural populations, is not advertised in Kathmandu (although it is available). The same marketing strategy is applied to the two identical condom products, Dhaal and Panther, which retail respectively for Rs 4 per six-pack and Rs 10 per five-pack. Again, pricing segments the market along class lines. The 'premium' products are marketed on television, with the target customer described as a 'lower B and C class person.' With regard to the premium Panther condoms, the target 'B class' customer is seen as earning a steady income of Rs 3,500–4,000 per month and owning a motorcycle and permanent cement home. 'A and upper B class' people are believed to buy the foreign brands of condoms available in Kathmandu and are regarded as being outside the premium marketing strategies of the CRS. The category of people described as 'D and E class', the users of Dhaal

---

[33] Personal communication, CRS management.

(which, among rural people, has become the generic name for condoms), are seen either as rural residents or as poor urbanites. In fact, to the elite marketing executives, it would seem that 'D and E class' is collapsible: the signifiers of 'poor and rural' function to flatten identity into a generic category that is all too familiar in development subtexts—the backward villager.[34]

The social differentiations between products for an urban middle class elite and the rural poor are reflected in both packaging and advertising. Even the sealed condom packets inside the Panther and Dhaal boxes reproduce nuances of social class, status and image, with the latter being packaged in plain white plastic and the former being distinguished by a gold circle. The politics of NGO programmes play a significant role in the distribution and sale of condoms. CSWs, for example, have little choice in the brand of condom they use because they are either distributed to them free or sold cheaply through social marketing projects. It is these people, who are both symbolically and corporeally linked to HIV discourses, that we must now discuss.

Badi Women as a Target Group

As we have seen, CSWs have become the focus of HIV/AIDS prevention efforts. NGO discourses have conflated a range of sex work practices, trafficking and HIV education, utilising moral, medical and cultural references to construct prostitution as a 'social evil'.[35] With prostitution generally seen as impeding 'social progress' and the 'healthy development of nationality', elite discourses of development oppose modern culture to a traditional past that is seen to be at odds with both national honour and development.

---

[34] See S. L. Pigg, 'Inventing Social Categories through Place: Social Representations and Development in Nepal', *Comparative Studies in Society and History*, Vol. 34, No. 3 (1992), pp. 491–513.

[35] K. Pandit, 'Let's Fight Against Social Perversity', in *Cheliko Byatha (Affliction of Female)* (Kathmandu, WOREC, 1997); V. L. Gurubacharya, 'HIV/AIDS—Everybody's Concern', in *Red Light Traffic: The Trade in Nepali Girls* (Kathmandu, ABC/Nepal, n.d.). For a critical commentary on the slippages in these discourses, see L. Pike, 'Innocence, Danger, and Desire: Representations of Sex Workers in Nepal', *Re/productions* 2, 1, http://www.hsph.harvard.edu/Organizations/healthnet/Sasia/repro2/issue2.htm.

The Badi, a previously obscure caste living in mid and far western Nepal, were soon identified as a target for HIV prevention and gender empowerment. The Badi became one of the archetypes of 'commercial sex work' in Nepal, serving as an example of what has been variously described as 'religious', 'cultural' or 'traditional' prostitution. NGOs based in Kathmandu inevitably refer to the Badi as part of an 'evil tradition'[36] and an instance of cultural exploitation, while INGOs often exoticise them, commissioning film crews to essentialise them for documentaries.

For the Badi themselves, donor and NGO perceptions of them as a community of CSWs has mixed implications. They do not perceive *pesaa* (the profession [i.e., prostitution]) as a caste occupation: originally, the caste profession was entertainment. According to oral histories, men wove fishing nets, fished, constructed and repaired *maadal* (drums) and made clay *chilim* (pipes). They formed small groups of musicians and, accompanied by female singers and dancers, contracted to perform music for high caste patrons, travelling seasonally between the hills of Nepal and the Terai and India. The Badi drift into sex work is related to socio- political changes that have occurred in Nepal over the last fifty years.[37] For younger members of the community, economic survival is determined along gender lines, with many young men seasonally migrating to India for wage labour and many women working as CSWs.

In 1993, the American Foundation for AIDS Research (AmFAR), the first large HIV/AIDS donor to enter into partnership with Nepali NGOs, provided major funding to an NGO that was working with the Badi on community development issues. This enabled the expansion of an existing HIV education and condom distribution programme. These types of programmes depended on the few twenty-something Badi men and women who were able to negotiate the formidable difficulties of caste discrimination

---

[36] See D. Ghimere, 'National Policy and Programme Regarding Control of Women Trafficking in Nepal: A Suggestion', in *Cheliko Byatha (Affliction of Female)* (Kathmandu, WOREC, 1997), p. 22; G. M. Gurung, 'Prostitution as a Way of Life', *Kathmandu Review*, Vol. 2, No. 7, pp. 5–8.

[37] See L. Pike, 'Sex Work and Socialisation in a Moral World: Change and Conflict in Badi Communities of West Nepal', in L. Manderson and P. Liamputtong Rice (eds), *Coming of Age: Youth, Courtship and Sexuality in South and Southeast Asia* (Richmond, Curzon, 2002).

(often at great emotional cost) in order to acquire a formal education. Several men working in Badi NGOs had the School Leaving Certificate (Class ten pass), while the few Badi women employed as field workers had, at most, a Class eight level of education. In discussions with Badi NGO workers, it became clear that they were particularly concerned with presenting an urban middle class identity. The reason for this is clear. As all Badi women are seen by outsiders as sex workers, their bodies function as sites of caste identity. This sexualisation of Badi identity resonates with other dimensions of high caste representations of low caste identities, resulting in a complex portrayal of status built on such referents as dress, immorality, alcohol use, violence and hygiene. Low caste people are often portrayed as 'backward', as lacking in 'awareness' and as 'impoverished'. In this way, the language of development serves to reinforce Badi difference.

The language of development also sets up a distinction between those who can deliver development, by virtue of their superior 'awareness', and those who can only receive it.[38] Development-based social distinctions are replicated within impoverished and marginalised communities. Badi women working in HIV education do not see themselves in the portrait of the archetypal Badini sex worker around which the programmes they serve are built. Their increasing engagement with the wider realm of health training, workshops and conferences is, for them, proof of this. And this interaction with the outside world of 'development' creates a certain social distance between them and their 'peers' within the community. This difference is significant to people at the local level, yet it is effaced by the model of 'peer education' that dominates international INGO/NGO approaches. The 'peer education' model assumes a homogeneity within categories of people that are poor and marginal, conflating the idea of 'community member' with 'peer'. Yet INGO bureaucratic protocols for monitoring and evaluation create a need for field workers with at least minimal record-keeping skills, thus creating a situation in which

---

[38] Pigg, *op. cit.* (1992); S. Pigg, 'Found in Most Traditional Societies: Traditional Medical Practitioners between Culture and Development', in F. Cooper and R. Packard (eds), *International Development and the Social Sciences: Essays on the History and Politics of Knowledge* (Berkeley, University of California Press, 1997), pp. 259–90.

only the most educated local people can be 'peer educators'. Very few women in the Badi community can, therefore, serve as 'peer educators' due to this community's historical exclusion from the educational system. In one locale, for instance, a 'peer educator' was a woman who had some schooling.but was not a sex worker.

Field workers and peer educators associate themselves with modernity both through their own self-evaluation and their alignment with biomedical knowledge and public health initiatives. Women in these roles are positioned within the hierarchy of knowledge associated with the twinned markers of education and development, and this obviates the very possibility of horizontal interactions among 'peers'. Thus rural village women, the recipients of 'peer education', are fixed as 'targets' who lack knowledge and awareness, while their 'peer educators' acquire a symbolic social mobility by being a link in a chain of personnel (field workers, trainers, programme managers) that leads back to the centre and the source of development.

As a sign of this social difference, different notions of knowledge permeate the interactions between peer educators and their targets. For example, in one Badi community, local women told Pike that, for a baby to be formed, female *raagat* (blood) must be joined with male *biu* (semen) and that the blood that would normally be shed in menstruation forms the resultant child.[39] When an older female informant was describing this model of conception, one of the peer educators interrupted and told her that it was male and female *andaa* (eggs) that joined together to form babies. At that time, the two peer educators were the only women in the community who held this view. Their divergent knowledge had been recently acquired from discussions with field workers— who themselves had only a very tentative notion of andaa and conception, because, the educational materials used in their training had focused primarily on HIV transmission and STDs. The peer educator's model of knowledge will no doubt come to prevail as 'truth', but how that will intersect with broader local understandings remains to be seen.[40]

---

[39] See L. Bennett, 'Sex and Motherhood among the Brahmins and Chhetri of East-Central Nepal', *Contributions to Nepalese Studies*, Vol. 3 (1976), pp. 1–51.

[40] Further fieldwork in Sept.–Oct. 1999 revealed a wider dissemination of the biomedical understanding of conception. Both peer educators and several other

In keeping with donor priorities based on research showing that STDs should be targeted as part of an effective HIV prevention strategy, Badi peer educators have focused on *youn rog* (the generic neologism for STDs, broadly translatable as 'sex disease', but, a term that was unfamiliar to most rural Nepalis) in their discussions with community members. Community education about youn rog follows the tenets of the officially endorsed model of treatment—syndromic management. According to this model, a given range of signs and symptoms (i.e., the syndrome) requires a set treatment. For youn rog, those signs and symptoms are *pisab polne, pet dukhyo*, and *seto paani* (burning urine, pain in the stomach and white discharge, respectively). As illustrated by the flow charts outlining STD treatment, youn rog is reified as a discrete box of signs and symptoms that is referentially connected to the new diseases of AIDS and STDs, but is unattached to other notions of the body.

Peer educators have been trained to carry the message of these new illnesses to the women seen to be at risk of contracting them. Questioned on diseases that may affect them, local women mention only those within the category of youn rog, as the educators have taught them to do. Moreover, the signs and symptoms are constructed as youn rog, and youn rog is constructed as those symptoms. In other words, educational efforts create a circular chain of information that excludes anything outside the category *youn rog*. Further probing elicits a range of symptoms and ideas beyond the discrete field of youn rog—one that, at times, conflicts with it.[41] For example, in both group discussion and informal

---

community women had attended a training session organised by the local NGO, and there was now agreement that male and female *andaa* joined together to create a child. Interestingly, attempts to tease out further understandings of the previous model of reproduction met with resistance, and several women drew diagrams and attempted to explain the biomedical model to Linnet Pike.

[41] For instance, the official information campaigns about *youn rog* emphasise *seto paani* (white discharge) as one of its main signs. Yet for Badi women, *seto paani* has a range of possible causations. It may stem from overheating or fever, too much hot food and too much sex, or manifest 'after doing something dirty'. It was suggested that white lime mixed with chewing tobacco caused *seto paani* and that Norplant was also a cause in some cases. Whereas in the frame of official health education, *seto paani* is a sign of STDs and nothing else, it is clearly much more in the world view of local women. Local women differentiated among many kinds of discharge and informally sought treatments of various kinds. The

interviews, women were adamant that *bhiringhi* (translated as 'syphilis' in the official reproductive health literature) was not a youn rog (and, indeed, in its local constitution bhiringhi does not conform to the biomedical construction of syphilis). Women further distinguished between bhiringhi and what they called '*syphilesh*,' seeing these two phenomena as different and distinct. From a planning perspective, the discrepancy between local categories of bhiringi, syphilesh and youn rog does not matter so long as the objective of increasing condom usage is achieved. However, educational campaigns may have the effect of bracketing 'knowledge' of AIDS and STDs from other knowledge about the body in ways that work against local recognition of actual symptoms and risks.

Since the early 1990s, Badi community informants, both male and female, CSWs or not, have been the target of intensive HIV/AIDS and STD 'awareness raising' and 'peer education'. Although these prevention campaigns have focused on the biomedical aetiology of the disease, there are a range of beliefs, behaviours and consequences that fall outside the biomedical frame. The rubric 'HIV/AIDS' creates social sites where local knowledge, practices of risk assessment and the political economy of community development converge. For example, although members of the Badi community were quick to state that condom use is the best way to prevent HIV transmission, and although official accounts hold that there is between 90 per cent and 100 per cent condom use in the Badi community,[42] CSWs, at least judging by the number of babies in the community, evidently do not use condoms on a regular basis. We know that negotiating HIV risks can be problematic with regard to personal relationships.[43] For CSWs, the boundaries between the categories of 'clients' and boyfriends/lovers are fluid. Indeed, the shifting boundaries between work and love are illustrative of the multiple human

increasingly narrow alignment of *seto paani* with STDs may serve as an additional barrier to women in seeking treatment from regional health centres or private clinics.

[42] His Majesty's Government of Nepal, Department of Health Services & National Centre for AIDS and STD Control, *Strategic Plan for HIV and AIDS in Nepal: 1997–2001* (Kathmandu, His Majesty's Government of Nepal, 1997); personal communications, NGO staff.

[43] See Manderson and Jolly, *op. cit.*, (1997).

nuances of everyday life—nuances that are often elided by the singularities of the global strategy of KABP studies, Information, Education, and Communication (IEC) strategies, training, peer education and community mobilisation.

The people working on HIV education and prevention in the Badi community are also caught up in shifting social representations and self-identifications, slipping back and forth between traditional and modern, between being part of development and being in need of it. There is a complex interplay between local beliefs, risk assessment and the political economy of relationships with NGOs and donors. All these factors come together to mediate both community and individual practices and experiences.

Conclusion

In 1990s Nepal, in order to communicate AIDS prevention it was deemed necessary to use images that make a social distinction between sexual respectability and sexual transgression. Such images helped to reinforce the view that AIDS is a sign of sexual deviance, a disease whose ultimate cause is immorality. This immorality, in turn, was clearly embodied by particular women, and these women came to figure as the locus of AIDS within Nepal's borders. It would be difficult to say whether AIDS prevention messages have enhanced this imagery or simply made use of it. Nonetheless, it permeates discussions of AIDS. As we have shown, questions of moral boundaries and personal respectability pervade not just awareness messages, but also the mechanics of AIDS prevention programmes. At the same time, AIDS prevention activities are slotted into the well-worn grooves of the development industry. Here the logic of difference relies on idioms of knowledge and ignorance to mark a hierarchy between agents of development and the people they target. AIDS and STD prevention activities involve the introduction of new terms and new, biomedically derived, conceptualisations of sexuality and health. Such activities are symbols of development and, as such, they become a site upon which both individual claims to status and collective claims to progress are contested.

12

Muscularity and its Ramifications

Mimetic Male Bodies in Indian Mass Culture

◆ Kajri Jain

In this essay I want to open up some questions about the links between masculinity, muscularity, power and the work of the mass-cultural image in post-independence India.[1] While my attempt to foreground the work of the image will mean that my discussion is centred on a particular set of iconic figures, I want to emphasise that the argument in which I situate these images by no means exhausts or adequately represents the work that they have done and will continue to do (indeed, I hope that my argument will make it clear just how and why this might be the case). As if to prove that the work of an image is never done, I shall proceed by revisiting the discussion, conducted over the previous decade, of a figure which began to appear in Indian 'bazaar' prints in the late 1980s, in confluence with the

---

[1] I should clarify at the outset that I am using the term 'mass-culture' not to mobilise a notion of 'the masses', but to refer to mass-produced cultural forms as distinguished from folk or popular culture.

Ramjanmabhoomi movement:[2] that of the god Ram as a muscular, aggressive, dynamic warrior (hence the irreverent pun in my title).[3]

A Reiteration

To begin with, I would like to go back to a wonderfully insightful and erudite article from 1993 by Anuradha Kapur, called 'Deity to Crusader: The Changing Iconography of Ram'.[4]

Here Kapur traces a marked iconographic shift in popular imagery from the earlier, textually-sanctioned depictions of Ram as soft, smooth-bodied, almost pudgy, smiling, benign and above all gentle and tranquil (see Plate 12.1), to the more recent muscular versions whose *rasa* or mood is—according to Kapur predominantly *ugra*: 'angry, exercised ... punishing', emphasising his bow and arrows in their capacity as weapons rather than as mere iconographic markers (Plate 12.2).[5] Kapur describes how the characterisation of Ram as compassionate, tender, composed and non-muscular spans several different textual, pictorial and performative cultural forms following the first written appearance of the Ramayana story sometime between 500 B.C. and 300 A.D. The departure from these established iconographic conventions, Kapur argues, is made possible by 'the making of a virile Hinduism' which accompanies the encroachment of 'realism', and particularly the depiction of a 'virile' physiognomy, onto the mythic or

---

[2] In the late 1980s the rallying point for the Hindu right was a call for the destruction of the Babri mosque at Ayodhya, allegedly built on the site of Ram's birthplace (*janmabhoomi*), and for its replacement by a Hindu temple. In October 1990 the BJP leader L. K. Advani led a *rath yatra* or chariot procession from Somnath (the site of well-known medieval attacks on Hindu temples by Muslim raiders) to Ayodhya to muster support for this cause; on 6 Dec. 1992, the Babri mosque was destroyed as the 'secular' state's forces stood by. Ensuing protests by the Muslim community were answered with organised attacks on Muslim persons and property by Hindu mobs, especially in Bombay which has a particular history of such violence.

[3] Evidently this is a particularly irresistible pun that readily presents itself to those of us working on Indian religion and popular culture: I have just learned that it has also been used by Philip Lutgendorf in the title of his forthcoming paper, 'The Tantrification of Hanuman, or, Further Ramifications of Rudra'.

[4] Anuradha Kapur, 'Deity to Crusader: The Changing Iconography of Ram', in Gyanendra Pandey (ed.), *Hindus and Others* (New Delhi, Viking, 1993), pp. 74–109.

[5] Anuradha Kapur, *op. cit.*, p. 75.

Plate 12.1 *Ram Raj Tilak* (Ram's Coronation) by Ramchandra, 1990s, publishe
by S. S. Brijbasi, New Delhi.

Plate 12.2 *Jai Shri Ram* (Praise to Lord Ram), *janmabhoomi* campaign propaganda sticker, New Delhi, 1994, artist and publisher unknown.

iconic image. This 'realism' was introduced during the colonial period by oil painting and the western pictorial convention of perspective, the proscenium stage, the technological mass-production and marketing of images, and a consequent 'standardisation', not just of images but also of the 'expectation' that they produce of a 'reality effect'.[6] For Kapur the 'realist' moment was inaugurated by the artist Ravi Varma and the playwright Radheyshyam Kathavachak, working around the turn of the previous century, whose 'humanised' depiction of physiognomy and placement of iconic figures within a recognisable, quotidian, sensually appealing *mise en scène* served to make the gods more accessible and more 'serviceable' to political ends.[7] The muscular Ram mobilised by the Hindu Right from the late 1980s onwards can thus, in Kapur's account, almost be read as a teleological consequence of this 'humanisation', even as she locates these later Ram images as 'images produced by a moment of violence', indexing a specific formation of Hindu absolutist aggression.

In his article, 'The Nation (Un)Pictured?', which also starts and ends with a reference to the recently muscularised Ram images, Christopher Pinney throws into productive disarray both the suggestion of a teleological progression in the work of images and the saliency of a 'physiognomic' reading which 'naively links formal content with ideological effect.'[8] Tracing a genealogy of 'commoditised propaganda' in India, Pinney convincingly

---

[6] *Ibid.*, pp. 96–97.

[7] This argument with regard to 'realism' is elaborated in greater detail in Anuradha Kapur, 'The Representation of Gods and Heroes: Parsi Mythological Drama of the Early Twentieth Century', *Journal of Arts and Ideas*, Nos. 23–24 (1993), pp. 85–107. A similar line is taken by Ashish Rajadhyaksha in 'The Phalke Era: Conflict of Traditional Form and Modern Technology', *Journal of Arts and Ideas*, Nos. 14–15 (1987), pp. 47–78. I have been placing the term 'realism' in scare quotes given that it is conceivably not the most accurate term to use in relation to pictures of the gods: my own preference is for 'illusionism'. However, Kapur's use of the term 'realism' points to a set of ideological underpinnings which are crucial to her argument across the articles I have been referring to. For a take on the way the term 'realism' is used by calendar artists, see K. Jain, 'Producing the Sacred: The Subjects of Calendar Art', in Tapati Guha-Thakurta (ed.), *Journal of Arts and Ideas* (issue entitled *Sites of Art History: Canons and Expositions*, Tapati Guha-Thakurta), Nos. 30–31 (1997), pp. 63–88.

[8] Christopher Pinney, 'The Nation (Un)Pictured? Chromolithography and "Popular" Politics in India, 1878–1995', *Critical Inquiry*, Vol. 23 (1997), pp. 834–67, p. 835.

demonstrates that mass-produced images are not sedimented into easily identifiable chronological and ideological strata, but instead their circulation, persistence, imitation, reuse and reconfiguration has meant that they inhabit a complex, disjunctive and recursive temporality.[9] To this extent I readily endorse Pinney's argument *contra* Basu et al. that the circulation of commoditised images, and their expression of a 'messianic' nationalism, has long posed an alternative to a nation (and a modernity) imagined as secular, so that in this respect the recent flood of Hindutva imagery does not index a radical qualitative change.[10] However, I do think that Kapur's much more specific observation about the muscularity of the Ram image is worth pursuing for what it might tell us about the enabling conditions for the permissibility of such an image within the iconographic canon, and the symbolic upheaval that is indexed both by this shift in the canon and by the violence that has accompanied it. In other words, I would like to hold open the possibility that thinking about change need not necessarily buy into a teleological narrative, even as I acknowledge that the inherent historicism of such an account makes it as 'inadequate' as it is 'indispensable'.[11]

Kapur is, in fact, at pains to emphasise the persistence of 'older' bazaar images and popular forms of performance which do not buy into the aggressive muscularisation of Ram, and to this extent she cannot be accused of deploying a logic of 'sedimentation' of images despite her narrative of colonially-imposed 'realism'. The problem with that narrative, to my mind, is that it makes too tight a connection between the visual convention of perspective, the 'humanisation' of the gods, a modernist notion of subjectivity, and a series of phenomena that Kapur seems to exclusively attribute to the colonial encounter with western modernity: the political 'serviceability' of images, their illusionism, commodification and imaginary identification via the gaze. I would contend that many

---

[9] *Ibid.*, p. 836.

[10] *Ibid.*, pp. 834–35; Tapan Basu, et al., *Khaki Shorts and Saffron Flags: A Critique of the Hindu Right* (New Delhi, Orient Longman, 1993).

[11] On the inadequacy of historicist thinking to non-secular notions of temporality and agency, and its simultaneous indispensability to critiques of secular governmentality and the quest for social justice, see Dipesh Chakrabarty, *Provincializing Europe: Postcolonial Thought and Historical Difference* (Princeton, NJ, Princeton University Press, 2000), particularly, p. 88.

of these phenomena were already occurring in some form (though obviously not in strict conformance with these modernist descriptors) before the colonial period, while others, like imaginary identification via a 'realist' gaze, have arguably never adequately described the engagement with popular images anywhere. What's missing here, for instance, is the history of kings and priests using icons to jockey for political power and/or material gain: a good example in this context is Norbert Peabody's account of how the Krishna images of the Pushtimarg cult (now based in Nathdwara) were ferried from one Rajput kingdom to another during the medieval period, as local kings vied with each other to shore up the legitimacy of their rule.[12] Or again, the 'humanising' aspects of the *bhakti* traditions, with their intense, sensual and personalised modes of attachment to the divine, could be said to pre-date and inflect both 'realism' and mass culture in the Indian context. Given these much broader continuities, more work needs to be done to specify the mechanics whereby these muscular images of Ram have become widely acceptable relatively suddenly *after* more than a century of 'realism' and mass-reproduction, despite the fact that an often violent Hindutva also formed a basis for earlier, anticolonial nationalism.[13] What might have changed since the earlier half of the century to allow for the circulation of these images?

In trying to address this issue I want to open up (at least) two parallel lines of exploration. One has to do with the figuration of masculinity in popular culture, developing on Kapur's insights into the delimited depiction of muscularity to ask to what extent the symbolic complex around masculine power, divine or mortal, has involved the figuration of muscularity as such. If muscularity

---

[12] Norbert Peabody, 'In Whose Turban Does the Lord Reside?: The Objectification of Charisma and the Fetishism of Objects in the Hindu Kingdom of Kota', *Comparative Studies in Society and History*, Vol. 33, No. 4 (1991), pp. 726–54.

[13] Here I should make it clear that I do not see Raja Ravi Varma's 'realistic' depictions of Ram as belonging to the same register as the images of late twentieth century Hindutva. It is, in fact, precisely their 'realism' that disallows Varma's images from presenting the kind of physiognomy that we see almost a century later: in paintings by Varma like 'Ram Breaking the Bow' or 'Ram Vanquishing the Sea' the body of Ram is more that of a relatively scrawny, albeit lithe and athletic, Malayali male (that is, from Ravi Varma's own milieu) than the power-packed, muscle-bound, post-Schwarzenegger body of the *janmabhoomi* prints.

has not always been a universal, privileged and defining attribute of masculinity in images—and I must insist that my concern here is with masculinity as actualised in images at their intersection with social performance, and not with some kind of general, idealised notion of masculinity (predicated on gender having a being prior to its embodied manifestation)—how might we historically locate the specific ideological nexus (in the field of the image) between muscularity, masculinity, sexuality and aggressive power, including state power (implied, for instance, in the term 'virility': *vir* in Sanskrit means warrior, while *viryam* is semen)?[14] Might it be possible that in certain constellations of images, visible bodily attributes are not primarily charged with the burden of figuring masculinity as such, given that there are plenty of other means available for performatively reinforcing the gendered structures of male power? Could this then mean that muscularity on the one hand, and male bodies on the other, are freed-up to do other kinds of symbolic work?

This ties in with the second strand of my exploration, which is to do with the way in which male bodies have, in turn, engaged with images. Here I hope to demonstrate the value of tracing the mechanisms whereby the work of images is concretely actualised at a material level, as an affective impact on other bodies (both human bodies and other images). If there is such a thing as an 'ideological effect' of an image it comes into being, and indeed can be countered, in and through such actualisations. To this extent I would argue that what is required is in fact a more, rather than less, 'physiognomic' reading of images, that would take into account not just the 'formal content' of images, but also their circulation as objects, and modes of relating to images that might exceed the visual and/or ideational. Particularly at the interface between the market-driven arena of mass culture and the habitual realm of everyday religious ritual, the acceptance of an iconographic shift in the depiction of a popular deity is highly significant. While it might be naive to see the mere presence of muscular Ram images as an index of a widespread belief in an aggressive *Hindutva*, I hope to show that attention to an image-driven logic, and to processes of actualisation in the wider visual field of mass-cultural images,

---

[14] I thank Philip Lutgendorf for pointing this out to me, as well as for numerous other invaluable comments and suggestions on several aspects of this paper.

could help to formulate a more productive spin on the significance of this shift.

Divine Muscularity

The first artist for the *Amar Chitra Katha* mythological comic series, Ram Waeerkar, told me that one of the first obstacles he faced was the publisher's insistence that the gods were not supposed to have muscles.[15] This was frustrating for Waeerkar, who had developed his early skill in figure drawing by copying from *Tarzan* comics, and it has been a similar story for all those 'calendar' or 'bazaar' artists who have studied anatomy, often at art school, but have not been able to use their grasp of proportion and musculature. To this extent my own interviews with artists bear out Anuradha Kapur's assertions as to the valency of textual injunctions against the depiction of deities like Ram and Krishna with muscles, but also simultaneously disrupt the centrality of western-style 'realism' within her narrative. The artists and picture publishers I spoke with saw iconographic accuracy, as opposed to 'realism', as a prerequisite for a picture to succeed in the marketplace; in this context muscularity explicitly figured as (if you will forgive the anatomically mixed metaphor) a bone of contention. According to the Nathdwara artist Indra Sharma, the reason why publishers sought him out to paint religious subjects, rather than the more 'realistic' (Sharma's term) Bombay artist S. M. Pandit, was that Pandit's figures looked like people rather than gods. 'Now the body is very strong, but we will not show the *anatomy*. For god's body, the description is of a gentle, beautiful (*sukomal*) body.... There won't be any *muscles*, we people avoid *muscles*.'[16]

Here Sharma is speaking in Hindi, but uses the English words 'anatomy' and 'muscles', and that too pretty much interchangeably.[17] Anatomy, the modern discipline of the body that brings

---

[15] Interview with Ram Waeerkar, Bombay, 4 Dec. 1995.
[16] Interview with Indra Sharma, Bombay, 13 Dec. 1994.
[17] Significantly, there seems to be no colloquial Hindi equivalent for muscles: the dictionary translation is *manspeshi*, which no-one I have asked has heard in everyday speech, while 'muscular' is *shaktishali*, or powerful; J. W. Raker and R. S. Shukla, *English–Hindi, Hindi–English* (New York, Hippocrene Books, 1995). Thus,

medical discourse into constellation with that of art, is cathected into this one forbidden area of musculature.

The textually specified iconography of divine bodies has also informed the representation of mythological figures in the cinema. This is particularly evident in the case of the star–politicians M. G. Ramachandran (also known as MGR, active in Tamil cinema from the 1950s to the 1970s) and N. T. Rama Rao (NTR, who acted in Telugu films from the 1950s to the early 1990s), both of whom started out by playing mythological roles and carried this iconography over to their portrayal of human heroes as well. Their physiognomies conformed closely to iconographic imperatives: soft and fleshy rather than muscular or skinny, with the face and eyes the most prominent feature, emphasised by make-up. NTR is quoted as saying, 'I realised that keeping a muscular body won't be nice, particularly for a character like Krishna. The body must look fine but not muscular. To keep that up, I took to *pranayam* [yogic breathing] and gave up physical exercises.'[18]

So why is divine muscularity such an oxymoron? Anuradha Kapur's essay elaborates how, in the numerous textual and pictorial traditions within which the Ram story has been told, divine agency unfolds within a framework of transcendent power, whose ultimate source does not lie in physical strength even as it might have a physical effect. The gods do not have warriors' bodies, in accordance with the characterisation of divine agency in the Vaishnava schema as more a matter of *lila*, sacred 'play' (in both senses of the word), than of labour.[19] As Ram Waeerkar put it,

---

for instance, Steve Derné cites a passage in the Hindi cinema fan magazine *Filmi Kaliyan* on actor Sunny Deol's display of his muscular body, in which the English word 'muscles' has been transliterated into Hindi. While Derné does not comment on this, I would suggest that it might indicate the relatively recent entry of muscularity as we know it into discourses of the male body. Steve Derné, *Movies, Masculinity and Modernity: An Ethnography of Men's Filmgoing in India* (Westport, Conn., Greenwood Press, 2000), p. 161.

[18] S. Venkat Narayan, 'The Phenomenon Called N.T.R., Actor-Turned-Politician', in T. M. Ramachandran (ed.), *70 Years of Indian Cinema, 1913-1983* (Bombay, Cinema India-International, 1985), p. 212.

[19] This does not preclude the possibility that Ram might appear to have terrifying strength in the eyes of his adversaries (again I thank Philip Lutgendorf for pointing out how this is evident in sections of the Tulsidas *Ramayana*); however, Kapur's emphasis here is on how the *devotional* address of verbal and visual icons of Ram has worked to inscribe him as primarily benevolent and sympathetic.

'Bhagwan Krishna, Prabhu Ram...they have succeeded in fighting, but they are not fighters.'

Accordingly, if power is manifested through bodily signs it is more in the radiance of the deity's eyes and smile, or the glow of the skin, all of which are highlighted in pictorial representations. It is primarily these attributes that have an impact on viewers, causing them, in Indra Sharma's words, to become *mugdh* (rapt) or *mohit* (seduced or enchanted). While a certain degree of muscularity is not inappropriate for Shiva given his association with yogic *tapasya* or penance, this too is not of the same order as instrumental human agency—and even in his case, muscular or lean depictions (such as a painting by S. M. Pandit from the 1950s, which adapted Hollywood's MGM poster style to recast Shiva in the Tarzan mould) are less commonly seen than more smooth and rounded representations.

For me, Kapur's most brilliant insight in this essay is in the distinction she posits between the power silently emanating from a still ('limpid'), disinterested, timeless, transcendent source and the noisy, aggressive force of a more instrumentalised, time-bound and goal-driven body.[20] I want to develop this distinction, shifting the emphasis in thinking about muscularity away from the much-discussed, primarily gender-inflected opposition in colonial discourse between 'martial' and 'effeminate' male bodies,[21] towards a more strongly caste and class-inflected consideration of the value assigned to the instrumentality of labouring bodies within Vaishnava image traditions, including 'calendar art' or 'bazaar art'.[22]

Monkey-see, Monkey-do

Consider, for instance, the one god for whom the depiction of musculature has been acceptable in calendar art since at least the

---

[20] Anuradha Kapur, 'Deity to Crusader', pp. 92–96.

[21] See, for instance, Mrinalini Sinha, *Colonial Masculinity: The 'Manly Englishman' and the 'Effeminate Bengali' in the Late Nineteenth Century* (Manchester and New York, Manchester University Press, 1995).

[22] For an elaboration of my argument that bazaar art, and to some extent the pan-Indian mass culture industry in general, has been characterised by a hegemony of northern Vaishnava visual idioms, see Kajri Jain, 'Gods in the Bazaar', *South Asia*, Vol. 21, No. 1 (1998), pp. 91–108.

early 1970s, the monkey-god Hanuman. Ram crucially depends on Hanuman's amazing strength: it is Hanuman whose monkeys construct a bridge across the ocean so that Ram's army can cross it, who spreads fire through the enemy's city with his tail, and who saves Lakshman's life by bringing him the life-giving *sanjivini* herb (as well as the entire mountain on which it grows). And yet Hanuman's powerful, muscular body poses no threat to the location of ultimate transcendent agency in the unlabouring, primarily affective body of Ram, for Hanuman's body is framed as that of an animal, a devotee and a servant. In calendar images the utter subservience of Hanuman's body to Ram is evident in the way his body is often made up of Ram's name, or an image of Ram (with or without Sita and Lakshman) is shown to be embedded within his chest or forehead (see Plate 12.3). If the expression of divine power in a transcendent, affective register delinks agency from muscularity, Hanuman's devotional body restores a certain value to muscular agency, but only to the extent that it is harnessed to the frame of abjection before the divine. Joseph Alter, in his seminal work on Indian wrestling, stresses that *shakti* (divine life-force or power, as opposed to *bal* or brute force) and *bhakti* (devotion), the two qualities that make Hanuman the exemplary 'warrior-devotee', cannot be thought apart, such that Hanuman's shakti can be seen as directly derived from his devotion to Ram.[23] In other words, there would appear to be a correlation between devotion and the conversion of the valueless, if not denigrated, bestial bal into the venerated and sought-after divine shakti.[24]

---

[23] Here Alter is following Leonard Wolcott, 'Hanuman, the Power Dispensing Monkey in Indian Folk Religion', *Journal of Asian Studies*, Vol. 37, No. 4 (1978), pp. 653–62. Joseph S. Alter, *The Wrestler's Body. Identity and Ideology in North India* (Berkeley, University of California Press, 1992), p. 208. See also p. 199, 'The more perfect his bhakti, the greater his strength; the more fabulous his strength the greater the magnitude of his bhakti.'

[24] I should emphasise that the denigration of *bal* is not to be conflated with a denigration of animality as such. However, it is possible that the scholarly narrative of a shift, between the twelfth and sixteenth centuries, from a courtly pre-Muslim Vishnu figured as Narasimha and Varaha to the pastoral/other-worldly Krishna, might be accompanied by a narrative of disentanglement of the world of animals, and their power, from that of men. On the historical context for the shift from kingly to romantic incarnations of Vishnu see David L. Haberman, *Acting as a Way of Salvation: A Study of Raganuga Bhakti Sadhana* (New York, Oxford University Press, 1988), pp. 40–45.

Plate 12.3 Ram embedded in the body of Hanuman, detail from poster by 'Appu' (?), published by Jain Picture Publishers, purchased at New Delhi, 1994.

Plate 12.4 Postcard by M. Baskar, Published by Vadhera Picture Publishers, purchased at New Delhi, 1994.

Between animal strength and divine power, where might human bodies stand? Before I consider how the delinking of muscularity from divine agency might inform the mass-cultural figuration of human masculinity, I want to spend a moment on the relationship between human bodies and iconic or divine images.

In Alter's ethnography, Hanuman is a central figure in the construction of a wrestler's identity, providing a model of shakti, bhakti and *brahmacharya* (celibacy). The wrestlers' relationship with this figure ranges across veneration of Hanuman's image, singing hymns or reciting poems in his praise, and worshipping and serving the guru, whose power is placed on a continuum with that of Hanuman. All of this amounts to what Alter describes as a 'deeply felt private identification with Hanuman on a personal level': ultimately these wrestlers worship Hanuman to be like him, to take on his qualities of devotion and strength.[25] While some form of ritual prayer is a common mode of relating to iconic images across the pantheon, it is characteristic of Vaishnava *bhakti*, and its mimetic relationship with models of devotion, that male devotees are able to identify with either Hanuman (in the case of Ram worship) or Radha (in the case of Krishna cults) at an embodied, performative level.[26] Thus, for instance, while wrestlers and devotees in general might worship Hanuman in order to take on certain of his qualities, the mendicants known as *bahurupias* (literally 'of many forms') actually adopt the monkey form (among others), with blackened bodies, their faces ringed by fur, wearing tails and often gibbering and jumping about for further effect.[27] Think also of the Bajrang Dal, the Hindu paramilitary group

---

[25] Alter, *The Wrestler's Body*, p. 201.

[26] This mimetic aspect of devotion is often theorised in cultic texts. For instance, *Raganuga bhakti sadhana* as described by David Haberman is a highly elaborated practice of devotional imitation, whose texts set out a schema of exemplars from the Krishna lila, hierarchically categorised according to types of devotional love (*ibid*). Here imitation of these exemplars becomes the starting point for a chain effect, wherein a particularly holy or accomplished practitioner himself becomes the model for other devotees.

[27] In the Valmiki Ramayana, monkeys have a privileged association with the capacity for metamorphosis or shape-shifting, as do *rakshasas* like Ravana and Surpanakha: the text often refers to them as *kamarupin*, able to take on the form they desire (Philip Lutgendorf, personal communication).

mobilised in the janmabhoomi campaign, whose young men styled themselves after Hanuman's monkey army (this group has been particularly reviled for vandalising a gallery carrying paintings by the celebrated modernist artist M. F. Husain, in 1996, on the grounds that his depictions of Hindu goddesses were 'obscene': again, a most emphatically embodied response to the image).

The wrestlers in Alter's ethnography are at pains to distinguish their practices, and their bodies, from those of their more overtly muscular counterparts in the mostly secular arena of bodybuilding.[28] This distinction mostly hinges around the bodybuilders' preoccupation with external form and their fragmentation of the body into distinct, bulging parts, as opposed to the wrestlers' holistic development of a 'smooth, integrated... ek rang ka sharir, a body of one colour and uniform texture', through attention to the matter that goes into and comes out of it, and an exercise regime that is inseparable from devotion.[29] Alter himself buys into this distinction in asserting that 'Hanuman's physique is not that of a bodybuilder, except as portrayed in some modern calendar art, but that of a wrestler.'[30] Alter is most likely referring here to the work of the Kolhapur artist P. Sardar, a Muslim, who was without doubt the most celebrated painter and fervent bhakta of Hanuman among calendar artists. In fact Sardar was himself a bodybuilder, and is reputed to have modelled in the mirror for his own paintings. Sardar's devotion to Hanuman is just one instance among countless others in the arena of Indian popular religion of an individual transcending religious boundaries. However, the mimetic aspect of this devotion, that is his identification with Hanuman through bodybuilding, also served to set up a dizzying mimetic concatenation whereby his own performative adoption of a muscular (because devotional) body, reflected in the mirror, transmuted onto paper, then replicated by the thousands, was able to turn it into the icon worshipped and identified with by devotees, be they wrestlers or bodybuilders, Hindus or Muslims.[31] Even as the anthropologist performatively reiterates the

---

[28] Alter, The Wrestler's Body, pp. 56–57.
[29] Ibid., p. 57.
[30] Ibid., p. 56.
[31] Here I am following the lead of Michael Taussig, who, by means of an enormously useful re-reading of Adorno and Benjamin, reanimates the notion of

codification of certain distinctions, the transgressive, exceptional devotee's body and its mimetic actualisation of Hanuman disrupts those distinctions, subtly but significantly reconfiguring the conventions of the (far from exceptional) medium of calendar art.

This, then, is one possible link in the visual logic whereby muscularity of the bodybuilding variety (which is how we might further specify the body of the *ugra* Ram) becomes acceptable in calendar art. This instance provides some sense of the way in which the arena of performance, and its experimentation with differently embodied 'speaking' positions (in this case, the devotee of Hanuman as a Muslim bodybuilder rather than a Hindu wrestler) can, in certain circumstances, reconfigure the canon by actualising a *reiterable version* of that new speaking position. (Here it is important to emphasise the often partial and conditional nature of that version, so that what is reproducible about Sardar's body is his muscularity, rather than his Muslimness.) Such experimental performances are often circumscribed by a ritual temporality, as in the case of carnivalesque 'inversions' or theatrical impersonations of the divine such as the Ramlila performances where the actors are worshipped as deities for the duration of the performance. However, technologies of mass-reproduction can enable images to migrate beyond such temporal boundaries, even as they might continue to be implicated within other forms of temporal, spatial and semiotic re-territorialisation.[32] To this extent,

mimesis as a productive, performative encounter rather than as a matter of accurate reproduction or verisimilitude, and elaborates on how technologies of mass reproduction have worked to reactivate a fundamental 'mimetic faculty' within the modern sensorium. See in particular Michael Taussig, *Mimesis and Alterity: A Particular History of the Senses* (New York and London, Routledge, 1993). I would also like to acknowledge a mimetic contagion from Laleen Jayamanne's work on the notion of mimesis in the cinema; see, for instance, Laleen Jayamanne, 'A Slapstick Time: Mimetic Convulsion, Convulsive Knowing', in George Kouvaros and Lesley Stern (eds), *Falling for You: Essays on Cinema and Performance* (Sydney, Power Publications, 1999).

[32] The terms de-territorialisation and re-territorialisation, as I understand them to be deployed by Deleuze and Guattari, refer as much to the regime of signs as to that of bodily movement, holding the two registers together in relation to an idea of society as a 'machine' that codes the flows of desire. The movement of de-territorialisation works to decode or liberate these flows from their spatial, institutional and conceptual overcoding by society. However, this movement is

even as the body of Sardar–Hanuman may have reconfigured certain physiognomic qualities of Hanuman that might continue to have a detailed symbolic significance for wrestlers, this body still works within the overall logic of devotional abjection, wherein the value and relevance of its instrumentality cannot be thought apart from its role in shoring up the greater value and power of a transcendent divine agency.[33]

A similar move from performative identification to a mimetic relay with images has also historically occurred in the male body's devotional engagement with the modality of Radha as a vehicle of feminine desire. While there are ample examples in bhakti poetry of male poets writing in the female voice, there have also been instances of male priests performing rituals dressed as women, particularly in Pushtimarg (a Krishna cult with a large Marwari following, based in Nathdwara, Rajasthan) and some

---

always and necessarily accompanied by re-territorialisation, a reinstatement of codes. Unlike the 'primitive territorial machine' and the 'barbarian despotic machine', capitalism is the only social machine which is predicated on the decoding of flows, furthering its own self-expansion by feeding off the re-territorialisations that impede its path. Trans. Robert Hurley, Mark Seem, Helen R. Lane, Gilles Deleuze and Felix Guattari, *Anti-Oedipus* (New York, Viking Books, 1977) and trans. Brian Massumi, *A Thousand Plateaus* (Minneapolis, University of Minnesota Press, 1987).

[33] I must emphasise that throughout I am using the term 'abjection' in its specific philosophical sense, as it unfolds via Georges Bataille, Julia Kristeva, and subsequent critiques of Kristeva by Hal Foster, Rosalind Krauss and others. If the abject is that which is cast out by society or the subject, for Kristeva this very operation of exclusion is crucial to the maintenance of normative sociality and to the integrity of an autonomous, bounded subjectivity. In other words, that which excludes the abject thereby also fundamentally depends on the abject for its very existence, and must, in denying this dependence, do a great deal of work to control it. Krauss and Foster complicate what Foster calls Kristeva's 'conservative, even defensive' formulation of the abject (and the normativity it enables) by attending not so much to the abject as substance or essence but to abjection as a process: an 'alteration' that renders unstable the very terms of exclusion and inclusion, remobilising the heterogeneity at the heart of the dominant order. My argument here can in part be seen as fleshing out this latter position: if the abjection of labouring and reproductive bodies is formalised in the devotional schema, the alteration enabled by devotional identification with abject bodies rebounds on symbolic conventions. See Rosalind Krauss, '*Informe* without Conclusion', *October*, Vol. 78 (1996), pp. 89–105; Hal Foster, 'Obscene, Abject, Traumatic', *October*, Vol. 78 (1996), pp. 107–24.

of the ecstatic Bengali Vaishnava sects.[34] In Renaldo Maduro's ethnography, Pushtimarg priests identifying with Radha reported intense sexual experiences before the image of Krishna.[35] An account of the Sakhi-bhava sect of Mathura and Brindavan, written behind an eighteenth century painting of one of its members, describes how male devotees wore red loin cloths every month to simulate menstruation, and after this period was over:

> In the manner of married women, anxious to be physically united with their husbands … they take to themselves … a painting of Shri Krishna, and stretch themselves, raising both their legs, utter 'ahs' and 'ohs', adopt woman-like coy manners, and cry aloud: 'Ah, Lalji [i.e., Krishna], I die! Oh Lalji, I die'![36]

Again, the relationship of the male body with the image in this instance exceeds the visual: if on the one hand the male *bhakta* performs an embodied identification with the image of Radha, the image of Krishna in its capacity as an object comes to stand in for what it represents, that is, Krishna himself.

What is significant about the Radha figure is that her affective and desiring body is not that of a wife (that is, not a wife to Krishna).[37] If Radha, as non-wife, expresses her desire for Krishna in excess of the imperative of wifely *duty* that defines social womanhood, Yashoda, as non-mother, provides a model for non-

---

[34] On debates in sixteenth century Gaudiya Vaishnavism over how literally male devotees should take the injunction to emulate the *gopis*, see David Haberman, *Acting as a Way of Salvation*, especially chapter 6.

[35] Renaldo Maduro, *Artistic Creativity in a Brahmin Painter Community* (Berkeley, University of California Press, 1976), p. 32.

[36] K. Goswamy, 'The Cult', in Enrico Isacco and Anna L. Dallapiccola (eds), *Krishna the Divine Lover: Myth and Legend in Indian Art* (Delhi, B.I. Publications, 1982), p. 142. Goswami cites B. N. Goswamy and A. L. Dallapiccola, 'Anmerkugen uber eine seri von indischen Miniaturen aus dem XVIII Jahrudert', in *Zeitschrift fur Religions—und Geistesgeschichte*, Bd. XXXIII, Heft 1 (1981), pp. 10–11.

[37] Again, see Haberman, *Acting as a Way of Salvation*, pp. 37–47, on the Gaudiya Vaishnava valorisation of the Krishna-love of the *gopis*, who are described as *parakiya* (belonging to another) over that of the *svakiya* women who are married to Krishna (the queens of Dwarka). See also Sudhir Kakar, 'Erotic Fantasy: the Secret Passion of Radha and Krishna', in Veena Das (ed.), *The Word and the World: Fantasy, Symbol and Record* (New Delhi, Sage, 1986), pp. 75–94, for an account of the significance of adultery and transgression in the Radha-Krishna narrative.

reproductive male bodies to affectively partake of maternal *vatsalya* (parental love).[38] In both cases, in a kind of Vaishnava version of immaculate conception, the reproductive body of woman is separated from the erotic, desiring body, eliding the relationship between woman's libidinal drives and her reproductive sexuality. This allows the sexually pure, iconic uxorial/maternal body to be strongly territorialised within the patriarchal symbolic structures of family, nation, religion and morality, while the de-territorialised, desiring feminine body (along with its necessary disregard for social convention) is freed up only to be re-territorialised, in the pastoral idyll of Braj, by the logic of devotional abjection. While Radha's body has been available for identification by both male and female devotees, the more performative and embodied modalities of identification have been largely reserved for male bodies: thus the moral suspicion to which the *devadasis* or temple dancers have been subject, as against the relative acceptance of devotionally-based cross-dressing by figures like Chaitanya, Ramakrishna and even, more recently, NTR (though perhaps with the increasing circulation in the Indian public sphere of relatively firm categories of identity based on gender and sexuality this acceptance may be on the decline).[39]

For it is precisely the social debasement and valuelessness of the desiring or libidinalised female body that enables it to be inscribed as a model of devotion. If this body was not always-already abject, it could not provide the basis for the valorisation within the devotional frame of an evacuated will and a surrendering body, one that is utterly seduced and enchanted (mohit, mugdh). In other

---

[38] I thank Kalpana Ram for reminding me that devotional excess is already built in to conceptions of maternal love, so maternal devotion and duty do not follow the pattern of tension between desire and wifely *dharma* (each of which also have their own modes of affective excess).

[39] This is not to say that devotional cross-dressing has not had a longer history of controversy and censure, one which deserves to be examined in greater detail. Haberman, for instance, describes how the ideas of the Gaudiya Vaishnava scholar Rupa Kaviraj, who advocated the literal, physical imitation of the *gopis*, were censured by a council in Jaipur in 1727; studying and teaching his works became a crime punishable by the Maharaja. Haberman, *Acting as a Way of Salvation*, pp. 98–104. On paradigms of 'transvestic' display in Hinduism see also Paroma Roy, 'As the Master Saw Her', in *Indian Traffic: Identities in Question in Colonial and Postcolonial India* (New Delhi, Sage, 1998), particularly pp. 96–100.

words, even as the mimetic mode has historically opened up a space for male bodies to legitimately inhabit the desiring femininity of Radha, it has also served to performatively reiterate the abjection and debasement of feminine desire within a patriarchal order. Similarly, I would suggest that what enables Hanuman's strong, muscular, agile male body to be inscribed as a model of devotional abjection is a symbolic schema where bodily force (bal) is denigrated—for instance, through its equation with animality. Thus even as Hanuman's devotion enables the conversion of the debased bal into the valorised shakti, this valorisation of shakti reinscribes bal as always-already subordinate, in a manner akin to the subordination of the labouring (rather than warring) human body within the schemata of caste.[40] Both these modalities of devotional embodiment, then, are consistent with the ultimate location of power in a transcendent, divine source, which crucially cannot coexist with a notion of labouring/productive or desiring/ reproductive bodies as immanent sources of instrumental agency or as *loci* of value. The delinking of devotional desire from reproductive sexuality doesn't only apply to the non-reproductive bodies of Radha and Yashoda: as I mentioned above, one of Hanuman's exemplary attributes is his strict brahmacharya or celibacy (a concept whose saliency I shall return to a bit later on).

My point in describing these structures of abjection is emphatically *not* to cast the power of patriarchal or caste hierarchies in totalising terms. On the contrary, if I am concerned with the ways in which the 'always-already' character of these structures is re/ produced by their reiteration in the arena of embodied practice, it is precisely because this performative arena is also where such structures can become vulnerable to reconfiguration, through

---

[40] Here I must thank Nita Kumar for her cautioning on the use of the terms 'labour' and 'work' in a manner that uncritically yokes them to a liberal—modernist understanding, one which has also inflected the reading of these categories in Marx. At the sametime, however, a historicist understanding of these terms is constantly reinscribed through the work of governmentality, the organisation of industrial labour and, indeed, the trade unions. As Dipesh Chakrabarty argues, the attempt of description must be to hold open the gap between such coexistent but heterogeneous forms of temporality, practice and understanding. See in particular Dipesh Chakrabarty, 'Translating Life-Worlds', chapter 3, *Provincializing Europe: Postcolonial Thought and Historical Difference* (Princeton, NJ, Princeton University Press, 2000).

differently articulated reiterations.[41] That is the thread I want to follow here. However, before doing so I just want to gesture towards another much more tenuous and enticing thread, where I would suggest that in fact even within these structures there is scope to develop more subtle and complex conceptions of power and agency. For example, there is a sense in which the very abjection of the desiring devotional body in the Krishna cult of Pushtimarg actually comes to exert some kind of power over the divine.[42] Krishna is practically held to ransom by the intensity of feeling in his devotees, who exercise something akin to the imperative of the prostitute in Lyotard's *Libidinal Economy*, 'Use me!': a power in abjection that renders undecideable the question of dominance and submission.[43] Radha takes on such centrality here that the Shrinathji image of Krishna in Pushtimarg has itself been painted in *sakhivesh*, that is, dressed as one of Radha's female companions (though, interestingly, painting such images has been forbidden since the early twentieth century).[44]

Human Masculinity

Here, however, I want to continue to track the mass-cultural images that lead us away from a cross-dressing Krishna towards

---

[41] For a discussion of performative reiteration as the site of linguistic vulnerability, see Judith Butler, *Excitable Speech: A Politics of the Performative* (London, Routledge, 1997).

[42] 'The nature of Pusti or God's Grace is that the Lord in a sportive manner assumes dependence on His devotees and transgresses the limit put by Himself on his own nature. Therein consists the real majesty of the Lord, in that He does not lose His sovereignty while going against the mandates pertaining to His nature'. Vitthalanatha, *Vidvanmandanam* (Bombay, 1926), p. 150, quoted in Mridula I. Marfatia, *The Philosophy of Vallabhacharya* (Delhi, Munshiram Manoharlal, 1967), p. 278. Vitthalanatha was the second son of Vallabhacharya, the founder of Pushtimarg, and it is to him that the high priests of Nathdwara, the Goswami Maharajas, trace their lineage.

[43] Trans. by I. H. Grant, J. F. Lyotard, *Libidinal Economy* (Bloomington and Indianapolis, Indiana University Press, 1993), pp. 60–66. This undecideability can be seen as an operation of abjection as process, resonating with the Bataillean notion of the *informe* (see note 25 above).

[44] Amit Ambalal, *Krishna as Shrinathji: Rajasthani Paintings from Nathdwara* (Ahmedabad, Mapin, 1987), pp. 144 and 160. There are also depictions of Radha dressed as Krishna, such as the miniature from Bundi (c. 1760), reproduced in Isacco and Dallapiccola, *op. cit.*, p. 141.

a muscular Ram—and indeed, towards a similarly muscular Krishna, for not long after the janmabhoomi images of Ram began to appear, Krishna, too, began to be figured in a martial, muscular incarnation (just as the janmabhoomi campaign's imagery of the infant Ram, itself based on the baby Krishna, led to the appearance of baby images of Shiva and Ganesh). But what of human men and babies in mass culture?[45]

I want to suggest that there is a sense in which the version I have been describing of transcendental patriarchal power within the Vaishnava visual schema extends to the post-independence nation-state, such that the mass-cultural figuration of the male subject of the state implicates him in an abject, devotional relationship with it. Again, my intention here is not to posit this configuration as part of an essentialised 'Indian culture', but to locate it at a particular historical conjuncture between the north Indian culture industry and the post/colonial state. I have argued elsewhere that the indigenous culture industry in northern and western India, whose extensive pan-national circulation gave it a hegemonic national character, has been centrally informed by what I have termed the 'ethos of the bazaar'.[46] This ethos, characterised by a particular set of interrelations between commercial, sacred, moral and libidinal economies, has been specific to the predominantly Vaishnava trading communities of the bazaar. However, through these communities' entrepreneurial development of the culture industry from the latter half of the nineteenth century onwards, the bazaar's Vaishnava devotional idioms came to inflect a visual print capitalism whose pan-Indian networks were integral to the rise of nationalism. Within this mass-cultural arena, then, the pre-independence and post-independence

---

[45] The seminal discussions of the mass-cultural representation of women, particularly in calendar art, are Patricia Uberoi, 'Feminine Identity and National Ethos in Indian Calendar Art', *Economic and Political Weekly*, Vol. 2, No. 2 (1990), WS41–48 and Tapati Guha-Thakurta, 'Women as Calendar Art Icons: Emergence of Pictorial Stereotype in Colonial India', *Economic and Political Weekly of India*, Vol. 26, No. 43 (1991), WS91–99.

[46] See footnote 18 above. In deploying the term 'bazaar' I am following the economic historian Rajat Kanta Ray. See, for instance, his 'The Bazaar: Indigenous Sector of the Indian Economy', in Dwijendra Tripathi, *Business Communities of India: A Historical Perspective* (Delhi, Manohar, 1984) and 'Introduction', in Rajat K. Ray (ed.), *Entrepreneurship and Industry in India 1800–1947* (New Delhi, Oxford University Press, 1992).

state came to source its moral authority and legitimacy within the terms of the sacred–commercial nationalist ethos of the bazaar, as its trading communities came to take on the lineaments of an indigenous bourgeoisie.

This nexus between the bazaar and the state was crystallised or actualised not just in the printed, cinematic and theatrical products of the culture industry, but also in the pre-eminently performative notion of Swadeshi, as well-heeled members of this indigenous bourgeoisie took up Gandhi's simultaneously moral–cultural and politico–economic imperative to boycott foreign manufactured goods and begin wearing—and ritually spinning—*khadi* (homespun cotton).

It is within this context that I want to show how an otherwise putatively socialist, secular post-independence state is able to take on the idiom of transcendental, divine power. Here, however, there is a temporal distinction to be made between the kinds of narrative that frame the printed bazaar images or calendar art on the one hand, and the cinema on the other. The predominantly iconic calendar images, with their enduring material presence and invocation of a mythic or ritual temporality, often held in place by textual and iconographic conventions, are relatively stable and slow to change (though this is not to say that printed images do not allow for change: the annually-produced calendars, in particular, tend to admit to a greater topicality of subjects than the framing pictures).[47] Calendar art has therefore tended to provide a continuing repository for the mythic basis of the nation, and concomitantly of the state's moral legitimacy and ultimately divine sources of power and authority.

Thus, for instance, the predominance in calendar art of religious imagery, and of the figure of woman as an iconic vehicle of national 'tradition'.[48]

---

[47] For example, in calendars from the 1960s and 1970s representations of women serve as the ground on which to conduct the negotiation with modernity, via depictions of women with bicycles, buses and scooters, or sitting on sofas with beehive hairdos, surrounded by modern household commodities. For some wonderful examples of these see the catalogue for Patricia Uberoi's show *From Goddess to Pin-Up: Icons of Femininity in Indian Calendar Art (Arts of People I)* (Fukuoka Asian Art Museum, 2000).

[48] See Patricia Uberoi, 'Feminine Identity', and Tapati Guha-Thakurta, 'Women as Calendar Art Icons'.

Plate 12.5 *Jai Jawan, Jai Kisan*, by 'R. Arts', 1967 calendar, publisher unknown, courtesy Patricia and J. P. S. Uberoi.

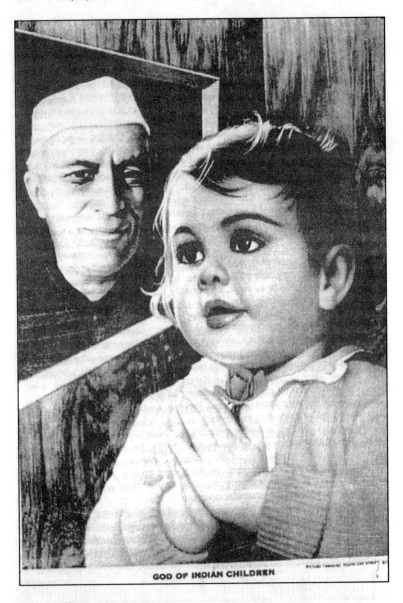

GOD OF INDIAN CHILDREN

Plate 12.6 *God of Indian Children*, artist unknown. Print, late twentieth century, published by Picture Paradise, Sivakasi, courtesy Patricia and J. P. S. Uberoi.

While his women negotiate 'tradition', 'culture' and domesticity, the male cinematic subject is, in this peculiar post-independence formation, set the task of mediating the historical, developmental axis of the secular state. While the Hindi cinema in the 1950s and 1960s has its share of nativist 'sons of the soil' (personified by Manoj Kumar), it also sees the emergence of the male protagonist that Sanjay Srivastava has called the 'Five Year Plan hero'.[49] This is an urbane, metropolitan (often 'foreign-returned'), actively modernising presence, whose framing within a melodramatic narrative enables him to negotiate the contradictions between a feudal patriarchal order and that of the vectoral modernity he embodies. However, even as he is the bearer of a secular, rational, scientific 'temper', it is also significant that the 'Five Year Plan' man is generally smooth and fair, predominantly romantic, his affects centred on his eyes, face and voice: again, more brains and heart than brawn, suggesting that the power of this modern male, and of the state that he represents, is, like that of the canonical Ram and Krishna, not located in the raw instrumentality of his body. This aesthetic convention, then, returns this embodiment of the state to its nexus with the bazaar. It also reminds us of the continuing relay between mass-cultural forms, across the temporal distinctions I have been making with respect to narrative framing: cinema has always been informed by the mythic iconography circulated by calendar art, and calendar art has adopted figures made available by the cinema (the most famous instance of this relay, outside the mythological cinema as such, is probably the iconography of Nargis as Mother India in the eponymous 1957 film).

That said, though, the importance of melodramatic narrative strategies for the 'Five Year Plan hero' would indicate that it is really hard for a similar representative of the modern state to emerge at all in calendar art. By and large, with the exception of a few backgrounds featuring lab-coated scientists or engineers, ordinary men or generic male subjects have only appeared in the

---

[49] See Sanjay Srivastava, 'The Idea of Lata Mangeshkar: Speculations of Voice, Masculinity and the Post-colonial Condition', in Ashis Nandy and Vinay Lal (eds), *Politics of Innocence and Culpability in Indian Popular Cinema* (New Delhi, Oxford University Press, forthcoming). The 'Five Year Plan' hero is so called after the planning model adopted by Nehru from the Soviets.

calendars as 'Jai Jawan, Jai Kisan'-type farmers and soldiers, men whose unstinting devotion to the state makes them worthy of praise and emulation ('jai') as model subjects (see Plate 12.4).[50] In other words, figuring these strapping male bodies is legitimised by their servile, devotional relationship to the state in much the same fashion as the muscular shakti of Hanuman's body becomes permissible, and indeed available for mimetic incorporation, within the framework of his bhakti. The Jai Jawan soldier and the Jai Kisan farmer (and, indeed, the nativist hero of the contemporaneous Manoj Kumar films) thus occupy an homologous position to that of Hanuman within a structure of devotional abjection. Indeed, these figures emerging from the 1965 war with Pakistan may have preceded and possibly enabled the muscular depiction of Hanuman in calendar art: either way, the bare-chested farmer, in particular (more than the uniform-clad soldier), provided a similar opportunity for calendar artists to hone their neglected skills in the anatomically correct depiction of musculature. By now, however, it should be clear that this muscular peasant body is not the subject of a 'realism' of the type embodied, say, by Courbet's stone-breakers, but relies for its existence on its incorporation within a sacred economy. The calendar industry's adoption of techniques from western oil painting does not inaugurate a western-style, modern, post-sacred subject that is seen as the putative *locus* of willing agency; instead it incorporates these techniques in a devotional address, with its logic of abjection, through the circulation of images in the sacred-commercial economy of the bazaar.

If the adult male devotees of the state of the mid-1960s onwards were farmers and soldiers, their children would be participants in the technologically functional, yet, culturally secure, future brought into being by the Five Year Plans. This is evident from the ever-popular calendars depicting androgynous infants playing at various forms of modernity: Soldier and Farmer Babies, equipped with fighter jets and tractors, but also Doctor and Engineer Babies, or Cricketer and Photographer Babies, as well as the more 'traditional' Namaste Baby or Qawwali Baby. Not just

---

[50] 'Jai Jawan, Jai Kisan (Victory/Praise to the Soldier, Victory/Praise to the Farmer)' was the slogan raised by Lal Bahadur Shastri in response to the 1965 war with Pakistan, emphasising the importance of food production alongside the defence of the nation.

babies but infantilised adults, they simultaneously promise, and substitute for, the adult subjecthood made impossible by a continued dependence on an iconic maternal nation (Mother India, Bharat Mata, Indira Gandhi) and a paternal state. The paternal state is embodied in specific iconic figures like Nehru, Gandhi, Ambedkar, the other Gandhis, and so on, known in the industry as 'leaders': not subjects of the state so much as quasi-sacred incarnations of it, their images imbued with its efficacy and its transcendental power.[51] The relationship between 'leaders' and 'babies' is established in the iconography of 'Chacha' (Paternal Uncle) Nehru, whose celebrated fondness for children is reciprocated, once again, by nationalist devotion: one calendar image depicting a child praying before a framed picture of Nehru is captioned 'God of Indian Children' (Plate 12.5).

The *Jai Jawan, Jai Kisan* images persisted into the 1980s, as did the heroisation of statesmen such as Gandhi and Nehru. Over the 1990s, however, the popularity of iconic 'framing pictures' and calendars depicting 'leaders' declined steeply, while demand grew for large, glossy posters of film stars as well as the usual deities (predominantly but not exclusively Hindu) in all shapes and sizes. Rajiv Gandhi was the last of the 'leaders' to be commercially viable as a calendar art icon. The increasing irrelevance of such incarnations of the state is most often linked to the rampant corruption of electoral politics and a disillusionment with the state's capacity to keep the nation together in the face of the violence accompanying various ethnic secessionist movements all over the country, the resurgence of a militant Hindutva, and the demonstrations in 1990 following the Mandal Commission's recommendation to increase job reservation for Dalits. But, I want to trace it back a bit further to the moment at which I would suggest the triumphal post-independence nexus between the bazaar and the state first comes under serious threat, and with it the possibility of deriving the moral legitimacy of the state from a transcendental *locus* of power: the Emergency of 1975–77, and the political movements to which it was an authoritarian response.

---

[51] For an elaboration of the sacred efficacy of images, and the iconographic attributes of national leaders, see K. Jain, 'The Efficacious Image: Pictures and Power in Indian Mass Culture', *Polygraph* 12, World Religions and Media Cultures, 2000, pp. 159–85.

Seemingly forgotten in the current preoccupation with globalisation, liberalisation and their spectacularly visible indices of change is the immense symbolic upheaval set in train by the politicisation in the early 1970s of the working classes and castes via, for instance, the trade unions, the Naxalite movement, Nav Nirman and Jaiprakash Narayan's Sampoorna Kranti. It is in the concerted assault by these movements on the existing structures of class and caste, and the state's collusion with these structures, that I want to look for the audience-driven re-valuing of the male body in mass culture, to which the muscular Ram images are, I would argue, a reactive (as well as reactionary), re-territorialising response. Specifically, I want to make the deliberately impertinent suggestion that the ugra or aggressive Ram of the Ayodhya campaign would neither have been possible, *nor necessary*, without the lean, active, hungry, fighting and labouring, libidinalised screen presence of the Bombay cinema superstar Amitabh Bachchan, and his resolutely non-abject embodiment of the urban working-class male from the early 1970s through the 1980s.

The Hero as *'Mard'*

Amitabh Bachchan was the Bombay cinema's first, and so far its biggest, superstar. Establishing an early reputation playing romantic heroes consistent with his own elite social background (his father was a celebrated Hindi poet; he himself had worked as a company executive), he quickly distanced himself from that image through his enormous popular success as what Rajadhyaksha and Willemen call a 'lumpen rebel-vigilante', or, as his defining cinematic persona is more commonly described in India, an 'angry young man' (Plate 12.6).[52] Indeed, by 1984 the director Manmohan Desai was saying that the only thing Bachchan lacked was 'an out and out romantic image'.[53] Bachchan—and from now on this will

---

[52] Ashish Rajadhyaksha and Paul Willemen (eds), *Encyclopedia of Indian Cinema* (New Delhi, Oxford University Press and BFI Publishing, 1994), p. 49.

[53] Interview with Manmohan Desai, *India Today*, 31 May 1984, quoted in Lalit Vachani, 'Bachchan-alias: The Many Faces of a Film Icon', in C. Brosius and M. Butcher (eds), *Image Journeys: Audio-Visual Media and Cultural Change in India* (New Delhi, Sage, 1999), p. 207.

primarily signify his defining film persona from the 1970s and 1980s (rather than that of his far less successful later films or his current televisual reincarnation, or, indeed, the 'real-life' Amitabh Bachchan)—has neither the divine, iconic body of an MGR or NTR, nor is he the soft, smooth hero of the Hindi cinema's 'social' melodrama. Tall, angular, with a trademark deep voice, and noticeably darker than preceding heroes, he cannot be described as muscular, but is acknowledged as the Bombay equivalent to the macho action heroes of Hollywood. One of his scenes in *Naseeb* (1981), for instance, is modelled on a Charles Bronson film, and as I recall in the late 1970s and 1980s autorickshaws would often be decorated with pictures of Bruce Lee or Sylvester Stallone on one side and Amitabh on the other.

But even as the Bachchan figure might be informed by Hollywood action cinema, it cannot be seen as a sheer transplant, or even a consistent imitation. Again, this is an instance of selective, productive mimesis, as has been the case throughout the Bombay cinema's long history of appropriations from Hollywood—or, for that matter, as has been the case with Indian popular art's appropriation of the conventions of oil painting, and the troubled relationship of the artists Ram Waeerkar and S. M. Pandit with the muscles of Tarzan. What is it that makes it desirable and possible at this moment for Bachchan to take on and reinterpret the action hero persona, when Bombay has been far less sanguine in adopting other aspects of Hollywood genre films (horror, for instance)? Rather than undertaking a comparison between Bachchan and the Hollywood action hero, which while potentially interesting would not be particularly useful for my argument, I shall focus here on how the Bachchan figure departs from both the transcendent and abject iconic bodies of a devotional economy to inaugurate a performative position hitherto unavailable to the male in Indian mass culture. I want to suggest that the Bachchan hero is a kind of crystal that refracts the political energies leading up to and away from the Emergency, and in particular the assertion of the value and power of working-class and working-caste male bodies, hitherto alienated from the Swadeshi-turned-totalitarian nexus between the power of the state and the morality of the bazaar.

The Bachchan film narratives often entail a quest for upward mobility or justice, but his means to success, and the code of honour according to which injustice is to be avenged, typically lie

Plate 12.7 Amitabh Bachchan in *Deewar*, as shown on the back cover of a pirated videotape.

outside the law of the state.[54] The state is often personified by a brother or friend in the police or army (as in the seminal *Deewar*, 1975, where his brother is played by the soft, romantic Shashi Kapoor), and the 'traditional' *locus* of ethics by the mother.[55] While the Bachchan hero fights to uphold 'feudal' codes of honour and kinship, he does so outside the nexus of moral-cum-governmental authority forged between the mother and brother figures, and thereby remains alienated from their universe: he often has no option within the narrative but to pay for his transgression and die (as in *Deewar*, *Sholay*, *Shakti*, *Muqaddar ka Sikandar*). To this extent Bachchan is possessed by the unquiet ghost of the Sunil Dutt character in *Mother India*, the son punished with death by his own beloved mother for breaking the law to defend her honour.[56]

[54] For a detailed structural analysis of what he terms Bachchan's 'Outsider' films, see Lalit Vachani, 'Bachchan-alias'.

[55] In his first 'angry young man' film, *Zanjeer* (1973), Bachchan starts out as a policeman who then forges alliances with the underworld; in the later films the policeman becomes a brother, like the Shashi Kapoor character in *Deewar*, from whom Bachchan is typically separated at birth to grow up fighting for survival on the streets.

[56] Here I am taking up Paroma Roy's trope of haunting in relation to identities that are repressed by an 'Indian (Hindu) psyche/polity': her instance is that of the 'good Muslim', to which I wish to add here the productive working-class/caste body. See Paroma Roy, 'Figuring Mother India: The Case of Nargis', in *Indian*

This time, however, in the pathos wrought from the abjection of the Bachchan figure before his mother, it is Bachchan and his unfulfilled thirst—for justice, but also for maternal affection—that occupy centre stage, not, as in *Mother India*, the mother's pain in choosing between love for her errant son and for the moral law.

I see this as a significant difference, precisely because what is so compelling about Bachchan is this propulsive thirst or desire. In this aspect of Bachchan we encounter the other of the body of brahmacharya or celibacy that the Banarasi wrestlers described above seek to emulate, and which, as Alter elaborates, forms the basis for a certain strand of discourse, and practice, of a virile yet celibate nationalism.[57] Here the biomoral imperative of celibacy, specified as the conservation of semen, automatically translates into progressive citizenship, not so much through a process of willed self-control triumphing over an errant body, but of material control over the substance of the body itself resulting in greater moral virtue.[58] This modern discourse of brahmacharya is explicitly directed against what is seen as an immoral western constellation of sexuality and individualism that manifests itself as self-gratification and self-indulgence.[59] Such debauchery includes not just sexual practices as such, but also a preoccupation with personal grooming, with *filmi* hairstyles and artificial scents, fashionable and in particular tight and synthetic clothing, smoking,

---

Traffic, p. 173. The plot of *Mother India*, as Rajadhyaksha and Willemen point out in the *Encyclopedia of Indian Cinema* (*op. cit.*, p. 326), was the model for *Deewar*; I think that there is also an uncanny resonance between the impotent armless patriarchs of both *Mother India* (Raaj Kumar) and *Sholay* (Sanjeev Kumar), the other seminal Bachchan film made in the same year as *Deewar* (1975).

[57] See Alter, *The Wrestler's Body*, particularly Chapter 10, 'Utopian Somatics and Nationalist Discourse', as well as his 'Celibacy, Sexuality and the Transformation of Gender into Nationalism in North India', *Journal of Asian Studies*, Vol. 53, No. 1 (1994), pp. 45–66. I must emphasise, however, that this represents just one strand of political discourse, for as Lawrence Cohen has shown, the metaphorics of sexual aggression are alive and kicking in the '*chhoti* line' political cartoons and editorials in the Banarasi popular press. Lawrence Cohen, 'Manmohan's Secret: Homosex and Indian Modernity', paper presented at conference on *Sexualities, Masculinities and Culture in South Asia: Practices, Popular Culture and the State* (Melbourne, 6–8 July, 1999).

[58] Alter, 'Celibacy, Sexuality and the Transformation of Gender', p. 52.

[59] *Ibid.*, p. 58.

drinking, chewing tobacco, riding motorcycles, loafing about in public places—and, of course, going to the cinema.[60]

Even as the Bachchan figure is hardly explicitly sexualised within the film narratives (though *Mard*, 1985, is a notable exception), he is the prototypical 'self-indulgent' young, urban, working-class 'loafer', replete with sartorial style (flared jeans, unbuttoned shirts, neckerchiefs, bow ties, longish hair), *beedi*-smoking, liquor-swilling attitude, motorbikes and girlfriends of occasionally borderline morality: indeed, it is conceivable that the Bachchan phenomenon helped the ideologues of *brahmacharya* to flesh out their descriptions. As a teenager in the 'Bachchan years' I remember vividly (most likely, it now occurs to me, because of the sense of vulnerability it engendered in me, as a relatively well-off young woman) the way in which young men and boys on the streets adopted Bachchan's hairstyle, clothing, stance, 'attitude' and gestures, punctuating their Bachchan-style fights with the obligatory '*dhishoom-dhishoom!*' sound-effects,[61] singing his songs and, of course, reciting his trademark 'dialogues' in an imitation of his deep, measured yet casual and colloquial, often cool and ironic delivery. Imitating the mannerisms and intonations of film stars, especially those of character actors, has always been part of Indian film culture: if it was mainly the street boys who imitated Bachchan, surely everyone imitated his foe in *Sholay* (1975), the villain Gabbar Singh, or slurred and hiccupped like the drunk comedian Johnny Walker, danced like the 'vamp' Helen or risked neck sprains tossing their heads like romantic heroes Shammi Kapoor and Dev Anand. But I know of no major hero before Bachchan to have entered such an intensive, and above all public, mimetic relay with the urban subaltern constituency represented by his screen persona.[62] While the young men on the street imitated him, his films drew on stories of pre-Emergency working-class agitations

---

[60] Alter, *The Wrestler's Body*, pp. 239–43.

[61] This became the commonly accepted onomatopoeia for the sound of fighting (punching, kicking and throwing things at people as well as shooting), as well as a metonym for the action film. I think it must be seen as specific to the Bachchan era, as it has been replaced through the 1990s by other phrases, particularly those circulated through advertising, such as *dhamaka* ('explosion': significantly, referring not to human force but to some kind of external agency).

[62] Something of this mimetic circuit can be illustrated by the Bachchan character's canny adoption of 786 as the number on his porter's badge in *Deewar*, 786 is a

and subaltern heroism: the 1974 railway strike in *Coolie* (1983), or the 1975 Chasnala mining disaster in *Kala Patthar* (1979). Crucial to this relay was a mutually imitable style, a mode of corporeal distinction that drew on the figure of the 'loafer' but gave it a cosmopolitan edge. Significant here was Bachchan's ability, emanating from his middle-class but also Hindi-speaking background, to fluently negotiate between various local Hindi dialects (Bombayya, Banarasi, 'Bihari') and impeccable English, often via humorous dialogues using Hindi-English word play, usually at the expense of English.

M. S. S. Pandian has described how MGR, too, drew on the idioms of subaltern heroism, particularly folk ballads, to shore up his popularity with subaltern-class audiences.[63] However, Pandian goes on to demonstrate how the appearance of social–political dissent in MGR films is counteracted by achieving narrative resolution within the 'moral economy of the system', thus preserving the *status quo* (69–73). Wicked Brahmins and landlords against whom MGR fought in his roles as a subaltern hero are simply given a chance to reform themselves as individuals, while in his elite roles MGR established his supreme virtue as a renouncer, giving away his wealth and status and marrying lower caste or lower class women. Even in his subaltern roles MGR is characterised by a certain *noblesse oblige*: even as he is oppressed, he is not desperate, not *hungry*. Thus despite giving up mythological roles in accordance with DMK ideology, his preservation of the moral order, combined with his fair, soft, plumpish body and a rhetoric of renunciation which presupposes an elite speaking position,[64] ultimately enabl 1 MGR to be deified

---

numerological formula for the first lines of the Quran: according to my observations around the city of Ahmedabad, after the film was released it acquired a new lease on life as a lucky charm among urban Muslims, as well as gaining more general recognition, reappearing on autorickshaws, keyrings, lockets, and of course as part of calendar images.

[63] M. S. S. Pandian, *The Image Trap: M. G. Ramachandran in Film and Politics* (New Delhi, Sage, 1992).

[64] Here Pandian quotes Dipesh Chakrabarty: 'The glory of the renouncer belonged to the—possessor'; to talk of sacrifice was to talk of possession, and hence of power'. *ibid.*, p. 72, quoting Dipesh Chakrabarty, 'Trade Unions in Hierarchical Culture: The Jute Workers of Calcutta, 1920–50', in Ranajit Guha (ed.), *Subaltern Studies III* (New Delhi, Oxford University Press), pp. 149–50.

by his fans, rather than becoming the subject of mimetic identification.[65]

Bachchan, on the other hand, cannot be described as a devotional icon in the manner of either MGR or NTR (who played predominantly mythological roles and, as suggested above, systematically shored up the image of himself as an avatar of Krishna). Even though Bachchan often does originally have a patrimony, he has not willingly given it up, it has been stolen from him. Far from being a morally unimpeachable renouncer who has earned the right to criticise society,[66] Bachchan's social critique stems from wanting more than he is legally allowed to have, even though it is justly his due. In this post-Emergency scenario where it is clear that the law and social justice are on opposite sides, with morality giving its blessing to the law, Bachchan does not emotionally preach moral reform (except to women), but uses his bodily force to fight for justice. But his bodily strength does not fit within a model of devotion, either: he is not a Hanuman-like 'Jai Kisan' or, indeed, the missing 'Jai Mazdoor' (worker). Even as he is abject before the mother-figures in his films, his relationship with them is impossible, fraught and alienated, for unlike the 'good' brother, he is no son of the paternal state: it is this deeply inscribed alienation that propels the narrative. In contrast, therefore, to the celibate wrestler whose strength derives from the moral purity, discipline and devotion of his body and the matter that flows in and out of it, or the canonical Ram images with their calm, timeless transcendental agency, Bachchan's is a goal-driven, instrumentalised body, its noisy (dhishoomdhishoom!) power derived from its own immanent hunger. Its aesthetic fascination is not so much that of the smooth, holistic 'body of one colour', or of the 'disengaged', effulgent radiation of affects from within via the eyes and face (Bachchan is not a star of the facial close-up), but precisely that of its engagement with other bodies and objects, and the varying intensities of these encounters: shooting mangoes off a tree or cavorting on a motorcycle (Sholay), leaping out of a giant Easter egg (Amar, Akbar, Anthony, 1977), looking for a lost shoe (Namak Halal, 1982), getting stuck in a yogic position while making an omelette, or fighting the capitalist villains with a hammer and sickle (Coolie).

---

[65] Ibid., pp. 113–17.
[66] Alter, 'Celibacy, Sexuality and the Transformation of Gender', p. 48.

The feeling generated across the Bachchan *oeuvre* is that once attention has finally been focussed on the body, there is a concerted attempt to explore just what that body can do. Despite his 'angry young man' rubric, it is not just the fight sequences that draw attention to Bachchan's body and its capacities, but also other 'para-narrative' elements such as his song and dance routines, where his long limbs are often used to comic effect, or his often very physical comic routines.[67] To this extent, even as Bachchan's body is not reducible to a signifier of lumpen assertion, it becomes a site for libidinal investments that are also not reducible to the kind of spectacular eroticisation or sexualisation that occurs with the overtly muscle-bound, singlet-wearing, body-building film heroes of the post liberalisation period. In *Silsila*, a 1981 romance, in a scene totally extraneous to the narrative, Amitabh is lying under a tree with Rekha draped over him, ostensibly running her fingers through his chest hair. He asks her *'Yeh tum kya kar rahi ho?'* ('What is this you're doing?'), to which she replies (something to the effect of) *'Aisa karna mujhe bahut achha lagta hai'* ('I really like doing this'). In this film, we not only see him (that is, his top half) nude in the shower with his bosom buddy Shashi Kapoor, but he almost never wears a shirt under his suit jacket, so his chest becomes an intense libidinal focus for both the camera and Rekha. This accords with a bodily schema in which the chest (in Hindi *chhati, seena*) is the privileged *locus* of a masculine essence and the qualities associated with it: devotion, friendship, bravery, pride and also loyalty, the quality that is centrally at issue in this film. The occurrences on Bachchan's

---

[67] Ravi Vasudevan has argued, following the work of Thomas Elsaesser on Hollywood family melodramas, that the Hindi film melodrama is characterised by strong 'para-narrative' elements, like the song and dance sequence, whose pleasures often run counter to the *status quo*-ist resolutions of the narrative—for instance in the song sequence the otherwise demure and submissive heroine gets to flaunt her body and declaim her desire in an open, if not always public, space. Ravi Vasudevan, 'The Melodramatic Mode and the Commercial Hindi Cinema: Notes on Film History, Narrative and Performance in the 1950s', *Screen*, Vol. 30, No. 3 (1989), pp. 29–50. Rajadhyaksha and Willemen seem to suggest that such para-narrative elements are crucial to Bachchan's 'brand image', particularly in the films directed by Manmohan Desai from *Amar Akbar Anthony* (1977) onwards, which are essentially conceived as a series of 'highlights' strung together with little regard for plot coherence. Rajadhyaksha and Willemen, *Encyclopedia of Indian Cinema*, p. 401.

chest across several films are particularly interesting when contrasted to the iconography of Hanuman, whose chest, as we have seen, is occupied by the image of Ram. In *Namak Halal*, for instance, Bachchan tears his shirt open to reveal the heroine Smita Patil's face: human, heterosexual love replaces abjection before the divine. Or again, in *Mard* (1985), set in the colonial period, he plays a *tangewalla* (horse-cart driver) whose princely father was captured by the British when Amitabh was a baby, and whose only patrimony therefore is the word his father had inscribed with a knife on his tiny son's chest: *mard*, man, not just a human but a sexual being (as we find out due to the sadomasochistic efforts of the whip-wielding heroine Amrita Singh).

Even as Bachchan's chest visually paves the way for later, more sexualised and muscularised figures of 'virile' masculinity, its resonance with the iconography of Hanuman maintains a tie with the visual idioms of the bazaar. Once again, despite the goal-driven 'individualism' and 'self-indulgence' that the ideologues of brahmacharya equate with the influence of the West, the figure of Bachchan does not invoke the kind of western realist subject associated with the paintings of Courbet, the psychological novel or drama, or even the imaginary identification said to characterise the 'classical' Hollywood narrative cinema. There is no sense in his films of an attempt to accurately portray subaltern life, no absorption of the viewer into the diegesis, no oblivion towards the facticity of the image, no preoccupation with the inner workings of the protagonist's mind. There are, instead, many instances of a non-realist, self-reflexive foregrounding in Bachchan films of the medium's own performativity: spectacular and 'para-narrative' elements, direct address to camera, comments about the cinema, or, famously, the freeze-frame in the film *Coolie* at the point where Amitabh was injured in an accident during the shoot.[68] Or again,

---

[68] For a listing of such instances, see Lalit Vachani, 'Bachchan-alias', pp. 218–21. However, I would have to disagree with Vachani's characterisation of these non-realist devices in Bachchan films as 'an appropriation of "Brechtian" techniques' (p. 219). I would contend that they are drawing on a much longer history of 'frontality' in Indian popular culture as elaborated by Geeta Kapur. See Geeta Kapur, 'Revelation and Doubt: Sant Tukaram and Devi', in Tejaswini Niranjana, P. Sudhir, Vivek Dhareshwar (eds), *Interrogating Modernity: Culture and Colonialism in India* (Calcutta, Seagull Books, 1993), p. 20. (Revised version of 'Mythic Material in Indian Cinema', *Journal of Arts and Ideas*, Nos. 14–15 [1987], pp. 79–108).

as part of the ongoing mimetic relay between Bachchan's virtual and actual personae, *Silsila*'s mirroring of Bachchan's real life romance with Rekha while being married to Jaya Bhaduri, with both women acting in corresponding roles in the film.

Plate 12.8 Self-portrait by Vikram, a boy studying at a municipal primary school in an underprivileged neighbourhood of Ahmedabad, produced at an art workshop I conducted there in 1984. Vikram had a picture of Amitabh Bachchan stuck on his shirt pocket; he had taken care to include it in his self-portrait, where it appears proportionally much larger than its actual size, possibly indicating its importance to him and his sense of self.

Indeed, I would argue that mimetic identification with the Bachchan figure is enabled not by 'realism' but, on the contrary, by the circuit this figure establishes between the facticity of the image—its material surface, its existence as an object in the present—and that which the image represents, refers to, resonates with and brings into being: that is, between its actual and virtual aspects, holding both in view at the same time and making it possible to see how the one might transmute into the other.[69]

It is in this respect that the mimetic engagement with Bachchan on the part of young urban men maintains its mass-cultural links with the devotional idiom of the bazaar, and with the genealogy of performative identification that I have traced above: wrestlers becoming the monkey-god through obeisance to the object that is his image, priests becoming desiring women clutching icons to themselves in ecstasy, the painter flexing his muscles in the mirror to become a calendar, the slum boy thrusting out his chin and chest, a picture of Amitabh stuck on his shirt pocket, next to his heart (see Plate 12.7).

Flexing the Canon

At this point I must attempt to curb my own libidinal engagement with the image by stating (what I hope by now is) the obvious. My argument has been that the Bachchan persona makes visible

---

[69] In his *User's Guide to Capitalism and Schizophrenia*, Brian Massumi provides a gloss on the 'plane of transcendence', which operates at a symbolic level to constitute the subject in terms of hierarchical, value-laden categories of identity. He offers a useful elaboration on how signs alone cannot institute the grid of transcendence in the social field, as this process requires a conversion to physicality, or from the virtual to the actual, via mediation in the realm of performance, an 'infolding into habit'. Brian Massumi, *User's Guide to Capitalism and Schizophrenia* (Cambridge, Mass., MIT Press, 1992), pp. 108–13. My use of the term 'virtual' is informed by the philosophy of Gilles Deleuze, for whom it seems to be a central and recurrent concept. The virtual is not opposed to the real, but to the actual; nor is it to be conflated with the possible. Trans. by Paul Patton, see Gilles Deleuze, *Difference and Repetition* (New York, Columbia University Press, 1994). I find this term particularly useful for the way in which it brooks no possibility of dismissing the image as 'false' or 'unreal'; on the contrary, it is seeing the falsity of the image in terms of a 'power that makes truth undecidable'. Trans. by Martin Joughin, see Gilles Deleuze, 'Doubts About the Imaginary', in *Negotiations, 1972–1990* (New York, Columbia University Press, 1995).

and available a bodily modality—and thereby a ground for subjectivity—where the male body becomes a libidinalised site for the production of value through its engagement with other bodies and objects, but my intention is not for a moment to celebrate Bachchan as an inherently progressive figure of working-class and working-caste resistance. Looking at the image as a circuit between its virtual and actual aspects is precisely a refusal to implicate it within the moral terms of good and evil (progressive/regressive) or true and false; instead, it helps to trace some of the different, often contradictory directions taken by the political currents passing through this circuit. I have argued that the Bachchan figure set in train a de-territorialising movement, and a mimetic circuit which returned to the bodies of young urban men a growing assertion of the value of bodily agency and labour, in response to the growing politicisation in the early 1970s of the working classes and castes. But the same figure was also subject to a re-territorialising movement, which recoded and re-harnessed this image and its energies.

For one, Bachchan has recently reappropriated his own screen persona to redress his financial woes by hosting Star TV's *Kaun Banega Crorepati* (the Indian version of *Who Wants to be a Millionaire*). But earlier, too, he had used it to help his real-life bosom buddy, the Shashi Kapoor-like (fair, smooth, pudgy, cow-eyed, full-lipped) Rajiv Gandhi. Bachchan's film *Coolie* blatantly paved the way for the 1984 elections in which he was elected as an MP for Rajiv Gandhi's Congress(I), the party that carried on Indira Gandhi's legacy. But, as I have suggested, part of the Congress legacy was a nexus between the bazaar and the state which allowed for the culture industry's perpetuation of certain symbolic aspects of caste and class hierarchy, including the inscription of state power as emanating from a transcendental source. The Bachchan icon, and its mimetic engagement with urban subaltern youths, posed a threat to this transcendental form of state authority by allowing for a non-abject performance of an instrumental, adult, human embodiment hitherto unavailable within the ethos of Indian mass culture.[70] Even as this modality of bodily agency

[70] This essay was written before I had read Madhava Prasad's illuminating discussion of Amitabh Bachchan's centrality to a populist 'aesthetics of mobilization', where Prasad formulates the film industry's deployment of Bachchan's

did not *replace* existing forms, its very availability in the field of images posed a threat to the canonical symbolic order, to which Hindutva's response was a *defensive reappropriation* of the muscular body in the form of the aggressive Ram.

If the ugra Ram is a way of harnessing the energies embodied in the figuration of a muscular, masculine, human force back to a sacred economy, this figure, in turn, engenders a new set of contradictions. The question to be asked of the tranquil Ram is how exactly he is able to vanquish his enemies without the use of bodily force; one might equally wonder why, if the muscular Ram really is all-powerful, he needs an army of human devotees to defend his birthplace in Ayodhya. But in both cases the issue could also be posed as one of how it becomes possible for a society to depend on the labour of the working castes without acknowledging this dependence, or the value of that labour. For what is at stake in the muscularity of Ram is not just how violence and aggression come to be made visible through the 'virile' male body, it is also how male labour comes to be devalued, abjected even as it is made visible—and women's labour doubly so. To overlook this context for mass-cultural images is to continue to function within the terms set up for us by the culture industry and the ethos of the bazaar. Anuradha Kapur, movingly searching for a redemptive note on which to end her essay, finds solace in the fact that the 'older', compassionate images of a benign and gentle Ram are

---

star image in terms of a response to the demands of a politically mobilised audience, and a push towards cultural segmentation arising from a fragmentation in the post-Independence political consensus. My argument similarly locates the Bachchan figure and its address to subaltern audiences within the context of this crisis (though Prasad dates it from the mid-1960s); to this extent the 'bazaar' in my account provides an institutional locus for the modes of pleasure and legitimation Prasad identifies with a maternalised 'community' counterposed to (and thereby perpetuating) a paternal Law. But while Prasad stresses the star vehicle's role in the film industry's ideological containment of 'centrifugal tendencies to segmentation' (p. 159), my emphasis on sites of actualisation seeks to keep open the gap between the viewer's interpellation by, and performative transformations of, institutionalised modes of corporeal engagement with images and the industry's interpellation of the subject-as-viewer (according to which, in contrast to my account, Prasad reads the populism of the Bachchan films as reinstating Bachchan as the transcendental object of a *'dars-hanic'* gaze, p. 77). See M. Madhava Prasad, *Ideology of the Hindi Film: An Historical Construction* (New Delhi, Oxford University Press, 1998), particularly Chapters 5 and 6.

still in circulation, unlikely to be driven out by the newer 'images produced by a moment of violence'. I have tried, through my own uncomfortably and unfashionably tight and synthetic narrative, to show how cultural critique doesn't necessarily have to choose between the new and the old versions, both of which have their regressive and progressive, de-territorialising and re-territorialising aspects. It also has the option to expropriate such iconic images and performatively re-imbue them with other, anti-canonical counter-meanings—even if it takes a bit of productive mimesis, or monkey-business, to do so.

13

Non-Gandhian Sexuality, Commodity Cultures and a 'Happy Married Life'

Masculine and Sexual Cultures in the Metropolis[1]

◆ Sanjay Srivastava

The Making of Sexual and Masculine Cultures

My effort in this essay is to present a preliminary outline towards an anthropological perspective on postcolonial modernity, with particular emphasis on the cultures of masculinity and sexuality. The conjoining of masculinity and sexuality and the focus on heterosexual contexts should be seen as analytical strategies rather than adherence to naturalised social categories. In the following discussion, then, I will utilise 'sexuality' as short hand for all those processes of heterosexual masculinity that gather

[1] A considerable amount of the groundwork for this research project was carried out by Veenapani Seksaria, the Mumbai based research assistant for this project. I think Veena for her assistance and would like to think that we have both learned from our joint visits to various ethnographic sites in Mumbai. Some part of the research was also carried out during an affiliation with the Institute of Economic Growth, Delhi. I thank the Institute for its facilities. Its director, the late Professor Praveen Visaria, was a generous host. My thanks also to Patricia Uberoi for securing the affiliation.

around this term. And, finally, my focus—ethnographic and 'textual'—on non-middle class contexts is also an attempt to insert a somewhat different postcolonised context into the rapidly consolidating canon of 'postcolonial studies' with its substantial focus on English-language sources, upon 'colonial discourse', and upon the cultural strategies of the transnational diaspora.

Over the past three decades or so, there has been considerable scholarly work done in the context of sexualities and culture. The focus of interest has ranged over the areas of power and knowledge, nationalism, the regulation of sexualities, queer theory, 'traditional' discourses of sexuality, psychoanalysis and sexuality, colonialism and sexuality and commodity cultures and sexuality. In the Indian context, perhaps the most dominant themes in the analysis of Indian sexuality have centred on semen-loss anxiety, the 'mother-goddess syndrome' and the Gandhian gloss on sexuality.[2] *Male* sexuality and a shared 'Hinduness' are the underlying assumptions of much of this research. In this discussion, I would like to move away both from the 'semen-loss' sexuality perspective, as well as the some what simplified postcolonial narrative of modernity that has been explored in some accounts.[3] My

[2] According to Mary John and Janaki Nair, 'questions of male sexuality have rarely been a focus of scholarly analysis, except for celebrated instances of celibacy'. 'A Question of Silence. An Introduction', in M. E. John and J. Nair (eds), *A Question of Silence: The Sexual Economies of Modern India* (Delhi, Kali for Women, 1998), p. 15. Their observations regarding celibacy are well made though it is more difficult to agree with the former point. See, for example, J. Alter, *The Wrestler's Body* (Chicago, University of Chicago Press, 1992); M. G. Carstairs, *The Twice Born* (London, Hogarth Press, 1958); S. Kakar, *Intimate Relations: Exploring Indian Sexuality* (Chicago, University of Chicago Press, 1990); B. Parekh, *Colonialism, Tradition and Reform. An Analysis of Gandhi's Political Discourse* (New Delhi, Sage, 1989).

[3] While one can not accuse Arjun Appadurai of being oblivious to the layered textuality of the postcolonised condition, it is possible that the following observation—unqualified as it is—might lend itself to a general conflation of disparate experiences of modernity and postcoloniality into a seamless whole. Appadurai says that as a boy he:

> saw and smelled modernity reading *Life* and American college catalogs at the United States Information Service Library, seeing B-grade films (and some A-grade ones) from Hollywood at the Eros theatre [...] I begged my brother at Stanford (in the early 1960s) to bring me back blue jeans and smelled America in his Right Guard.... I gradually lost the England that I had earlier imbibed in my Victorian schoolbooks, in rumors of Rhodes

intent is to explore an emerging culture of sexuality in India as the complex site for the overlapping narratives of modern subjectivity that encompasses the metropolitan–provincial divide, the culture of urban spaces, the anxieties of masculine immigrant life in the metropolis, the relationship between 'official' and 'unofficial' knowledge systems, the rise of commodity cultures, and the creation of a 'subterranean' civil society. I do not in particular wish to state 'this is Indian sexuality and masculinity', rather, my aim is to follow the contours of the seams opened up—and those contexts that become apparent—when sexuality and masculinity are evoked as a topic of thought and expression.

In addition to its influence in orienting recent scholarship on the production of modern subjectivity through medical, penal and other discourses, the work of Michel Foucault has been particularly important in its impact upon research on sexuality.[4] It has served, most importantly, to move the focus away from empiricist and psychologised frameworks that have played a key role in consolidating discourses of the norm. However, as I have recently argued elsewhere,[5] it is not clear that Foucault's insights, linked as they are exclusively to European history and society, can be substantially, and unproblematically, applied to the Indian postcolonised contexts. Further, I am in agreement with Bryan Turner's comments that:

> although Foucault has provided a model of the self in modern culture through his historical analyses, the [Foucaultian] perspective neglects the significance of consumerism, fashion and life-style

scholars from my college, and in Billy Bunter and Biggles books devoured indiscriminately.

A. Appadurai, *Modernity at Large: Cultural Dimensions of Globalization* (Minneapolis, University of Minnesota Press, 1999), p. 2. I do not mean to discount individual experiences, or the experiences of *particular* groups, rather, my objective is to point to this very aspect of such sensory (and other) experiences of non-Western modernity. This is important to counter the tendency towards a universalised category of the 'postcolonial' [for further discussion, see Chapter 7 of my *Constructing Post-Colonial India: National Character and the Doon School* (London, Routledge, 1998)].

[4] M. Foucault, *The History of Sexuality, Volume I. An Introduction* (London, Penguin Books, 1990).

[5] *Op. cit.* (1998). See also A. L. Stoler, *Race and the Education of Desire: Foucault's History of Sexuality and the Colonial Order of Things* (Durham, Duke University Press, 1995).

on contemporary notions of selfhood … [and,] that the new self is far more mobile, uncertain and fragmentary than the bureaucratic image of the disciplined self in the work of Weber and Foucault because the modern self corresponds to and is produced by a new uncertainty, differentiation and the fragmentation of the risk society [Beck, 1992].[6]

How do we then think anthropologically about these additional contexts of uncertainty, consumer culture, the production of new spaces and the anxieties of contemporary non-western modernity? This paper, part of a larger ongoing project, is concerned with the situation of notions of Indian masculinities and sexualities within the contexts of uncertainty and differentiation that Turner and others[7] describe.

I would like to emphasise that my project is also an exploration in methodology: that is, it attempts to bridge the gap between exclusively historical and textual analyses of the socio-cultural context of Indian sexuality and masculinity, and ethnographic work that engages with contemporary issues of modernity and subjectivity. This essay is really an attempt to think aloud about a methodological framework which can borrow from developments in, say, history and cultural studies whilst at the same time trying to work out how to also 'do' anthropology; one that can pay attention, in other words, to the cultural and social specificities of non-Western spaces which have tended to merely become the site of interdisciplinary struggles in some versions of cultural studies and globalisation theory.

A certain kind of anthropological project is, I think, of increasing importance in an era when the conditions of possibility of knowledge are increasingly narrowly defined: now is perhaps a good time to think of what it would mean, for instance, to argue for an anthropological project within cultural and 'postcolonial' studies; not least to rescue the latter from a kind of disciplinary parochialism and the frequently simpleminded desire to be 'theoretical'. My attempt is to contribute to an anthropological theory of modernity, as distinct from a sociological one, as attached, for

---

[6] B. Turner, *The Body and Society: Explorations in Social Theory* (London, Sage, 1996), p. 21.
[7] U. Beck, *Risk Society: Towards a New Modernity* (London, Sage, 1992).

example, to names such as Giddens and Habermas,[8] that is also distinguishable from the frameworks of 'postcolonial theory'. An anthropological theory of modernity—in as much as some kind of fieldwork is a part of it—should also attempt to find a way between hermeneutic and phenomenological emphases on the one hand and the place of social structure in the structure of our feelings; we also need to address the divide between 'structure' in Althusserian and Levi-Straussian positions, and the so called culturalist position that places its analytical faith upon consciousness and experience.

Scholarly research on Indian masculinities and sexualities has moved along several trajectories. Analyses of classical texts such as the *Kamasutra* and Kalyanamalla's *Ananga Ranga*[9] have, of course, a very long history in Indological literature and beyond. Such works—insightful and suggestive though they may be—tell us little, however, about contemporary gender relations. An understanding of the latter must also turn upon ethnographic work rather than remain an exclusively hermeneutic project, for, Indian society (no more than any other) does not simply order its existence according to scriptural codes and canonical texts. Hence, a theoretically sensitive ethnographic analysis can provide a more complex and dynamic picture of *everyday practices* that result from the interface between 'tradition' and the realities of late twentieth century life.

Psycho-social studies of Indian masculinity—such as those by M. G. Carstairs[10]—have usually been organised around the theme of the 'obsessive' male fear of the physical consequences of the 'waste' of semen. In addition, these studies have also focused on the ambivalence towards sexual desire in as much as it becomes linked to a loss of spiritual potency. The exploration of these fears and anxieties are usually also positioned in the context of the role of the (Hindu) mother, and her relationship to the male child. The

---

[8] See, for example, A. Giddens, *The Consequences of Modernity* (Stanford, California, Stanford University Press, 1990); and J. Habermas, *The Philosophical Discourse of Modernity* (Cambridge, Polity Press, 1987).

[9] Trans. by Sir Richard Burton and F. F. Arbuthnot, introduction by Dom Moraes, John Muirhead–Gold (ed.), Vatsayayana, *The Kamasutra of Vatsayaana* (London, Kimber, 1963); Trans. by Sir Richard Burton and F.F. Arbuthnot, Kalyanamalla, *The Ananga Ranga of Kalyana Malla* (London, Kimber, 1963).

[10] M. G. Carstairs, *op. cit..*

argument then unfolds through an emphasis on the importance of religious maternal imagery in the lives of Indian men.

Another type of literature—and the influence of psychologists is also noticeable here—has turned its attention towards the colonial sphere and the indigenous responses to the 'feminisation' of the native. This line of investigation has been carried forward in the recent work of historians and sociologists examining aspects of colonial and postcolonised politics and culture. For example, in Mrinalini Sinha's recent book on colonial masculinity and the imperial stereotype of the 'manly Englishman' in relation to the 'effeminate Bengali', in John Rosselli's work on physical culture movements in Bengal at the turn of the century, in M. S. S. Pandian's recent essay on the regulation of hunting in the Nilgiris, in Joseph Alter's writings on the Indian wrestling tradition, and in my own work on middle class contexts of 'epistemological masculinity'.[11]

Finally, and this largely unexamined sphere points to the overlap between Indian and Western modernity, the opening decades of the twentieth century in India witnessed a body of sex-literature inspired by the work of European writers and activists such as Havelock Ellis and Margaret Sanger (the 'pioneer birth controller'[12]). Though not strictly 'analytical' or 'scholarly', such writings attracted an educated readership, and found support from a wide cross section of the English-speaking, modernising intelligentsia in India, as well as influential men and women in other parts of the world. The corpus—pioneered most energetically by the medical doctor turned sexologist A. P. Pillay—sought to promote the ideas of 'rational' sexual and gender identities towards a 'modern' social life.

[11] A. Nandy, *The Intimate Enemy: Loss and Recovery of the Self Under Colonialism* (New Delhi, Oxford University Press, 1983); M. Sinha, *The 'Manly Englishman' and the 'Effeminate Bengali' in the Late Nineteenth Century* (Manchester, Manchester University Press, 1995); J. Rosselli, 'The Self-image of Effeteness: Physical Education and Rationalism in Nineteenth Century Bengal', *Past and Present*, Vol. 86 (1980); M.S.S. Pandian 'Gendered Negotiations: Hunting and Colonialism in Late Nineteenth Century Nilgiris', in P. Uberoi (ed.), *Social Reform, Sexuality and the State* (New Delhi, Sage, 1996); J. Alter, *op. cit.*; and, S. Srivastava, 'The Garden of Rational Delights: The Nation as Experiment, Science as Masculinity', *Social Analysis*, Vol. 39 (1996).
[12] C. Haste *Rules of Desire, Sex in Britain. World War I to the Present* (London, Pimlico, 1992), p. 24.

Pillay's *The Art of Love and Sane Sex Living*, which carried glowing endorsements from, among others, the anthropologist Verrier
Elwin, sought to inform the public that 'the irksome religious
dogmatism and anti-sexual taboos and tyranny still persisting
are incompatible with biological needs and scientific findings.'[13]
The issue of the ideal (middle class) masculine identity is explored
here through a combination of scientific and psycho-social discourses, with a particular regard to the sexual 'satisfaction' of
women as constitutive of such identity. Going by the fact that this
publication achieved fifteen editions—and that Pillay was one of
the guiding lights behind the Family Planning Association of
India—we may assume that such works were extremely popular
among a certain class fraction in early twentieth century India. The
precise nature of its popularity—located at the various intersections of 'modernity' and 'tradition', science, 'ancient' wisdom, and
so forth—remains to be analysed at greater length.

Pillay's monograph was published in Bombay, and Maharashtra
was a particularly fertile site for negotiations of modernity that
were elaborated through explorations of sexual and masculine
cultures. So, for example, sex and sexuality were also part of
another, more curious register, a context that brought together
sexuality, *swarajya* ('self-rule') and eugenics. This was the field
explored by N. S. Phadke, Professor of Mental and Moral Philosophy at Rajaram College in Kolhapur. The foreword to his book *Sex
Problem in India. Being a Plea for a Eugenic Movement in India and
a Study of all Theoretical and Practical Questions Pertaining to Eugenics* (published 1927)[14] was written by Margaret Sanger, a fact that
once again illustrates quite nicely the localisation of a Western
movement in an altogether different context within the colonial
sphere. Phadke pointed out that his discussion was concerned
with the issue of how to maintain the vigour of a 'declining race',
for 'who could deny that physical strength and military power
will be for us an indispensable instrument to keep *Swarajya* after
it is won?.' The subtext here, we can speculate, is both a concern

---

[13] A. P. Pillay, *The Art of Love and Sane Sex Living: Based on Ancient Precepts and
Modern Teachings* (Bombay, D. B. Taraporevala Sons, 1948).
[14] N. S. Phadke, *Sex Problem in India. Being a Plea for a Eugenic Movement in India
and a Study of all Theoretical and Practical Questions Pertaining to Eugenics* (Bombay,
D. B. Taraporevala Sons, 1927).

for the nature of India masculinity after swarajya, but also the politics of *upper caste masculinity* at a time of a number of social reform movements in South India that expressed their concerns through the matrices of caste oppression and 'self-respect'. A 'plea for a Eugenic movement' in this context should alert us, then, to a number of overlapping contexts and anxieties of early twentieth century Indian life.

Curiously enough, despite the obvious theoretical sophistication of the scholarly works on the topic, research into sexuality and masculinity appears to have suffered a somewhat 'textual' fate, with a strong allegiance to a notion of 'deep structures' suggesting that there is a body of unchanging Indian 'tradition' to which an undifferentiated Indian mass consensually subscribes. We are now increasingly familiar with critiques of this position both from the historical and anthropological perspectives, and this discussion owes considerable debt to the fragmentation of disciplinary and analytical boundaries that has been the consequence of such critiques.

I am not suggesting, however, that the kinds of work represented in the 'semen-loss anxiety' school,[15] and Indian variations on the Oedipal theme analysis are wrong—for they certainly represent important themes in Indian culture—[16] only that they may represent very specific cultural formations, and that 'out there' there are a wide variety of discourses that gather around sexuality and masculinity that may pay little heed to the supposedly dominant themes of Indian (Hindu?) sexuality and masculinity. Moreover, the cultural modernity of contemporary capitalism gives rise to a number of ways of conceptualising the masculine self; it is in this context that analyses such as that by Steve Derné on the connections between 'movies, masculinity, and modernity'

---

[15] But see the critique of 'semen-anxiety' by Filippo and Caroline Osella in their 'Contextualising Sexuality: Young men in Kerala, South India', in L. Manderson and Pranee Liamputtong (eds), *Coming of Age in South Asia and South-East Asia. Youth, Courtship and Sexuality* (London, Curzon Press, 2002).

[16] Certainly, a particular kind of research into sexual behaviour informs us that 'semen-loss' still carries important cultural connotations in the construction of male identities in India. See, for example, Ravi Verma 'Beliefs Concerning Sexual Health Problems and Treatment Among Men in an Indian Slum Community', paper presented at the third Conference of the International Association for the Study of Sexuality, Culture and Society, 1–3 October 2001, Melbourne.

are of considerable interest.[17] The work of R. W. Connell is, of course, exemplary in its attention to theoretical and ethnographic frameworks appropriate for the study of masculinity and the cultures of capitalism.[18]

Beginning in 1999, I have been carrying out 'fieldwork' in Delhi and Mumbai on a research project tentatively called 'Masculinity, Sexuality and Modernity in India' and this paper is a preliminary attempt at outlining what I believe to be some important contexts for the study of sexualities and masculinities in the Indian context. However, at this stage all that I am really able to do is to provide a *sketch* of what appear to be fruitful areas of inquiry. Further, though my main objective through this research is the outlining of the formation of modern masculine subjectivity, it is also my aim to develop alternatives to Foucaultian concerns of self-discipline and surveillance as constituents in the production of modern subjectivity. The body and human actions are, of course, a site for administrative control and regimes of self-discipline; however, these intersect with and are, at different times, both subverted and reinforced by the play of the different processes and fantasies of modernity such as commodity cultures, the cultural divide—in India—between the metropolis and the province, and the different forms of masculinity politics (as well as gender politics in general).

Scholars have begun to remark upon the fact that there is no dearth of 'talk' about sexuality in India. Speaking of her earliest fieldwork experience, the anthropologist Ann Grodzins Gold says that she 'had been led to expect extreme reticence about sexual matters and about women's bodily processes', but that 'to the contrary, … both marital sexuality and scandalous love affairs were subjects of frequent discussion.'[19] This lack of reticence has been, in different ways, a more general feature of Indian life. The important thing is to engage with the diversity of themes and

---

[17] Steve Derné, *Movies, Masculinity, and Modernity: An Ethnography of Men's Filmgoing in India* (Westport, Greenwood Press, 2000). It is fair to say that ethnographic studies of masculinity for the Indian context are still a nascent genre and display a degree of unevenness that requires attention; one of the issues that needs to be addressed is the shifting nature of (masculine) gender identity that is played out according to social, political and economic contexts.

[18] See, for example, his *Masculinities* (Sydney, Allen and Unwin, 1995).

[19] G. G. Raheja and A. G. Gold, *Listen to the Heron's Words: Reimagining Gender and Kinship in North India* (Berkeley, University of California Press, 1994), p. 28.

preoccupations that proliferate under the rubric of 'the sexual'. My research has dealt with three different sites. First, I looked at specific instances of discourses on sexuality and 'indecency' in the nineteenth century, primarily in the context of discussion and debates on prostitution, *hijras* ('eunuchs') and instances of 'public immorality'. The latter includes cases such as the one reported in 1875 concerning the pregnancy of a woman confined to the Nagpur Lunatic Asylum,[20] and an account of 1882 ('An Extraordinary Case of Indecency') concerning an 'old woman of sixty' and 'a young man of 30' discovered having sex in public, with the former claiming to be following the orders of her spiritual guru.[21] In this part of my research, I have been primarily concerned with exploring the continuities and ruptures with contemporary discourses of morality and indecency in India.

Second, I carried out 'fieldwork' in the sex-clinics of Delhi and Mumbai. Readers who use public (rail or bus) transport in India, will be familiar with their advertisements scrawled in large letters, in both Hindi and English, at entrance points to urban areas and on various walls within cities, at bus depots and along railway tracks. 'Sex and Vitality Clinics', as they are sometimes known, are, *in their present form*, mainly an urban phenomenon with a large clientele of *men* (and sometimes, women) from the lower socio-economic categories. The clinics offer a variety of services to their clients: among them, 'cures' for sexually transmitted diseases, impotence and premature ejaculation, ways of enhancing sexual 'performance', and the promise of male progeny. Those who run these clinics, deploy medical and scientific terminology in conjunction with 'traditional' notions of masculinity, sexuality and sexual well-being to attract their clientele. Perhaps, the best known of all the sex-clinic's in North India is the Khandani Shafakhana, and the starch-turbanned image of it's founder Hakim Hari Kishan Lal that beams down majestically from a plethora of billboards in Delhi and is a familiar part of the visual landscape. The Hakim is no longer alive and the clinic is now operated by his sons,

---

[20] Home Department Proceedings, Nos. 16–21, November 1875. Dr. Beatson's Management of the Nagpur Lunatic Asylum.

[21] Legislative Department Proceedings, February 1895. No. 136; Extract from the Proceedings of the Government of Madras, Judicial Department, No. 258 (Misc.), dated 4 March 1882. *An Extraordinary Case of Indecency.*

though quite clearly the image of the patriarch—with its embodiment of a certain kind of masculinity—is still seen as crucial to defining the clinic's public presence. I will also return to the Hakim and his masculinity later in this paper.

The larger context of the public presence of the sex-clinics is the arena of a host of non-western healing systems, such as Ayurveda and the Unani system. Hence, in addition to the relatively low cost of 'treatment' offered by the clinics, their historical legitimacy also derives from popular memory as well as the surviving practices of traditional healing systems. I will have more to say on this aspect later in this paper. I have noted above that their clientele is mainly the urban poor, however, this is not always strictly true, and there are increasingly those that also serve a better-off clientele.[22] Sex-clinics are usually located in/near three kinds of places: near major transport nodes such as railway stations and interstate bus depots; in newly established outlying 'colonies' of the metropolis which may contain a mixture of slum dwellings, light industrial units (such as dyeing businesses) and new and old *pucca* housing; and in older and established commercial localities, such as Chandni Chowk in central Delhi and Dadar in Mumbai, that are also home to an industrial and semi-industrial labour force from the non-urban areas. There is quite clearly work to be done on the geography of sexuality, in it's literal spatialised sense.

It is possible to view the sex-clinics as alternative sites of communication, knowledge and treatment, one's that belong to the non-formal sector of the political and cultural economy of the postcolonised state. These sites of informal communication both interrogate and conform to the dominant modes of transaction such as the formal medical system, and the authorised modes of communication (specialist journals, governmental communication, and so forth). The clinics are, then, one of the several sites of the articulation of masculinity, gender relations, class, the national and commodity cultures of modernity, the tension of urban life for the poor and discourses on communicable diseases.

---

[22] For the moment, I am leaving aside medically qualified sexologists, the best known of whom is Mumbai based Dr Prakash Kothari. Their clientele is usually well-educated and engaged in middle and upper middle class professions. In the present discussion, I am concerned with the modernity strategies of those not part of this group. The larger research agenda includes, however, the therapeutic world of the 'formal' sexologist and will be addressed in other articles.

They are, therefore, vital sources of information on these issues. However, they have not thus far been a focus of analysis in social science research and this project hopes to open up a new source of information for this area of research.[23]

The third aspect of my research has dealt with the vast body of Hindi language 'footpath' pornography available in most areas of Delhi. My method of analysis of the contexts of masculinity and sexuality borrows, as far as I am explicitly able to outline the distinct influences upon this research, from two quite different sources. First, I proceed from a kind of a method outlined by Rahul Sankritayayan (1893–1963). The method I refer to is 'ghummakkadi' as explored in his *Ghummakkad Shashtra*.[24] Second, while I have stated my intention to move away from specifically Foucaultian concerns with self-discipline and the play of dominations, I am nevertheless indebted to his genealogical analyses in as much as these open the way for an exploration of seemingly unrelated contexts, in order to explore the play of forces rather than the sovereign actions of individuals.

One way of proceeding with this discussion is to think of the notion of the 'subterranean civil-society', or a non-Habermasian civil society,[25] as fundamental to the processes of postcolonised modernity: an arena of secret but public modernity, and silent though thick circulation of knowledges. This is a milieu of debate and discussion aligned to sites such as the sex-clinics, non-English language pornography written by such 'legendary' authors as Mast Ram and Kamini Devi, with titles such as *Sexy, Sexy, Sexy, Mujhe Log Bole* ('Sexy, Sexy, Sexy,' people call me), *Sulagati Chahat, Machalte Arman* (Burning Desire, Uncontrollable Wishes), *Kaam Samasyane* (Sex Problems) and *How To Increase Sex Power*.

It is a forum that is constituted through the spaces of the 'Unauthorised Regularised' housing localities of Delhi, and the

---

[23] It should also be said that given their reach among 'at-risk' populations, their neglect in the formulation of anti-AIDS strategies is also incomprehensible.

[24] R. Sankrityayan, *Ghummakkad Shashtra* (Delhi, Kitab Mahal, 1948/1994). Briefly, my reading of, Sankrityayan's method of cultural analysis is one where the analyst seeks to uncover contiguities and resonances among a wide range of phenomena such that 'modernity' is seen to be a haphazard and irregular process rather than an overarching and formal category that has a clear address; it is difficult to say, in other words, where one might find it.

[25] Habermas, *op. cit.*.

unauthorised regularised discussions that gather around the sex-clinics may tell us something about contemporary urban subjectivities. In the following discussion I will move between the sex-clinics and footpath pornography. Sex-clinics and Hindi pornography are part of the same complex in the sense of a shared clientele. Some clinics also publish 'advice' manuals and other literature that share the commercial footpath space with pornographic literature. The important thing is that they are both part of a wide-ranging site for the discussion of many aspects of modern subjectivity in India. A salient aspect of this discussion forum, however, is that most of it's participants have little or no voice in the metropolitan postcolonial culture of the nation-state: it is not the 'reading-formation' of the civil-society constituted through *India Today* or *The Times of India*, nor does it take part in the formation of the idea of 'postcoloniality' that has gathered around its 'real' voices such as Salman Rushdie and Vikram Seth. It does find some voice, however, in the writings of authors such as Manjul Bhagat, Nagarajun, and Faniswarnath Renu.[26]

An important context for the study of contemporary masculine sexuality—hetero homo and others—is, following from the above, the consolidation of 'provincial' culture within the metropolis through the process of rural–urban migration, the most visible manifestations of which are the *Jhuggi–Jhopri* colonies and the Unauthorised Regularised Colonies of Indian cities. We need to pay greater attention to the relationship between the various cultures of capitalism (and not just those of, say, different 'ethnic' groups) *within* national societies. I think this is an important characteristic of many postcolonised societies that can be usefully analysed as consisting of metropolitan and provincial cultures that have a particular relationship with respect to each other as well as to the wider changes we now characterise as 'globalisation'. This research is a move, then, towards an ethnography of the human topography of the city carved out by informal bureaucracies, haphazard economics, erratic knowledge regimes and their savants, dislocated gender positions and hybrid commodity cultures; a territory—and sense of being—somewhere out of sight of

---

[26] See, for example, M. Bhagat, *Anaro* (Delhi, Rajkamal Paperbacks, 1977/1996); Nagararjun, *Ugratara* (Delhi, Rajkamal, 1987); F. Renu, *Maila Anchal* (Delhi, Rajkamal, 1954/1984).

Ritzer's McDonaldised socius, and yet also seemingly contiguous with it.[27]

It is within this context that new questions about modern subjectivity are being asked through a framework which is a complex configuration of commodity desire, masculine anxiety, and a new urban spatial sensibility that is also formed by but not reducible to global flows. Now, it is true that what some scholars have identified as other discourses on sexuality and masculinities—such as the Gandhian and the Hindu fundamentalist one's, for example—also make an appearance on this stage, but their presence does not appear to be either overarching or determining. They do not, in other words, form master-narratives of discourse and opinion.

Before proceeding to a more detailed outline of the contexts of sexuality, let me make an additional methodological point. My interest in the present study also lies in the social life of emotions and sentiments, most obviously in the cultural construction of love and intimacy. However, the majority of the studies I have come across that deal with the social construction of emotions in India seem to proceed from the premise that there exists an unbroken and undisturbed world of emotions that have been passed down to Indians through an ancestral cultural bequest, such that 'Hindu emotions' are the heritage of all those living in the geo-political place called India. In such studies, commodity cultures, globalisation and the media, for example, appear to have little role as supplements.[28]

No doubt cultural difference—and the different history of cultures—provides us with radically different conceptualisations of emotions, but these differences cannot be understood as the simple heritage of something called 'Hindu culture'; rather, they

[27] G. Ritzer, *The McDonaldization of Society. An Investigation into the Changing Character of Contemporary Social Life* (London, Sage, 1993). Even though at times Ritzer's case for 'rationalisation' seems somewhat overstated, his basic premise that' McDonald's has utilized bureaucratic principles, and others have combined with them to help create the process of McDonaldization' (p. 24) would seem to offer ample opportunities for comparison with the situation in India. I hope to deal more fully with this aspect of the discussion in other articles.

[28] See, for example, S. Kakar *op. cit.*; O. M. Lynch (ed.), *Divine Passions. The Social Construction of Emotion in India* (Berkeley, University of California Press, 1990); M. Trawick, *Notes on Love in a Tamil Family* (Berkeley, University of California Press, 1990).

must be conceptualised as the constant (re)conceptualisation of 'Hindu culture' itself by Hindus (and others) in the broader context of the forces of modernity. So, 'Indian notions of family and what mother's love in it means'[29] during contemporary modernity need referents further afield than references to the theory of *rasas*. Rural–urban migration, popular literature, almost fifty years of advertisements for Farex baby food and Johnson's baby powder in magazines such as *Dharmyug* (now ceased publication), as well as Indian films, advice columns, the media, and Family Planning Programmes are also important parts of the picture. What counts, then, as emotion in the Indian context is itself, it need hardly be said, historical and contingent rather than unchanging and attached in a monolithic manner to 'Hindu life'. It is therefore, subject to the major processes of different eras, in as much as we might be able to demarcate these in terms of major influences. These processes must, therefore, be incorporated into analysis. My discussion here is an attempt to move towards such a position.

Footpath Modernity: Sexualities and Commodities

I will first consider the interaction between a particular kind of commodity culture, urban anxieties and 'traditional' remedies, each serving as contiguous, and overlapping contexts. This is the interactional space of ex-prime minister Rajiv Gandhi's economic liberalisation, Bollywood versions of masculinity of the small-town man come to make a living in the industrial metropolis (typified by actor Amitabh Bachchan's provincial masculinity-come-to-the-city), and the entrepreneurial mainstreaming of 'traditional' remedies in the service of a 'traditional modernity'. Now, quite clearly, the middle (and upper middle) class context for herbal remedies such as those marketed by the entrepreneur Shahnaz Hussain is quite different from the marketplaces—and the lifeways—that concern me here. These are, however, contiguous territories in as much as they are both part of the cultural mechanics of the transformation of 'traditional' use-values into

---

[29] O. M. Lynch, 'Introduction: Emotion in Theoretical Contexts', in Lynch, *op. cit.*, p. 24.

the goods and processes through which the 'modern' self might come to be.[30] Though I have no formal studies to draw upon, Hindi language footpath pornography appears to have a huge market all over North India. The booklets generally have poor production values (including missing pages and inexplicable endings to climactic narratives), and it is common practice to haggle over the 'official' price printed on the cover, making them quite cheap to acquire; being an intrinsic part of the accoutrements of urban footpaths, customers can, literally, obtain these on the run, or opt for leisurely perusal while killing time waiting, say, for the next bus. Cover photographs often portray either European women, or some version of westernised images of Indian women, in various poses of desire/seduction or 'availability', an aspect that requires separate discussion. Both the authors and readers of these booklets would appear to be primarily male—an observation based on participatory fieldwork in the traditional sense of the term—though it is difficult to be certain about this. However, given their *public life* as commodities—subject to a myriad casual and passing inspections—it can safely be said that at least most of the purchasers are males; they may, however, be part of secondary routes of circulation whose participants include both men and women.[31] They are usually published by small scale, city-based presses such as the Bansal Press in Seelampur, New Delhi, and sometimes also by the publishers of provincial newspapers.

The booklets combine a wide range of functions: as a bridge between 'tradition' and 'modernity', as a window to the world of contemporary commodity culture, as the complex sites of the

---

[30] I should point out that my use of the idea of the self does not mean to suggest a 'bed-rock' of 'concrete' subjectivity to which analysis has access. Rather, the 'self' finds articulation in public discourse, and we need to attend to its multiple contours, contexts, manifestations and dissolutions. So, it is not 'sovereignty' I wish to posit, but rather, the *idea* of sovereignty. I am grateful to Kajri Jain for comments on this aspect.

[31] I base this conclusion on the nature of some of the content of the booklets. There is a considerable amount of material which consists of advice to women on 'women's health' issues, on 'satisfactory' sexual relationships with men, and articles and letters, supposedly by women, on 'proper' sexual conduct , and on premarital and extramarital relationships. Whether such writings are 'actually' authored by women may not be as interesting a question as the one seeking to identify the audience for such work, and its appeal for this readership.

fantasy culture of modernity and as propaganda vehicles for a 'modern' nuclear family. A wide variety of 'goods' are advertised in these publications (most often toward, the end); the list below provides some indication of the nature of the advertisements:

(a) The founder editor of the daily *Taj Times* and *Basant Prakashan* says in an advertisement that on the 3rd of December 1996 some men robbed him of his Maruti car after threatening to kill him and his wife, at a particular location in Agra. And, that he is willing to provide a reward of Rs 25,000 for information leading to their apprehension.

(b) A firm from Gaya (in Bihar) advertises for a ring which is 'capable of giving its wearer complete control over any man or woman; can ensure success in business, legal matters, in exams, a good job, marriage according to personal wish, protection against bad spirits, successes in lotteries and gambling, freedom from debt, the ability to see buried treasure in dreams, bad *grah* (luck) will improve, power of memory will improve, recover lost goods, health will improve. Tantrik ring Rs 51; A tantrik ring made according to your horoscope Rs 151; A special strong silver ring for those who have faced disappointment in all aspects of life', Rs 251'. Further, the advertisement points out, 'All letters are treated as confidential, so please do not hide anything from us, and provide all details. Our address: Lalita Ashram, (BA/9) PO Lal Bigha, Gaya.'

(c) An advertisement for Ayurvedic treatment: 'For *safed daag*, and sexual diseases, and piles; Vaidhya Shri Jwala Prashad (regi.), PO Katri Sarai, Gaya. Note: if you want to visit, please write and receive instructions on getting here.'

(d) 'Lion Zorro automatic folding revolver, no licence required; Gupta Trading Co., 4995 Rehman Street, Chandni Chowk. For security, theatre, picnics etc.; emits a loud bang along with smoke and sparks.'

(e) 'Asli bara harmonium', a book written by an expert, contains many new types of songs, *raginis, ghazal, thumri, dadra, quawalli,* film songs etc. taught through a numbering system so that even those without any knowledge can learn. Rs 50 excluding cost of postage.'

(f) 'New sabun-tel shiksha course: make different types of oils and soap and sell for profit. Market purchased oil often smells of kerosene and is harmful to use, get rid of all that.'

(g) 'Colourful photo album: Despite possessing physical beauty, millions around the world are unhappy, many pictures of smiling women; contains many thing worth knowing both before and after marriage.'

(h) '325 secrets to great wealth. Learn to establish industries which require little capital but generate great profit, such as detergent powder, paint varnish, dhoop batti, textiles, pharmacy, electrical goods, autoparts, phenyle, tinopal, vim, neel, etc. the secrets of manufacturing, how to get loans etc..'

(i) 'sure ways of increasing height; based on many successful experiments in America and Europe.'

(j) 'Sex course with naked pictures: published for the first time in India; 600 colour photos; successful suhagraat, lack of children, swapandosh; how to have enjoyable sex, etc..'

(k) 'Judo karate: based on Japanese techniques (Rs 50) (Can be bought through V. P, Ashoka Prakashan, Chandni Chowk).'

(l) '*Asli prachin maha brahad hast likhit Indrajal* : If you have not been able to find the real Indrajal book, buy it from us. It contains various yantras such as Bhairon, Kali, Durga etc. Also contain spells to bring others into your control; contains bhoot vidya ('spirit knowledge') etc..'

(m) 'A mala [necklace] with 108 beads: takes away all your troubles, cast spells, spirit possession, pass exams, rid of debts and diseases, success in business, in lotteries and in gambling; we'll refund double to cost if not satisfied (Krishna Jyotish Bhandar).'

(n) 'Purchase these books from us: (a) film acting guide; (b) Assam–Bengal ka jaadu: how to make humans disappear, turn people into dogs, monkeys etc., conjure a magical *pari*.'

(o) 'Genuine spell for putting people under your control, genuine crow magic; ancient owl magic; mantra for worldly success; card tricks.'

(p) 'Now in India a new age 35 mm camera (Gupta trading company suhaag-raat course with pictures.'

(q) 'Learn to speak English in 50 days.'[32]

---

[32] Sources: Mast Ram, *Sexy, Sexy, Sexy, Mujhe Log Boley* (Delhi, Raju Publication, n.d.); Kamini Devi, *Kaam Samasyaen* (Delhi, Raju Publications, n.d.).

Commodities, as anthropologists have long realised, 'represent a subject on which anthropology may have something to offer to its neighbouring disciplines, as well as one about which it has a good deal to learn from them.'[33] It is this aspect of 'learning from commodities' that requires attention in the present context. What is the connection between sexual culture and these bewildering variety of advertisements that vie for the reader's attention? What is the relationship between the consumer and the objects and processes for sale? How do we understand the 'moral economy that stands behind the objective economy of visible transactions'?[34] As Kopytoff also points out, the sharp distinction between 'things' and humans has not always been—as the case of slavery demonstrates—a historical fact. What is required, Kopytoff says, is a biography of things. However, in the context of my discussion, I think it might be more fruitful to think of a biography of 'thingness': the simultaneous (and inextricable) life of humans and commodities in the contemporary world, such that each grants the other subjectivity. In one sense, this proposition may stand accused of 'commodity fetishism', however, if we conceive of things as having a 'social life',[35] then a way must be found to conceive of the subjectivity of 'objects'.

Proceeding from the work of the historian Ferdinand Braudel, Kopytoff suggests that 'the extensive commoditization we associate with capitalism is thus not a feature of capitalism *per se*, but of the exchange technology that, historically, was associated with it and that sets dramatically wider limits to maximum feasible commoditization.'[36] There is then, according to this formulation, an 'internal logic of exchange' that is a characteristic of collective human existence itself. Kopytoff's discussion is useful for my own, however, before building upon it, let me point to what appears to be a somewhat idiosyncratic position in his argument. 'The counterdrive to this potential onrush of commoditization' he says, 'is culture. In the sense that culture is discrimination, excessive

---

[33] A. Appadurai, 'Introduction: Commodities and the Politics of Value', in A. Appadurai (ed.), *The Social Life of Things. Commodities in Cultural Perspective* (Cambridge, Cambridge University Press, 1997), p. 5.

[34] I. Kopytoff, 'The Cultural Biography of Things: Commoditization as a Process', in A. Appadurai (ed.), *op. cit.*, p. 65.

[35] Appadurai (ed.), *op. cit.*.

[36] Kopytoff, *op. cit.*, p. 72.

commoditisation is anti-cultural—as indeed so many have perceived it or sensed it to be.'[37] But the problem is, in what sense does there exist *a* culture that is separable from commoditisation, such that it exists above it, rather than being enmeshed within it, influencing as well as being transformed by it? And, how do we separate 'cultural rules' (that govern 'small-scale societies') from 'biographical idiosyncracies'[38] (that apply to industrial societies'), so as to assert that subjecthood in 'complex' societies exists outside 'cultural rules'? What is at issue is whether we can speak of, say, 'commodity culture' as separate from an 'uber-culture' that acts as a check upon the 'wayward' tendencies of the latter. In what follows, I will attempt to build upon Kopytoff's valuable insights through regarding culture as the *grounds* upon which all activity takes place, rather than a discrete *deus ex machina* of human actions.

Now, one context for the inventory of advertisements I have listed above is that this a market for—by the standards of mainstream capitalism—slightly soiled goods, the belief in miraculous cures and what have you. In one sense, this is card-trick capitalism, where the 'devil and commodity fetishism' come together.[39] However, in another important way, it may contain the potential to problematise the notion of 'commodity fetishism' in as much as the commodities *are* the subjects since the project of human subjectivity is inextricably bound with the perceived aspects of commodities.[40] So, one might say that in this context, the commodity does *not* become ' a very queer thing, abounding in metaphysical subtleties and theological niceties…[taking on] an enigmatical character'.[41] Instead, it gains its character concurrently with the

[37] *Ibid.*, p. 73.
[38] *Ibid.*, p. 89.
[39] M. Taussig, *The Devil and Commodity Fetishism in South America* (Chapel Hill, University of North Carolina Press, 1980). But, on the other hand, these beliefs are no more or less odd than the belief in futures trading on the stock market.
[40] I have in mind here the kind of discussion Marriott provides through his notion of the 'dividual', one that broaches the possibility of the 'divisible' character of persons. However, greater attention to this aspect will have to await another discussion. McKim Marriott, 'Hindu Transaction: Diversity Without Dualism', in B. Kapferer (ed.), *Transaction and Meaning* (Philadelphia, ISHI Publications, 1976).
[41] K. Marx, *Capital Vol. I*, (Moscow, Progress Publishers, 1978), p. 76. I have borrowed this quote from another piece where I analyse 'the sentiments of the metropolis' in India. See my *Constructing Post-Colonial India. National Character and the Doon School* (London, Routledge, 1998), Chapter 6.

character that is sought to be secured for the self. As Kopytoff point out, 'even things that unambiguously carry an exchange value—formally speaking, therefore, commodities,—do absorb the other kind of worth. We may take this to be the missing non-economic side of what Marx called commodity fetishism.'[42]

The relevant point, for my discussion is the one Kopytoff makes regarding the drive towards the 'singularization' of commodities, the other side of the commoditisation imperative. He suggests that commodities may acquire their 'social power' (Marx's notion of their 'fetishisation') *after* they are produced, and this by way of an autonomous cognitive and cultural process of singularization'.[43] Notwithstanding my discomfort with the split Kopytoff posits between 'culture' as a master-narrative separable from processes within it, this is a productive entry into the interactional world of things and humans. For, it suggests an active relationship between things and humans, produced and reproduced by cultural and historical circumstance.

Hence, the magical cures, the Lion Zorro automatic revolver, the colourful picture album, the film acting guides, and the judo–karate course—not all of them commodities in the classic exchange-value sense[44]—are both objects and processes of culture, rather than merely occupying the status of fetishes, *once and for all* defined by the existence of an exchange-value system. In the context of this discussion, this means that different commodities are singularised—given an 'additional' individual valuations in the face of their homogenised nature—during and through the processes of postcolonised existence. That is, their lives unfold through the themes, procedures, and structures we summarise under the rubrics of (though not exhausted by) 'tradition', 'modernity', 'the province', 'the metropolis', 'class', and 'commodity culture'.

The other point of relevance follows from Kopytoff's observation that the subject (humans) and object (things) dichotomy may

---

[42] Kopytoff, *op. cit.*, p. 83.

[43] *Ibid.*, emphasis added.

[44] Appadurai's makes an important observation in this context: 'Let us start with the idea that a commodity is *any thing intended for exchange*' (1997: 9); this, as he points out, 'gets us away from the exclusive preoccupation with the 'product,' 'production,' and the original or dominant intent of the 'producer' and permits us to focus on the dynamics of exchange', Appadurai, *op. cit.*.

be a 'disposition' peculiar to the West; that in other cultural contexts, the moral dilemmas over the objectification of subjects may not marked by the same anguish. This does not necessarily imply a 'devaluation' of human life, rather, that there may be other senses of the self in non-Western contexts that we have yet to explore, and which may render uncertain the universal validity of the subject–object dichotomy as a moral and political position. Marilyn Strathern's comments on the anthropomorphic nature of objects in Melanesian societies are of relevance here. 'To state that these wealth objects are "personifications" is not', she says, 'to set them *against* "objectifications", for that implies an unwarranted double participation in the equation between subjects and persons, and the separation of subjects from objects, promoted by commodity fetishism. Objects are created not in contradistinction to persons but out of persons.'[45]

It is to these 'other' senses of the 'self' being elaborated under the current regimes of capital that we must turn our attention, and whilst this discussion cannot do justice to this suggestion, it should be seen as a preliminary step in that direction. For this project, we need recourse to an ethnohistory of postcolonised life in its myriad aspects. To be more specific, then, the market that searches for custom in the pages of the pornography booklets[46] described above is the transactional space of the *intra-national* male diasporic subject, for whom the promises of capitalism— liberalisation, whatever,—seem always out of reach. It is a market on the margins of capitalism and yet one that seeks to domesticate 'mainstream' capitalism through casting its strategies as widely as possible. Here, the masculine–sexual self is the consuming subject: but consumption of what? How to become the ideal subject of

---

[45] M. Strathern, *The Gender of the Gift* (Berkeley, University of California Press, 1988), p. 171. Moreover, Kopytoff points to the pro- and anti-abortion positions in the West as an apt illustration of the debate over 'things' and 'persons' and adds that this is in striking contrast to those found in Japan. In this regard, he might also have added India. However, the influence of Christian theology has also to be factored into the analysis. My thinking in this context was stimulated by some comments made by Nita Kumar during a discussion on different senses of the self. I am also grateful to editors of Vol. 24 of the journal *South Asia* for reminding me of the Strathern volume.

[46] Given the analytical load I am placing upon it, this description of the printed material might prove increasingly difficult to sustain, but I will stay with it for the moment for want of a more suitable short-hand.

neoclassical economics, a course not open to everyone? Perhaps through a strategy of 'excessive' consumption, or an *all*-consuming (male) subject.

Of course, we need to pay close attention to the *kinds* of commodities available for purchase, as well as to the commoditisation of those 'goods' (such as goal oriented magic) which may earlier have belonged to the non-commoditised sector of transactions. The significance of the Lion Zorro automatic revolver and the 'Colourful Photo Album' can only be understood within the framework of the political and cultural economy of the readership of these booklets, rather than as a straightforward desire for more commodities by those with limited buying power; the specific *meaning* of each commodity—or categories of commodities—holds the key to consumption, or collection.

The desire for greater consumption, or a changed consumption pattern, may well be a factor in the process of commoditisation. But, as Gell usefully reminds us, it may also be a manifestation for something other than commodity desire.[47] Speaking of the Muria 'tribe' of central India, Gell points out that their attitude towards 'prestige consumption goods available in the markets'[48] can be best understood with reference to traditional Muria attitudes towards consumption and towards group solidarity. So, if Muria men and women have adopted the commodity cultures of the surrounding Hindu populations, competitiveness is not an explanatory factor. Rather, 'in taking over elements of a set of non-Muria prestige goods for internal consumption, the Muria have imposed their own set of social evaluations on them, which are quite distinct from the one's operative among the groups with whom these goods originated.'[49] Hence, Muria's consumption of 'Hindu' goods 'is in order to express conformity, not originality or individuality';[50] it articulates group loyalty and identity and the desire to maintain the prestige of the collective in the face of changing scales of prestige introduced by Hindu outsiders. It is in this sense, then, that non-commodity variables might be

---

[47] A. Gell, 'Newcomers to the World of Goods: Consumption Among the Muria Gonds', in Appadurai (ed.), *op. cit.*, (1997).

[48] *Ibid.*, p. 121.

[49] *Loc. cit.*.

[50] *Ibid.*, p. 122.

introduced into the analysis of commodities in the (sexual) sphere of the pornography booklets.

The 'success' that is being imagined in the commerce of greater height, magic potions to pacify one's enemies, miraculous rings for overwhelming power, a course for successful *suhaag-raat*, 'a new age 35 mm camera', and learning to speak English 'in 50 days' within the shared space of sex-stories says something about the contiguity of the narratives of consumption and those of masculine–sexual culture. It speaks of a strategy of achieving and maintaining a sense of the masculine self in a hostile environment through participation in the rapacity of capital, *seemingly* at the margins of its processes; modernity's male equivalent of the voracious Hindu goddess that putatively haunts the Hindu male psyche. Suffice to say that it is a context that provides us with rich material for analysing the parallel civil society that exists on the margins of the 'mainstream' one, and one whose strategies and influences must be taken account of when 'we' discuss 'our' civil society.

Let me provide one example of the point of suture between consumption and masculine sexual culture in order to point to the collaborative social text that is its consequence; this is the process of the establishment of meanings in the post-production phase, through the social acts within which corporeal transactions, consumption trajectories and cultural frameworks are sought to be joined. It is the space where consumption, appears in the guise of 'proper' consumption in an age of bewildering choices. It is here that there develops a version of sexual economics. 'There is a wrong impression among certain young men' an 'advice' booklet of the Khandani Shafakhana points out, 'that all time erection, repeated erection or over excitement for intercourse are the signs of complete and perfect man-hood but in fact this condition soon turns into impotency.'[51] Here, the discourse of deferral is ensconced within the larger narrative of consumption culture (i.e., 'proper' sexuality can be purchased in the marketplace, from us, and that it is an aspect of the 'good' life in contemporary capitalism). This is also the interface between the emerging cultures of globalisation and the attempt to define the local: an unstable equilibrium where commodity culture is good, but only

---

[51] Hakim Hari Kishan Lal, *The Message of Youth* (Delhi, Khandani Shafakhana, n.d.), p. 27.

if reshaped according to a different—'traditional'—consumption
pattern than that in the west and that promoted by the forces of
globalisation. So, women are recognised as possessing 'the sex
urge'. However, Hakim Hari Kishan Lal warns that 'young men
should be careful on their first wedding night. They often think
it is essential to intercourse [sic] on the first night to prove their
manhood. Due to their ignorance they fail to excite their brides
on the first night.'[52] A proper, *Indian* course of consumption is best
advised for a 'happy married life'.

Sexuality, Masculinity and Space: The Global and the Local

The issue of the anxiety (or perhaps, just debate) over the most
appropriate milieu for the expression of Indianness moves us to
the next domain of inquiry: the mutually-reinforcing relationship
between the intra-national and the inter-national diasporic Indian
male subject. In my conversations with those who operate the
Khandani Shafakhana, I was told that a considerable number of
its clientele are Non-Resident Indians (NRI's) and their 'treatment'
is often carried out through correspondence. A letter from the
Shafakhana addressed to potential NRI clients notes that 'our
medicines are exported to America, England, the Persian Gulf,
Nairobi, Africa, Singapore, Malaya, Thailand, etc., and we receive
hundreds of thousands of Pounds and Dollars from these places.'
Further, NRI clients are offered treatments such as 'London Shahana
Special treatment', 'London Special Treatment' or the 'Africa
Special Treatment'.[53]

Among other things, the sex-clinic milieu presents us with a
scenario where 'traditional' ways of predicting the future—through
the commoditisation of charms and *mantras*[54]—engage with the
possible future that appears to circulate within 'rational' laws of

---

[52] *Loc cit..*

[53] From material gathered by the author. My own position as a NRI did not really
come into play in terms of an attempt to impress me with evidence of the
international demand for the 'cures' offered. For, at this point of time I was
affiliated with a Delhi based research institute and had not discussed my non-
Indian affiliations. Of course, it is correct to say that in this instance the 'foreign'
as an important source of legitimation for the 'local'.

[54] Which also have, at other times and places, non-commoditised lives.

supply and demand. One of the traditions is invoked through a particularly well-known public image, that of Hakim Hari Kishan Lal, beaming down from countless billboards in Delhi and is also emblazoned upon the clinic's stationary. In the age of the free-market, the muscular film hero, and westernised head-gear (if any), the Hakim's image is even more striking for the imagined markets it may be directed at (Plate 13.1).

For here is a *zamindar*-like, mustaschioed, double-chinned and starch-turbanned figure that appears to borrow its representational codes from an entirely different era; it is an image of masculinity that would appear to be curiously out of synch with contemporary ideas of metropolitan male identity, both in India and in NRI host nations. What then is the appeal of this image? The masculine code represented here, it could be suggested, has a very particular appeal to the dislocated male. It is the appeal of restoration, and the promise of relocation at a time of dislocatory anxiety. For, both the internal and the external immigrant male must engage with an environment where his 'authority' (as a male) is frequently questioned by women who go out to work, daughters who have boy-friends or move away from home, and by the nation-state—both the host and the 'local' one—which proscribes

Plate 13.1 Hakim Hari Kishan Lal.

the kinds of action a man might take to assert his 'natural' patri-archal rights.

An aspect of the Hakim's therapy is, then, the possibility of the maintenance of 'Indian' traditions in 'threatening' environments, and the appeal of maintaining ones *khandan* (lineage) through the agency of the Khandani Shafakhana. In the case of the 'overseas' migrant, it is the promise of reformulating the demands of the host nation-state through a private contract with one's 'own' commu-nity. And, for the locally displaced man, the Hakim holds out the possibility of the (existential) return to the more controllable milieu of the province and the village. And, of course, publicity regarding the 'global' and 'local' aspects of the clinic's business serves as a powerful legitimising strategy; in the Indian market, the foreign demand for its therapies can be marketed as proof of their efficacy, and the overseas clientele is reassured in the know-ledge of their local roots. So, sex-clinics may be part of the prolix processes we have to come to call 'globalisation'. And, the articu-lation of an India-based sex-clinic—and hence of a fraction of its sexual culture—with the stocks and flows of global forces is also transcribed by the fluctuating fortunes of traditional—'local'—knowledge systems and structures, and the work of the imagina-tion in conjuring a consciousness community of *de facto* male prerogatives.

In order to more clearly delineate the contours of urban non-middle class masculinity in India there are a number of variables that require attention in terms of the biographies of the group, including its status in the city (recently arrived, slum dwellers, those displaced from work due to technological changes, and so forth).[55] For the Indian situation, the swirl of commodities that speak to the sense of modern subjecthood—the circumstances I have outlined in earlier paragraphs—is an extra variable. For, here, subjectivity—traditional strategies, modern means, what-ever—is also woven into a broad canvas of non-exclusive choices, a very pure form of capitalism itself, the promise of *everything*.

Dis-location carries within it a narrative of space. The cultural meaning of space has tended to remain somewhat marginal to the efforts of scholars of South Asia. Spatial metaphors, as I have

---

[55] I provide a discussion on some of these aspects in the section on Mumbai's *Kaya Kalp* sex-clinic.

discussed elsewhere,[56] can be fruitful sites of engagement with the dominant themes of Indian modernity. This is true with just as much force for the present discussion. The discourse of space and a contest over space is, I would like to suggest, a crucial aspect of the sexual culture that gathers around the sex-clinics.

This consists in the increasing 'occupation' of the public spaces of the well-off for the enactment of the fantasies of those without much private space; in the meanwhile, the well-off themselves retreat to walled residential estates with names like Garden Estate and Qutub Enclave. Both the sex-clinic literature and the footpath pornography are replete with spatialised discussions of modern subjectivity. By this I mean a discourse of public parks, gardens, picnic grounds, tourist sites, fast food outlets, and so forth, around which Indian modernity is sought to be gathered. Both through words and images, readers and clients are urged upon these spaces as places of therapy, self-expression, communion with 'nature', and so on. For most young people from non-middle class backgrounds, the only private spaces are, in fact, public ones such as the Lodi Gardens in New Delhi. Here, various long established fantasies of modernity (romance, filmic style) are played out: readers who have observed the photography sessions around the Qutub Minar and the Lodi Gardens will know what I mean. Within the pornographic literature, the cultural strategy of space plays upon the search for a pastoral idyll within the city as a fundamental aspect of contemporary modernity. The various farms, advertisements for housing estates that go by names such as Garden Estate, and Aravali Estate are part of this fantasy. If the poor can't actually afford the materiality of this fantasy, at least they can exercise a spatial imagination.

Semen, Saving, Expenditure, Development and Filmic Culture

In another discussion on the career of India's most famous 'playback' singer, Lata Mangeshkar, I have noted the emergence during

---

[56] Srivastava, op. cit., (1998), and 'The Idea of Lata Mangeshkar: Speculations of Voice, Masculinity and the Post-Colonial Condition', in Ashis Nandy and Vinay Lal (eds), Politics of Innocence and Culpability in Indian Cinema (New Delhi, Oxford University Press, in press).

the immediate post-independence period of a masculine type I referred to as the Five Year Plan (FYP) Hero, and have suggested that Lata's little girl voice should be counterpoised not just to any postcolonised masculinity, but to quite a specific one, that of the FYP hero.[57] The FYP hero of Indian films represented a particular formulation of Indian masculinity where manliness came to attach not to bodily representations or aggressive behaviour but, rather, to being 'scientific',[58] the idea of a middle class 'epistemological masculinity' as it emerged from sites as the Doon School. One of the ways in which this came to be represented on the screen was through the operation of very specific spatial strategies, where roads and highways and metropolitan spaces came to be the 'natural' habitat of the FYP hero, and an important strand in 1950s and 1960s films was the profession of the hero: quite often he was an engineer (building roads or dams), a doctor, a scientist or a bureaucrat. The filmic presence of the hero was one which could be quite easily characterised as camp, for the camp persona of the heterosexual hero could coexist quite comfortably with a nationalist ideology which identified post-independence manliness as aligned to the 'new' knowledges of science and rationality which, it was held, would transform the 'irrational' native into the modern citizen.[59] In the field of popular culture the immediate post-independence period was particularly important in terms of the representations of what could be called the aesthetic and the ethic of planning and development.

The context under discussion here seems to mark a move away from the FYP hero model of masculinity that gained some of its legitimacy through both the Keynesian *and* the neoclassical models of economic thought. The FYP (male) hero stood both for government intervention and for delayed gratification through the reinvestment of savings for the 'national' good.[60] The FYP hero,

---

[57] 'The Idea of Lata Mangeshkar: Speculations on Voice, Masculinity and the Post-colonial Condition', see footnote 56.

[58] S. Srivastava, *op. cit.*, (1996).

[59] S. Srivastava, 'The Management of Water: Modernity, Technocracy and the Citizen at the Doon School', *South Asia* (n.s.), Vol. 16, (1992); Srivastava, *op. cit.*, (1996).

[60] I am following standard and somewhat simplified notions of 'Keynesian' and 'neo-classical' models of economic thought. See for example, P. A. Samuelson, *Economics*, Ninth edition (New York, McGraw Hill, 1973).

whose death throes began with film star Amitabh Bachchan's rise to fame, finds almost no resonance in the non-middle class contexts under discussion here; his funerary rites are, as if, administered through the sex-clinic discourse on male masturbation: several of their publications routinely point to its 'harmful' effects, whilst the majority of the operators I spoke to said that they did not condemn it in their discussions with their clients, and usually regarded it as harmless pastime that was surrounded by many myths. I have suggested in my Lata discussion that in the context of FYP hero, the discourse on semen-conservation and that on 'nation-building' were conjoined and represented an aspect of the over-all schema of frugality and saving that was characteristic of the planning ethos. If such a perspective was *ever* shared during the early life of the nation-state, it certainly appears to be part of a more ambivalent context in the milieu of the sex-clinics and their clients. Delayed gratification for the 'national' good, or whatever, may hold little attraction for those whose gratifications seem perpetually delayed. Instead of 'epistemological masculinity', we are now in the era of corporeal masculinity where the male body is the shining surface of the commodity: and unlike the 'intellectual' FYP, the qualities of the male commodity are more immediately expressible. It is in this sense that we might speak of a *new* commodity culture that differs from the old one within which the advertisements discussed above also made an appearance: the shift from Keynesian sexualities to neoclassical one's.

There is, a more general point to be made concerning the confluence between the sex-clinics, filmic culture and sexual culture. In publications such as *Safal Jiwan* (also published in English as *Happy Married Life*),[61] monogamous relationships and 'love' are important thematic devices, and the most common points of suture between filmic culture and the sexual culture of footpath pornography and the sex-clinics. It might be tempting to borrow the terms of the discussion here from works such as Radway's *Reading the Romance* (1987), where, for example, 'many of the writers and readers of romances interpret these stories as chronicles of triumph.'[62] However, the validity of the conclusions drawn for relatively affluent women readers from a small mid-western community

---

[61] *Safal Jiwan* (Delhi, Ashok Prakashan, n.d.)
[62] J. Radway, *Reading the Romance* (London, Verso, 1987), p. 54.

in the United States may be questionable when thinking about non-middle class Indian male readership in a large metropolis. So, in contrast to Radway's suggestion that 'romances are valuable to [the women] in proportion to their lack of resemblance to the real world', I would like to suggest that in the present context, romance provides a way through which non-middle class men (and women) attempt to find a place in a world that otherwise discounts their agency and well-being; what we can, however, say is that the social and say cultural—ethnographic—contexts within which ideas on love and romance are elaborated are, indeed, important for understanding the meaning of this activity. On the other hand, it is, probably, just as problematic to utilise the argument made by Giddens that romance (and romantic literature) is 'the counterfactual thinking of the deprived'[63] since this reduces both the complexity of the social and cultural conditions within which the 'deprived' live and makes their motivations transparent.

For the present, and in the absence of any well developed body of theory on romantic love *under the conditions of contemporary capitalism* in India,[64] I will have to be satisfied with a speculative argument, one that introduces political economy in order to track its cultural contours. One way of thinking about ideas of romance and love that congregate in the present context is that they elaborate a narrative for the 'future development' of the individual; they point to the discourse of agency that is connected to the 'economic' but not reducible to it. Now, if we keep in mind the economic and political asymmetry between Indian metropolitan and provincial cultural spheres, and my suggestion that the milieu of the sex-clinics is also the site of a relationship between the metropolitan and provincial cultures of postcoloniality, then it is not difficult to speak of the provincial male (and female) as the subject of the movie romance such that it provides a narrative of 'future development' denied by economic processes. To be 'in love', then, operates as a metonym for 'freedom': the freedom to 'achieve', to exercise individual choice, to be part of the 'real'

---

[63] A. Giddens, *The Transformation of Intimacy. Sexuality, Love and Eroticism in Modern Societies* (Cambridge, Polity, 1993), p. 45.

[64] I have recently been alerted to Laura Ahearn's, *Invitations to Love: Literacy, Love Letters and Social Change in Nepal* (Ann Arbor, University of Michigan Press, 2001). However, at the time of writing, this book was not available to me and I am unable to draw upon its discussion.

world, and, finally, to attain 'fulfilment'. In this sense, the idea of 'triumph' that romance speaks to in the Indian context differs substantially from its American mid-western counterpart: for the former is also heir to a trajectory of colonial and postcolonised political and cultural economy that has little resonance in the latter. 'From its earliest origins', Giddens says, romantic love raises the question of intimacy. It is incompatible with lust and earthly sexuality, not so much because the loved one is idealised—although this part of the story—but because it presumes a psychic communication, a meeting of souls which is reparative in character.'[65] However, in the context of the sex-clinics, earthly sexuality and romantic love present themselves as part of the same discourse: perhaps because of the mediating context of consumption under contemporary capitalism—i.e., sex is a 'good' and good sex can be purchased.[66]

Ramesh Vishwakarma: Carpenter, Believer in Spirits, Sex-Clinic Client

The marginalisation of traditional systems of healing and experience from 'respectable' therapy and 'validated' knowledge, and the role of the former in the life of the immigrant to the city, is the next context we need to explore. Despite the existence of government funded universities and hospitals, medical systems such as Ayurveda suffer low prestige in terms of the status of their practitioners (even though they have a very wide clientele, and Ayurveda is widely regarded as 'household medicine'). Almost all sex-clinic operators are either qualified Ayurvedic doctors or

---

[65] A. Giddens, loc. cit.. Radway appears to make a similar suggestions—though in the context of *female* readership—through her observations on 'the relative unimportance of detailed reports about sexual encounters' in the romance novel, and that 'Smithton readers are interested in the verbal working out of a romance ... rather than in the portrayal of sexual contact through visual imagery', J. Radway, op. cit., p. 66.

[66] Filippo Osella has also suggested that the gloss provided by Giddens might be too sparse to take account of the Indian situation, certainly, as evidenced in his and Caroline Osella's researches in South India. For example, love as an embodied state also needs to be considered. And, he quite rightly points out that, the many different types of affect, 'sneham, prem, kama, and so on need to be differentiated and are not glossed happily as "love".' Personal communication.

represent themselves as relying upon Ayurvedic or Unani or Tibbi medicine. For example, the following discussion comes occurs in Hakim Hari Kishan Lal's booklet on the treatment of impotency:

> ...some medicine for the rich production of semen and thickening the semen should be used. For this purpose some of the Indian Herbes [sic] such as Asgandh (Withania Somnifera), Kouch (seeds of Coucharge), Vidari Kand, Talmakhana (Hygrophila Spenosa) and Musli in due proportion are of unique efficiency.[67]

Through such attempts at self-identification, it is possible to view the sex-clinics as sites where non-allopathic systems of medicines continue to exist and find a place of elaboration.

The official suspicions that keep watch over 'traditional' systems of medicine need to be juxtaposed with the material and cultural conditions of life for the marginal populations of the metropolis in order track the emergence of the 'regularised unauthorised' milieu of the city I have earlier referred to. The uncertainties of metropolitan life with its official promises—and everyday denials—of the 'rule of law' and an urban space of contractual existence are most saliently articulated through the competition between 'official' and 'unofficial' knowledge regimes. For the non-middle class clients of the Kaya Kalp[68] sex-clinic in Mumbai (with branches in the suburbs of Dadar and Borivili), it is this which seemed to be the most palpable experience of the metropolis: the attempt on the part of the economically and culturally marginal to anchor the self in the bewildering swirl of urban processes and oppressions through recourse to familiar experiential and knowledge systems; the postcolonised city as a scattered locale of knowing and being that not so much authorises the law-and-order legends of the modernity as places them in confrontation with 'other' knowledges through the agency of the migrant who forever dreams of a return to the province. As precarious Mumbai hillside locations provide tenuous slum-shelter to an increasingly large number of migrants from states such as Uttar Pradesh, they also serve as the grounds

---

[67] Hakim Hari Kishan Lal, op. cit., p. 19.
[68] I was given access to various facets of the working of Kaya Kalp clinic by its owner Dr Arun Kumar. I am extremely grateful to Dr Kumar for his co-operation and generosity. My thanks also to Dr Ashok Gupta of Ashok Clinic, Delhi, for his help during the course of this research.

upon which the charisma of the state is met with the supernaturalism of a displaced people.

Kaya Kalp is the most widely advertised and perhaps the most successful of Mumbai's larger sex-clinics. Its hoardings and posters can be found on almost all of Mumbai's suburban railway stations, as well as inside many train carriages that service the suburban routes. The red, yellow and black graphic with its motif of a lion and a silhouetted naked woman in a standing posture is a pervasive part of Mumbai's visual landscape. It is, quite simply, everywhere. The owner, Dr Kumar, is the son of a dentist and trained as an Ayurvedic doctor from the Satya Sai Murlidhar Ayurvedic College, Moga, Punjab. He had become a sexologist, his father told me in a separate conversation, at the latter's insistence. The Borivili clinic has morning sessions, whereas the Dadar one opens at three in the afternoon. In general, Dr. Kumar works from around nine in the morning to 10:30 at night, with a break of about two hours in between. I had the opportunity of observing the functioning of both the clinics in June–July 2000, December 2000 and in January 2001. At all times, the sitting rooms at both clinics were full to overflowing. The Dadar clinic had a separate, air-conditioned room to gather the overflow from the regular waiting area, and this too was invariably crowded with patients.

The walls of both the Dadar and Borivili clinics are adorned with a number of framed clippings of newspaper articles written by Dr Kumar for Marathi and Hindi newspapers, medals and trophies, photographic stills from television talk shows that Dr Kumar has appeared on and certificates and endorsements from a number of Indian and international organizations. The latter include the Royal Society of Health, U.K.; The [Indian] Board of Alternative Medicine; Sexuality Information and Education Council of the United States; Kurukshetra University; Satya Sai Murlidhar Ayurvedic College, Moga, Punjab; Special Executive Magistrates Directory Committee; Punjab State Faculty of Ayurvedic and Unani System of Medicine; and the Maharashtra Council of Indian Medicine. Photographs show Dr Kumar on popular television programmes such as *Bindas Bol* ('Carefree Conversations') and the Priya Tendulkar Show where Dr Kumar shares the dais with other 'formal' (i.e., medically qualified) sexologists such as Prakash Kothari of Mumbai, another shows him receiving an award from the Sheriff of Mumbai, with the Maharashtra Finance Minister looking on, and there is one from an appearance on the programme *Purush Shetra* (Man's World).

Both on his letterhead as well on the ubiquitous billboards advertising his services, Dr Kumar provides an elaborate inventory of his qualifications and affiliations. In this way the walls of his clinic become part of a contiguous visual landscape that includes Mumbai's suburban train stations, railway coaches, and highways; the clinic is the world, and the world the clinic, no less, and no more unfamiliar than the promises, seductions and fulfilments of Mumbai itself. During one of my visits to his clinic I asked a man why he had chosen to come to *Kaya Kalp* over others and he mentioned the many 'foreign' degrees listed in the advertisements for the clinic.

My first meeting with Dr Kumar was in June 2000 and I was asked to come to his Dadar clinic at nine in the evening. My wait to see him eventually lasted some two hours till he had finished all consultations. There was a television set switched on just above the door to his office with the sound turned off or at very low volume. The reception was quite poor, but a lot of the men watched the song and dance programme, almost mesmerised by the glowing hues of an out of focus screen. A long bench had been placed along the narrow gallery that formed the waiting area of the clinic, and on this we all sat waiting for our turn in the inner sanctum of the clinic, the consulting room itself. We might have been at a railway station, anxiously hoping for our turn at the ticket counter, and willing the night to a special dispensation so that we would reach the counter before it closed for the day. The doctor's employees wore white coats, and inside the clinic there was a small reception area, a 'History' room, an 'Examination' room, a 'Dispensary' and finally the doctor's consultation room. When a new patient arrives, he is first taken to the History room, his 'history' recorded on a form,[69] then to the examination room for a physical examination by one of the staff, and then finally— after a wait of anywhere from fifteen minutes to an hour—he

---

[69] The form elicits information on the age, married status, occupation, the nature of the complaint, whether both the male patient and spouse achieve sexual 'satisfaction', and the 'progress of disease' which is a column for symptoms of the malady.

consults with the doctor. The consultation fee for a new patient is Rs 300, every subsequent visits costs around Rs 100.

At first glace, Dr. Kumar's office is like any other doctor's clinic, promotional material from medical companies on his desk, a stethoscope by his side, and a bed to conduct physical examinations against the back wall. However, it is also quite different. One of the walls is lined with a glass cupboard that contains an extensive collection of labelled jars of herbs and prepared medicines. The labels—written in Hindi—are easily read by the naked eye: *Ghamasa, Samudraphen, Santra Chala, Mashparni, Punarnara, Devdar, Chalispatra, Neempatra, Adras, Triphala, Dhatriphal, Chausapad, Raie AasuriRagika, Sanaya, Sankhnami, Sariwa, Hiraksis, Harnaumool, Kadachal, Mahanfal Chitrak* and *Makparni*, among others. Also unlike other clinics there closed circuit television monitor on his desk, connected to an unobstrusively mounted camera in the waiting room. Neither the doctor nor his patients seemed particularly clear (or concerned) about its role in the life of the clinic.

Typically, consultations last around ten to fifteen minutes and, based on the figures contained in the *Kaya Kalp* record books, during January 2001 the Borivili clinic (morning shift only) was visited by approximately 200 clients, whereas the corresponding figure at Dadar (afternoon shift only) was around 300.[70] For the same month, the youngest of the clients was 19 years old, and the eldest 57. Approximately 60 per cent of the visitors indicated that they were married, and apart from one woman and four couples, all the other clients were men. Almost all the clients came from the outer suburbs of Mumbai such as Bhayandar, Ghatkopar, Goregaon, Jogeshwari, Kandivili, Malad and Wadala,[71] and the occupational categories present a picture consistent with the

---

[70] Dr Kumar was kind enough to give me access to his records for January 2001, however, I should point out that at the time of my consultation of the same, these were incomplete. Not wishing to strain the hospitality I has already been afforded, I felt unable to ask him for further access to completed record books. I don't believe that the observations of this paragraph are substantially affected by this fact.

[71] It is impossible to generalize about a city as historically complex as Bombay/Mumbai, however, most of these areas are home to substantial migrant populations of non-white collar workers; localities such as Ghatkopar are also characterized by large slum and shanty town developments and were also affected by the riots that enveloped Mumbai in the wake of the 1992 demolition of the Babri Masjid in Ayodhya (see the *Srikrishna Commisson Report*, 1998).

non-middle class milieu of the clinic, including as they do 'machine operator', 'peon', (auto?) 'rickshaw driver', 'furniture work' and 'tailor'. While a large proportion of men I spoke to were either first or second generation migrants to the city—from states such as Uttar Pradesh, as well as regional Maharashtra—what is more analytically significant is their location within the unstable cultural and political economy of the metropolis. They are not merely migrants to the city, they are also migrants *within* it, located in spaces that are rapidly transforming, often hostile, bewilderingly unfamiliar, out-of-reach, and depending upon how often one is 'cleared out' out of urban slums and shanty towns, literally shifting beneath one's feet; 'migrancy' here is more than a change of place, it is the instability of space through which certain forms of unstable male subjectivities emerge. The urban biography of *Kaya Kalp's* male clients consists, then, of a series of untimely passages.

The 'history' sheets at *Kaya Kalp* list 'premature ejaculation' as by far the most common 'chief complaint', and the separate column for 'satisfaction' records an overwhelming 'no' across the age groups. 'Masturbation' and 'issueless' occur infrequently as complaints. Once the consultation is concluded, two kinds of remedial options are offered: Ayurvedic medicine prepared at the premises if the nature of the complaint warrants it, or, referral to one of the several medical doctors on *Kaya Kalp's* 'Specialist Panel'.[72] Recourse is normally taken to the latter where specific kinds of medical technology is required, for example, in procedures requiring X-ray reports, and blood and semen examinations.

The space and processes of the clinic consist, then, of a number of over-lapping contexts: 'scientific' enterprise, 'ancient' Indian wisdom,[73] contemporary everyday culture, foreign expertise, and the informal–formal system of awards and honours whose epaulettes, shields, and cups are the staple of countless glass cabinets in innumerable sitting rooms around the country. The clinic is never a purely formal space, like a medical hospital, nor is it a

---

[72] At the time of writing, these included a specialists in 'Gastro Intestinal Surgery' and 'Colorectal Surgery', a gynaecologist, an 'Oro-Dental Surgeon', and a 'Consultant Sonologist and Radiologist' (information from the *Kaya Kalp* letterhead).
[73] Joseph Alter also makes a similar point in the context of science and early twentieth century discourse of 'yogic physiology'. J. S. Alter, *Gandhi's Body: Sex, Diet, and the Politics of Nationalism* (Philadelphia, University of Pennsylvania Press), pp. 65–66.

place of total informaility. The clients move between formality and familiarity in a space that is not the street but is contiguous to it. Here, matters of the body are conjoined with the bodily contexts that are the norm for the men who visit. The clinic does not dissimulate: it does not seek to remove its therapy from the world of profit and commerce, there is no hyphen here between 'sexual' and 'economy'; I think it is this that, among other things, contributes towards its attractiveness for its clients.

The clinic premises in Dadar are on the second floor of commercial block next to the railway station. The clinic sign is also visible from a flyover next to the building. On the first floor are situated the offices of Gemini Arts and Om Graphics (companies making wedding cards), Nutan Beauty Collection (a jewellery shop), The Deccan Merchants Co-operative Bank and the Dadar Commercial Institute (a secretarial training institute). On the second floor, the clinic shares space with Chitalia Infotech Academy, and Bhartiya Kala Sangeet Mandir (a music school). The small lanes below that surround the *Kaya Kalp* building and the railway station are full of a variety of shops selling electrical goods, cheap clothing, plastic shopping bags printed with (unauthorised) versions of internationally and locally recognisable lables/logos, and stalls selling fruit and vegetables, fruit juices and soft drinks. Itinerant hawkers crowd the streets with their wares of handkerchiefs, travel bags, belts, ties and a multitude of other goods whose quality marks them as destined for a lower middle class market as well as towards the consumption capacities of Mumbai's migrant labour force. At night, say after ten, the entire area gets converted into an open-air market for different kinds of herbs, vegetables and plants used in religious ceremonies. The periods of a lull in the activity of the area appear to be quite brief, perhaps a few hours late at night and very early in the morning.[74]

It is at this juncture—where the promise of contract is modified through the *personal* economies of small-scale commerce, space, intimacy and the dreams of going back 'home'—that the sex-clinics are located as metropolitan sites of therapy *par excellence*.

---

[74] On my first visit to the Dadar clinic I was accompanied by Veenapani Seksaria. We left the clinic at around 11.30 p.m., the signs of unabated commercial and social activity still around us.

I was introduced to 21 year old Ramesh Vishwakarma by *Kaya Kalp's* Dr. Kumar in response to my request to meet some of his clients. We met at the clinic's Borivili premises in North Mumbai. Ramesh has lived in Mumbai for about two years, leaving behind a young wife and the rest of his family in a village in the district of Azamgarh in Uttar Pradesh. At our first meeting at the clinic, he was relaxed and keen to seek an answer to his 'problems' of the lack of a sustained erection leaving both him and his wife 'unsatisfied' and childless.[75] After our discussion, I asked him if we could meet again, to which he readily agreed, and we met again in a small tea-shop near the Andheri railway station. We could hardly hear each other for the noise of the fellow-guests, the waiters, the whirring fan, the occasional train and the sounds of the street, but the 'Ideal Railway Restaraunt' was Ramesh's preferred option as a meeting place. This time he was accompanied by an 'uncle', a man of perhaps forty, and our conversation was more wide-ranging. He told me that after he had saved up enough money he wished to return to Azamgarh, that he stays in the semi-slum locality of Kranti Nagar with some people from 'home', and that, like the majority of the others from his region, he frequently consults *tantriks* and *ojhas* for a variety of complaints. Of course, there is a ghost world, both he and the uncle tell me over *samosas* and tea, the city is full of malevolent spirits, and those that deny people like them a decent life despite their unrelenting labour. The milieus of the 'formal' political economy of the city with its circuits of 'social capital'[76]—or those of criminality with its own systems of distribution and redistribution of resources—are inaccessible to men (and women) of Ramesh's background, and it is in this context that there emerges the sphere of the ghost-city, and alternative landscape of knowledges and experiences, to which the metropolis of the official master-plans and tourist brochures is merely an adjunct.

In the unofficial city, then, we find the project of the 'ayurvedic body': a proliferation of advertisements by pharmaceutical companies and sex-clinic operators that promises to overcome the

---

[75] My discussion of the ethnography carried out at the sex-clinics will necessarily be brief and more detailed analysis will be provided in the larger work of which this research is part.

[76] P. Bourdieu, 'The Forms of Capital', in J. G. Richardson (ed.), *Handbook of Theory and Research in the Sociology of Education* (New York, Greenwood Press, 1986).

nutritional constraints of the political economy through recourse to the therapy of tradition. Most of clients of the sex-clinics milieu lack the means to a healthy body available to better-off Indians, including, adequate nutrition, a clean environment, and functioning medical facilities. So here, a marginalised medical system has become aligned with the body strategies of a marginal people. Perhaps the most important of these strategies is the one where the body is sought to exceed the limits imposed upon it by the political economy of the nation-state. In such cases, the physical body may suffer the pangs of hunger, but hunger is sought to be overcome by the social process of the remedies offered by the sex-clinics. These remedies consist of 'advice' on maintaining masculinity and on leading a fulfilling family life, on how to avoid contracting sexually transmitted diseases (STDs), on eating proper food, on the 'good' thoughts and on brightly coloured medication.

The youthfulness of the Ayurvedic body is often an important area of discussion: 'Youth is the most vital period of life of any human being. At this stage only, a man comes to know about the real happiness of life.'[77] Here, there is a shift from any scriptural notion of Indian (Hindu) existence, where 'youthfulness' is not necessarily valorised over old age, a shift linked to the emerging culture of consumption and contemporary capitalism. The narrative of lost youth appears to be common to the different booklets from the different sex-clinics, and we need to position it, among other things, in the context of the political economy of hunger and poverty when 'youth' and vigour for the majority of the sex-clinics' clientele is indeed a fleeting experience. The youth angle is also reiterated in other ways: at the end of Hakim Hari Kishan Lal's *Message of Youth*, there are a series of photos of the Hakim either with Indian political leaders or being awarded some mark of public recognition. In these he features with, among others, Nehru, Indira Gandhi, ex-presidents Sanjeeva Reddy, Zakir Husain and a very startled Gyani Zail Singh. And whilst the captions describe those the 'Hakim Sahib' is in the act of greeting as the late so-and-so, his own mortality is never mentioned. In fact, it appears that the pictures all belong to the same era and in only one of them, the one taken with Zail Singh, does he actually look old.

---

[77] Hakim Hari Kishan Lal, *op. cit.*, p. 2.

Youth also figures in the context of 'unnatural means' of satisfying desire viz., masturbation and homosexuality:[78] so that by
the time they marry, young males are 'totally incapable to enjoy
[sic] marital bliss.'[79] The latter being linked to 'complete control
over momentary pleasures' and preservation of semen 'which is
a valuable treasure of life'.[80] Here, the discourse of consumption—
to which youthfulness belongs—is combined with that of the
deferral of pleasure, so that pleasure becomes available at a later
point within a sanctioned framework. Enjoyment-consumption-
saving-deferral-proper enjoyment constitutes here the discourse
of modernity. On the front cover of the booklet *Safal Jiwan*, published by Delhi's Ashok Clinic, is a colour drawing of an 'ideal'
modern family: facing the 'camera', the young father with a son
on his shoulder, his pretty wife just behind him, and all of them
in a garden/forest setting: the nuclear family, happiness, through
consumption, but also through its deferral.

There may be a temptation to dismiss all this as 'bad' modernity,
except that the sex-clinics and their literature are often part of a
larger context of discourses which actually question our stereo-
typic ideas abut the 'backward' modernity of the urban poor. Quite
often, the discourse on sexuality offers confronting perspectives—
instances that confront traditional views regarding the conserva-
tism of such literature—through quite explicit discussions on the
normality of the sexually active and desiring woman. Indeed the
notion of desire itself is usually presented as normal, and healthy.

Women, Pleasure and Subjectivity in a Masculine World

Here, I want to touch upon some of the quite contradictory ways
in which female subjectivity, particularly in the field of sexuality
and pleasure is dealt with in footpath literature. I will proceed

---

[78] I should reiterate that the description of masturbation as 'unnatural' in sex-clinic
literature does not necessarily lead to a similar discourse during consultations
between doctors and their clients. In fact, most doctors speak of it, as I have
already pointed out, as being quite 'harmless'.

[79] Hakim Hari Kishan Lal, *op. cit.*, p. 2.

[80] *Ibid.*, p. 3; the *caveat* noted in footnote 47 also applies in the case of the 'semen
conservation' perspective.

from the implicit assumption that this corpus is largely written and read by men and hence representations of female subjectivity need to explored as an aspect of 'footpath masculinity'. In a discussion on rape, Rajeshwari Sunder Rajan notes that 'wife-murder as a widespread social phenomenon in India expresses the socially sanctioned violence against women that reinforces and is reinforced by the ideology of husband-worship (*pativrata*).'[81] There is a truism to this statement that appears to require little reflection. For we have been made increasingly aware of the imbrication of this 'tradition' with, *inter alia,* the discourses of nationalism, those of the family in filmic and other contexts, and in contemporary exhortations to a 'new' nationhood by the votaries of *Ram Rajya*. It is not incorrect to say that, the notion of pativrata is part and parcel of the social and cultural contexts of the postcolonial civil society. Anthropologists, sociologists and historians have noted its particular significance in Indian society, and feminists have provided critiques as part of the larger projects of feminism in the social sciences. 'Above all, in the ideals of the traditional [Indian/Hindu] culture', Sudhir Kakar points out, 'the "good" woman is a pativrata, subordinating her life to her husband's welfare and needs in a way demanded of no other woman in any other part of the world with which I am familiar.'[82]

The point I would like to make is not that pativrata is not a significant aspect of the Indian women's lives, rather, that notwithstanding this, there are other, unexplored, sites of popular culture where pativrata is in fact significantly contested as defining aspects of the relationship between men and women. The footpath pornography can also be, I would like to argue, a possible site of recalcitrance against bourgeois norms of domesticity (summarised as pativrata), and the control of female sexuality.

Of course, this does not refer to some unambiguous feminist position, a subalternist resistance to hegemonic formulations on gender and sexuality. It does, however, point to the less than complete hegemony of dominant ideas among those—the readers and writers of these texts—who are usually seen to be their most natural constituency. There is, in other words, an 'underworld'

---

[81] R. Sunder Rajan, *Real and Imagined Women: Gender, Culture and Postcolonialism* (London, Routledge, 1993), p. 83.
[82] S. Kakar, *op. cit.*, p. 66.

civil society where ideas of gender, sexuality, power and resistance circulate and are debated upon, and often complexly inflected. There are, we can speculate, a wide variety of pleasures that are generated for the male audience of these texts: these may range from reading about rape, multi-partner or 'unnatural' sex, or about fantasies of relationships with prohibited kin and social and economic superiors (the bosses wife or the landlord's daughter). The political complexity—for the analyst at least—arises from the manner in which such pleasures are often made to culminate in the humiliation of the either a patriarchal ideology or the male body itself. What I am trying to do, in other words, is to work out a path between the pleasures of the 'reactionary' text and the paradoxes of its sometimes quite contrary messages of female resistance to oppression. An exploration of this paradox requires a problematisation of the taken for granted subjectivity of the male reader, as well as of the apparent act of the granting of subjectivity to the violated woman. It calls for an engagement with the political and social contexts of both verbal and non-verbal speech.

The following example comes from a collection by Mast Ram.[83] In the story, called 'Zulm Ko Mita Doongi' (Oppression will be Stopped/The Injustice will be Addressed), a man abducts a college girl, Reshma, while she is travelling in a rickshaw. She is bundled into a car and taken to a bungalow, where she threatens and then pleads with her tormentor to release her, but is helpless against his sexual advances. These scenes are meant, we might speculate, for the reader's titillation rather than as a strategy for generating anger against sexual violence. Here, sexual violence with its themes of the forced undressing of the woman, biting and scratching, and the abductor's rising excitement at the resistance he encounters, becomes the site for male sexual fantasy. After raping her the man asks Reshma whether it wasn't so bad after all and further informs her that he had desired her for a long time. Reshma responds positively and agrees to meet him again for more 'good times'. These further encounters culminate in Reshma winning the rapist's confidence, getting him drunk at one of their subsequent encounters and cutting off his penis with a razor blade. The story concludes with the sentiments that Reshma had regained her lost 'izzat' (honour) and the man's evil deeds have been wiped out.

---

[83] Mast Ram, *Machalti Jawani* (Delhi, Vinod Prakashan, n.d.).

Now, on the one hand, the castration story could be read as an advance warning of the possible 'insurrection' of the subaltern and hence the need for greater vigilance—i.e., measures to keep them 'in check'—against revolutionary acts. According to this argument, the avenging woman/wife is imagined in order to 'serve as such a prophylactic strategy'.[84] As the readership of these books, is in all probability, predominantly male, this is a suggestive line of reasoning. There are, of course, the added dimensions of women as avenging goddesses (Durga/Kali), and a commentary on 'law and order' and its 'breakdown' that such stories encapsulate: that justice can (now) only be achieved through individual action rather than by relying on the state. The Hindi vigilante film genre is, of course, based around this idea. However, it also important to keep in mind another angle: the context of an emerging commodity culture, with its emphasis on individual action, as another important context of the castration story. Resistance in this context, is not a political issue, in the usual sense of politics as collective action based on reflection, rather, it is concomitant to developments in the political economy of urban life, the unintended politics of changing patterns of consumption.

Ideas of female chastity as the norm seem to be most often challenged in 'advice' booklets such as *Kaam Samasyane* by Kamini Devi which leads me to speculate that some of these booklets may, in addition to men, also be targeted at non-middle class urban women.[85] An 18 year old woman, 'Santosh Verma from Nagpur', narrates the following story to Kamini Devi and asks for her advice. Santosh says that she has had a relationship with a cousin of her *bhabhi's* (sister-in-law) after they both witnessed the bhabhi and her husband having intercourse. She further points out that she was responsible for initiating the relationship. Prior to this, she had fantasised about sex in front of a mirror, and here the text seems to suggest masturbation: 'I leant against the wall and began to stroke my stomach and navel. My hands began to stray. My fingers [now] wandered uncontrollably all over my body. I began to moan'.[86] However, Santosh discovers that the young man is, in

---

[84] R. Sunder Rajan, *op. cit.*, p. 94.
[85] Kamini Devi, *op. cit.*.
[86] *Ibid.*, p. 84.

fact, in an illicit relationship with his supposed sister (i.e., the bhabhi), and has been since before the marriage. What should she do? Kamini Devi advises her to 'warn your bhabhi to desist, otherwise tell your brother'. In this scenario, the woman takes the lead in instigating a relationship with a man that is not likely to lead to marriage, and, is not condemned for it on the grounds of morality or a 'woman's modesty'. This is one of *several* such stories where 'forward' women are represented as also exercising choice and being within their rights to do so. There is a context here, then—and with all the usual qualifications regarding circumspection with respect to 'resistance' in popular culture—which leads to the conclusion that we cannot come to definite conclusions about the *pervasiveness* of the ideals of Indian (or Hindu) feminine behaviour; that, in fact, the question needs fresh investigation in light of the cultural and economic (or, rather, the cultural contexts of the 'economic') developments of the past few decades.

Stories of the humiliation of the male body and female auto-eroticism require a further comment with respect to the issue of male identification and subjectivity.[87] The occurrence of such narratives in popular literature addressed mainly to men may also say something about the uncertainty of locating (or discovering) a unified male subject that is their object. Or, put another way, that men respond in a monolithic manner to the narratives to which they are subject. One way of thinking about 'humiliation' in the Indian context might be consider it as a trope that serves to remind economically and culturally marginal men about their marginality. That, for men like them, the city is, indeed, a place of many dangers and repeated humiliations at the hands of others more powerful; that within the hierarchy of masculinities, theirs may stand at a precipice, teetering between feminisation and re-masculinisation, not always allowing for a stable, delimited sense of the masculine. This is the juncture where the self-that-wants-to-be is mortified by the actual experiences of 'being' towards an anxious—fluctuating—subjectivity. It is also the moment where the masculine self may experience itself as member of a class, its masculinity inscribed and restrained by the rules of inter-class intercourse. For, Reshma, as the embodiment of the 'modern'

[87] I am grateful to Filippo Osella for suggesting that I provide a more detailed discussion in this context.

woman is not, of course, a déclassé figure and the reader's engagement with her is also in the nature of a social lesson in the proprieties (and improprieties) of such interaction.

In a discussion of 'male masochism in the [Hollywood] horror film', Barbara Creed makes the point that the signifying strategies of the genre work through feminising the (male) 'monster' and thereby linking 'monstrosity' to the 'socially denigrated' and 'abject' feminine.[88] Julia Kristeva's discussion of the 'abject' is fundamental to Creed's own argument on the 'othering' of the feminine and the feminisation of the monstrous male body that is accomplished through the narrative and visual strategies of horror films. To uncritically accept Kristeva's argument on the 'origins' of abjection *in toto*, and seek to apply them to the Indian context would be a violence to ethnographic complexity that is often a mark of psychoanalytic engagements with India. However, there are aspects of Creed's discussion that are pertinent for the present context.

The first of these is the glimpse it offers into the complexity of desire. Or, to pose it as a question: how does masochism as (male) desire serve to further complicate the relationship between the text and the audience? Creed also goes on to suggest that 'while some horror films explore man's desire for castration in order to become a woman, others explore castration as part of a male death wish.'[89] A refractive interpretation of this position for the Indian case might be possible. We can say that the castration narrative in the Indian case is better seen as an engagement with a 'death wish' that has an ethnosocial rather than—or exclusively—a psychoanalytic dimension. It is, to reiterate the argument made above from another angle, the recognition of the fragile mortality of the non-middle class male self and expresses one of the strategies for continued (masculinsed) survival under conditions of perceived hostility.

The fragmenting of the audience in terms of its commitment (or loyalty) to the male protagonist and hence to the masculine trajectory of domination represented by the latter is another

---

[88] Barbara Creed 'Dark Desires. Male Masochism in the Horror Film', in S. Cohan and I. R. Hark (eds), *Screening the Male: Exploring Masculinities in Hollywood Cinema* (London and New York, Routledge, 1993), p. 131.
[89] *Ibid.*, p. 129.

possible context that needs to be explored. I have noted above that in a variety of contexts—A. P. Pillay's 'serious' sexology, footpath pornography and advice booklets, *Kaya Kalp's* patient's records, Ramesh Vishwakarma's comments—sexual 'satisfaction' for *both* men and women finds a prominent place as a topic of discussion, instruction and anxiety. There is, in another words, an incipient male subject position that—erratically, to be sure—engages with concerns not always reducible to the masculine. And, in this sense, both the humiliation of the male body and the space of female autoeroticism may speak to the irregularity, the splitting and the multiplicity of identification itself.

Finally, in this context, at its most analytically intractable, which is most likely the actual state of affairs, the realisation of male vulnerability-in-the-city, and the splintering and multiplying of identity positions and of male desire, come together to make *any* notion of stable masculinity under the contemporary regime of capital a chimera of the analytical will to stabilise.

The State of Knowledge

What is at issue is the ability to view non-Western modernity— one that involves unprecedented population movements *within* such societies (the issues of international movements is really of secondary concern here) from primarily the rural and semi-rural areas to the urban—in terms of a series of fractures such that the framework outlined by, say, Giddens, where all aspects of society move in concert to articulate a consistent whole, no longer holds true. So, for example, Giddens suggests that 'the consequence of modernity' is that 'we' move from a embedded pre-modernity to a disembedded modernity and various social, economic and political aspects change in a consistent manner to produce this state.[90] The discourses and sites surrounding sexualities and sexual cultures in Indian non-middle class contexts suggests, I think, that *even if* this is true for western modernity, non-western modernities may be quite different from this. And, further, that we need to *critically* analyse the manner and extent to which the milieu of contemporary 'Indian' male (and indeed female) sexualities can

---

[90] A. Giddens, *op. cit.*, (1990).

be understood through an analysis of Gandhian ideas or through psychoanalytic frameworks, rather than accept their explanatory value.

I would like to suggest that analyses of Gandhian ideas, and critiques of the influence of Hindu 'mythological stories' upon the 'Indian psyche', may be of uncertain value in discussions of the milieu of contemporary 'Indian' masculinity and sexuality. So, when one writer suggests that the 'inherently contradictory quality of these representations of female sexuality are part of a cultural subconscious for the *majority* of the population',[91] then we have to ask whether she isn't, in fact, confusing the *public* nature of certain perspectives with '*majority*' opinion. The other critical issue concerns the gap between the circulation of discourses, not least within the realms of scholarly research, and their uneven absorption into the everyday due to their refraction through a *multitude* of cultural processes and sites. It is an added problem that our reliance on English-language material can often lead us to opinions about the 'majority' (which, as Raymond Williams' critique of the notion of the 'masses' pointed out, may be a problematic term anyway[92]) that may not tell us very much about the unstable nature of culture and cultural change in contemporary postcolonised societies. For, the 'majority', if one goes by the popularity of the kinds of literature I am analysing here, do not, any longer, have much time for Gandhi nor do they seek to emulate or desire, Swami Vivekananda's exhortations notwithstanding,[93] the archetypal 'virtuous' women of Hindu mythology such as Draupadi or Savitri; their energies are taken up with the daily task of theorising culture as a process influenced by contexts such as the marginalisation of old knowledges (such as Ayurveda), the tensions of urban life for the poor, the desire to be part of an emerging commodity culture, and the proliferation of new tastes, styles and fashions of contemporary non-Western modernity. To assume that Gandhi, Draupadi and Savitri continue to reside with any degree of consistency in the dwellings of the Indian

---

[91] K. H. Katrak 'Indian Nationalism, Gandhian "Satyagraha", and Representations of Female Sexuality', in A. Parker, M. Russo, D. Sommer, and P. Yaeger (eds), *Nationalism and Sexualities* (New York, Routledge, 1992), p. 399. Emphasis added.

[92] R. Williams 'Culture is Ordinary', in R. Gable (ed.), *Resources of Hope: Culture, Democracy, Socialism* (London, Verso, 1989).

[93] Swami Vivekananda, *Our Women* (Calcutta, Advaita Ashram, 1974).

social psyche is to simply revert to a model of society where public ideologies and narrowly textual analyses usurp the complexities of *practice*.

Date: January 2001, I am talking to young 'sex-counsellor' at a government run clinic in the 'red-light' area of Kamathipura in Mumbai. He informs me that he discusses different meanings of 'sex' with visitors to the clinic: it could be touching, it could be masturbation, it could be kissing. And homosexuality? Yes, he says, that's another option. I'm taken aback and ask if there are no official objections to this 'advice'. He smiles and says that the state isn't really as monolithic and all-knowing as I assume. Like the fractured state, the 'sex-question' in India may not have a unified ground upon which we can build a theory of 'Indian' sexuality and masculinity, and an exploration of male subjectivity requires close attention to the shifting cultures of contemporary capitalism and the production of the 'all-consuming male subject'. Perhaps the most productive way of navigating the issue is through an under-standing of postcolonised modernity as it unfolds across the reg-isters of political economy, commodity cultures, the displacement of peoples within and without the nation-state, the attrition of traditional masculinity politics and the competition between 'authorised' and 'non-authorised' knowledges within national and global contexts.

About the Editor

Sanjay Srivastava is Associate Professor, Faculty of Arts, and Associate Head of School, School of Communications and Creative Arts, Deakin University, Melbourne, Australia. He is also a member of the editorial committee of the journal *South Asia*. His research interests include masculinities, sexualities, popular culture and the city. His previous publications are *Constructing Post-Colonial India: National Character and the Doon School* and *Asia: Cultural Politics in the Global Age* (co-authored).

About the Series Editor and the Contributors

Series Editor

Howard Brasted is Professor in modern South Asian history, University of New England, Armidale, Australia, and Director of the UNE Asia Centre. He also holds the position of Secretary of the South Asian Studies Association, and from 1984 to 2001 was the editor of its scholarly journal *South Asia*. He has published widely on topics ranging from Indian nationalism and the Indian National Congress to the processes of decolonisation. He has recently completed projects on child labour and female labour in South and South East Asia and has begun working and publishing on aspects of Islamic history.

Contributors

Leena Abraham is Reader, Department of Sociology of Education, The Tata Institute of Social Sciences, Mumbai, India. She has carried out research and has published in the areas of youth sexuality, development and gender issues in education, the social history of education, health education and alternatives in education.

Chandra S. Balachandran, a cultural geographer by training, has taught for several years in the USA and now lives in Bangalore, India. He is the founder and Chairman of The Dharani Trust, a Bangalore based non-governmental organisation, that acts as a forum bringing together academic and activist work. The trust has recently initiated a number of projects that cover areas such as inter-cultural studies and the human rights of marginalised peoples. He is also the founder and Chairman of the trust's first initiative, The Indian Institute of Geographical Studies, Bangalore. His interests include pilgrimages, geographic education, epidemics, religion and sexualities and their intersections with geography.

Zahid Chaudhary is currently finishing his PhD in the Department of English, Cornell University, Ithaca, USA. He has written a dissertation on colonial photography in India and has contributed an essay to a forthcoming book on 'Mutiny' photographs to be published by Sepia International and the Al-Kazi Collection of Photographs. His essay in this book has emerged from an earlier study on British travel writing in India.

Kathryn Hansen is Professor, Department of Asian Studies, The University of Texas at Austin, USA. She has published widely on Hindi and Urdu language and literature and on drama, popular culture and the performing arts in India. She is the author of *Grounds for Play: The Nautanki Theatre of North India*.

Kajri Jain is a Post-Doctoral Fellow, Faculty of Arts, Deakin University, Melbourne, Australia. Her research interests include popular culture, including film, television and calendar art, and globalisation in India.

Sushma Joshi has a master's degree in cultural anthropology from New School for Social Research, New York City, USA, and a bachelor's degree in international relations from Brown University, Providence, Rhode Island, USA. She was the coordinator of the Global Reproductive Health Forum in South Asia, a project of Harvard University, from 1992 to 2000. She has worked with documentaries, including *PANI*, a documentary examining the gender and caste issues surrounding drinking water, which was featured on *Q and A with Riz Khan* on CNN International. She has taught at Eugene Lang and La Guardia colleges in New York City, USA. Her research interests include gender and development, technology and new media and the intersection between health and rights. Her recent publications include an essay on women's rights in Nepal in *Greenwood's Encyclopedia of Women's Issues Worldwide*. She also writes a weekly opted for *The Kathmandu Post*, Nepal's leading English daily.

Vikash N. Pandey (1959–2003) was Reader, Unit for Rural Studies, The Tata Institute of Social Sciences, Mumbai, India. His research interests were agrarian legislation and property relations in colonial Awadh. Later, he explored theories of the self and freedom in post-structuralist analyses, ideas surrounding the rural–urban dichotomy and the uses of critical realism in contemporary social analysis. He also wrote on the relationship between the state and civil society in India. At the time of his death he was working on issues of 'structural determinism' in the study of rural society in India.

Carla Petievich is Associate Professor, Department of History, Montclair State University, USA. She has carried out research and has published in the areas of Indo-Muslim cultural history, classical and modern Urdu languages, contemporary of Pakistani culture and gender issues in the Muslim cultures of South Asia.

Stacy Leigh Pigg is Associate Professor, Department of Sociology and Anthropology, Simon Fraser University, Vancouver, Canada. She has carried out research and has published on medicine and transnational processes, relations between cosmopolitan and local medical systems, discourses , ideologies and practices of international development and all these issues in the context of AIDS. She is the editor of the journal *Medical Anthropology: Cross Cultural Studies in Health and Illness*.

Linnet Pike has studied anthropology and history at the universities of Melbourne and Queensland. She has conducted fieldwork in Kathmandu and in the mid-western region of Nepal between 1996–98. Her fieldwork explored sex work and HIV/AIDS, with particular focus on the programmes of non-governmental organisations related to HIV and STD education, prostitution issues and community development. She is currently writing her doctoral thesis titled, 'Women and HIV Education in the Sex Industry of Nepal: The Politics and Culture of Prostitution', at the Key Centre for Women's Health in Society, University of Melbourne, Australia.

Gayatri Reddy is Assistant Professor, Center for Gender and Women's Studies, the University of Illinois at Chicago, USA. She has published in the area of gender and non-heterosexual contexts in India and is currently working on a project titled,

'Queer Bodies: Construction of South Asian (Male) Queer Identities in the USA'.

Sudipta Sen is Associate Professor, Department of History, Syracuse University, USA. He is the author of *Empires of Trade: The East India Company and the Making of the Colonial Market Place* and *A Distant Sovereignty: National Imperialism and the Origins of British India.*

Index